ALL NEW SECOND EDITION

THE
DANCE
EXPERIENCE

INSIGHTS INTO
HISTORY, CULTURE
AND
CREATIVITY

ALL NEW SECOND EDITION

THE DANCE EXPERIENCE

INSIGHTS INTO HISTORY, CULTURE AND CREATIVITY

Myron Howard Nadel
and Marc Raymond Strauss

Princeton Book Company, Publishers

Princeton Book Company, Publishers
PO Box 831
Hightstown, NJ 08520-0831

Book design and cover by Lisa Denham
Cover photograph "The Ascension" by Charles S. Klabunde
Printed in Canada.

Library of Congress Cataloging–in–Publication Data
Nadel, Myron Howard and Strauss, Marc Raymond.
    The Dance Experience: Insights into History, Culture and
Creativity. /Myron Howard Nadel and Marc Raymond Strauss— 2nd ed.
        p. cm.
        ISBN 0-87127-251-2
        1. Dance—

DEDICATION

To the memory of Martha Hill, pioneering dance educator.

M.H.N.

To my mother, who always wanted to be a dancer.

M.R.S.

CONTENTS

SECTION ONE:
APPRECIATING THE WORLD OF DANCE

SECTION TWO
THE DANCE EXPERIENCE

APPENDICES

FOREWORD

WHY DANCE?

Edward Villella
Founding Artistic Director, Miami City Ballet

Why dance? Well, you might as well ask, Why sing? Why listen to music? Because the arts are wonderful extensions of the sensitivities of the human spirit.

One of the most interesting things to do is to watch young kids when they are happy. They are so physically animated that they begin to tell us things with their bodies. They speak a physical language to us. Dance is an extension of that childlike physical activity, in which we express ourselves, speak, and make others understand how we feel about things.

Who are we dancers? First and foremost, we are physical human beings. In a way, we are similar to athletes, in that the basis upon which we proceed is the investigation of movement, and the role it plays in whatever we are doing. But there are differences. For an athlete, the question is: How far can I throw the ball? For a dancer, the question is how you throw the ball. Dance involves quality more than quantity. That quality is called "aesthetics."

The aesthetics of ballet, the field of dance art in which I work, distinguishes that art from popular culture. Most popular culture has not put a premium on the aesthetics of structure and form, so it is dispensable because it lacks staying power. For dancers, the technique that we have—our alphabet—gives us our structure, and artistic direction gives us our form. Once we have the structure and form, then we seek to extend them. In dance, we extend them to the point that we pass through space in relation to time. Our art is not dispensable because, based as it is on aesthetic values, it endures.

Exercises in ballet are formal: we take human gesture and pass it through predetermined positions—our alphabet of movement. This passing through from position to position creates the foundation for dance, and this lovely process leads us to see how far we can stretch ourselves, not only physically but aesthetically.

However, you still might say, well, athletes do the same in their exercise and practice, don't they? Yes, but dancers go further. We relate our forms to style, and we add theatrics. Ballet dancers also seek to make the difficult look easy, and that's one of their great challenges. Athletes certainly don't mind if something looks difficult.

Classical ballet is classic only because it has been previously accepted. Built on a sense of tradition, it goes beyond tradition because it's also tied to the ever-growing potential of physicality. Years ago, to break the four-minute mile was impossible. Now, many people regularly run the mile in under four minutes. In ballet, we're constantly seeking to discover how much further our bodies can become more expressive.

From a very basic point of view, then, understanding dance involves how one presents the body. How many people have an awareness of their bodies? For instance, how you sit and how you eat are taken for granted. The point of dance, particularly ballet, is to show what is possible for the body in relation to an ideal of perfection. This doesn't mean you have to be a dancer to appreciate its value and meaning. An awareness of its form, structure, lines—all making some kind of logical sense—offers an understanding of a language involving the fullest potential of mind and body.

Why do I like to dance? So I can analyze with my mind. So that when I stand there, I have the ability to know how to be always prepared to move. In ballet, we have a very, very basic way to move, which is to open the body out and anticipate movement. If I'm going to turn to the right, I have to open my shoulders, open the right side of my body, incorporate my mind and my whole being, and not just think "turn right."

Watching ballet dancers warm up at the barre has been called "boring" by many of the young people at our lecture-demonstrations in the school systems, until they see the incredible tricks and turns and spins and lifts our dancers do soon afterwards. The process of this so-called boredom at the barre allows us to do what these young people get so excited about.

Being exposed to dance at a later time in life, such as in college and by reading a book like this one, off the bookstore shelves or in class, permits you to better appreciate the incredible challenges that dance presents. For you, it doesn't just involve what I said earlier, simply "to make the difficult look easy." You will look at the barre exercises, perhaps experience them for yourself, and then realize that without them, there can be no ease. You must prepare yourself, like for an exam. You don't start the night before.

Why dance? For me, I always loved to move, I had to move, and so I had to speak not only with my hands and arms but also with my whole body. One of the most satisfying aspects of learning and knowing how to dance is the sensual feeling of having full physical control. And it's very much a sensual idea, if you can finally do it right. For instance, in ballroom, I love the masculine idea of guiding a woman correctly, presenting a woman, taking care of woman on a dance floor. For me, there is a very nice lesson involved. You invite a woman to dance through your gentility, sensitivity, and awareness—it's the other side of aggression. We are hit in the face with aggression all the time in our culture. If you want to release some aggression, guide a woman on a dance floor expertly.

When I was in college, I was a hero because I could dance. Every bar I went to, I got a table of ladies to join my table of classmates, because I asked them to dance one at a time. Women respect men who can dance. They seek out dancing partners. And you always knew the guy who was the best dancer, because he was the one with all the most gorgeous women!

PREFACE

Myron Howard Nadel

At first, I saw no particular reason to update *The Dance Experience*. The first edition was a high point in one of my lives, but I had already gone on to the next. During that earlier time, I had founded the dance department at the University of Wisconsin/Milwaukee and created the first three-credit, university humanities course in dance. This class became accepted for core academic credit as the equal to any introduction to art, music or theater course—a still proud accomplishment of mine. With the collaboration of Constance Miller, I designed the original 1969 book to accompany that course. I am very happy to see that these types of courses, some with studio work, some pure lecture, are quite common now.

For over thirty years, I have ignored colleagues, friends, and even my wife, who regularly asked me why I didn't create a new edition. I figured that others were writing material for these courses by now, so there must be plenty of books on dance available out there. Why should I? I was also quite busy as a professor and administrator, with a pointed interest in promoting programs in music theater and inter-arts courses at several universities around the country.

Then, at the year 2000 meeting of the International Council of Fine Arts Deans (ICFAD), I met Dr. Marc Strauss, who was serving at the time as Associate Dean in the College of Liberal Arts at Southeast Missouri State University. "Hey, I had your book in college!" said Marc, "It was great!" Since he appeared to be nearing fifty years of age, his very flattering statement hit me right in my gut, where I firmly believed I was still a teenager. Marc, just like the others, asked why I had not written a new edition, and so I gave him all of my predetermined, rote answers.

Then, for some reason, I impulsively blurted, "Why don't you write it, if you think that it is such a good idea?"

"Really?" said Marc.

Stunned by my own utterance, and still protective of my thirty-something-year-old baby, I said, "Well, I might like to help, of course."

It took us about an hour and a beer or two but, on the spot, we decided to collaborate as equals. He would act as the guy who was really up on things, and I would be the grumpy traditionalist. As it turned out, Marc's philosophy is nearer to mine than I could have hoped. Of course, he had the benefit of reading my first edition.

But Marc also had his own unique approach to introducing the art of dance. On the one hand, he is more academically inclined than I, but he is also enamored with popular culture, particularly dance in Hollywood films. I wondered if that kind of perspective could work with a new edition. Then I thought, "Wait a minute, I myself have been called, though not always in complimentary fashion, 'Professor Musical Comedy.'" Perhaps Marc and I could put together an all-new *Dance Experience* that would open wide the boundaries of the art form by including some of the more accessible and popular cultural arenas, and thereby attract new and contemporary audiences. By doing this, a new edition could even have a certain appeal to the general-interest browser at those big national bookstore chains, the ones that sell coffee and pastries.

We returned to our respective Texas and Missouri homes after making a pact to see if any publisher would be interested in such a book. Charles Woodford at Princeton Books was, and he became a real mentor to both of us in terms of the tone and organization of the new edition. I became more excited each day to learn new things about dance from our contributors, including Marc, and to discover that I still wanted and needed to share my seasoned perspectives on dance. Although I had always taught dance, and still do, this fresh project renewed my love for dance's multitude of viewpoints—historical, technical, critical, theoretical, artistic, aesthetic, educational, expressive, and joy-filled—all of which make dance a truly universal art.

As you read through this book, the editors/authors and all of our contributors wish for you a similar sense of fascination and love for dance. If you also decide to go into the dance studio, that will be a blessing.

ACKNOWLEDGMENTS

The editors would like to thank Edward Villella, for giving this book a head start, and to all of our contributors, who shared their expertise in this endeavor. We would be thrilled to have any of them lecture for us in an Introduction to the Art of Dance course, and are extremely pleased to have their lectures in print. Thanks also to Constance Miller, for her permission to create a new edition.

M.H.N. and M.R.S.

Special thanks must go to my greatest helpers: Jane Ellen Poss, my wife, for her patience; Annie, the cat, for sitting on my lap; and Marcia Daudistel, for her editing expertise.

M.H.N.

First and foremost, I want to thank my co-author, Myron Howard Nadel, for taking the plunge, wholly on faith, to collaborate on this new edition of his seminal 1970s text. From the start, Myron has unselfconsciously trusted in our equal contributions to this project, and it has been a great pleasure and honor for me to work with him, a true colleague. Thanks, too, must go to Southeast Missouri State University, for granting me the time to work on this book during sabbatical. I also want to thank my mother, Ann Louise Dalmas Berk, for all of her unconditional love and support throughout her gracious, generous, and all-too-brief life. Her angelic presence hovers over all I do, as we both keep dancing to the music of the spheres.

M.R.S.

INTRODUCTION

THE DANCE EXPERIENCE AND THE 21ST CENTURY:
THEN AND NOW

Myron Howard Nadel
and Marc Raymond Strauss

You have been invited, or have asked someone, to go to your first dance concert. You haven't a clue what to expect, and may feel quite nervous about the upcoming experience. It is one big unknown, and you are not all that certain you even want to go. But, you like the person you're going with, or heard something interesting about this particular dance style or performer or musical accompaniment, or have to go due to a class assignment, so you are on your way, sink or swim.

As soon as you step into the performance building, you know something unique is going to happen. If you don't have your ticket, you wait in line, and notice that you are in a different kind of crowd from any other. There is excitement and anticipation in the air, maybe even perfume, and people seem to be bright, intelligent, and eager to see the concert. You may feel that everyone except you knows what is going to happen. They don't, unless the whole audience has been to all the rehearsals.

You hand your ticket to the usher and find your seat. You can't decide if you should sit near the back of the house in order to get a complete picture of the dances, in the balcony to get a bird's eye view, or up close where you can clearly see the dancers' faces. I prefer being somewhere near the fifth or sixth row, where I have a wide enough panorama of the proceedings and yet feel near to the spirit of the dancers, the dance, and the choreographer.

You look at the program, and may be astonished that there aren't reams of explanations. You worry that you might not be able to understand what is going to happen. What, pray tell, is going to happen? No one really knows! Neither the dance aficionado, who has seen hundreds of performances, nor you, a novice, can say for sure, because every dance is different. You may read the names of the dance pieces and think they're rather obscure, or you may see the names of the dancers and read their "bios," notice the names of the choreographers, composers, musicians, and costume and lighting designers. Who are these people? Some may be professors and students you know or have heard of, while others are total strangers. Nervousness and excitement increase as you feel your own eagerness build.

You may hear a rustle of feet behind the stage curtain, feel the lights dim to "half," and then blink your eyes as the whole auditorium goes black. You fiddle with your note pad so you can take notes. I say, "Skip that part." If you want to write a word or two to remind you of something, well, ok. Just don't miss the magic onstage because you are writing, when you should be seeing and hearing and feeling.

The dance begins, and—presto—all sorts of things start to happen before your very eyes. Some startle, others make you wonder, and still others turn you on. Allow yourself to fully experience the dance. After each piece, go ahead and jot down something if you have to write a report but, even better, just mull over some of the visual, musical, and dramatic images that are so fresh in your mind. However you respond or react, you are now participating in your first dance experience.

Fully appreciating the dances you just experienced calls into play intellectual skills that accompany your sensory and emotional intercourse with that experience. But, while you are involved, you do not want to provide obstacles to that involvement by analyzing what you are seeing at the time that it is happening. If at all possible, you will want to have what might be called a transcendent experience during the performance—something "out of the ordinary" in your life. Afterwards, your analytic skills may then be called into action, along with your memory of that experience—what dance critic Arlene Croce calls one's "afterimages."

An afterimage is "what we are left with when the performance is over. Dancing leaves nothing else behind—no record, no text—and so the afterimage becomes the subject [of our musings about] the performance."

"Wow, what was that?" we might exclaim. "What was that movement or feeling?" "That was different!" At that point, immediately after the experience, it is the time for you to figure out what it was that made you feel a certain way during the performance. You will need verbal skills to describe the memory of what you saw and heard, and you will want to have the ability to research facts about the choreographer, the company, the style or history of the work, and the process of the choreography, in order to support your statements.

Whether you realize it or not, you will also be assessing and broadening your own life experiences, and how they relate to what you have just seen. Why? Because viewing live dance is always a very personal experience. You are seeing and sensing bodies moving in space before you in unique ways, just as in sports competitions; and, as humans, we automatically engage our emotions, thoughts, and even bodies when our human compatriots are doing actions of any kind in close proximity to us.

Can we appreciate dance without dancing ourselves? Yes, if what we intend is to sharpen our sensibilities as audience members in the company of dance on stage or on a screen. No, if we think that any book or video or performance can actually teach us how to dance. The book you hold in your hands is unlikely to improve your own dance technique, but anyone can appreciate a painting or a sculpture or a song without being a painter or a sculptor or a singer.

For those readers fortunate to be dancing and learning about dance at the same time, that is the best possible dance experience. Why wouldn't all dance appreciation courses include both dancing and reading? Likewise, why wouldn't appreciation courses in art, music, and theater also include such hands-on familiarity? Quite simply, it is too expensive and impractical. If students in art appreciation courses all had easels, class sizes would be severely limiting, and too many art professors would be needed to teach those beginner courses. In a reasonably sized dance studio, a class of 20-25 is the maximum number of students any instructor can justly accommodate, in order to have enough room to move with the personal and professional attention necessary.

In spite of these restrictions, the editors of this book have endeavored to provide as close an approximation to the actual dance experience as is possible through the words and expertise of our contributors. We have brought together a rich diversity of artist-teachers who practice what they preach, and who are sharing with you from the inside out their own perspectives on this highly engaging art form.

The twenty-two chapters in this book are presented in two sections. The first, "Appreciating the World of Dance," introduces both the "horizontal" and "vertical" approaches toward dance—a many cultured perspective of a variety of dance styles set within their approximate historical contexts. If readers can better understand the interconnectedness among disparate cultures and their histories within today's 21st century global culture, they should be better able to appreciate the province we call dance.

All of the contributors to this book strongly believe that dance is an essential part of this world culture, and that increasingly integrated ideas continue to come together from all of its areas. The writers share many understandings about these world "subcultures." One category, for instance, is dance as performance, the presentation of dance for an audience. Another involves dance as religious expression. A third concerns the preservation of the customs of an ethnic group. There are also subcultures of people who dance for pure enjoyment, meeting partners, and winning contests.

Transcending any categorization is an overall sense of oneness for those who dance. Dancers are aware of the vitality of their movements, and of dance's binding and energizing value. They want to do it and sense its deep, intrinsic worth. Dance is a nourishing and quite pleasant experience. While dancing, we may have more in common with dancers in other countries than with our classmates, business associates, friends, and even relatives!

The current edition of *The Dance Experience* leans primarily toward a preparation of its readers for a rich appreciation of concert dance, while also stressing the idea that world dance and the professional dance world are as intimately connected as threads in a brilliant tapestry. Not only are the boundaries between dance styles in our 21st century world increasingly blurred, but the artificial distancing of the popular from the artistic has also narrowed. These separations were never a part of the profession of dance, anyway. After all, a concert dancer who can get a job in a Broadway musical or on a television show will often do so. Serious choreographers throughout history have contributed to both the concert and commercial realm.

The arbitrary separation of "high" and "low" art occurs mainly at universities, usually for purposes of analysis and comparison, where professors have sometimes eschewed such forms as musicals, jazz, and tap dance as threatening to the lofty status of more "rarefied" art forms, such as ballet or classical music. Fortunately, professors of the arts have come a long way. Universities around the world now include studies in jazz, tap, the graphic arts, advertising, and web page design in their curricula. Majors in musical theater abound. The fluidity and ease of crossing over from the so-called "serious" to the commercial arts are partly a function of performers and choreographers simply training in the same places: high school arts magnet schools, private conservatories, university dance departments, and in the "real" world. Dance is dance and a job is a job.

Until recently, few authors dared espouse commercial dance and dance in musicals as a viable source of arts experience for students. Now, in this introductory volume for the 21st century, we are taking a more profane—and, we believe, more inclusive—approach. Several of our contributors proudly use commercial dance ideas and musical theater examples to emphasize their points.

Inclusion and the importance of all cultural ideas are essential tenets of the American ethos. Although African, Hispanic, and indigenous American heritages had been until recently treated as part of a homogenous melting pot in our country, these and many other groups are now understood as singular threads of a heterogeneous multicultural tapestry. Such intricate lacework and vivid textures are reflected in the current edition; in fact, the field of dance has often led this advance towards egalitarian respect among disparate people and groups, at both the professional and educational levels.

The first nine chapters of Section One detail the vibrant diversity of dance styles, cultures, and histories on our planet by representing world dance, ancient Greek dance, African, folk, Japanese, and social dance, jazz and tap, ballet, and current forms, such as modern, postmodern, and the avant-garde, from the 20th century on. In any introductory book, even a list as diverse as ours can only give readers a small taste of the dance world's flavors. Still, we feel your appetite will be whetted. The section concludes with a reminder that it is a sense of spirituality and oneness with our neighbors that is fundamental to the world of dance. When that spirituality rises to the surface, it suffuses dance with an ennobling energy, allowing all people to tap into its vitalizing essence in their own ways as equals.

In Section Two, "The Dance Experience," some very seasoned and practical examples are provided for you to consider as you approach your own dance experience, whether it is on a stage or screen or as a participant. From both a personal and professional perspective, the chapters feature distinct ingredients that support dance both as a theatrical and visual/media art, such as technique, choreography, collaborations among the arts, costuming, lighting, and the performing arts, as well as issues that address the preservation of dance (on screen and via notation), gender, sexuality, the waning relationship between dance education and physical education, and the usefulness of dance criticism. Scrutinizing and learning about these perspectives, which are basic to the practice of primarily Western concert dance, will increase your opportunity for delight and reward.

Our hope with this book is to encourage you to enjoy and understand not only what you see and hear but what you feel. As you enter into a dance experience of any kind, release any previous knowledge or conscious assessment you may want to bring to that moment and just let the dance happen, with you as a part of the experience. The knowledge you cultivate by taking in these chapters will be there, waiting, for your "afterimage" reflections.

Dance and the other arts involve an offering (in the best sense of the word) from the creators to their audience—you. Accept the gift, devour it with your senses, and recuse your intellect for a time. A "serious" dance is not automatically better than a "popular" one, and vice versa. After the experience, you can enrich your pleasurable, puzzling, even troubled memories of your participation by applying the examples and lessons in this book. By then, such musings will hopefully be a delightful complement to—not impersonal substitute for—your dance experience.

THE
DANCE
EXPERIENCE

SECTION ONE

APPRECIATING
THE WORLD OF DANCE

CHAPTER ONE
introduction

Carl Wolz's insights testify to a world that has been becoming more and more interconnected or globalized. In North America, Europe and Australia, the recent Cold War and post–Cold War migration flood from the old Soviet bloc, as well from third world countries, has put Asian, African and Central American cultures next door to each other and to both indigenous and long-standing immigrant cultures. Although the United States and Canada lead the world in diversity of cultures, almost all nations and areas around the globe reflect multicultural influences from far away places.

THROUGH WORLD EYES
Carl Wolz

Internationalism, a buzzword to describe many aspects of contemporary global culture, has been a major characteristic of life since the 1990s. For several years, interculturalism, cross-culturalism and multiculturalism have been popular topics in a number of academic and artistic fields, including dance. In all cases, people are concerned with and fascinated by the emerging international culture that has resulted from technological advances in travel and communication systems. We are clearly becoming a global village.

In the world of dance, some forms have become truly international. Major companies worldwide present styles as diverse as classical ballet, ballroom dancing, hip-hop, tango and tap, and their participants literally know no societal boundaries.

In contrast to this burgeoning international culture, a return to and a strengthening of ethnic differences have occurred in many areas of the world, sometimes with disastrous results. One need only read the daily newspapers for mention of places where people have no respect for each other's cultures or even for their own lives. A major factor at work here is a lack of understanding and acceptance of other lifestyles. We must find a way to combat this intolerance and hate, especially in the youth of the world, for they will always inherit the earth. We can change prejudice, a kind of thought pollution, but only through education that starts at an early age. Part of this education can be through dance, the art that gives form and deep meaning to humans' common ability and need to move. The human body in movement is not only an important part of communication, but also a vital factor in discovering cultural roots, as well as a basic key to understanding and appreciating human differences.

The strengthening of ethnic identities in all areas of the world can also have a positive side, however, when groups strive to maintain or revive traditional cultures, including dance. These efforts contribute to the richness of our global culture. In recent years, more and more people are studying dances from cultures other than their own. Examples of cross-cultural study of dance are as old as history but have been on the increase in this international age. Whenever people learn a style of dance distinct from their own culture—for example, students from the West going to India to study Kathakali Dance, or Asians studying classical ballet and contemporary dance—they touch the universal in humankind's experience. Such activities promote international connections, creating an invisible network that reinforces the idea of one world, with all people as one family of infinite variety. Every instance of learning dance from other cultures involves an inherent respect for the people of that culture. Each person who participates in such dances contributes to the preservation of the multicultural life on this planet. We all are enriched by these wide varieties of dance experiences, and through them we learn to celebrate our differences.

Perhaps the United States, as a pluralistic society, can be seen as a case study for the world in its rush toward globalization—with both positive and negative results. Several images have been used in the United States to represent this phenomenon. During the large waves of immigration through the first half of the 20th century, the country was seen as a melting pot, an alchemist's cauldron in which various elements came together to create a new golden society. After World War II, however, this concept began to change so that images emerged of groups retaining their ethnic identity but still being a part of the whole: the country was instead a patchwork quilt, a salad bowl, a mosaic.

All of these images suggest that two processes are happening simultaneously. On the one hand, we have fusion, interculturalism and other similar processes that indicate an emerging global style. On the other hand, we have separation and distance in the recognition and celebration of ethnic and national identities.

Opportunities for the study of world dance are on the increase today in colleges and in urban community centers, especially where cultural minorities live. Courses on dance in world cultures are also on the increase not only in the United States but also around the globe, and they address the need for a greater understanding of cultural diversity. The syllabi for these courses include guidelines and checklists for relating the form, function, content and context of different dance traditions to the socioeconomic milieu in which they were created. In addition, more and more students are participating in junior-year study abroad programs in which dance is the major or minor field of study.

One of the roles of education is to prepare students for life, to teach them respect for other peoples and their cultural traditions. Multicultural learning broadens these students' worldview and emphasizes an attitude of caring for others. It is not an easy task to balance their self-esteem and ethnic identity with an assimilation of something different, new and perhaps even strange. A sound education in a multicultural context should prepare them to understand and function within our dichotomous world culture. Dance can play a vital role in contributing positively to this understanding of a global society.

Perhaps the most important value that international dance study can provide is an affirmation of the spirit of cooperation and mutual respect necessary to the idea and existence of one world, what Buckminster Fuller (1895–1983) called "this space ship earth," on which we are hurtling toward a common destiny.

CHECKLIST FOR LOOKING AT CROSS–CULTURAL DANCE

A brief checklist can help anyone to approach any type of dance in any cultural context. It can be used in a dance appreciation course and is offered here as a guide to some issues an individual should consider when participating in a new dance experience, either as a viewer or as a doer. The five stages of looking are: observation, description, explanation, interpretation and evaluation.[1]

OBSERVATION: HOW DO WE SEE DANCE?

1. Movement: theoretical framework—concepts and vocabulary

2. Methods of understanding: viewing (active, not passive audience) and doing (participation as a mover)

3. Point of view: inside or outside of the culture?

DESCRIPTION: WHAT ARE THE VISIBLE ELEMENTS?

1. The dancer: body type, age, social class, etc.

2. The dance: movement vocabulary of the genre or the work or both

3. The music: performers, instruments, structure, etc.

4. Objects worn: costumes, shoes, headgear (masks, etc.)

5. Objects carried: musical instruments, properties, etc.

6. Environment: stage, sets, scenery, lighting, etc.

Note: Creators of the movement, the music, the objects, and the environment also can be described.

EXPLANATION: WHAT ARE THE VIRTUAL STRUCTURES?

1. Form: structure in time, relationship of parts, content (from narrative to abstract movement), function, uses in the parent or adopted culture (ritual, entertainment, expression, etc.) and context (historical and contemporary periods, places and events where performed)

Note: Form, function, content and context can be evaluated for aspects of continuity and change within a given culture.

INTERPRETATION: WHAT ARE STYLE AND MEANING?

1. Core characteristics: summary of important elements

2. Style: What is the basic style? What is style?

3. Significance: the meaning of the genre or of the work in a cultural context

EVALUATION: HOW DO WE ASSESS DANCE?

1. The former/creator: criteria for the creator/choreographer— training, experience, creativity, reputation and biographical information

2. The performer: criteria for the dancer/actor/musician—body type, technical skill, talent, virtuosity, musicality, discipline, artistry, commitment, knowledge and experience

3. The work: criteria for the dance piece—form and function, content and context, approach or point of view, evaluation in relation to genre and innovation

Note: Criteria for evaluation of dance in a multicultural world change as the world changes. There is thus a real and ongoing need to train and develop culturally sensitive dance critics and theorists.

REFERENCES

Copeland, Roger, and Marshall Cohen, eds. *What is dance?* New York: Oxford University Press, 1983.

Gere, David, ed. *Looking out: Perspectives on dance and criticism in a multicultural world.* New York: Schirmer Books, 1995.

Hanna, Judith Lynne. *To dance is human: A theory of nonverbal communication.* Chicago: University of Chicago Press, 1979.

Jonas, Gerald. *Dancing: The pleasure, power, and art of movement.* New York: Harry N. Abrams, 1992.

Martin, John. *Introduction to the dance.* New York: W. W. Norton, 1939.

Nadel, Myron Howard, and Constance Nadel Miller, eds. *The dance experience: Readings in dance appreciation.* New York: Praeger, 1969.

Sorell, Walter, ed. *The dance has many faces.* New York: World Publishing, 1951.

ENDNOTES

[1] *Editors' Note:* Wolz's "five stages of looking" are a variant on the same four or five categories that visual arts researchers have used for centuries to investigate, analyze and critique painting, sculpture, ceramics and many other arts objects. Whereas Wolz pres-

ents his "stages" in the form of a self-guiding checklist here at the beginning of this book, each of the chapters in Section Two investigate detailed examples of many of the signposts he introduces in his list. In particular, chapter twenty-one, "Dance Criticism," completes the circle Wolz begins by taking his conventional arts categories into perhaps more representative 21st century areas of *description, contextualization, interpretation* and *evaluation*. It also presents a critical analysis of a variety of dance performances, which readers can subsequently practice for themselves. Self-guiding checklists or critical analyses can be useful for any student of dance.

CHAPTER TWO

introduction

The great minds of the Western world's first classical period, such as Socrates (469–399 B.C.E.) and Aristotle (384–322 B.C.E.), considered questions concerning the role dance should play in the education of a good citizen and the value of all the arts as entertainment, spectacle and therapy. Western theater and theatrical dance can be traced to the ancient Greeks' performance rituals, so it is no surprise that these acute minds examined the essence of the theatrical experience. They concluded that seeing a drama where terrible tragedy befalls the characters is cathartic or therapeutic to its audience. When a contemporary dance work is based on a Greek tragedy, do we also receive the satisfying feelings of that cathartic release? Can we see in our current forms of classical ballet technique or in the vocabulary of more "natural" styles of dance any relation to the theater of the ancient Greeks? George Balanchine and Isadora Duncan certainly did!

DANCE IN EARLY GREEK SOCIETY

Marc Raymond Strauss

What are the requirements for being a good citizen in 21st century America? We all might agree at least on the following: obeying the laws, supporting the country in times of peace and war, experiencing and contributing to the rights and responsibilities of our democratic system and pursuing the benefits of life, liberty and happiness.

All of these actions were also appropriate in ancient Greek society of the 5th and 4th centuries B.C.E., when well-known philosophers such as Socrates, Plato and Aristotle did their thinking and teaching. In fact, today's system of government and society in the United States can trace much of its structure to ancient Greece.

These two systems have interesting differences, of course. Although laws in ancient Greece nominally seemed to provide the same rights for everyone, their "equality" in truth excluded women, slaves and foreigners. Today, we have erased two of the three exclusions, at least on the book. The ancient Greek Olympics also showcased only men, and any women caught competing would be thrown off a cliff (none were discovered, fortunately). This practice, too, has changed, although women and men still do not yet compete against each other.

The sphere of the fine and performing arts is where the most intriguing differences reside between then and now. Many people today consider sports the most popular form of entertainment, but in 5th century B.C.E. Greece, dance, music, sports, poetry, sculpture and all the fine arts not only were equal in value, but were required and rigorous study for all citizens. In his works *The Republic, Laws,* and *The Symposium,* the seminal Greek philosopher Plato (c. 427–347 B.C.E.) viewed dance

> as an integral part of mousiké, "the art of the muses," hence as one facet of a triad that includes music and poetry. Dance . . . was to be an essential part of the young person's education, and as such it was meant to help inculcate into the future citizen a rhythm and harmony which, once developed and augmented by other studies, would amount to justice. Plato did not think of dance as an optional course of instruction, but as a required disciplining of the physical movement so natural to young children. And, he would insist, any dancing—like any music playing, poetry reciting, or storytelling—that failed to contribute to a harmonious psyche in the individual and thus to a well-organized community would be disallowed in a proper polis [city].[1]

Plato's equally insightful student Aristotle (384–322 B.C.E.) found the arts so important to daily Greek life that he composed what many consider the first—if not the richest and most detailed—description and analysis of the literary arts of dramatic (epic) tragedy and comedy: his unparalleled *Poetics.* In this one book, we find an illuminating and comprehensive treatise of Western philosophical thought on all the arts. Much later thinking on the use and value of the arts in the West owes its inspiration to Aristotle.

A primary tenet of the *Poetics* is the ancient Greek notion of *katharsis* (catharsis), loosely translated to mean clarification, purification, purgation and therapeutic cleansing. In a pertinent passage from *The Politics,* Aristotle makes a strong argument for the existence of catharsis in all the arts, specifically music and poetry:

Music [poetry, dance] should be studied . . . for the sake of . . . many ben-efits, one of which is purgation. For feelings such as pity and fear, or, again, enthusiasm, exist very strongly in some souls, and have more or less influ-ence over all. Some persons fall into a religious frenzy, whom we see . . . when they have used the sacred melodies, restored as though they had found healing and purgation. Those who are influenced by pity or fear, and every emotional nature, must have a like experience, and others in so far as each is susceptible to such emotions, and all are in a manner purged and their souls lightened and delighted.[2]

One example of a 20th century dance that created such a purgative feeling of release is popular British contemporary ballet choreographer Kenneth MacMillan's (1929–1992) signature 1966 Royal Ballet version of Shake-speare's 1595 tragedy *Romeo and Juliet*, with poignant and powerful per-formances by Rudolf Nureyev (1938–1993) and Dame Margot Fonteyn (1919–1991) in the lead roles. This story of lovers who kill themselves in order to remain together forever has perhaps no greater embodiment. As audience members, we know what is going to happen but cannot do any-thing to stop it. We watch the lovers dance inexorably toward their tragic end, and pity and fear for them well up in our throats.[3]

What Aristotle meant was that through our empathy for characters in such tragic circumstances, we *vicariously* experience their struggles *as if* we were they. We know we could be in their shoes, and our sympathy for them is real. We feel relieved and purged of their pain. Our soul is indeed "lightened and delighted."

Another important concept from the *Poetics* is the notion of mimesis, or *poētikēs*, which doesn't mean imitation in the way that we use the term today, but more accurately translates into "things that are made, invented or crafted." Our contemporary term *artistry* fits better. The original Greek word resembles our word *poetry*, of course, which certainly has remained a uniquely inventive and crafted art form to this day. Aristotle treated all the poetic arts—dance, music, theater, the visual arts, rhetoric and even poli-tics—as essentially "creative acts."

One reason poetics cannot be simple copying is that art involves the trans-lation of reality into another medium. Just as the portrait sculptor trans-lates the human countenance into clay or stone, the poet translates action into language [or the dancer translates thoughts and feelings and themes into movement]. Nor can the poet merely translate his materials raw. Even if he does not invent his plots but takes them, as many Greek tragedians did, from the historical or mythological record, he selectively reshapes the action to make it more universal, and thus more powerfully tragic. . . . [A]rtists must disregard incidental facts to search for deeper universal truths.[4]

Any number of dances exemplify Aristotelian mimesis as a creative, even transformative embodiment of some universal truth(s): *The Green Table* (1932), by German choreographer Kurt Jooss (1901–1979), remains to this day a scathing testament to the innocent and unnecessary deaths that war invariably brings. The signature work *Revelations* (1960), by Alvin Ailey (1931–1989), set to a number of compelling and emotionally charged spirituals and gospel songs, embodies a "communal journey from baptism through despair to salvation."[5] *Prodigal Son* (1929), George Balanchine's (1904–1983) last work for Serge Diaghilev's (1872–1929) Ballets Russes recapitulates the biblical story of unconditional love of a father for his son. These dances and a host of others embody universal truths in ways that also may evoke a cathartic response.

Many past and contemporary choreographers have looked to ancient Greece for inspiration, knowing of the rich lode of timeless ideas embedded in that culture. American Isadora Duncan (1877–1927), often referred to as the mother of modern dance, traveled to Greece to spend time at the original sites where many of its artists and philosophers practiced their disciplines. Absorbing their aesthetic through her study of sculpture and other arts, she considered herself a Greek goddess and felt destined to liberate her own culture from the strictures of its self-proclaimed sophistication. She worked throughout her life to elevate dance to the level of other art forms, such as theater, music and the visual arts, as the Greeks had done twenty-five centuries earlier. Duncan's belief in self-expression and commitment to the nobility of the Greek arts remains an inspiration for many dancers and choreographers.

Martha Graham (1894–1991), one of the most influential forces in modern dance, also went to the myths of ancient Greece for the universal truths she investigated in her richly psychological dance dramas. *Cave of the Heart* (1946), *Night Journey* (1947), *Errand into the Maze* (1947) and *Clytemnestra* (1958) focus on the themes of incest, suicide, murder, betrayal and tormented sexuality. Her presentation of these tragic stories on stage was consistent with Aristotle's explanations of mimesis and catharsis. Through universally sympathetic but ill-fated, deeply flawed characters such as Oedipus,

Medea, Jocasta and Ariadne, Graham drew deep from the Greek tragedians' embodiments of humanity's eternal struggles.

Can we imagine what dance might have been like in ancient Greece? Probably not. Although "several types of dances are known to have existed"—such as the *hypōrchema* (sung choric poems with movement); the vigorous, soldier-based pyrrhic dances; the *gymnopaedia* (wrestling-based dances); and the comedic *kordax*, which apparently involved "lewd rotations of the abdomen and buttocks"[6]—from our view twenty-five centuries later we can only guess what these dances looked like. The value of dance in that society cannot be disputed, for it "is best proved by the inclusion of Terpsichore as one of the nine Muses."[7] We also know that the dramatists Aeschylus, Euripides and Sophocles often were the choreographers for and at times dancers in the stagings of their own works.

Dance, along with the other arts, served at least a dual function in early Greek society—to provide a cleansing, cathartic release and to educate good citizens. Not only did Aristotle illuminate the essential aesthetic qualities of his own culture's literature, but, it turns out, he was more than prescient about the artistry to come, millennia distant. We can continue to use his artistic rubric in understanding dance works performed today.

ENDNOTES

[1] John E. Atwell, The significance of dance in Nietzsche's thought. In *Illuminating dance: Philosophical explorations*, edited by Maxine Sheets-Johnstone (London: Associated University Presses, 1984), p. 19.

[2] *Politics*, ll. 1341–1342; quoted in David H. Richter, ed., *The critical tradition: Classic texts and contemporary trends* (New York: St. Martin's, 1989), p. 41.

[3] For an evocative and educational discussion of MacMillan's popular 1966 full-length film, please refer to chapter 12, "Romantic, Small 'r,' Big Emotions—*Romeo and Juliet*," in Robert Greskovic's very readable 1998 book *Ballet 101: A complete guide to learning and loving the ballet* (New York: Hyperion), pp. 448–480.

[4] Richter, *Critical tradition*, p. 40.

[5] Allen Robertson and Donald Hutera, *The dance handbook* (Boston: G. K. Hall, 1988), p. 149.

[6] Lillian Lawler, cited in Jack Anderson, *Ballet and modern dance: A concise history*, 2d ed. (Pennington, N.J.: Princeton Book Company, 1992), p. 18.

[7] Walter Sorell, *The dance through the ages* (New York: Grosset and Dunlap, 1967), p. 22.

CHAPTER THREE

introduction

The "Western" culture that Ferne Yangyeitie Caulker refers to in this chapter is Judeo-Christian, western European, and American. As Caulker points out, the assumptions and biases of this culture have colored its accounts of other cultures. Although she acknowledges some progress over prejudice in our society in recent decades, she also correctly notes that one of the best ways to break out of one's cultural biases, however "right" they may feel to the bearer at the time, is to experience another people's culture, either through geographical travel to the country of origin or through virtual travel—for instance, a dance class in that "other" culture. It is only when one enters into another society and becomes a different person—a foreigner—for a while that one can learn what otherness really means.

AFRICAN DANCE: DIVINE MOTION

Ferne Yangyeitie Caulker

The Yoruba people of Nigeria, West Africa, believe that when God came down to the world, he gave his most precious gift, *Ashé* (ah-shey), a living power activated by and through the embodiment of a divine, universal force. For the Yoruba, as throughout Africa, movement is the vehicle through which the divine nature in each person can be expressed.

FINDING THE ASHÉ IN YOU

We stand in parallel position, our arms by our sides, head aligned, back and chest lifted. We take a deep breath, lifting our arms up to the sides of our torso as we inhale. Journeying to Mother Earth, we release through the back, bend our knees and roll to the floor. We touch the earth, paying homage to Mother. We stretch our arms, fingers and palms, caressing earth. We begin a tracing with our fingers from earth upward through our body until we reach

the sky, paying homage to the ancestors. We arch, releasing both our torso
and pelvis to the back, stretching our torso, arms in parallel position above
the head, hands flexed, fingers pointing toward the back, palms flat to the
sky, knees bent, chest held high, head back. We assume the posture of a tra-
ditional piece of African sculpture. We release our torso to the earth, keep-
ing our torso flat and parallel to earth Mother. Torso and legs are at right
angles. We stretch. With a release of breath we continue rolling to the floor,
rebounding in a roll back up to our original beginning position. We take a
deep breath and contemplate our completeness and connectedness to Mother
Earth and Father Sky.

This act of salutation is the beginning of each of my classes in African dance.
It is an opportunity for students to commit their bodies and awareness to the
experience of a new aesthetic. It is a unique way of seeing and feeling the
world. If I salute myself each day, then I can salute other living creatures. I
begin to celebrate the divine in myself and in others.

The best way to understand and appreciate another culture is to study, discover and experience its people and the role that the arts play in its society.
Without having to travel to specific destinations, which would be the ideal
scenario, one can achieve this appreciation by experiencing what I refer to as
the mind-body culture map. The study of African dance, not unlike the study
of any cultural form, serves as an opportunity to let go of safe and familiar
notions, perceptions and preferences. This process is an act of surrender that
allows one to "flow" into new shapes, rhythms and levels of understanding.

The dictionary defines *surrender* as "relinquishing control or possession of
another by force or demand." I refer instead to the surrender of the individual to himself or herself in a process toward enlightenment through the
merging of body, mind and spirit. Such a passage in African dance employs
movement, rhythm, text and song. The end result is a transformation
toward comprehension and placement of the individual in a tribe, a space, a
time and, most important, a sense of spiritual unity. The African understanding of body positioning and surrender is linked with a divine essence
through the ancestors. Many traditional African societies believe that "when
they dance or strike an honorific pose, they are standing in the image of their
ancient divine fathers."[1]

In many dance forms, and Western dance in particular, the dancer's essence
is separated into distinct mind and body. In the West, technique and body
form have traditionally been held in highest esteem, but in the African tra-

ditional view the human body is revered as a combination of spirit, emotion and motion. In other words, technique in African dance is a vibrant composite of mind-body and soul-spirit.

From a physical perspective, in African dance one sees the body articulated in its most natural state. Legs and arms work in parallel lines, centered from the torso, knees bent to provide a rebounding effect with the earth. The torso is often held in a forty-five-degree angle with the pelvis, to allow a more fluid range of movements. Polyrhythmic motions occur among the arms, legs, head and torso. Knees are often lifted, kept close to the torso, to allow more flexibility and coordination with the back and arms. Limbs explode centrifugally from the torso as center. In jumps, the body does not try to defy gravity, but rather to embrace it. African dancers do not attempt to hesitate in the air, as in a ballet's *ballon*, but to create texture and to shape the air space before returning back to earth for revitalization. They often repeat highly developed rhythmic movement sentences to confirm cultural, historical and ceremonial contexts, leading toward spiritual alignment. Dance and music serve to codify and preserve the living community and its history.

In African dance, each area of the body is brought to heightened awareness and execution; it is allowed to articulate within a rhythmic percussive flow independent of the other parts, but it remains firmly connected to a larger context. Within this percussive flow is what I refer to as the "tubular effect": the execution of movement in a vertical up-and-down plane. The dancer focuses on sculpting content through space, rather than on conquering space. Elements of weight, density and rebound are more important than the appearance of being weightless, ethereal or sparse.

One cannot discuss African dance without touching on the relationship and influence of African rhythms. Rhythm and motion reside in a symbiotic relationship. Each element gives to the other life energies beneficial to both. The dance is, as I like to call it, "drumatic." Through highly developed systems of musical virtuosity, African rhythms—combined with historic, societal contexts and movement—result in a spiritually and physically dynamic aesthetic form. The dance functions, therefore, as history. Even when it is not accompanied by musical instrumentation, as in many traditional forms, the body itself becomes the accompaniment.

Repetition is one of the cornerstones of African and African American dance and music. The untrained observer may see only simple, monotonous repetitions of one particular element, but these repetitions serve as a conduit through a multitude of thresholds that elevate the dancer to heightened levels of awareness of the spirit and body "self." For example, although the rungs of a ladder may look the same, each step up or down changes the climber's level and creates new perspectives. At each of these rungs, whether spiritual or secular, specific codified rituals or benchmarks prescribe body positioning, rhythms, vocalization, costuming and protocol. The act of repetition confirms and enforces elements of rhythmic "drive," Mother Earth and Father Sky.

The Western aesthetic previously assumed that anything not written was not codified, a dominant academic view throughout the 19th and much of the 20th centuries. As a result, early explorers and scholars defined the dance and music of the African technique or form in their *own* ways. Seeing through their own culture's eyes, these observers assumed that because the African arts had no written text, as in ballet dance, they had no form. Westerners at this time did not yet understand or appreciate the processes of oral traditions. When viewing African and other non-Western dance forms, most critics and scholars throughout the Western world held this accepted position.

This strange and devastating relationship between the West and Africa has its foundation in the institution of slavery. In most slavers and slave owners' view, enslaved Africans, sold as livestock, were not human and thus were without culture, aesthetics or spiritual essence. The African arts, dance in particular, were often described as "primitive," meaning simple, crude, savage, hedonistic or idolatrous in nature. Even as late as 1979, anthropologist John Miller Chernoff, while in Ghana, West Africa, overheard an old man say, "Most Westerners cannot find anything particularly musical about a group of drums, and their judgments, therefore, seem to only demonstrate their ethnocentric biases."[2]

In the United States during the middle to late 1800s, mockery of African Americans developed in the form of minstrelsy. As far back as the mid-1700s, African Americans performed in segregated theaters with segregated audiences. But it was through one of the most famous figures in early white American theater, Thomas Dartmouth Rice (1806–1860), known as Daddy "Jim Crow" Rice, that such entertainments took a turn. A white man fascinated with the dance of African Americans, Rice began to research and copy their steps and improvisations. Painting his face with black cork, with exaggerated lips and bug eyes, and employing grossly stereotyped vocal and floppy body language, he began what was to become a standard caricature of African Americans. An even more ironically painful tragedy is that black artists were forced to perform in blackface in front of white audiences to maintain jobs, thus beginning their own form of minstrelsy in the latter part of that century.

In the early part of the 20th century, some artists in the Western world became fascinated with the sheer abstraction and emotional contours of African sculpture, dance and music. Many of them regularly employed African aesthetics as a point of departure and inspiration. Imitated and duplicated, the African performing and visual arts became the foundation for many new global art trends and genres.

One of the earliest examples of the influence of African arts on the Western world is the development of the cubist movement in the visual arts between 1907 and 1914. To the cubists, the body or form was to be seen from "within and without, [so that it was] not . . . deformed but re-formed."[3] This view of the body was very African in concept: the body in African dance flows in polycentric and curvilinear planes, wherein circles and cross energies operate simultaneously, embraced by natural rhythmic accompaniment. There is often no distinction between the outside veneer of a form and its inner essence. The dances of Africa create balance among motion, emotion, form, content and purpose.

African art greatly influenced one of Europe's most famous artists, Pablo Picasso (1881–1973). In his later years, Picasso admitted that his first viewing of an exhibit on African art sculpture during the early 1900s threw him into a new phase of his creative spirit. At the time, he was working on a large canvas featuring a group of nude women. After exposure to the exhibit, he returned to the canvas and completely reconfigured the work. The painting, known as *Les demoiselles d'Avignon* (1907), demonstrates this stark realization. Two of the women's faces and bodies are abstracted and have an indisputable resemblance to traditional African masks and sculpture.

Many American dance forms derive from traditional African dance as well. In Nigeria, West Africa, for example, a dance characterized by the shaking of shoulders and muscles throughout the body, known as *shika*, surfaced in the Americas as the shimmy. In the early 1900s, a young black dancer by the name of Earl "Snake Hips" Tucker (d. 1937) redefined the concept of smooth, fast, gliding and gyrating hips. Years later a young white artist from the South, Elvis Presley (1935–1977), became an overnight success with his gyrating, "sexual" hip movements. Also, let us not forget American tap: a combination of Irish clogging and African dance. The creation of tap dance

21

in America is a beautiful example of cross-fertilization between two cultures brought together in the New World.

African dance is not just movement for movement's sake, but the embodiment of poetry, history, community and transformation. About the African continent's contribution to Western art, Robert Farris Thompson says, "[Africa] introduces a different art history, a history of danced art, defined in the blending of movement and sculpture, textiles and other forms, bringing into being their own inherent goodness and vitality. [It completes] the transformation of cryptic objects into doctrine. [I]f motion conveys stature to music and art, sculpture deepens motion by condensation of several actions into one."[4]

This "transformation of cryptic objects" (things with a hidden meaning) into a doctrine of danced art and community self-affirmation is clearly demonstrated in the women's secret society called Sande, among the Mende people of Sierra Leone and the Vai of Liberia, West Africa. Similarly, one can observe this process among the Egungun ancestral dancers of Nigeria's Yoruba people and in the gravity-defying stilt dances of the Dan of eastern Liberia and western Ivory Coast.

Doctrine and communal belief systems are transformed into visual movement mechanisms through which epic memories are triggered. These mechanisms—dance, music, costumes and masks—are mnemonic devices that serve to preserve and transmit cultural values, while simultaneously helping to expand traditional notions of art. A mnemonic device can be any object (the U.S. flag), a melody, a song, a rhythm or a dance. In African culture, masks appeal to a conditioned and communal understanding of psychic consciousness. For the Mende people of Sierra Leone, a mask serves as a conduit through which the person is transformed into a tangible mystical representation. The unexplained then becomes explainable.

The approximately one million Mende of Sierra Leone have developed a sophisticated system of societal and behavioral etiquette through a codified system of instruction called Sande. This system is exceptional in that it uses the art of dance as a vehicle for the transmission of lessons. Concepts of beauty, religious expression, moral guidance and training in medicinal treatments, ethics and laws are transmitted to young girls as they transition into womanhood. Sande is the keeper of the arts. The sculptural abstraction of this embodiment is in the masked character Bundu. Her hooded helmet mask—clearly defined by an elaborately carved coiffure of braided hair known as *ngufele*, a characteristically small nose, tiny slits for eyes and a large forehead, which symbolizes poise and success—is constructed of bombax, a light wood painted in "luminous" black, symbolizing purity and beauty. From the neck down, the mask is dressed in rich layers of dyed black raffia grass and cloth. A characteristic series of pronounced neck rings (sowo-wui), or coils of fat symbolizing wealth and status, reflect the Mende view of beauty. This masked character (the mnemonic device) is ever present whenever the initiates appear, providing a link between Mende culture and its people. The community is affirmed through a celebration of Mende womanhood.

The stilt dancers, known as Kwuya, from the Dan people of Liberia, defy laws of physical gravity and control. Their dance involves a conical hat covered with cowrie shells and stilts covered by long pants and a raffia skirt.[5] In their challenge to the laws of gravity and power of illusion, these masked dances assert the community's need to control natural forces in the environment—creating what I call the principle of "controlled uncontrol," the fine balance between human life on earth and natural, psychic forces.

At the root of traditional African art is the joint importance of art and morality. Many masked dance traditions embody this interwoven sense of public scrutiny, criticism, behavior and societal standards. The Egungun dancers of Nigeria's Yoruba people provide continuity between the world of their ancestors and the world of the living. Wearing layers upon layers of shiny, textured and expensive cloth panels that whirl and twirl through space, Egungun masked dancers, as Thompson says, convey "the spirit of the dead. These masked dancers represent a wisdom beyond all human understanding. Their shapes are otherworldly and very strange. They are creatures of two worlds, the purifying wind of coolness [and] the wind of God, balanced briefly upon the head of man."[6] They serve as both representations of ancestors and tangible embodiments of the divine; they are also mnemonic devices that remind the community of its divine connection to the past and its responsibility to the future.

African dance is a powerful spiritual journey colored with a diverse palette of cultures and languages. The African continent is steeped in history, mythology and legend, rich in cultural and aesthetic diversity. Its arts provide visual, verbal, physical and musical texts that are tied together through sophisticated codified systems. These texts are executed through intricate and deeply rooted cultural, religious, philosophical, kinesthetic and aesthetic matrices.

If we view the art of dance as a language, a means of visual communication, then Africa is abundant in both oral and body movement languages. It covers more than 12 million square miles, with a population of more than 350 million people speaking more than two thousand languages, and is divided into fifty-five modern nation states. Africa defies the notion of generalization in any subject. Add to the spoken word an infinite number of dance styles, and one can begin to understand the magnitude of the danced "languages" represented on the continent. A professor of mine once said that the only consistent thing about Africa is its inconsistency. But Africa is not inconsistent! If anything, one must be careful not to oversimplify definitions of the African experience. I would say that Africa is consistently diverse, a diversity that is lush with context and timbered with historic, sociopolitical and geographical influences.

Through all movement in Africa and its diaspora, there is a continent-wide synergy of time, movement and space, most eloquently demonstrated in the form of danced art. For the sake of classification, danced art in Africa can be divided into six regions, within which there are subregions and microregions, all distinguishable by ethnic and sociopolitical identities. In *The Dances of Africa* (1994), anthropologist Michael Huet focuses on just four of these regions: the Saharan and northern Sahelian zones (Niger, Nigeria, Chad, Mali); western Dry Savanna and southern Sahel (Mali, Burkina Faso, Cote D'Ivoire, Cameroon, Chad); Atlantic Coast and Western Wood Savanna (Senegal, Guinea, Cote D'Ivoire, Nigeria, Sierra Leone, Liberia); and central and eastern Africa (Cameroon, Central African Republic, Republic of Congo, Kenya, Tanzania, Rwanda, Ethiopia). Let us add two others: southern Africa (Angola, Zambia, South Africa) and northern Africa (Egypt, Libya, Algeria, Morocco, Tunisia).

Each of these geographic regions has a distinct cultural patterning. Africans brought these ancient regional and cultural patterns to the New World, transforming them alongside and within existing New World forms.

The clearest example of this transformation is West Africa's traditional Vodun system of worship, which metamorphosed into vibrant religious forms such as Vodou in Haiti, Santería in Cuba and *candomblé* in Brazil. Each of these New World spiritual systems carried within them the embodiment of traditional African concepts of meaning, forms and abstracted information. Certain principles and guidelines regarding behavior, relationship to the deceased and forces of the universe remained consistent. To this day in each of these New World religions, dance and music perform major roles in the communication with the divine, connecting the human spirit and mind-body to a kinetic interpretation of abstract natural forces. They make the intangible tangible, the unseen vivid and understood.

In 1935–1936, a young African American dancer by the name of Katherine Dunham (b. 1909) received a fellowship from the Rosenwald and Guggenheim Foundation to support her research in the West Indies. In Haiti, she discovered a personal passion and mission through the Vodou dances. Her book *Island Possessed* (1969) chronicles her spiritual and artistic journey. Through her study of the gods of Haiti—or Loas, as they are called—she introduced a "new" pantheon of dance, song, rhythm and spirituality into mainstream American and European culture.

The story of Vodou has its origin in the journey of enslaved Africans from the regions of Dahomey and Nigeria. It is interesting to note that *Vodun* is the Fon people's word for spirit or deity. Mostly misunderstood, this vibrant and healing religion is often associated with evil practices such as sorcery and witchcraft. Nothing could be further from the truth! Its main purpose is to define the human connections to the universe. It consists of a complex pantheon of gods, rituals and laws. How different is this system from the Western world's acceptance of Greek and Roman gods and goddesses as vehicles to control and manipulate human destiny?

The dances of Haiti are a metaphor for self-definition, divine spiritual connection and even freedom, personified through movement and rhythm. A codified system of movements, rhythms and songs, each with a defined purpose and series of orderly, prescribed events, dance in Haiti embraces the characteristics of African art in order to transform experience into doctrine and doctrine into living visible practice.

Possession is another misunderstood phenomenon in African religions throughout the world. In these religions, the soul is believed to be nonmaterial, transient and transformable, capable of existing on its own. It therefore has the power to displace the physical body and to reveal itself through a set of prescribed representations dictated by a series of codified, religious controls. During possession, the human body (masked or unmasked) transcends itself, creating a visual image in which merge surrender, transformation and connection with the divine and through all time.

Another profound example of African dance in the New World is in the African American dance form the ring shout, from the early 1900s. In it, we can observe the ability of African dance to transform and reinvent itself, ensuring spiritual survival against severe atrocities. The ring shout, more than a dance, functioned as a prayer meeting performed in a circle and incorporated percussive "shouting" and hand clapping as a main feature. It is not a coincidence that the Arabic word *saut* is pronounced like and has the same meaning as our word *shout*, as many enslaved Africans came from the Arabic area of West Africa.

Ever since the first enslaved Africans landed in the Americas, their dances became a major influence in the redefinition of the American body and map landscape. Off the Carolina coast, on Sea Island, also known as "the Ellis Island of black America," West African and European languages were combined into what we now know as Gullah. Heavily influenced with an aesthetic legacy from the Mende people of Sierra Leone, this vibrant culture still demonstrates the connectedness of African people throughout the world. Gullah dancers, in the ancient African tradition, are often inspired to "Gimme de kneebone bent." In his article with this phrase as its title, Peter H. Wood says, "many West Africans believed that straightened knees, hips and elbows epitomized death and rigidity, while flexed joints embodied energy and life. The bent kneebone symbolized the ability to 'get down.'"[7]

At the beginning of the 21st century, choreographers of African descent continue to celebrate their heritage and psychic bonds with the continent of Africa. Trained in Western dance, many work to create a new and exciting vocabulary that preserves and renews definitions of traditional forms. These choreographers and their companies have developed a genre of dance language in the West that is a unique blend of traditional African and modern dance. On any given day in *The New York Times*, one can read reviews of new and exciting dance artists working within the modern dance genre, while delving deep into their ancestral roots for inspiration in both form and context.

In *Children of the Passage* (2001), choreographer Ronald K. Brown (b. 1966) blends traditional African movement with modern expression to paint a spiritual picture of the Middle Passage (the travel of slaves across the Atlantic Ocean to the Americas). Rennie Harris (b. 1964) connects contemporary street life to the stage in his solo work *Endangered Species*, with his hip-hop movement poetry. Urban Bush Women, a company formed by Jawole Willa Jo Zollar (b. 1950), performs works that break barriers and stereotypes, such as in Zollar's solo work *Batty Moves* (1995), a humorous yet political work that features the derrière as a tribute to the prominent hip and pelvic movements of Afro-Caribbean dance. These artists are not an anomaly, but part of a long line of inventors who use Africa's myriad cultures as an eternal spring for their creative spirits. They are recipients of a legacy with deep and ancient roots.

Equally and even more critically important are choreographers who, in contrast to others who reinvent movement within this newly discovered vocabulary, work to preserve, stimulate and promulgate ancient traditions for future generations. Asadata Dafora (1890–1965), Pearl Primus (1919–1994) and Chuck Davis (b. 1937) are just a few of the individuals who have contributed to the African presence on the American dance scene.

It is essential that this cross-cultural pollination of African and Western dance does not backfire by consigning traditional African forms to oblivion in the haze of trendy redefinitions. The study of history might make one skeptical, however. I hope that these ancient forms are allowed to stand on their own as viable and fully nonnegotiable genres.

At its best, dance heals. It transforms and elevates. The body is a vessel through which the divine resides, waiting to be made tangible. Dance is a path through which spirit, mind and body merge. African dance exemplifies this thread between the psyche and the body as instrument. It catapults the psyche into boundless possibilities. It not only serves to make horrific situations understandable and tolerable, but, more important, provides divine connections to a higher presence.

African Dance: It is celebration. It is divine. It is *Ashé!*

REFERENCES

Ajayi, Omofolabo S. *Yoruba dance: The semiotics of movement and body attitude in Nigerian culture.* New York: African World, 1998.

Ardyn Boone, Sylvia. *Radiance from the waters: Ideals of feminine beauty in Mende art.* New Haven, Conn.: Yale University Press, 1986.

Aschenbrenner, Joyce. *Katherine Dunham: Reflections on the social and political contexts of Afro-American dance.* New York: Congress on Research in Dance, 1981.

Bellegarde-Smith, Patrick. *Haiti: The breached citadel.* New York: Westview, 1990.

Brown, Tony. *Black lies, white lies: The truth according to Tony Brown.* New York: William Morrow, 1995.

Deren, Maya. *Divine horsemen: The living gods of Haiti.* London: Thames and Hudson, 1953.

Dunham, Katherine. *Island possessed.* Chicago: University of Chicago Press, 1969.

Haskins, James. *Black dance in America: A history through its people.* New York: Harper Trophy, 1992.

Oliver, Roland. *The African experience: Major themes in African history from earliest times to the present.* London: Weidenfeld and Nicolson, 1991.

Williams, Lavinia. Master teacher and mentor. Conversations and correspondence. Unpublished material, late 1960s, early 1970s.

ENDNOTES

[1] Robert Farris Thompson, *African art in motion* (Berkeley: University of California Press, 1974), p. 47.

[2] John Miller Chernoff, *African rhythm and sensibility* (Chicago: University of Chicago Press, 1979), p. 27.

[3] Albert E. Elsen, *Purposes of art* (New York: Holt, Rinehart and Winston, 1967), p. 366.

[4] Thompson, *African art,* p. xii.

[5] *Raffia* grass comes from the forests of sub-Saharan Africa. The raffia palm, known as *Raffia vinifera,* yields young fiber-type leaves five or six feet long that can be sliced into small strips and dried lengthwise for a grasslike texture. The *cowry shell* is a small marine snail of the Cypraeidae family. Its characteristics are a thick humped back and a slit underside with corrugated edges. Traditionally used as money in parts of Asia and Africa, this shell has become a much sought-after item in today's world, where it is predominantly used as ornamentation.

[6] Thompson, *African art,* p. 127.

[7] Peter H. Wood, *Gimme de kneebone bent: African body language and the evolution of African dance forms* (project booklet for American Dance Festival: The Black Tradition in American Modern Dance, 1993), p. 7.

CHAPTER FOUR

introduction

Folk dance actively embodies vital aspects of a peoples' character. Rosa Guerrero is a well-known Texas dance educator who brings a passion to the subject through personal reminiscences about her experiences with dance and about the conditions of Mexican Americans. Her expertise in a wide variety of the world's folk forms and her vast experience in both modern dance and dance for children allow her to chronicle her stories in intimate and professional ways. Folk dances of all types bring people together to celebrate their differences as equals. Such communal activities create mutual respect, where we look into each other's minds and spirits and embrace both our differences and similarities. As the eminent musicologist and folklorist Alan Lomax (1915–2002) once said, "It is the voiceless people of the planet who really have in their memories the 90,000 years of human life and wisdom."[1] In chapter three on African dance, Caulker calls the earth our mother and the sky our father, images that both overlap and diverge with Guerrero's parental metaphors for folk dance.

FOLK DANCE: FATHER MUSIC, MOTHER DANCE

Rosa Guerrero

Ah, Father Music, beckon your wife, Dance.

Call forth your beautiful children created from your wedded bliss.

Let them spin, twirl, and move throughout the earth to join with

nature's song. Let them laugh, play,

and make joyous sounds named after you, Father Music.[2]

The United States has often been called a melting pot, but it is really a multicultural tapestry. In a melting pot, immigrants and all indigenous peoples lose their Old World identity and language in order to become "Americans." But a true American, I believe, is made up of a combination of many beautiful cultural groups and individuals, all of which contribute to a shared weaving.

As a former educator for the El Paso Public Schools for twenty years, I always told my students how beautiful they were. Whether black, brown or white, each was special. In the classroom and during my cultural dance presentations, I tried to show them that we all are part of the great cultural flow of humanity. Because of our respective and mixed cultural heritages, we all are Americans who bring something unique to the fabric of American life. We are threads woven into a multicultural tapestry or notes in a chord of music; if all the threads or the notes were the same, there could be no harmony, no real beauty, because harmony is based on differences, not similarities. This is as true in human relationships as it is in music and dance. So I try to teach my students how to be proud of our differences and how to respect the differentness of others. This notion, to me, is what my country is all about.

Folk dances in this country and around the world truly embody these differences. For example, Afro-Latin and Afro-Caribbean sounds easily bring everyone together on a dance floor. You see *cumbias*, mambos, meringues, rumbas and sambas all danced with their flavors and rhythms. When the balladlike boleros (soft, slow music) are played and sung, we all come together as one species of human beings. At these times, music and dance become truly universal.

Latinos like me who live in the El Paso area represent the largest minority in the United States. If we do not teach our students to have pride in their original culture, to believe in and educate themselves in order to better their lives, to learn both *their* languages and others, thereby becoming truly bilingual and multicultural, then we are going to have continuing problems.

In the 1970s, I started the first *folklorico* dance group in El Paso, and it was not easy. Amelia Hernandez (1917–2000), from Mexico City's famous Ballet Folklorico, first coined the word *folklorico*, which comes from the words *folk*, meaning "people," and *lore*, meaning "the life and history of the people." Thus, the Spanish word *folklorico* is tied to strong feelings of affection, pride and cohesiveness.

Back then, students refused to speak Spanish or learn it, thinking it an inferior and "dirty" language. They would say they did not want to lower themselves to the level of the Juárez, Tijuana, Nogales and Matamoros Mexicans right across the border. They did not want to have an accent. I believe that an accent is like a folk dance step, however: each person does it differently— we all turn, hop, jump, leap, smile and enjoy the dance in uniquely different ways. The person "who has an accent knows another language," says the Mexican American actor Ricardo Montalban (b. 1920).

Fifty percent of the students I worked with hated their culture, the Spanish language, themselves and their parents' heritage and country. They did not know who they were. Some Mexican people use a special word, *pocho*, to refer to Mexican American Latinos who do not have a language, a culture, a country or a sense of being and belonging. *Pochos* do not belong to either Mexico or the United States, and definitely not to Texas. That is why so many changed their names, such as Vicky Carr and Richie Valens to Victoria Cardoza, Ricardo Valenzuela—although marketing and public relations were also important reasons. Which names are easier to pronounce, more "American"? Again, what is "American"? More than ever, since September 11, 2001, we need to learn how to celebrate diversity, not oppress it, if we are to remain and grow as one nation.

In the 1940s, many teachers in our schools did not really know any better. "Assimilate before we lose them" was often the rule in the educational system. But we all have borrowed from each other in this tapestry, mosaic, salad bowl, bouquet, quilt and rainbow—this culture wrongly called a "melting pot."

When I was young, dances taught to elementary school children were called "rhythms" and "singing games." We learned the Looby Lou (a predecessor to the Hokey Pokey), the Paw-Paw Patch, Skip to My Lou, the Virginia reel, and How Do You Do, My Partner? Some of these dances came from England, some were from other European countries, and some were influenced by African American folk songs. In spite of these influences, many of us chose to retain our heritage, roots and culture.

Since my first efforts at developing and spreading the *folklorico* dance, more than fifty *folkloricos* have sprung up in El Paso alone. In Ciudad Juárez, our sister city right across the Rio Grande, there are hundreds. El Paso schools now include *folkloricos* in their curricula, allowing students to get credit in fine arts or in physical education and wellness programs. Folk dancing is actually an all-around wellness program. All I did was plant a *folklorico* seed to help prevent students from dropping out of school or becoming a nuisance in our society. Pushed out of school by some educators who had little cultural understanding or sensitivity, many of these kids had no self-pride.

Because many of our folk dances today come from other countries, opportunities to preserve these beautiful dance forms have never been greater. With the blending of the cultures through the national bicentennial celebrations and the Sesquicentennial in Texas, many Americans have developed pride in their ethnic and racial heritages. There has been a rediscovery of "ethnic identity" in our communities. We are truly a land of immigrants, and the diversity of our peoples is evident in our folkways and folklore—our foods, music, dance, languages, customs, religions and traditions.

Folk dances developed in different countries for various reasons, but all of them reflect the essence of the people and their ways of life. There are dances about birth, death, hunting, fishing, marriage, fertility, coming of age, war, religion, nature, flowers, the universe, and astronomy. For example, the Yaqui Deer Dance celebrates animal life, and the Corn Dance of Central and North America celebrates the harvest. Folk dances are like languages. They are the souls and spirits of their peoples. A community that sings and dances is a happy community.

Folk dances have many formations: circle, semicircle, circle within a circle, lines, squares, parallel lines and patterned positions. The variety of formations depends on the culture and the country. Folk dances can be intergenerational and cross-cultural, and anyone can dance them and be included. The basic steps include walking, running, skipping, galloping, sliding, hopping, jumping and leaping, and these simple steps are used in the folk dances of all countries.

Traditional folk dance steps progress from the simple walk in many directions to intricate choreographies that only very skilled performers can produce. Such movements can be found in the Russian Cossack or Slavic dances with their leaps, jumps and fast turns. Amateurs can observe and enjoy these dances until a simpler version is introduced, when they can again be participants.

Because folk dances evolve from a broad range of countries and cultures, a few definitions are in order. According to anthropologists, an *ethnic group* is a people with the same folkways, language, music, dance, customs and food. Ethnic dances are actually specialized folk dances, such as flamenco and the aforementioned Russian Cossack dance. As the world gets smaller and smaller, we now have multiracial, multiethnic and multicultural peoples everywhere. Their dances, like their cultures and languages, are a hybridization of styles and character.

In some countries and cultures, folk dances have been transformed into social dances. In 1920s and 1930s America, for example, the tango, rumba, fox-trot, fandango, *paso doble* and a variety of other still current ballroom dances became very popular. The lively swing and jitterbug followed in the late 1930s and 1940s. Today, ballroom dance competitions and exhibitions all over the world include dances that originated here—the jitterbug, the fox-trot and swing, which I consider to be American folk dances.

Square dances originated in the French and Spanish quadrilles, formations of squares with eight people. Other national folk dances from different parts of the world include: the *jota* from Spain, the *fado* from Portugal, the tarantella from Italy, the hora from Israel, the *cueca* from Chile, the *cumbia* from Colombia, the merengue from the Dominican Republic, the rumba from Cuba, the *jarabe tapatio* (Mexican hat dance) from Mexico and the polonaise from Poland. Many of these dances can be used for ballroom dances.

Because we are largely a land of immigrants, the only true indigenous folk dance is that of the Native Americans. Pre-Columbian cultures highly regarded music and dance, seeing them as inseparable from and necessary to daily life. Dance was so important to Mexican Aztec society that teachers taught it to people who were twelve years and older in special houses. Young students were required to attend classes so that they would be able to perform at dance festivals. Many hours of practice were essential before they were ready to present these dances. If they made a mistake in the dance, they were severely punished and sometimes even executed!

The difference between Spanish and English and Dutch colonists was that the Spanish were a very spirited people who loved dancing, music and life. The English and Dutch tended to be quieter and more low-key in personality.

The Spanish explorer Juan de Oñate crossed the Rio Grande more than four hundred years ago on the Royal Kings Highway (Camino Real) from the Zacatecas area in Mexico and traveled to the Santa Fe area in New Mexico. Many people in the Southwest have roots that go back twenty-four generations to ancestors such as Oñate. People in New Mexico have preserved many of their original folk dances, cultural traditions and folk groups. Quadrilles are still traditionally performed first by the oldest eight senior citizens in New Mexican towns. In *la marcha,* or "the march," the eldest couple starts by traveling down the center of a ballroom followed by the other couples, who then peel off alternately to the right and left in twos and then fours as they move toward the front two couples. In eights and sixteens, the entire group walks all together down the center of the ballroom. Likewise, other *danzas* and music from New Mexico continue to be preserved with pride and dignity, and are passed down to the children by their elders.

Many other traditional folk dances from Europe and Spain are danced throughout the Southwest. The isolated geographic location of many towns has helped in the preservation of these cultures and traditions. Even the Spanish language has been preserved, and some of the archaic words used in these dances can be traced to the early settlers. On the other hand, this same isolation has been a reason why many immigrants have been cut off from their original cultural roots and heritage. Another reason, of course, is the distance from their mother countries. Ironically, although many Latinos did not cross the Rio Grande, the Rio Grande crossed us, so to speak, and we therefore live in two worlds, two countries and two cultures. We speak two languages, have two distinct lives and live them out in two different and wonderful ways. Preserving both cultures is a major challenge for all of us.

Other European peoples brought their social dances to the United States, the Caribbean and Latin America, including Mexico. These dances include the polka from Bohemia, a part of the former Czechoslovakia; the schottische from Germany, which became the *chotis* in Mexico and Spain; and the waltz from Austria and Germany. Mexico has its own waltz, which many believe is indigenous to the country, called *sobre las olas*, or "over the waves." It was created by Juventino Rosas, a Zapotec from Oaxaca. *La varsouvienna*, originally the *varsouvienne* from Austria, later became "Put Your Little Foot In" in the United States. The mazurka from Poland was a forerunner of the *varsouvienne*.

Like so many of the folk dances we practice today, ballroom steps remain relatively simple and nearly universal. The basic waltz includes a movement called the *balance* (from the French *balancé*), as well as a forward and backward step. With just these three steps, one can lead any partner all around the dance floor. This same three-quarter rhythm is utilized in the Philippines with a dance done between two poles, called *tinikling*. They, too, have their own waltz, in which they balance candles or coconuts on their heads and hit them together like Spanish castanets to the waltz rhythm. In the United States, waltzes are named for states, such as the Tennessee waltz, the Missouri waltz, and the Beautiful Ohio waltz.

34

There may be no greater heritage of folk dance, music, folklore and other influences than that absorbed by Texas, because of its more than one-thousand-mile border with Mexico. Mexican states along this huge US state include Chihuahua, Coahuila, Nuevo León and Tamaulipas. One small example of the acceptance and incorporation of dance into the mixed cultures along this border is the polka. With the addition of an accordion, the Mexican American *conjuntos* were born. The *conjuntos* are a small group of musicians who formed their own styles of music called Mex-Tex, or Tex-Mex, depending on which side of the border one lives. There is a certain "twang" to the *conjunto* music, very much like the Texas twang in speaking. These groups play for the dances, gatherings and fiestas of South Texas.

As they followed the crop harvests, migrant workers and their families brought these songs and dances to other parts of the United States. Other forms of *conjuntos* were developed in Chihuahua. West Texas, in particular, merged styles from that Mexican state with influences from Austria, Germany, France and other European nations.

The cattle industry gave birth to the *vaquero* ("buckaroo" or "cowboy"), and dances using the lariat, such as *la reata*, were created and subsequently used in Mexican rodeos. The word *rodeo* comes from the Spanish *rodear*, meaning "roundup." In the Mexican state of Tamaulipas, the horsewhip is still used in some dances, such as the *caballito*. Intricate footwork called *zapateado* is danced with boots and influenced the development of beautiful, handmade leather costumes. The music used in this dance has a falsetto sound in both the violin and the voice of the singer.

Ireland, with its lively fiddle music and energetic jigs, reels and clogging, contributed much to hillbilly and mountain music and dance. American hybrids were born in the Ozarks, Appalachia and the Southwest. The hoedown, for example, came from the cotton fields, where farmers, after working very hard, said, "Let's put the hoe down and dance." And clogging transformed into flamenco in Spain and tap dance in the United States.

The polka is still one of the most popular dances on both sides of the border. The basic polka step is from Bohemia, but the traditional Polish polka uses high jump steps involving the rapid movement of the body from side to side. The German polka involves maintaining low steps and appears more conservative, but still quite merry. Yells and shouts (in Spanish, *gritos*) are heard during folk dancing in all cultures, but the Mexican and Mex-Tex polkas add quite a bit of salsa *(chilitio)* to their dances. Starting with the basic European step, Mexicans developed a kind of shuffle to go all around the dance floor on wobbly, bent knees in a relaxed way. If you really dance the European polka with stamina and real polka hop steps, then you are literally running the half-mile or mile in some cases, but in Mexico you do a sort of shuffle, much more relaxed and easy-going. It is said that *"El reloj corre en los Estados Unidos y anda en Mexico"*: the clock runs in the United States and walks in Mexico!

In the Rio Grande Valley, the polka is called *el tacuachito* (the "possum shuffle"); in Colorado and New Mexico it is called *"rancherito* dancing" ("ranchstyle dancing"); and in the El Paso/Juárez and Chihuahuan Desert areas it is the *corridito* ("little *corrido"*). *Corridos* are Mexican ballads, folk songs and music for people who do not generally get their news from the media, but hear it passed on vocally from village to village.

My parents were my first teachers. I started to dance in my mother's womb and will continue to dance in my tomb. I was three years old when my father put my feet on top of his feet so I could feel the rhythm and tempo of the music as he held my hands. By the time I was five, I knew my waltz, polka, schottische, mazurka, *varsouvienne, paso doble,* rumba and *danza.* My teachers in school called me "culturally deprived." I was not culturally deprived; I was culturally different, like all of us humans on earth. I did not and could not speak English, so I was punished severely for speaking my mother's tongue, Spanish—just as all the Italians, Germans, Czechs, Scandinavians, American Indians, Asian Americans and Latinos everywhere, especially the migrants and immigrants, were punished for speaking their languages.

In order to make us melt into the pot, many of our ancestors, grandparents and parents sadly abandoned their mother tongue. We were told that we did not need French, German, Chinese, Japanese, Navajo and Spanish in our lives and that we needed to speak "English only." Educators now, not realizing the degree of their former ignorance (or ours!), are finally beginning to learn. If folk dance is the spirit and soul of a people, so is one's native language. Although it was very difficult for me in the 1970s to try to teach our dances, our beautiful history and culture, and the richness of our roots and heritage to Mexican Americans, Chicanos and Latinos, we now see mariachis and *folkloricos* blossoming everywhere.

Folk dance and music nourished and protected me from all the negatives in the world. If you touch a child with music and dance, you touch a soul and spirit. You make that child so happy and proud of who he or she is. For me, dance and music opened the doors to life itself. For more than sixty years,

I have tried to do the same thing for all people. Folk dancing is simply a great way to have fun, a genuine cultural wellness program that is recreational, social and therapeutic. If all the economic, political, social, business and technology summits and conferences could include a seminar in folk dancing, the participants would leave with a spirit of clean fun and a clearer understanding of cultural diversity. Movement releases tension, depression, anxiety and grouchiness. Because our fast, stressful world does not always permit us to enjoy life to its fullest, we should consider folk dancing as a recreation. Easier than jogging and aerobics, it is a culturally enriching, wonderful experience.

ENDNOTES

[1] Jon Pareles, "Alan Lomax, who raised voice of folk music in U.S., dies at 87," *The New York Times*, July 21, 2002, A1.

[2] Excerpted from a poem dedicated to Rosa Guerrero by Loretta Diane Walker, music teacher and poet at Reagan Magnet School in Odessa, Texas (1999).

CHAPTER FIVE

introduction

American Helen Myers has found much artistic and aesthetic value in Japan's vastly different dance forms. However foreign Japanese dance theater must still seem to 21st century Western sensibilities, it should recall a more familiar history and tradition, ballet, which is merely one-fourth as old as some of its Japanese counterparts. Both ballet and Japanese dance owe their complexities to their intricate historical developments. The fourth and most current style Myers discusses, Butoh, has some surprising affinities with Western postmodern dance. Envisioning other traditions alongside one's own can bring one's understanding of dance into sharper focus.

PIERCING THE MASK OF JAPANESE DANCE THEATER

Helen Myers

This chapter provides a brief historical, cultural and aesthetic overview of the Japanese dance theater forms of Bugaku, Noh, Kabuki and Butoh. It explores these forms through a Western audience member's eyes and compares and contrasts the four forms.

In any attempt to understand the historical roots of Bugaku, Noh, Kabuki and Butoh, it is useful to take a brief look at the history of Japanese folk culture, which often took the form of grotesquery. Ghost stories, demons and Dionysian-like dances could be found in the seasonal festivities throughout the Japanese countryside. One of that country's central creation myths involves the sun goddess, Amaterasu, who, insulted by another god and withdrawing to a cave, plunged the whole world into darkness. All attempts to draw her out were to no avail, until other spirits gathered outside and performed a wild dance, after which she returned to the world, restoring warmth and light. "Thus light and darkness, dance and grotesquerie have been closely intertwined in Japan since the dawn of time."[1]

Before Confucianism and Buddhism were brought to Japan beginning in the 5th century, forms of naturism (worship of the forces of nature) and animism (belief that inanimate objects possess a spirit) were practiced.[2] Japanese culture has a history of synthesizing outside influences, as early cultural waves came from China, Tibet and India via Korea. Bugaku developed in the 8th century as a stately dance for the emperor's court. It has been performed continuously in Japan since that time, making Bugaku the oldest institutionalized dance form in the world.[3] During the 14th through the 16th centuries, Japan entered a period of civil wars and feuding between rival fiefs. Noh developed during this time period from an earlier theater form called Sangaku, which was crude, realistic and often humorous. It subsequently became a more refined dance theater for a sophisticated and aristocratic audience.

In 1603, a period of shogun (warrior-lord) governments began when Shogun Tokugawa Ieyasu seized control. This period of government lasted until the emperor was returned to power in 1868;[4] it was during this time that Kabuki emerged and developed. Butoh began in the late 1950s, partially as a reaction to these earlier forms, but also to the strict social boundaries in Japanese society. Butoh emanated from a society reeling from the horrors of the bombs dropped on Hiroshima and Nagasaki at the end of World War II in 1945.

BUGAKU

Bugaku has survived in Japan from the 8th century to the present day. It developed out of the imperial court rituals, themselves influenced by earlier Chinese, Indian and Tibetan dances. Bugaku originally flowered during the Tang dynasty (618–906 C.E.) in China. Chinese culture had absorbed influences from other cultures and at its height greatly influenced the arts of Japan. During its initial period of development, Bugaku was a highly creative and dramatic form, with specific characters and story lines. However, beginning in the 11th century, the Japanese court slowly codified Bugaku into a more elegant and stylized form in keeping with the highly ceremonial court etiquette of the time.[5] Bugaku eventually lost its dramatic quality and became abstracted into a more ritualized, courtly dance form.

The name *bugaku* comes from the Japanese characters *bu*, for "dance," and *gaku*, which is generally translated as "music." It is always performed with a form of music known as *gagaku* (elegant music). *Gagaku* was the traditional court music that was brought to Japan from China, and it reached its greatest popularity in the Japanese imperial court during the 10th century. Bugaku is still performed today with its corresponding *gagaku;* the music and dance styles are divided into categories of "left" and "right" music and dances. The origin of these categories is not known, although it has been suggested that some connection with Confucian ideals is possible. It is common practice in Bugaku to alternate entrances for dances, from dressing rooms located on the left and right sides of the stage.

The various types of Bugaku include: Bubu (military dances), Bunbu (court dances), Warawamai (children's dances), Onnamai (women's dances) and Hashirimono (running dances). One should note that all of these dances are performed by males, including the Onnamai.[6] Bugaku performances vary according to the seasons and combine various types of dances, alternating styles and numbers of dancers. Each type of Bugaku is proscribed for two, four or six dancers. The dancers move slowly, symmetrically and forcefully in this ceremonial dance form. The stately *gagaku* provides a solemn musical background, repeating the musical theme with slight variations to suggest the cyclic flow of evolutionary time. Bugaku exemplifies imperial court demeanor, with the dancers showing honor, restraint, conformity, emotional detachment and strength in their movements.

Bugaku dancers wear exquisite, brightly colored silk brocade costumes. The dances originally were performed in the official uniform of the imperial court, which designated the dancer's court rank. Today, elaborate pieces dating back three hundred years are still in use. Bugaku dancers often wear masks that represent supernatural beings, animal gods from Indian and Chinese mythology or faces of people from other Asian cultures. Unlike Noh masks, Bugaku masks are used for one dance only. The dancers use props such as swords, oversized jewels and branches in symbolic gestures. A traditional Bugaku stage is built of a square wooden platform elevated from the floor, with two dressing-room tents set up on either side of the stage. The stage is covered by a heavy cloth and framed by a brightly painted, two-foot-high rail. When Bugaku is performed outdoors or at a shrine, a temporary stage is set up, so this type of stage may vary somewhat.

After the splendor of the aristocratic culture surrounding the emperor's court during the Heian period (1185–1392 C.E.), the power of the aristocracy was greatly reduced, as Japan came under the influence of the samurai (military) class. Consequently, Bugaku, which was an expression of the vanishing aristocratic supremacy, fell into decline until after World War II, when the Japanese government finally recognized it and *gagaku* as important national treasures.[7] Performances in the United States and Europe in the 1960s and 1970s left a grand impression abroad, further enhancing the status of Bugaku in Japan. Once observed only by members of the imperial court, it may now be seen three times a year on the grounds of the imperial palace in Tokyo or occasionally at major shrines around Japan. These public performances, often televised, have helped make Bugaku available to millions of Japanese citizens and will help to ensure its future.

NOH

Noh developed from the earlier form of Sangaku in the 14th century. Sangaku was first performed in shrines and temples and sometimes at court, but it also became popular among the common people.[8] It was not a polished theater form and so was considered beneath the dignity of the ruling class. Noh, however, developed with an aesthetic designed to please the taste of refined patrons. All Noh plays combine dance, music and acting and are based on morality themes. Unlike most Western theater, a Noh play unfolds very slowly, as the performers dance, speak and sing in a very deliberate and controlled manner. Such a pace in a Noh performance is part of the aesthetic experience for its audience.

The two greatest Noh theoreticians, Kan-Ami (1333–1384), also referred to as Kannami, and his eldest son Ke-Ami (1363–1443), or Zeami, developed Noh into an elegant, sophisticated art form. It is from Japanese aristocratic and warrior aesthetics that the Noh concepts of Bushido (the samurai code of ethics, which includes honor, loyalty, courage, discipline and military training), Miyako (the code of manners for the imperial court) and Zen (spiritual training) were developed.[9]

Masaru Sekine, a Noh scholar, states that "the Noh theater, now six hundred years old, can be studied today not only in its own right but as an introduction to and explanation of Japanese culture in a wider sense."[10] Noh distills emotions and gestures into simple, subtle and stylized forms of expression. Its lack of realistic presentation and extensive use of symbolism require a high degree of understanding and sophistication from the audience. "The dramatic element is the least important," explains P. G. O'Neill, "for the main aim of No [sic] is not to unfold a story scene by scene in as vivid a way as possible, but rather to capture the mood of a moment and to represent it in an aesthetically satisfying way."[11]

Noh emphasizes tradition, repetition and the translucence of *hana* (spiritual beauty). The great Noh theoretician Ke-Ami brought this concept of *hana* to full fruition.

At age twenty-two and upon the death of his father, Ke-Ami took over leadership of the Kanze-ze Noh troupe. He stated that *"hana* is the life of Noh" and described it in a Noh performance: "All plants and trees flower at their appropriate season, and people appreciate their flowers because they are fresh and novel. Noh is the same as these flowers."[12] Great artists can find spontaneity and individual expression in the mastery of this six-hundred-year-old tradition, and it is through this experience that the audience comes to sense *hana*. Both the performer and the audience share *hana* as an ultimate spiritual performance experience. It was common for older Noh actors to become monks near the end of their lives and to devote themselves to spiritual awakening.[13] As Ke-Ami aged, he, too, became more interested in spiritual rather than physical beauty, and contemporary writings indicate that he became a Zen monk in his later life.

In order to bring freshness to this very traditional form, Noh companies organize their performances so as to present a unique program each time. A typical Noh program consists of two Noh plays, separated by a short comedy skit known as a Kyogen. The two plays are chosen carefully, the time of year taken into consideration and a unique combination of the two plays arranged. Noh actors must have a large repertoire of characters so that they can act in a wide variety of Noh plays. Even so, Noh actors specialize in certain roles and perform them year after year.

Five predominant types of Noh plays are grouped according to their subject matter. The first group, Waki Noh, is a god play, whose main character praises the peace and prosperity of the land. The second, Shura Noh, is a warrior play, in which the ghost of the warrior usually appears and, with quiet elegance, tells of the torments it is suffering. The third group, Kazura Noh, includes plays about well-born ladies, in which an atmosphere of gentle, elegant beauty pervades the action. Contained in the fourth group, Kurui Noh are dramatic plays that deal with mentally disoriented persons and are more like traditional plays than those of any other group. The fifth group of Noh plays, Kiri Noh, portrays supernatural beings, gods or devils in some form. They usually have a faster tempo than the other types.[14]

Also important to the Noh theater is the symbolic stage area of cedar boards and the entranceway leading in from the left, with three pine trees on both sides of the bridge. Clay pots are carefully distributed under the stage to enhance the sound of the actors' stomping. The pine trees on the entrance bridge and painted on the back wall of the stage had, and still have, superstitious beliefs attached to them; it is unthinkable not to have them in a Noh theater in some form. The Japanese people believe them to be symbols of eternity, longevity and peace because of their durability, beautiful form and evergreen leaves. In the Noh theater, they represent not only everlasting physical beauty, but also the Noh actors' desire for the "everlasting prosperity of their theatre."[15]

The Noh stance incorporates a straight spine, with a slight lean forward from the hips. The main movement action is walking, a precise, gliding action with heels barely leaving the floor and feet flexed. As the leg steps forward onto the whole foot, "motion flows out of a totally centered, earth-drawn body, which appears to hover inches above the floor."[16] The movements of Noh are designed for the elaborate and bulky traditional costumes. Performers often wear masks, which are stylized representations of different characters. Props, such as fans, also have symbolic meanings and serve as extensions of the hands, which are hidden by long sleeves. Each gesture or traveling phrase has a timing aspect to it: *jo*, the introduction or prelude, has a slow and steady tempo; *ha*, the development or exposition, has a moderate pace; and *kyu*, the climax or finale, is quick, with a dramatic ending.[17] These *jo-ha-kyu* movement sequences are codified into *katas*, each of which has many different meanings that an informed Noh audience clearly understands.

One of the most common *katas* is *hiraki*, meaning "to open." *Hiraki* consists of three steps traveling backward at a medium level, as the arms rise out to the sides with the elbows higher than the wrists. At no time do the arms reach outside of the body's kinesphere (the sphere of space surrounding the body). After a brief stillness, the arms return in a slow and sustained manner to their original position.[18] This *kata* is characteristic of Noh's movement vocabulary of sustained, controlled and elegant gestures, and of its traveling patterns designed to exemplify an aristocratic aesthetic. Noh is meant to be enjoyed by a sophisticated audience that appreciates tradition and detail.

KABUKI

Kabuki emerged in the latter part of the 16th century as a popular theater form. Although Noh had remained throughout its development primarily a theater for the intellectual and wealthy, Kabuki began with a more imprecise dramatic form and embodied various styles of acting. It was at times racy, violent and sensationalistic. Kabuki reflected the average Japanese person's tastes at the time of its development. Like Noh, it combines dance, music and drama. Unlike Noh, it uses more elaborate scenery, costumes and makeup, incorporates quicker movements, and is a more dramatic spectacle.

The word *kabuki* is derived from *kabuku*, an obsolete verb meaning "to incline," but by the early 17th century it had come to mean "unusual or out of the ordinary." It is generally agreed that the first Kabuki performance occurred in Kyoto in 1596. This early style of Kabuki, known as Onna-Kabuki (women's Kabuki), was started by a woman named Okuni. In 1629, the warrior-lord Iemitsu prohibited Onna-Kabuki on the grounds that it was immoral; women did not appear again on a public stage in Japan until after 1868. Young, attractive boys took the place of the women in female roles, but then certain samurai warriors became attracted to the young boys, so the shogun also forbade this form of Kabuki in 1652.[19] After this date, men began performing all of the female roles, a practice that continues to this day. This custom of all-male performers is common to many traditional Japanese dance theater forms, including Bugaku, Noh, Kabuki and others. It was one of the traditions that Butoh groups rebelled against in the 20th century. It is interesting to note the similarity to the Western theater of 16th and 17th century England, where the men performed all the roles in plays by Shakespeare and other playwrights of the era.

The shogun governments enacted a series of laws designed to control this popular art form, which had attracted the attention of a newly forming *chonin* (townsperson) social class, the equivalent of our American middle class. One of these laws, enacted in the mid–17th century, required Kabuki performers to register officially as actors for specific types of roles. "This practice led to the stereotyping of Kabuki characters by age, sex, and personality."[20] A male hero character is known as a *tachiyaku*, whereas a young female character is called a *wakaonnagata*.

As early as 1587, laws were enacted to control the society at large, thereby squelching rebellion and ridding Japan of outside missionary influences. By 1637, Japanese people were not allowed to leave the country, and Japan became isolated from the rest of the world. Even travel within Japan was discouraged by guards at roadblocks who carefully examined each traveler. Roads and bridges were deliberately kept in poor repair. Towns became more and more isolated from each other, and careers subsequently tended to become hereditary. This practice still exists in Noh and Kabuki theater today, with a *gekidan* theater family carefully protecting its acting techniques and passing roles down from father to son. One must be born into or adopted by a theater family in order to perform Noh or Kabuki professionally.

Along with the rise of the *chonin* social class came the rise of Kabuki theater, as this newly important economic class came to comprise the principal audience members. Kabuki became an expression of middle-class artistic tastes and ethical beliefs: "Kabuki, existing in the forefront of popular taste, was particularly susceptible to the waves of novelty which swept its audience. . . . And so there is in the Kabuki not only unrestraint, lavish detail, and almost uncontrolled line, but simultaneously, restraint, economy of statement, and exquisite control."[21]

Kabuki audiences come to the theater to see a succession of striking images. "The audience requires that the Kabuki be an eye-filling spectacle. Stage decoration, costuming, makeup are colorful, bold, rich, and luxuriant."[22] The movements and gestures of Kabuki are larger and broader than those of Noh, but are nevertheless precise in design and execution. For example, a rhythmical movement of the head and precise gestures of the hand demonstrate weeping. Kabuki scholar Dr. Shigetoshi Kawatake states: "Kabuki acting and dancing are as inseparable as rain and snow. They melt and fuse into each other."[23]

The dancing in Kabuki theater is different from Western dance forms. Kabuki dance movement, though fluid and graceful, tends finally toward a static position. Its most significant moments are not realized through movement, but through a final dramatic posture. Stylized movements or gestures carry specific meanings and are used to further the narration of the story. A special codified posture, which an actor strikes at an exciting moment in the story, is known as a *mie* and is typified by the "cessation of movement and glaring expression."[24] Movements, postures and gestures are grouped into sequences called *katas*, as in Noh theater, and young Kabuki actors learn the *katas* by imitation. These young actors first appear on stage at the age of five or six and continue on to a very advanced age. Kabuki actors are judged truly accomplished only by the age of fifty or so, when they are considered mature enough to allow their own personal expression to emerge through the conventional form of the characters they play.

Characters in a Kabuki play are designated by elaborate makeup, costume, movement style and wig. Because white skin has always been prized in Japan as evidence of social superiority, well-born characters have a white-based makeup, whereas peasant characters wear darker makeup. Stage assistants are dressed in black, which by Japanese theater convention makes them invisible. They deliver or remove props, scenery or other stage effects, help the actors manipulate their costumes and care for the actors by supplying them with tea or handkerchiefs during a long scene, all the while making themselves as inconspicuous as possible.[25] Kabuki actors today play several types of roles and often are on stage six to eight hours per day, seven days a week. Only star actors receive vacation time.

A typical Kabuki theater contains a wide proscenium arch stage (approximately ninety feet wide) and a rectangular auditorium with balconies on three sides. An elevated passageway, called a *hanamichi* (flower way) connects the back of the auditorium with stage right and is used for entrances and exits and as an additional stage area. Musicians and narrator-singers share the stage with the actors.

Attending a Kabuki performance has always been an informal social affair. Theatergoers often come in large groups and during the play sometimes leave their seats to visit with other audience members. Tea, cake and food are served at the theater, and boisterous audience members shout approval or jeers at the actors. As it did from the beginning, Kabuki performance goes forward to the constant accompaniment of eating, talking and traveling audience members; the actors accept this activity as a natural occurrence. Earle Ernst states that the "hold of the Kabuki on the Japanese people is strong today, and there is every evidence that its strength will continue."[26]

BUTOH

"Butoh is not for the frail."[27] The avant-garde dance theater form known as Butoh has been called Japan's most startling cultural export. The word *butoh* comes from two Japanese characters: *bu,* for "dance," and *toh,* for "step," and both are derived from terms signifying ancient ritualistic dance. *Buyoh* is the neutral word for dance, implying a sense of leaping or jumping, but the addition of *toh* connotes stomping. The element of stomping is commonly found in traditional Japanese mythology and in other Japanese theater forms, such as Bugaku, Noh and Kabuki.

Butoh themes center around creation and destruction. Ushio Amagatsu (b. 1949), artistic director and founder of the Butoh group Sankai Juku, states that "Butoh belongs both to life and death."[28] Often mistakenly associated with all forms of Butoh is Ankoku Butoh, meaning black or dark dance.

This form of Butoh was developed through the work of Butoh pioneer Tatsumi Hijikata (1928–1986), who first used the term in 1961. The "dance of darkness" in Hijikata's work referred to social taboos and forbidden zones not traditionally acknowledged in polite Japanese society. The dark side of Butoh drew inspiration from the underprivileged, exploited and neglected persons in society, those "drenched in an atmosphere of spiritual and physical darkness."[29] Noted Butoh choreographer and artist Min Tanaka (b. 1945) has said of Hijikata, "He was always angry about how our bodies are controlled historically. Behind the social face, we have many faces. He tried to take them off."[30]

The aesthetic of Butoh is "[a] compound of the grotesque and the beautiful, the nightmarish and the poetic, the erotic and the austere, the streetwise and the spiritual."[31] Butoh is often characterized by full body paint, full or partial nudity, primal images and expressive faces with mouths open in silent screams. Although Butoh performers usually do not wear masks, their expressive and often exaggerated use of facial gestures lends an eerie, masklike countenance to their performance. According to Tanaka, "My actual work is to awaken emotions of the body sleeping in the depth of history. . . . I wish to become an artist who shoots an arrow into everyday life."[32] Earlier, Hijikata had proclaimed, "In our body, history is hidden . . . and will appear in each detail of our expression. In Butoh we can find, touch our hidden reality."[33] Butoh artists strive to evoke memories buried in our subconscious.

In the late 1950s and early 1960s, Japan was in the throes of social upheaval. Butoh emerged as the country was still reeling from the horrors of Hiroshima and Nagasaki, and it became a powerful means of protest. Butoh seeks to erase the heavy imprint of Japan's strict society, offering unprecedented freedom of artistic expression for those Japanese artists who turned away from the traditional forms after World War II.[34]

The two pioneering forces in Butoh were Kazuo Ohno (b. 1906) and his younger avant-garde thinker and onetime student Tatsumi Hijikata. The two shared the anguish of seeing their country devastated by war and decided to highlight ugliness and fragility in a culture noted for its appreciation of visual beauty. They met in 1954 and briefly collaborated in 1959, but developed dramatically different styles during the late 1960s and early 1970s.

Kazuo Ohno studied modern dance with Takaya Eguchi, a well-known dancer-choreographer who had studied with Mary Wigman (1886–1973), the noted German modern dance pioneer. Ohno traces his influences to

German expressionism, Christianity and the lifelong inspiration he found in a 1929 performance by La Argentina, a Spanish flamenco dancer who, to him, represented "dance, literature, music and art, love and the pain of living."[35] Ohno performed for the first time in 1949 at the age of forty-three. His performances are structured improvisations around a theme or narrative, and his aesthetic is concerned with spirituality, generosity and the fragility of the soul. His "work magnifies details—a ribbon, an ornament, precise articulation of feet or a finger or an eye. [He] gently reveals the minutiae of human existence."[36] In his late nineties today, he is still performing and is known as the "grand old man of Butoh" as he looks into the human soul and finds not darkness but light.

Tanaka has said, "Kazuo Ohno is a god and Hijikata is the devil." Tatsumi Hijikata, whose given name is Kunio Motofuji, was born in 1928 in the remote northern region of Tohoku. Hijikata came to Tokyo at the age of twenty-four to study dance. He once stated that his work was influenced by Dadaism, surrealism, the French experimental theater director Antonin Artaud, the rural culture of his youth and German expressionism. His aesthetic "integrated eroticism, nudity, provocation, and social criticism with other elements of Japanese culture: classical dance, Japanese body postures, prewar vulgar entertainment, medieval grotesque paintings."[37] His work was shocking, antagonistic, brutal, violent, dark and erotic. His movement style was characterized by flexed legs, grounded body weight, rolled-back eyes, twisted faces and the tortured bodies of the *oni-babas* (old witches of folk mythology).[38]

Hijikata's ideas attracted the attention of the intellectual avant-garde in Japan, including the author Mishima, the photographer Eikoh Hosoe, the film director Nagisa Oshima, the poet Shuji Terayama, the graphic designer Tadanori Yokoo and many others. Japanese art in the mid-1960s was suffused by Hijikata's Ankoku Butoh style. He withdrew from performing in 1974 but continued to choreograph and teach until his death in 1986. Among those important Butoh artists who acknowledge Hijikata as *sensei* (master/teacher) are Yoko Ashikawa, Ushio Amagatsu of Sankai Juku, Akaji Maro of Dai Rakuda Kan, Eiko and Koma, Min Tanaka and Natsu Nakajima of Muteki-sha.

The second generation of Butoh artists includes Akaji Maro (b. 1943), a former actor with the experimental theater group Joyko Gekijo and Hijikata's student for nearly three years. He founded the Dai Rakuda Kan Company in 1972. The name means "great camel battleship," chosen for the image of the camel not only as a misshapen creature, but also as the animal who had walked the Silk Route, the main communication line between the East and the West.[39] Dai Rakuda Kan, the first major Butoh group to perform in the United States, appeared at the American Dance Festival in 1982.[40]

Maro's work is illustrative and theatrical, consisting of choreographed large group tableaus with elaborate stage scenery and props. He is an actor and director first and offers a hallucinatory vision of the theater. His company was the first in Japan to appropriate elements from nightclub and cabaret acts. His work "attacks the audience with provocative, often grotesque images that prompt shock and revulsion. [Maro] combines carefully nurtured movements with deliberate theatricality to create works that verge on performance art. Haunting, even jarring music heightens the visual aspect of the troupe's performances."[41]

In a 1986 essay, Maro wrote that Butoh is "a total rejection of the values of materialism . . . therefore a dangerous force. The way of Butoh is dangerous."[42] Ushio Amagatsu (b. 1949), artistic director and founder of Sankai Juku (which is one of the most commercially accepted Butoh companies in the world), has a different opinion, however: "Our work is not dangerous. It is dangerous to think that it is."[43]

Amagatsu began his training in classical and modern dance before becoming involved with Butoh. He trained with Butoh master Hijikata before joining Maro's group, Dai Rakuda Kan. Sankai Juku, which means "school of mountain and sea," was founded in 1975, and its first performance, *Amagatsu Sho*, took place in Tokyo in 1977. The company performed in the West for the first time in 1980 at the Nancy Festival in France, performing *Kinkan Shonen* (1978) and *Sholiba* (1979), and since that time it has been based in Paris.[44]

Sankai Juku's type of Butoh combines breathtaking visual imagery with universal themes. Amagatsu presents a more mystical, sophisticated, delicate and harmonious aesthetic than that of his predecessors. The elements of white body paint, shaved heads, detailed gestures and the stretching of time common to Butoh remain part of Sankai Juku's style, but the company's work represents a departure from the Ankoku Butoh roots, evolving as an elegant expression from rebellious origins. Some critics believe that Sankai Juku has marred the tradition of Butoh, whereas others believe it embodies Butoh's highest development.

Butoh has received much attention in the West in general. Kazuko Kuniyoshi, Japanese dance historian and writer, offered this explanation for its popularity: "Western theater and dance has not reached beyond technique and expression as means of communication. The cosmic elements of Butoh, its violence and nonsense, eroticism and metamorphic qualities, are welcomed by Western artists because they are forced to use their imaginations when confronted with mystery. Butoh acts as a kind of code to something deeper, something beyond themselves."[45]

In Japan, Butoh was not widely accepted until attention from the West brought it prominence in its own country. The Japanese refer to this phenomenon as *gyaku-yunya*, which means "to go out and come back." Until artists gain recognition abroad, they are unlikely to win approval in Japan. Today in Japan, "after a history of rejection followed by acceptance on the part of the Japanese audience, there is a general boredom with Butoh on the part of many of its former fans."[46] Many younger artists feel that the form has not evolved far enough and has run its course. Another possibility for the shift in attention is the rampant consumerism and attraction to current popular styles, which is part of contemporary Japanese life in the cosmopolitan areas.

What lies in the future for Butoh? Marcia Siegel, noted dance scholar, writes: "Having worked its way through Cunninghamesque formalist abstraction, anti-choreographic expressionism, and new-wave linguistic apparatuses, the contemporary dance is returning to movement as an expressive medium. Just dancing is no longer enough."[47] As all historical movements have their moment, perhaps Butoh's survival will be determined by the degree to which it is able to change and reinvent itself. Although Bugaku, Noh and Kabuki have endured virtually unchanged for hundreds of years, only time will tell how long they will survive. At its worst, Butoh remains pure spectacle, but in its pure form it exceeds its own history by touching within all of us something deep, primal and transcendent.

SUMMARY

There are some obvious similarities between Bugaku, Kabuki, Noh and Butoh. All four dance theater forms employ a similar use of time, expanding it through a predominance of slow, sustained movements punctuated by quick, sharp moments. All four also use the human face as an exaggerated mask, showing impassivity or utilizing very active and emotional facial expressions. Bugaku and Noh employ the use of masks or face make-up, and Kabuki's wildly elaborate makeup appears as a mask. Butoh sometimes employs full body makeup or no makeup, but also uses the face in a highly expressive manner.

These four dance theater forms are different in some ways as well. In Bugaku, Noh and Kabuki, costumes, movement style and makeup delineate character. Gestures are symbolic, and informed audience members easily understand their meanings. This codification of gesture and costume is not present in Butoh. Whereas Bugaku, Noh and Kabuki are performed in specialized theaters, Butoh is performed outdoors, in cabarets, on rooftops and in other nontraditional spaces, as well as in traditional theaters.

The three older forms receive government funding and are widely accepted in Japan. In fact, a very strong traditional performing arts consciousness exists today in Japan, nurtured by decades of scholarship, community support and public policies.[48] The general public can now view Bugaku on stately occasions throughout the country, although it originally was restricted to members of the imperial court. The public can even study Bugaku on an amateur basis at a university, shrine or private club. Noh and Kabuki companies are inherited or adopted family organizations, so the average Japanese citizen, as in Bugaku, is able to perform these forms only as a hobby. Most Butoh groups, however, do not receive government funds. Some, such as Dai Rakuda Kan and Manijuku, live and work communally, although members of the company are usually not blood relatives. Another difference between the three older forms and Butoh is that all professional performers of Bugaku, Noh and Kabuki are males and begin their training as children. Both men and women can be Butoh performers, and most begin their Butoh training as adolescents or adults. Whereas Bugaku, Noh and Kabuki use the language of stylized gestures and codified aristocratic postures, Butoh incorporates primal and sometimes disturbing images, and is described as "the language of the body."

All four dance theater forms have their unique place in Japanese society. We all must hope that they will continue to survive and enrich the artistic life not only of Japan, but of the rest of the world as well.

ENDNOTES

[1] Jean-Marc Adolphe, Tatsumi Hijikata, founder of Butoh Darkness, was created by meteor, in *Festival International de Nouvelle Danse* (official program of events) (Montreal: Commission d'initiative et de développement culturels, 1989), p. 76.

2 Rika Ohara, Butoh as another outbreak of Japanese paganism, *High Performance* (summer 1990), 44.

3 Eleanor King, Bugaku: The dance two thousand years young, *Mime, Mask and Marionette Journal* 2, nos. 3–4 (1980), p. 234.

4 Earle Ernst, *The Kabuki theatre* (New York: Oxford University Press, 1956), p. 3.

5 Benito Ortolani, *The Japanese theatre: From shamanistic ritual to contemporary pluralism* (Princeton, N.J.: Princeton University Press, 1990), p. 39.

6 Ibid., pp. 44–45.

7 Benito Ortolani, Bugaku: The traditional dance of the Japanese Imperial Court, *Monographs on music, dance and theatre in Asia* 5 (1978), p. 3.

8 Margaret H. Young, *Kabuki Japanese drama* (Bloomington, Ind.: Eastern, 1985), p. 27.

9 Carl Wolz, Dance in Noh theatre, *The World of Music* 17 (1978), p. 75.

10 Masaru Sekine, *Ze-Ami and his theories of Noh drama* (Gerrards Cross, Great Britain: Colin Smythe, 1985), p. 19.

11 P. G. O'Neill, *A guide to No* (Tokyo: Hinoki Shoten, 1953), p. 1.

12 Sekine, *Ze-Ami*, p. 144.

13 Ibid., p. 152.

14 Ibid., pp. 45–56; O'Neill, *A guide to No*, pp. 9–10.

15 Sekine, *Ze-Ami*, pp. 48–50.

16 Monica Berthe and Karen Brazell, *No as performance: An analysis of the Kuse scene of Yamamba* (Ithaca, N.Y.: Cornell University Press, 1978), p. 79.

17 Sekine, *Ze-Ami*, p. 161.

18 Berthe and Brazell, *No as performance*, pp. 80–81.

19 Ernst, *The Kabuki theatre*, pp. 10–11.

20 Samuel L. Leiter, trans., with commentary, *The art of Kabuki: Famous plays in performance* (Berkeley: University of California Press, 1979), p. 260.

21 Ernst, *The Kabuki theatre*, p. 71.

22 Ibid., p. 86.

23 Shigetoshi Kawatake, *Kabukishi no Kenkyu* (Tokyo: Tokyodo, 1948), p. 312.

24 Leiter, *The art of Kabuki*, p. 257.

25 Ernst, *The Kabuki theatre*, pp. 107–109.

26 Ibid., p. 16.

27 Margaret Loke, Butoh: Dance of darkness, *The New York Times*, November 1, 1987, F41.

28 Qtd. in Ethan Hoffman, photographer, Mark Holborn, Tatsumi Hijikata, and Yukio Mishima, commentaries, *Butoh: Dance of the dark soul* (New York: Garden Limited, 1987), p. 121.

29 Richard Philp, Out of darkness: Butoh, part I, *Dance Magazine* (April 1986), p. 61.

30 Min Tanaka, Farmer/dancer or dancer/farmer: An interview by Bonnie Sue Stein, *Drama Review* 30 (1986), p. 146.

31 Philp, Out of darkness: Butoh, part I, p. 61.

[32] Min Tanaka, I am an avant-garde who crawls the earth, *Drama Review* 30 (1986), pp. 154–155.

[33] Bonnie Sue Stein, Twenty years ago we were crazy, dirty, and mad, *Drama Review* 30 (1986), p. 125.

[34] Ibid., p. 111.

[35] Kazuo Ohno, in *Festival International de Nouvelle Danse* (official program of events, Montreal: Commission d'initiative et de développement culturels, 1989), p. 82.

[36] Philp, Out of darkness, p. 61.

[37] Stein, Twenty years ago, p. 116.

[38] Jean Viala, Butoh: Identity rediscovered. In *Festival International de Nouvelle Danse* (official program of events, Montreal: Commission d'initiative et de développement culturels, 1989), p. 73.

[39] Hoffman et al., *Butoh*, p. 33.

[40] Anna Kisselgoff, Dai Rakuda Kan's theatre of raw images, *The New York Times*, April 19, 1987, B8.

[41] Susan Chira, Japanese troupe seeks to shock, *The New York Times*, April 19, 1987, B39.

[42] Qtd. in Hoffman et al., *Butoh*, p. 76.

[43] Bonnie Sue Stein, Out of darkness: Butoh, part II, *Dance Magazine* (April 1986), p. 68.

[44] Jean Viala, *Butoh: Shades of darkness*, edited by Nourit Masson-Sekine (Tokyo: Shufunotomo, 1988), p. 108.

[45] Qtd. in Stein, Twenty years ago, p. 114.

[46] Steven Durland, Contemporary art in Japan, *High Performance* (summer 1990), p. 27.

[47] Marcia Siegel, The truth about apples and oranges, *Drama Review* 32 (1988), p. 3.

[48] Barbara E. Thornbury, Behind the mask: Community and performance in Japan's folk performing arts, *Asian Theatre Journal* 12, no. 1 (spring 1995), p. 145.

CHAPTER SIX

introduction

It is likely that at one time or another you have socialized, chatted or relaxed around a dance floor. The dancing on that floor is called *social dance* or sometimes *ballroom*, referring to European and American social dance palaces. In a 1995 American Movie Classics television special entitled *Gotta Dance!* a group of everyday ballroom enthusiasts of all ages and abilities were filmed partner dancing to the sounds of a live orchestra. Between dances, they talked about the hypnotic waltz, the sensuality of the tango and the roles of gender within different dances. Such a TV program demonstrates the compelling nature of social dance for people of all ages and how through acquirable skills and enjoyable exercise it can transform anyone into a socially adept, civil human being. Knowing something about social dance forms and their milieu also gives audiences entrée to a richer understanding of concert dance because choreographers have referred to and employed social dance forms for centuries.

SOCIAL DANCE: A PORTRAIT OF PEOPLE AT PLAY

Myron Howard Nadel

Social dance has an intimate and many-faceted relationship with dance for the concert and theatrical stages. Although it is different from the communicative and entertaining nature of theatrical and concert dance, its forms and content provide concert and Broadway choreographers with an important reservoir of gestures, manners and procedures from which to choose. Tapping the reservoir of social dance by concert and Broadway choreographers is at least as common as musical composers' use of folk and popular tunes to compose their works.

Not surprisingly, European social dances, beginning from the time of the Renaissance (14th to 16th centuries), continue to remain closely aligned with theatrical dance in America and Europe in many ways: their steps are composed of basic units of weight shifts that appear in all Western theatrical dances; their patterns are the root steps of ballet technique; they provide a way to differentiate historical periods; and their varied styles and tempi provide a framework for many dynamic and rhythmic devices used in all theatrical dance.

Social dance is often referred to as *ballroom dance* because of the extensive introduction of popular ballroom palaces in 19th century Europe, when the influence of a new middle-class society of traders, bankers, scientists and business people began to dominate the political world. Social or ballroom dance derives from the practiced civility of the courts, the romance of post-Napoleonic Europe, the manners of the Victorian age and the entire 20th century.

To be enjoyed, social dance requires varying levels of skill. The minuet of the baroque era required training as exacting as sword fighting. Many of the rock and salsa dances today have shed such precision for individuality and spontaneity, but still mirror a need for genuine human contact. The vitality and abandoned natural skills of the twist and of post-twist rock dances created a compelling style that became synthesized and codified for Broadway and Hollywood entertainments. As ballroom dance continues to evolve, its technical demands will continue to reflect its society's values and level of sophistication.

Each social dance form has a character or style notable in its specificity of rhythms, foot patterns and body attitudes, degree of formality and exactness, distance between partners, degree of touching, gender roles, unison or counterpoint and relationships with other couples. These characteristics evidence themselves in "period" dances because their qualities are linked to expressions unique to certain places during certain historical periods. The way an individual could act was well defined in the social dancing of a specific period, for it allowed a permissible amount of contact and communication within the social settings of the time.

Certain indicators point to the whole dances, dance fragments and subject matter or motifs from specific social dance forms that contemporary choreographers in concert, Broadway and filmed dance continue to use. Two people dancing together does not always indicate a social dance form any more than a dancer pointing his feet or shaking his shoulders or standing in a square with three other couples indicates a ballet, a jazz piece or a square dance. These indicators, however, offer a start in categorizing the type of social dances you may see in ballrooms or even in concert or Broadway dance.

¤ *Invitations.* Does one party invite the other to dance? Many social dances begin after a prospective partner asks another to join him or her on the dance floor. Note, however, that many ballet pas de deux (duets) begin by the man asking the woman to dance in the same way that a gentleman at a ball will ask a lady to dance.

¤ *Farewells.* What was done at the conclusion of the particular dance? A bow or curtsey might indicate one era, but turning and applauding for a dance band will indicate another era.

¤ *Reverse symmetry.* Are the dancers doing the exact same steps in reverse; that is, when ones goes forward, does the other move backward, or if one moves to the right, does the other move to the left? The back-and-forth momentum of the Latin cha-cha is a good metaphor of marital relationships in any period.

¤ *Contact.* Do the partners touch? Many social dances include touching, but some do not. Many rock dances are performed along with but not in contact with a partner. The typical dance pose of a ballroom dance style has the man's right hand and arm supporting the woman's lower back, and his left hand and arm stretched to the side holding and guiding the woman's right hand and arm, while she rests her left hand on his right shoulder.

¤ *Facing.* Are the partners facing each other, side by side, or back to back? Dances from different eras feature different facings.

¤ *Body part touching.* What parts of the bodies touch? Dances often involve touching, but certain dances allow for bodies to be glued to each other. Others limit touching to only light hand support.

¤ *Leading/following.* Does someone appear to be "leading?" In most social dances, the dominant figure is the man, so it is significant when a woman takes this role.

¤ *Music.* Do the rhythms of the music resemble those used in a certain social dance form?

¤ *Changing partners.* Do the dancers switch partners? How is this done? In some two-person social dance contexts, an outsider may ask to break in, with permission of the current leader. One can easily imagine the dramatic tension if permission is denied or given reluctantly.

◻ *Isolated or whole body movements.* What parts of the dancers' bodies are normally moving or still? In a waltz, the couples may be twirling with vigor, but their two bodies move as a whole in a fairly vertical plane. The Cuban rumba, however, promotes the articulation of the pelvis, and the swing involves leaning.

◻ *Appearance of a dance plan.* Do the participants appear to be following a plan? In some dances, the leader decides what to do and when to do it. That is a form of improvisation that involves deference. Sometimes both partners plan their patterns. Competition ballroom dance demands such precision planning. Most rock partner dances emphasize improvisation.

◻ *Floor paths.* Is a path for the dancers around the floor part of a movement design? Some dances occupy very little space. Others feature movement in circular paths, as in some waltz and polka forms.

◻ *Group patterns.* Are more than two people organizing their movements together with others? This characteristic of social dances has its origins in folk dance, such as square or contra dancing.

◻ *Stamina.* What degree of fitness does the dance require? The Charleston, for example, is so vigorous that it nearly eliminates the unfit, but a slow waltz might be suitable for the elderly.

◻ *Social status.* What social status does the dance indicate? Lower classes historically were not able to afford or were not accepted into the ballroom milieu, and the upper classes presumably would not frequent the brothels, where ragtime and jazz dances got their start.

◻ *Costume.* Do the costumes suggest that the performers are at a dance or a ball? Saddle shoes say "jitterbug," a man's stiff collar says "ragtime," and tight bell-bottomed pants scream "disco."

⌐ *Place.* Does the dance suggest a specific country or locale? The folk forms adapted for ballroom usage, such as the Polish mazurka or the Brazilian samba, indicate a geographic place of origin.

⌐ *Period and moral atmosphere.* Is a time period suggested? Does the dance form promote or denigrate a certain society's mores? Knowing the era when a social dance was introduced or lost favor is helpful. In some times or places, religious leaders railed against dancing as the work of the devil, while many others believed it to be a celebration of life.

The history of social dance is fraught with contradictions; only the most careful academic research can unearth the facts. Even so, we can never see or participate in the original dances themselves; we can only reproduce them with integrity by relying on the scholarship of great dance detectives such as Elizabeth Aldrich, who also reconstructs and choreographs period dances for the stage. She points out that dance "existed in and interacted as part of its culture rather than as an independent system."[1] Therefore, we must understand the culture that supports the dance system.

However, unlike Aldrich, choreographers who reach back to the more generalized historical pool of known social dances are often drawing on *reflected* images of these forms from films, paintings, literature, musical compositions and oral histories, perhaps handed down through previous choreographies, which themselves were images. Aldrich warns that to appreciate dance one should not "limit oneself only to a list of dances and steps—or, worse, to a 'feeling' of how it might have been performed."[2]

Most dances made popular before the 19th century were group dances, which required clever organization for the movements of the entire group to be safely coordinated. The groups were often, but not always, paired in couples as well. According to the patterns of the group and the socially accepted rules of behavior, couples might be able to change partners. At the beginning of the 19th century, it was improper for betrothed couples to dance together because of the informality and heightened desires such behavior might provoke. It was preferable to match them with their more formal acquaintances within the group.

GROUP FORMS: THE COURTS, COURTIERS AND MINUET

Social dancing historically was a highly organized affair, with complicated steps that were part of both ballet and folk vocabularies. As a rule, social dance implied (and still implies) a higher social stratum than folk dance because of its origins in the courts of Europe and the growth of wealth in the courts of the Renaissance. It also included the use of folk materials refined for more civilized and artificial recreations.

Renaissance social dances held great interest in a time of humanistic concerns, in part because they projected a sense of well-being counter to the deprecating view of humans in the Middle Ages (c. 500–1453). The period's interest in classicism included dances of antiquity, even if the "ancient" dances seemed to be newly invented. The nobles believed the crude habits of the commoners did not suit the proper deportment of a courtier. Nevertheless, the dances of the Renaissance had their basis in these common dances, although paid dancing masters redevised them to make them suitable for court costumes and other refinements. Renaissance court dances based on folk forms tended to be less ribald than their original or common versions, but still satisfied both the desire for dance in a social setting and the need for elegant behavior, self-control and the sense of authority that precisely planned movements can provide. Social dance also seemed humanistic—it was fun and challenging.

Movement in most dance formats prior to the 20th century gave pleasure to the participants through a strengthened sense of pride, physical commitment and social acceptance. In fact, pleasure remains the primary ethos of social dance. Because each strata of society has its own parameters for social behavior, the process of cleaning up more common dance forms for acceptance into a higher social strata has continued throughout social dance history.

The preclassic allemande, for instance, bore little resemblance to its earthy German folk dance cousins, and the 19th century waltz was considerably different than the rustic and lustier *landler* from which it originated. Likewise, the turkey trot of the early 20th century ragtime dance era was a sanitized version of the slaves' mime dance of the same name from the previous century.

Ballets or spectacle entertainments of the Renaissance employed dances that were considered social inasmuch as the dancers were members of the court. These dances can be divided into two main categories (from the French): the *basse* or low dances and the *haute* or high dances. *Basse* dances are usually slow and contain steps, touches, draws, glides, bows and curtsies, whereas the *haute* dances include hopping, light running and even clapping and stomping, all elegantly done at a faster tempo than the *basse* dances.

A *basse* dance selection followed by an *haute* dance represented an attempt at dance programming in a satisfying suite format. This juxtapositional sequencing of various styles and speeds in music and dance has been an essential factor in programming dance suites not only in social dance venues, but also in concert and commercial venues. Dances from the Renaissance include the pavan, a slow and stately dance in duple meter built primarily with walking steps; the galliard, a jumping dance in quick three-quarter time, with a jump on the fourth count of every six beats; the allemande, a dance in which much attention was given to the smooth interweaving of a couple's arms; and the courante, a running dance in three-quarter time.

Dance groupings and patterns of the baroque (17th and early 18th centuries) and rococo (mid– to late 18th century) eras became a standard part of choreographic protocol for manipulating groups in theatrical dance. Dances were elaborately organized as an expression of an increasingly mannered court life. The ornate rococo style brought more intricate configurations to the social dance scene. Attention to minute details coincided with a time when the lace on a man's sleeve revealed an aversion to manual labor and a fixation on intellectual adroitness. The dance gestures and steps of this age reflected the effete court life: "French courtiers who mastered the courante went on to spend three months learning the minuet."[3]

The minuet's basically unaccented rhythmic structure was in a slow three-quarter time. In a contained mode, beats in the musical measures were often treated with pauses and controlled balances. Although the minuet was slow, stately and ornate, it was not without strength and authority. Group patterns were also cleverly planned to add to the complexity of the activity.

Group forms, including the minuet, were called contra dances (from the French word, *contre*), which "countered" couples against couples in genteel and sophisticated versions of common dances. Today's Virginia reel is a folk dance version of a still popular contra dance. Social dancing in the 17th and 18th centuries was oriented more toward organized communal dances, which allowed couples to face and dance in relation to other couples and to switch partners within the form.

Because of the couple countering and the group patterns in folk or country dancing, these forms are often misnamed "English country" dances. Some figures from folk dance that appear in contra and country dances are circles, rounds (movement on a circular path), rings (movement toward and away from the center of a circle), squares and lines—patterns commonly used from the Renaissance onward. They eventually formed a vocabulary of group designs for theater dance, even as they were adjusted to face audiences seated in proscenium theaters. Contemporary choreographer-dancer Mark Morris (b. 1956) has incorporated social, folk and country dance forms into a number of his works, most notably *New Love Song Waltzes* (1982, music by Brahms), *Going Away Party* (1990, music by Bob Wills and His Texas Playboys) and *Somebody's Coming to See Me Tonight* (1995, music by Stephen Foster).

Colonists brought both folk dance and social dance to North America as a part of their former traditions and social graces. Even the Puritans tolerated social dance and justified its use "because [it] taught manners, and manners were considered a part of morals."[4] Despite some pockets of bitter religious opposition, country dancing became a leading social custom in New England, which encouraged the immigration of social and theatrical dance masters who quickly became deeply entrenched in colonial America. New England country dance traditions are very much alive today, particularly in summer with weekly contra or square dances held on village greens or squares.

The adaptability of country dances appealed to colonists of various classes because the dances could include steps out of their own folk traditions. During the American Revolution (1775–1783), taverns all over New England competed for business by including country dancing in an evening's entertainment. These dances were rejuvenated by new patriotic themes such as "Hull's Victory" and by movement patterns brought from various homelands. By combining traditions from various countries, these jigs, hornpipes and reels allowed for a rich spirit of community.

Almost anywhere that square, country or social dances still flourish, they are planned, not improvised, and create a closed social group no matter the class. Yet for the upper classes of the 18th and early 19th centuries, whether in the Old or the New World, the minuet became the longest-lasting foreign social dance import because its intricacies of style, movements and figures reflected the dancers' high social status.

The dance challenges of minuets and gavottes also required the import of foreign dance masters to oversee these rococo court remnants. The southern colonies were more predisposed to this type of dance, although when the waves of French ballet masters, who were self-imposed exiles of the French Revolution (1789–1799), opened schools or taught privately during this time period, the fancier ballet steps associated with minuets and gavottes were taught in the North as well. Teachers of ballroom dance often were former ballet dancers or ballet masters vying for students by giving exhibitions at balls or exploiting their reputations in theatricals.

Country dances also provided a structure for solo dancing, usually in the form of jigs or hornpipes, which translated onto the stages of England and later to its colonies. The jig has a long and complex history as an intricate solo folk dance form, including as it does combinations of turns and leg gestures that feature repeated hops on one leg. Popular in Ireland and Scotland, it also appeared as the "gigue," a French court dance. The hornpipe, popular in England and Scotland, was also used in country dancing and theatricals because of its vigorously complex rhythms. Double hops and leg gestures known as "cuts" were not too different from those in Scottish highland dancing.

Reels from Scottish folk dancing included formal versions of ancient group weaving patterns, while the individual dancers performed sliding and hopping steps along their paths, sometimes in the form of a "grand right and left." The group formations and movements of European contra and country dance—such as circles, squares, weavings and threading figures—provided the sources for group figures in American country dancing. The combination of leg gestures, hops, cuts, weavings and other interesting group, couple and solo patterns from jigs, reels and hornpipes made the country dances of America full of exciting and varied patterns.

Homesteaders who settled the western territories of the United States also came together in social events that featured the evolving country dancing, quadrilles and folk steps from many European countries. As immigrant members from one European group became part of the social fabric, movements from their national dances further ensured the freshness of country dance. Because of the many complex figures and the limited time the dancers could spend on perfecting steps, callers were needed to organize and run the squares. The neoclassical Russian American George Balanchine (1904–1983), enamored as he was with all things American, used country western–inflected music for his 1954 ballet *Western Symphony* and even hired a real caller to holler instructions on stage for his *Square Dance* (1957), set to period music by Antonio Vivaldi (1678–1741) and Arcangelo Corelli (1653–1713).

The changing nature of country dancing became the basis for early American theatrical dancing. Soloists used jigs and hornpipes in play afterpieces and in cultural programs of song, recitation, dance and even lectures. These solo forms, the mainstay of dancers, gradually developed into the "buck and wing" and tap dance.

Social dance in 19th century America sometimes represented an instantaneously created upper-class society. Many people made quick fortunes in this century, but the new American rich knew very few of the social rules governing the upper class. So rules of social dance behaviors were published in hundreds of manuals and were enthusiastically acknowledged and obeyed not only for dancing but for the protocol of socially acceptable behaviors. One's behavior at public and private balls was a strong indicator of one's life at home. Vulgarity was considered to be a breach of manners, and the rigid rules that covered all aspects of the balls and dancing held together an entire class of landed gentry, businessmen, manufacturers, politicians and their spouses.

Within the five basic types of group dances—the contra, the English country, the quadrille, the French cotillion and the German cotillion—a few characteristics indicate the ideas emanating from the 19th century upper-class group dances after the French and American Revolutions—although roots of these dances were established well before that time:

- ♯ a ball was an evening's program that could include dances from various national and folk origins

- ♯ dance steps, figures and group patterns were difficult to learn and had to be memorized

- ♯ group patterns resembled folk dance arrangements

- ♯ couple dancing did not often feature dancing between the betrothed or married

- ♯ dancers could change partners in the course of a dance

- ♯ someone might "call" the next dance or even the next figure

- ♯ the group of dancers could not improvise, so dance masters were required

- ♯ there was a strict separation of the classes

Although the phenomenon of group dancing changed gradually in the United States during the first half of the 19th century, the practice of dancing minuets, gavottes, courantes and bourrées continued. The ongoing transformation to couple dancing paralleled the rise of a working class in the Industrial Revolution (beginning in the early 19th century).

Social dance became more widespread and popular among greater numbers of people, who found its graces to be a signal of a newly acquired
middle-class standing. By the middle of the 19th century, however, group
dances began to lose their luster as the spirit of individualism grew in this
new and larger society. Heartier dances were bred into the contra forms,
and the essence of the burgeoning romantic movement was found in the
steps and turns of the waltz, which first found its way into group dances
at the end of the 18th century.

THE WALTZ: A TRANSITION TO COUPLE DANCING

Waltzing came to overshadow all other social couple dance forms in the
19th century. By 1797, just two years before the end of the French Revolution, new characteristics such as facing, clasping and turning a partner
had taken over the nearly seven hundred public dance halls in Paris. A
growing working class was embracing a new social dance form. The
appealing distinctions of the waltz grew from German folk dances such as
the *waltzer, landler, dreyer* and *weller,* but in their cruder ancient folk settings these dances had been associated with kissing, lifting partners, vigorous circling and other low-class behavior.

According to the old-fashioned, previously court-connected and well-heeled
dancing masters, the waltz represented a popular revolution. Among the
spoils of war from Napoleon Bonaparte's (1767–1821) military successes on
Teutonic lands were some seemingly dangerous elements extracted from the
rough German dances. Although waltz fundamentals became more refined
in the ballrooms of Paris and Vienna early in the 19th century, its most
incendiary element, close couple facings, influenced all ballroom dancing forever. The waltz endured in popularity throughout the 19th century, even
though quadrilles, polkas and galops occasionally replaced it as favorite.

The waltz owed its refinement in part to the music written for it, which
reshaped the phrases of music and movement into longer, more "rounded"
sections. When composers such as Franz Schubert (1797–1828) wrote art
pieces called German waltzes for concert consumption in the first decades of
the 19th century—the romantic era—the musical products were treated in
eight-measure phrases of three-quarter time, more similar to their heavier
German dance antecedents. Johann Strauss Sr. (1804–1849) and Johann
Strauss Jr. (1825–1899) were really classy dance musicians whose music for
ballroom waltzes of the mid- to late century extended melodic phrasing

beyond the typical sixteen-measure lengths, creating a fellowship of movement and music with an ongoing, smooth, curvilinear and increasingly dynamic feel.

Another characteristic of the waltz became a central dance metaphor: the counterclockwise circling of couples on the ballroom floor. This movement symbolically represented the earth revolving around the sun, while the rotary movement or circling of a couple represented the spinning of the earth on its axis. Deliberately developed or not, an understanding of the universe and of humans' relation with the heavens is part of the romantic and postromantic eras. The root *volv* refers to rolling or turning, as in "revolve." When the waltz was first introduced, the turning was limited, but as it became a couple dance, the repeated turning, especially in the Viennese waltz, created a great challenge for dancers as they attempted to retain control of their bodies' deportment while approaching a state of vertigo.

Many consider the waltz to be the world's first ballroom dance. Americans waltzed the Boston waltz and the Tennessee waltz, both of which appeared in the 19th century ballrooms of Boston, New York and New Orleans. Although these homegrown American variations were received in Europe with less enthusiasm than their continental counterparts, they remain popular in American ballrooms to this day.

Besides turning and close couple facing, the European ballroom waltz included elements such as elegant dance phrasing to lovely melodies and clothing that allowed a freer flow of movement in order to smoothly glide on the polished ballroom floors. Three beats in each measure, with an accent on the downbeat, give a rounded flow demanding a step on each beat. When, as in the swift Viennese waltzes, the three beats are compressed, or counted as one, the speed of steps creates a great whirling effect and gives the illusion of a long suspension on the second and third beats, as if the dancers are floating. No other social dance form is associated with such transcendent, romantic energy more than this one.

When waltzing is used in ballet and musical theater, it is often a metaphor for romance, spiritual or financial wealth or all three. Its tempi have become part of the otherworldliness of romantic and classical ballet. The ballets *Sleeping Beauty* (1890) and *Swan Lake* (1895), the operetta *The Merry Widow* (1907) and the musical *A Little Night Music* (1973), among many others, depend on the lifted, lilting waltz for their atmosphere of romantic ideals and lofty society. Nearly all professional actors and dancers have been confronted with the need to waltz because its meanings are so closely related to emotional, social or historical contexts of much romantic subject matter. Mark Morris and George Balanchine created several dances with waltzes as an important musical theme, such as in *New Love Song Waltzes* (1982, music by Brahms) and *Vienna Waltzes* (1977, music by Strauss Jr.), respectively.

Next to the waltz, the dance performed most often in the 19th century was the polka, a pseudo-Bohemian dance. The polka answered the need for even more physical commitment than its close cousin. It followed the same circling patterns but also added hopping steps and seemed to be in a constant state of rapid, traveling motion. Unlike the waltz's three-quarter time, the polka is in two-quarter (duple) meter, giving a more jarring and athletic feel to its aerobic repetitions.

The dances of the 19th century, whether encased in novelty or acceptable delirium, were more physically demanding than the dances of the 18th century. One of the minor dances introduced to the ballrooms of America and Europe by the mid– to late 19th century was the galop, a dance full of *chassé* (sliding) steps that careened up and down the room.

From Vienna, Paris and London to the public dance halls of New York, urban gentry, less likely to be swayed by the rigid dictates of conservative religious philosophies, began to influence dance. The sheer excitement of social dances and the perils of participating in those that were contrary to a prudish Victorian mentality contributed to the popularity of American social dancing among many classes.

Entrepreneurial dance teachers seized the opportunities inherent in this burgeoning popularity. In 1835, Allen Dodworth (1817–1876) opened a private dancing academy in New York City, where he taught for more than forty years and wrote on the relationship of social dance to education. He set the highest standards for private academies to follow by teaching dance in a rigorous and precise manner and even encouraged the teaching of social dance in physical education curricula. Social dance classes are still thought to be a way for school-age boys and girls to learn useful forms of social etiquette.

AMERICAN SOCIAL DANCE:
HOMEGROWN AND TRANSPLANTED

In the United States, creating novelty became a commercial enterprise with an enduring effect on the 20th century social dance scene as it substituted social dance imports from Europe with exportable dances that would themselves influence the Western world. Such "dance novelties" were linked to or based on a national or ethnic source, but they were also contrived to be popular. The success of dance novelties was driven largely by the sales of dance-related sheet music, items of clothing, movies and, later, audio and video recordings. Homegrown styles and dance ideas grew from grassroots dance, primarily performed by blacks and Hispanics, and were promoted within commercial ventures. Even before today's instantaneous communication, oceangoing steamships and train transportation allowed speedy promulgation of dance articles, dance news, sheet music, dance fashions and, of course, living dance personalities.

The One-Step and Two-Step

One of the first popular American dance music exploiters and exporters was the composer-conductor John Phillip Sousa (1854–1932), who took his brand of popular marches, such as the durable "Stars and Stripes Forever" (1896), to Europe after introducing them in the American dance scene. The foot patterns and spins in the old dances of the 19th century, such as the polka and the waltz, seemed too complicated for Sousa's music, which was more naturally suited to marching, skipping and stepping in six-eighths tempo.

The imprecisely named upbeat dance steps that fit Sousa's rhythms and tempos were called the "one-step" and the "two-step." Their simplicity became the basis for all sorts of floor patterns and variations of couple facings, such as front-to-back and back-to-back. Even the side-to-side open facing once characteristic within European court dances now offered the new bourgeoisie variations in the one-step and two-step dances that everyone could do. The one-step was formed on the simple skip, and the two-step, which required a modicum of skill, used the three-step foot pattern borrowed from the less-demanding and slower Boston waltz form, transformed from three-quarter time to duple meter. Balanchine, a lover of many things American, also tackled Sousa in his rousing 1958 ballet *Stars and Stripes.*

The new dances required even more vigor than former social dances, and the dance teachers of the early 1900s saw this individuality, simplicity and uncontrolled physical exertion as a threat to their business of teaching the complexities and controls necessary in the 19th century social dances.

Rag Dances

Early in the 1900s, the stream of American novelty dances swelled, first here and then abroad. In its prime, between 1899 and 1915, ragtime dancing used classical music and marches with a strong sense of syncopation and compositional structure. Composers as varied as Scott Joplin (1868–1917) and Igor Stravinsky (1882–1971) composed ragtime dance music. The vaudeville team of Bert Williams (1874–1922) and George Walker (1873–1911) made popular the first of these dances, the cakewalk, which was favored mostly by young people. The cakewalk was followed by the turkey trot, said to be an invention of Joseph Smith (1875–1932), son of the 19th century premier American dancer George Washington Smith (c. 1815–1899). The bunny hug and the grisly bear were two other rag dance excuses for "animalistic" behavior.

At the time, the Organization of Dance Teachers of America refused to teach these syncopated dances. They were considered vulgar because of the daring physical contact between partners. More relevant was the paucity of skills necessary to perform these simple dances, thus making their services obsolete. In addition, the powerful commercial symbiosis between America's youth and the rapidly growing music businesses in the early 20th century, primarily centered in New York's downtown area known as Tin Pan Alley, took the control of dance inventions away from the dance teachers. Close physical contact and a rebellious sense of self were but a part of young people's social statements through these syncopated dances.

Dance and social graces formerly were taught as one and the same, but the ragtime era degenerated that historic European and American practice. The rag dances were closely linked to the emerging rhythms of blacks, making large portions of a bigoted society shudder, but Europeans, removed from America's social reality, were attracted to these exotic American exports. America's participation in World War I (1914–1918) and the continued presence in Europe of expatriate Americans of some social rank certainly increased the influence of American social dance and music in Europe in the rag dance era and in the gestating jazz era that followed.

A Return to Elegance

The foxtrot was a transitional rag-to-jazz dance style, an animal imitation dance in name only. There are two possible origins of this dance. One form of foxtrot contained hopping gestures similar to those made by English music hall star Harry Fox (1882–1959); the other was like the *vaux-droite*, a simple Norman folk dance that involved simple shifts of weight and walking foot patterns, easily performed by anyone who could walk across the dance floor. The second form, when accompanied by sophisticated syncopations of the jazz era, effectively concluded the rag period.

The 1910s brought the personal elegance of the Broadway and vaudeville dance team Vernon Castle (1887–1918) and his wife Irene Castle (1893–1969) to popularity. Vernon embodied the sophisticated, urbane man, and Irene the liberated woman, with her own opinions, expressive clothing and chic hair-styles. Their elegant approach was applied to all sorts of social dance forms, which quickly offset the youthful rag dances. Through their teaching, the Castles codified the social dance steps and styles of the early 20th century and became the emblematic couple of class for their era. Their look became de rigueur for ballroom dancing, and their influence renewed the use of ballroom dance as an acceptable public pastime for adults.

Fred Astaire (1899–1987) once said that the Castles "were a tremendous influence on our careers [his career with sister Adele Astaire (1898–1981)], not that we copied them completely, but we did approximate some of the ballroom steps and style for our vaudeville act."[5] Astaire, along with Ginger Rogers (1911–1995), his most famous dance partner, paid generous and rich-ly deserved homage to the Castles in 1939 with the historically accurate RKO musical "The Story of Vernon and Irene Castle." By using tap dance with a balletic overtone in Broadway shows such as "Lady, Be Good!" (1924) and "The Gay Divorce" (1932; RKO film "The Gay Divorcee," 1934, with Fred and Ginger), Fred Astaire and his partners further stylized the forms of ballroom dance previously created by the Castles.

Arthur Murray (1895–1991), with his wife and partner Kathryn Murray (1897–1999), were also influential ballroom teachers. Together they codified the infusion of jazz and Latin American social dances into the American pub-lic's ballroom dancing lexicon of the 1930s through the 1960s. The Murrays' rather impossible task was completed by a mostly dry and unlikely synthe-sis of simple foot patterns that have become the blueprint for society's social dance steps to this day. Arthur Murray's more than two hundred dance stu-dios in the United States still compete with studios under Fred Astaire's name. At best, the Murrays superficially regarded elements of authentic black and Latin dance; they perceived social dance forms as inventions, so authenticity was no priority. Nevertheless, the standardization of the steps of the Lindy, the Jitterbug, the foxtrot and Latin dances such as the tango, the rumba, the mambo and the cha-cha gave American society formulas with which to enjoy the new rhythms of the 20th century.

The Tango: An Import

The tango was the first Latin American dance to gain favor in America. An indirect importation from the slums of Buenos Aires, Argentina, and based on even earlier dances brought to South America by African slaves, it entered the civility of Parisian ballrooms around 1911. The tango's unbroken life, like that of the waltz, has remained a part of contemporary ballroom dance. Authentic tango orchestras presented new rhythms, dynamics and costuming to accompany "tango teas," as this phenomenon became the dance rage of Europe and America at private dinner dance clubs and cabarets. By the time of its import to the states, it had developed into a sexy love dance, involving fiery passions and close physical contact.

The tango, like most ballroom dances before it, had to be purified of its own lower-class elements, but it also had used various elements from traditional Spanish dance. Its image, refined and codified by the Castles before World War I, subsequently became the model of movie screen romance, when Rudolph Valentino's (1895–1926) tango became the vogue, first seen in the silent film "The Sheik" (1921). The tango was also popularized in Hollywood's "Flying Down to Rio" (1933; Fred and Ginger's first film together) and "Down Argentine Way" (1940, with Carmen Miranda and the Nicholas Brothers).

The tango follows the minuet and the waltz as a principal social self-portrait. Its combination of strong, slow movements and sharp punctuations motivated by sexual tension between partners portrayed the society's new and cherished decadence. Its movements depicted unbridled passions suppressed by Victorian society's sustained conventions. It was the closest approximation to the love act heretofore seen in polite society. Its sophisticated complexities made its threat to proper society exceedingly more dangerous than that of the childish ragtime dances. But its more respectable Arthur Murray version was less exhausting and more inviting to older couples, who wished to experience the passion it offered. The completely acceptable waltz from the 19th century continued to open doors for a condoned and expressive romanticism, but the tango, some protested, opened the bedroom doors.

The tango's popularity in Paris further increased its disrepute and sense of danger. Two other dances from the underbelly of society marked all French-grown dances as lewd, lascivious and horrifying. The *chahut*, a folk dance full of high kicks much like the black American cakewalk, supplied the movement ideas for the can-can, a women's dance popularized in seedy cabarets and nightspots such as the Moulin Rouge (as exemplified in the 1960 film "Can-Can" and the 2001 film "Moulin Rouge!"; artist Henri de Toulouse-Lautrec [1864–1901] painted its picture near the end of the 19th century). Legend tells that wild kicks, full body bends as the women faced away from the audience, skirt waving and cartwheels of the can-can revealed unmentionable portions of the dancers' unclothed anatomy.

A commercially presented nightclub variant was the *apache*, an aberrant couple dance about male dominance and battery. The woman played a cat-like creature in a masochistic role. Joseph Smith, of turkey trot popularity, is also credited with introducing the *apache* to America. The seductive and perverse themes from tangos and *apache* dances were showcased in the *Pickpocket Tango* in Bob Fosse's (1927–1987) Broadway musical "Redhead" (1959) and as the Valentino/*apache* spoof called *The Carnival Tango* in the 1954 Broadway musical "The Boyfriend" (adapted to film in 1971).

Long and slinky gliding steps provide a thrilling smoothness and suavity to the tango. Tightly pressed to each other, partners often move in very direct, straight paths, with their eyes either sharply focused on each other or on the direction in which they are moving. The action of a tango easily serves to express sexual tension, as can be seen in Al Pacino's (b. 1940) mock-blind tango duet in the popular film "Scent of a Woman" (1992).

Jazz Dances

The Charleston was the first jazz dance to reach the popular social dance audience. It was introduced to audiences in the black musical "Runnin' Wild" (1923). The door for jazz dancing had already been opened in the first all-black Broadway production "Shuffle Along" in 1921 (although the performers had to wear blackface to perform!). The Charleston, following the interrupted thread begun by the ragtime dances, was the next major social dance of black origin, except that it paralleled the explosive world of music called jazz. The most basic ground rhythm of the Charleston is a double-dotted quarter, followed by an accented sixteenth note. The Lindy, the big apple and the black bottom followed this idea. The famous black dancer and singer Josephine Baker (1906–1975) helped popularize the Charleston, particularly in Europe.

The word *jazz* literally means the sex act (from the word *jism*), but came to mean "stuff," "junk," "enlivening," "unrestrained" or "improvising on a theme." Therein lies the problem: once something is "captured" for study, it is tamed and domesticated. Pinpointing jazz social dances can be confusing because of the various definitions and unique qualities of jazz. We also have to consider the educated musician-composers who create serious and sophisticated jazz music in subgenres such as mainstream, classic, New Orleans, swing, bebop, cool and even Latin (or Afro-Cuban) jazz.

The steps of the Charleston emanated from movements accompanying black work songs on the docks of Charleston, South Carolina. They had appeared in many work and play dances far back in African history and would appear again in the "mashed potato" of the 1960s, long after the Charleston's popularity had waned. The actual steps are less important than the syncopation of this dance and its music. The Charleston also involved frenetic movements of the legs, arms and body—in one variation, the legs seem to cross through each other, exchanging right and left sides—but the free isolation of torso parts, so common in African dances, was significantly missing.

In the Charleston, which was white society's incorporation of a black style into a popular novelty dance, the entire body often quickly tilts toward the floor and then abruptly recovers. More varied patterns of arm, leg and body movements were packed into this dance than in any before it, and the Charleston seemed to represent a society that with carefree abandon was attempting to compact all of life into a high-energy fling following World War I and through the 1920s.

New York City's uptown Harlem neighborhood, broadly located between 110th and 155th Street, became the coordinating ground for the next stage of social dance growth. Whites went uptown to predominately black Harlem for dance and musical inspiration in jazz clubs, including the famous Cotton Club, where blacks were welcome at that time only as entertainers and workers, although many other clubs—such as Barron's, Leroy's, the Lafayette, the Paradise and even the famous Savoy Ballroom—remained unsegregated. The population of Harlem, originally a white suburb of uptown Manhattan, grew from a few thousand blacks at the turn of the 20th century to a few hundred thousand by the 1930s owing primarily to their mass migration from the South after World War I. In spite of (or perhaps because of) Prohibition in 1920 and even the Great Depression beginning in 1929, black vaudeville houses, night clubs and ballrooms provided a home for what came to be known as the Harlem Renaissance. Great black and white swing bands, such as those directed by Duke Ellington (1899–1974), Fletcher Henderson (1898–1952), Cab Calloway (1907–1994) and Tommy Dorsey (1905–1956), led the way in this musical and multiarts explosion. Black dances with moves such as the mooch, the eagle rock, the buzzard lope and the pigeon wing, straight from old slave dances, were used in variations of a new dance called the Lindy hop, named after Charles Lindbergh's (1902–1974) first solo airplane flight (hop) across the Atlantic in 1927. Improvisation, fast taplike steps, ball changes (two quick changes of weight) and shuffling, sliding feet were all part of the pre–World War II Lindy mania.

Accompanying America's entry into World War II, the swinging Lindy was quickened with solo and duet acrobatic feats and soon became the jitterbug, done to boogie woogie music, which depended on a grinding, "walking" bass. The term *boogie woogie* was taken from the rocking motion of hands walking over lower octaves of a piano in marked repetitive sequences. The swinging jitterbug was fast—it used kicks, turns, cartwheels and just about any pattern of foot and body movements imaginable. The dancers could jump off of and fall onto the floor, a far cry from the slithering of the tango, the incessant revolutions of the waltz, the upright posture of rag dances and the tilted movements of the Charleston. Jitterbugging was "down and dirty," boogie jitterbugging was lower and dirtier still, and both were fully conscious of the sophisticated and syncopated rhythms and swinging motions in the band music of the time. The Lindy utilized established foot patterns, but the jitterbug was more improvisational and unabashedly jazzy.

Jitterbugging and Lindy hopping were significant in the second jazz social dance period because of their unique movements, but, even more important, because of their many participants, both black and white. World War II brought the races together, as military necessity dictated, and increased the adoption of additional black vernacular dance steps into this synthesized black-and-white social dance form. Still missing, however, were the sinuous and segmented movements of the spine and torso, which would complete the investment of a unified body into a social dance form.

Rock

Rock dances linked the spine, pelvis, ribs and shoulders to the rest of the body in an energetic discharge of primary gestures, but were significantly less intricate and sophisticated than the steps of the jitterbug. The communication of raw libido in rock has little concern for social nuance and no need for dance masters or a system of steps. Technical, creative and sophisticated crafts that were part of jazz music and dance were ignored in favor of instinctual movements on the dance floor. Rock dances took people back to a primal ecstasy. Germinated in jitterbugging, which accompanied the white rock 'n' roll of the 1950s, and evolving from the twist and the mime dances of the early 1960s, rock dances were primeval remembrances of the rhythmic intensity and deeply felt motion that reside in the core of the spine and instinctual animal brain.

To keep up with society, modern social dancing masters at Arthur Murray or Fred Astaire schools have reluctantly put rock dances in ballroom dance curriculums. In addition, many of the formalized movements of the torso taught in professional and recreational jazz dance classes today more precisely replicate these untrained and unconscious rock dances.

Authentic rock and jazz dances should include improvisation and natural motions foreign to bodies accustomed to poor neuromuscular habits. Driving rock rhythms have the power to dig through social problems, reaching primitive proportions and encouraging abandon even in trained dancers. Today's mosh pits, with their slam-dancing bodies flung against and upon each other with often breakneck force, embody this wholly preternatural energy.

Five distinct stages of the rock dance period have emerged so far:

1. *The "Grease" era, 1950s.* The initial rock period was characterized by a tentative trading of black and white rock 'n' roll, the significant features of which were electric amplifiers, national TV exposure and jukeboxes from a previous era. The music had a driving rhythm under an often countrylike sound. Huge audiences, garbled words, unsophisticated rhythms, bands in showy costumes and group dances such as the locomotor, the freeze and the bunny hop (not really rock) were part of the scene. Bobby socks, pleated skirts and saddle shoes from the 1940s were still in vogue. Following the music's insistent primitive rhythms, the dances were heavy and boldly simplistic, like the hand jive dance. Musicals such as "Bye Bye Birdie" (1960; film, 1964), "Grease" (1972; film, 1978) and "Little Shop of Horrors" (1982; film, 1986) are about this period of the 1950s.

2. *The Twist to the Hullabaloo.* The main rock period began when singer Elvis Presley (1935–1977) was made into a superstar by the ubiquitous acquisi-

tion of television sets in early 1950s homes. Once Elvis appeared on national TV—using movements appropriated from the black, jazz-inflected dance forms of the previous generation—his affirmation of the expressiveness of the entire body finally made it acceptable for the white community to enjoy many types of organically charged dances. The Broadway musical "Hairspray" (2000; film, 1988) illuminates musical ideas from the early 1960s.

The twist, popularized by Chubby Checker (b. 1941) in 1960, started a slew of mimic dances both individual and communal. The shake, the jerk, the monkey, the hitch-hike and the pony entered the scene with the speed of new records hot off the press. Black and white musical groups accompanied the social dancing of both ethnic groups on television dance shows like Dick Clark's (b. 1932) "American Bandstand," NBC's "Hullabaloo," ABC's "Shindig!" and the syndicated "Hollywood A Go Go," where girls in cages danced to new rock sounds. Dances from the 1960s can be seen in Bob Fosse's Broadway musical production "Sweet Charity" (1966; made into a film two years later with dancer Shirley MacLaine [b. 1934] in the lead) or in the many generic "beach" movies of the time, such as "Beach Party" (1963) and "Beach Blanket Bingo" (1965).

3. *The love children can dance without technique.* With President Lyndon Johnson's Great Society came the very unpopular Vietnam War. Body, mind and spirit seemed to be unified in the vocal and dance expressions of the street protests, especially of the era's flower children. This rock period offered a communal statement of peace, freedom, brotherhood, love, drugs and open sexuality. Rock became the loudly amplified accompaniment to a super social dance for thousands at open-air concerts, with the steps not as important as all participants' immersion in a universal community of sheer energy. The Beatles were one of the many groups that sparked feelings grown out of social struggles. The themes for this type of dance appeared on Broadway in rock musicals such as "Hair" (1968; film musical, 1979, with choreography by Twyla Tharp) and "Jesus Christ Superstar" (1971; film version, 1973). Everyday social dancers needed no training and no set steps, and their Broadway and concert counterparts were often nondancers.

4. *Disco and break dance: technique is back.* The popular social dances of the late 1970s and early 1980s saw a resurgence of technical proficiency. Social dance–oriented movies such as "Saturday Night Fever" (1977), "Flashdance" (1983) and "Footloose" (1984) projected the notion that dance was a difficult and worthy skill. The disco style of "Fever" demanded body control and difficult partnered sequences.

Staging elements derived from break dancing have two basic forms: one includes a gymnastic style with falls, twirls and acrobatic stunts, performed mostly at floor level. Its complementary form, the electric boogie, is more mimetic and uses gestures that evoke images of robots and machines facing a hostile world, with no human emotional investment. The complexities of human life and the struggle to get a piece of the American pie were so overwhelming that emotional nonreaction, inward concentration and dedication to physical accomplishment became the primary manifestations of the black ghettos of the 1980s.

5. *Later developments*. Break dancing and hip-hop continued to foster skill, daring and creative competition. The often antisocial rock and alternative music such as acid, punk, heavy metal and rap have coexisted with mainstream rock music, but their influence on movement has pushed free dance form into undeveloped spasmodic gestures. Like the music, punk, heavy metal and rap dance is often an expression of anger strangely close in energy to the earlier French *apache* dances, with their sadomasochism. Although created long after the punk period, the 1996 musical "Rent," in its sophisticated, pseudo-operatic style, captured a punk rock musical style with a very disciplined and talented group of triple-threat performers.

Like break dancing, rap music is also the proud, rhythmic and poetic expression of the frustrating black ghetto experience. Multiple verses of rhyming couplets are its most pronounced feature. Its sister dance form is hip-hop, where pugilistic gestures reminiscent of karate are accompanied by a type of nervous hopping-jumping not unlike the footwork of boxers. This form has developed into an exciting visual, aural and literary expression.

Other Latin Influences

Salsa. Salsa is a spicy sauce made up of many ingredients. The original dance began in Cuba in the 1940s. It combined African Yoruba drumming and response vocals with indigenous movements and music from the dances of Spain, France and England. When further combined with the Puerto Rican, Mexican and Central and South American dance elements within popular jazz forms found in Miami, New York, Los Angeles and other American cities, this mixture, called *mexcla*, produces a characteristic Latin flavor with two distinct sounds and tempi. Salsa *caliente* (hot) is the faster, Colombian-sounding music, whereas salsa *romantica* favors sentimental love lyrics.

The rumba. Supposedly Cuban, the rumba gained popularity beginning in the 1930s when revelers and business people could easily fly to Havana for the evening and get back to the States before the sun came up, like the characters in the 1950 Broadway show "Guys and Dolls" (film, 1955). The Cuban Revolution in the 1960s ended that advantage. Because of the rumba's tilting of the pelvis in a side-to-side plane while the dancers' hips are touching, this dance has more obvious sexual overtones than the suggestive tango. In the basic rumba, the dancers face each other, and their chests and shoulders may follow in swaying, seductive unison. Its long-short-short repeated counts, with a foot pattern similar to a box step, make it distinctly different from the marchlike tango. It was meant to be a "sexy" ballroom dance in the 1930s and 1940s.

The samba. The samba features a sloping and swinging torso over a kind of running-foot pattern. The dancers' bodies seem to rock back and forth, individually or together. When partners are not touching, a ballroom samba convention is to hold the arms as if the dancers are carrying small rattlelike gourds called *maracas.* Three equal running steps, followed by a rest beat and accompanied by complex patterns of percussion sounds and syncopation, provide a rich rhythmic motif for the dancers in this exuberant dance. The samba has Brazilian origins, and its combination of vigor and a slower-than-jitterbug tempo make it a good alternative for dancers who want to retain a bit of formality reminiscent of more restrained ballroom dances. The Brazilian samba is still danced at carnival in Rio, primarily as a solo dance. You might recognize the samba *Argentina* from the show "Evita" (1979; film, 1996) or via the popular song "Brazil."

The mambo. Often considered a combination of jazz and Latin dances, the mambo is a powerful, flamenco-like dance that can include flicking kicks and hip thrusts. Like the Haitian *mambo,* the tribal queen of war and pride, it is regal and upright, and no physical contact between partners is quite common. The authentic rhythmic pattern of the fast-paced mambo is rest-quick-quick-quick. The beginning pause of each dance measure is a strong holding action, which makes the three-step sequence that follows seem very quick and marked, but light. Throwing the beat in this manner is a crucial skill for handling the jazzy syncopations. A simpler form, with the dancers moving quick-quick-quick-rest, is suitable for less-skilled couples and for those who do not feel the syncopated Latin rest on the first beat. The band's guttural "ugh" can often be heard at the end of a long phrase.

The cha-cha. Like the mambo, the considerably slower cha-cha has two basic rhythmic forms: the slow-slow-slow-quick-quick style and the easier slow-slow-quick-quick-quick version. Both feature steps that travel either forward and backward or cross over and back to place. The couple maintains contact either in a conventional dance position or at least with the hands touching. Both the faster mambo and the slower cha-cha offer great opportunities for sharp jutting foot patterns, quick turning combinations and interesting couple patterns. The cha-cha's two or three quick steps, when varied in direction and height, offer unlimited patterns. The "ugh" sound is also likely to be heard in the music for this dance.

The merengue. From the Dominican Republic, the merengue features a limping movement and is said to be derived from the movement of workers as they cut the sugar cane. It is a true work dance, with simple, evenly paced, insistent steps set against the wonderfully syncopated rhythm of a strong, flowing upbeat falling into a heavy downbeat, indicative of the limping motion. With its very steady and heavy steps, in contrast to the syncopation, dancers can find multiple variations of arm, head and torso movements.

The conga. From a serpentine procession formally associated with both pagan symbol and religious *fêtes* (festivals) in Spain and other Christian countries, where participants would wend their way through city streets on their way to hallowed ground, the conga is the longest-lasting group dance to appear on the modern social dance scene. The movements of the 20th century conga consist of three marching steps followed by a step or gesture accented by a syncopated delivery just prior to the fourth musical count. The rhythm is slow-slow-quick-quick-rest. The percussion similarly accents the second quick beat of each truncated section, giving dancers the opportunity for a side or diagonally backward hip thrust.

Nearly any punched, sharp movement is acceptable, limited only by the dancer's imagination. The repeated use of the conga's single percussive pushed beat makes it a valuable tool for exploring this essential jazz rhythm device. The energetic variety of individualized gestures make the snaking conga line an inviting dance for anyone who wants to join.

The rhythms and culture of millions of Latinos from all over Mexico, the Caribbean, Central America and South America will undoubtedly continue to influence jazz music and dances far into the 21st century.

ENDNOTES

[1] Elizabeth Aldrich, *From the ballroom to hell: Grace and folly in nineteenth-century dance* (Evanston, Ill.: Northwestern University Press, 1991), p. 36.

[2] Ibid.

[3] Peter Buckman, *Let's dance* (London: Paddington, 1978), p. 1.

[4] Joseph E. Marks, *America learns to dance: A historical study of dance education in America before 1900* (Brooklyn, N.Y.: Dance Horizons, 1957), p. 28.

[5] Fred Astaire, *Steps in time* (New York: Harper and Brothers, 1959), p. 239.

CHAPTER SEVEN

introduction

This chapter offers a historical overview of jazz and tap dance in America. A variety of influences contributed both deliberately and inadvertently to the development of these extraordinary art forms indigenous to the United States. The obvious flash and power of jazz and tap may be the easiest way for viewers to begin to appreciate these styles, but the eloquent and energizing life forces in their practice and performance remain their greatest contribution to world culture.

AND "ALL THAT JAZZ" DANCE

Myron Howard Nadel

What is this thing we call *jazz?* The word has various meanings: a type of music and dance, fornication, lively vernacular speech or objects and activities that the speaker feels no need to label carefully (i.e., "stuff"). Jazz may seem indefinable precisely because it is so pervasive. When asked "What is jazz?" famous jazz trumpeter Louis Armstrong (1900–1971) replied, "Man, if you gotta ask, you ain't never gonna know."

Dance audiences may see whole dances and think, "Yes, that is jazz dance!" For certain stylistic elements or movements, they point and say, "That step was jazzy." If a ballet or contemporary dance work contains jazz elements as a metaphor for our lives and times, but uses music by a composer who never thought of himself as a jazz musician, is that jazz dance? Or if a ballet choreographer designs unmistakable classical steps to a piece of music heralded as a bebop classic, is that jazz dance? What if a tap dancer hoofs and jams with a jazz harmonica or taps to a Bach composition from the 1700s? Is that jazz dance?

So many variables are included in this thing called jazz dance that it would be misleading and unjazzlike to provide only one definition. This chapter instead concentrates on essential elements from the many varied sources that have contributed to the feel and vocabulary of the jazz that is in dance today.

Instructors of jazz dance have created a form primarily for teaching dancers who want to command a broad vocabulary of movement in commercial and concert venues. This vocabulary combines movements from ballet, modern dance, various African, Caribbean and Latin American dance forms and even East Indian dance. Like jazz music, which can include a wide array of sub-forms, jazz dance is eclectic and inclusive.

Jazz dance has its most immediate roots in the social dances that grew out of the Jazz Age of the 1920s. We know that social dances such as the pavan, the galliard and the allemande—which were founded in European folk dances with roots in antiquity—provided the basis for ballet movements. Like ballet, theatrical jazz dance commandeered the Americanized versions of African and European dances and transformed them into movements for the stage.

Tap dance, with its inclusion of sounds from metal-plated shoes striking man-made floors, is also closely related to the history of jazz dance because many of the stepping movements are similar.

ELEMENTS OF BLACK MOVEMENT CULTURE

Jazz dance, tap dance and, by association, jazz music are indigenous American art forms, but they would not exist at all if it were not for the contribution of America's African ancestors, who practiced a love of life and spirituality through movement and music long before the beginning of the slave trade in the 17th century. The combined influences of the musical and dance traditions of Africans and of the various peoples who emigrated from Europe contributed to the development of jazz dance, jazz music and tap dance. The characteristic African dance elements amalgamated into jazz dance exhibit a number of recurring qualities:

Gliding, dragging or shuffling footwork, often in low, crouched attitudes. This close-to-earth footwork originated in the slaves' barefoot dancing on dirt and is just a tap shoe away from many famous black entertainers' "getting down" type of tapping.

A tilting and fluid spine. These postures led to a style of social dancing that was to alter the upright stance of the European-based dances, allowing for the generous fluctuations of individual parts of the torso, ribs, shoulders and pelvis to be highlighted. Dancing from and in a crouched position is a protocol for the jazz dance styles of Eugene (Luigi) Facciuto (b. 1925) and Jack Cole (1914–1974), for example, which often include a bent-knee position, known in ballet as *plié*.

Animal dances. Animal dances are closely linked with the many slave dances that served as an impetus for ragtime dances in the early 20th century, such as the turkey trot and the bunny hug. The mime dances of the 1960s, such as the monkey and the pony, are similarly linked. Gestures that imitate animal movements, like the leveled isolation of the skull on the neck in a chicken's feeding attitude, are part of a pool of standard isolation movements of jazz dancing today.

Propulsive, swinging, loping and hard-driving percussive gestures. Such gestures of the whole or parts of the body describe a plethora of high-energy dynamics within jazz dance.

Centrifugal, outward-exploding movements. In these movements, initiated in the hips, the pelvis becomes the impetus for scattered and convulsive or controlled follow through.[1]

EARLY CULTURAL EXCHANGES

The mixing of artistic practices among the immigrants and slaves from the early 17th century through the 19th century—particularly among the African, Irish, South American and Caribbean peoples—led to the development of what anthropologists call *syncretism*, or "the blending together of cultural elements that previously existed separately."[2]

Even before the time of the American Revolution (1775–1783), there existed a small number of black "freedmen" who were able to settle in some of the northern cities. In New York City, freedmen and whites mixed in bars and brothels in a depressed area called the Five Points District, where blacks could hear the tunes and see the steps of Irish jigs and English clogging, and whites could see the unique ways that blacks performed their dances and songs.

William Henry Lane (1825–1852) was a freedman who bravely toured as a dancer with white minstrel players. Known as "Massa Juba," Lane took his nickname from the "Juba," a plantation dance that included many of the dance and music elements that contributed to his projected image of a happy dancing Negro. Although he didn't wear taps, he made intricate and syncopated sounds with his hard shoes, paving the way for tap dancing. Before Lane's popularity, white entertainer Thomas Dartmouth "Daddy" Rice

(1806–1860) was the leading mimic of black dance. Daddy Rice's 1820s theater intermission act, known as "Jim Crow," combined his reputedly skilled Irish clogging with an imitation of a lame Negro.

In the South, slaves were refused use of their drums for fear that they might be secretly communicating possible rebellion through the drumming and dancing, but many still found ways to be rhythmically creative with sticks, bones, clapping and stamping. Slave owners inadvertently nurtured this artistry, particularly around the holidays and on Sundays, the one day slaves did not have to work as hard. The slaves would often include satirical imitations of the white social dance forms they saw regularly, such as the minuet and the quadrille. In Louisiana, black freedmen who immigrated from independent Haiti and other areas of the Caribbean adopted a version of European Catholicism but kept their own ritual traditions alive through a singing, dancing and drumming activity known as Vodun or Vodou. In 1817, fearing secret meetings among the blacks, white authorities restricted these public rituals to Sundays only in Congo Square, New Orleans.

Because one drop of "white" blood was enough to keep a person from indentured servitude, the results of interracial sexual intercourse created a whole class of "colored" folk, mulattos, many of whom gained financial independence. Their social life included its own theater, an opera company and evening balls in imitations of white society. White gentlemen danced and otherwise mingled with the lovely "women of color" in fashionable and expertly executed quadrilles and cotillions.

EARLY THEATRICAL SOURCES

White audiences in the 19th and early 20th centuries were willing to buy tickets to hear black music, see black dances and enjoy jokes at the expense of blacks in a theatrical form called *minstrelsy*. In white minstrel shows, performers would blacken their faces with burnt cork, presenting the black man as either a foolish dandy or an ignoramus. These white impersonations ironically captured some of the energy inherent in the dance of many fine black entertainers of the time. By the late 19th century, some minstrel shows began to employ blacks, who also had to wear blackface, but who slowly began to transform this perverse art form into a somewhat reputable trade, creating their own more "realistic" variety acts such as "Coon Shows" and eventually a few all-black revues and Broadway productions. (For an uncomfortable yet thought-provoking take on a modernized, "fairy tale" version of the "Coon Shows," see Spike Lee's [b. 1957] fascinating 2000 film "Bamboozled.")

Minstrel shows captured the attention of American audiences through their high-pitched energies and variety acts, especially in the middle section, known as the Olio. They embraced a large vocabulary of dance steps and styles, including the essence, sand dancing, buck and wing (later called tap) and eccentric dance. Minstrel shows culminated in a climactic walkaround: a high-strutting dance called the cakewalk. The cakewalk became the first black dance to appear not only on stage but within the social dance fabric of the ragtime era.

Unfortunately, blackface persisted well into the 20th century, and early sound films of the 1930s and 1940s still highlighted the occasional blackface number (see the films of Eddie Cantor, Al Jolson, Bing Crosby and even Fred Astaire in the "Video/Film Resources" appendix).

Jazz Dance Elements from the Theater

The buck and wing. Important general types of vernacular theater dance emerged from minstrelsy: white and black vaudeville, "race" musicals and early musical comedies called revues. The most inclusive black-white exchange was what was known mainly in the South as the buck and wing and as tap dancing in the North.

Each buck and wing dancer found his unique style, where speed, agility and a sense of the weight being dropped into the floor were the most common. The *buck* was the shuffling or stepping part combined with the tappy, eventually syncopated, sound-producing part; the *wing*, probably derived from the authentic slave dance the pigeon wing, was the part in which dancers stretched their arms sideways and flapped them as they bent over for some difficult tapping tricks. "In the buck and wing," said concert tap artist Paul Draper (1909–1996), "the arms never went over the head, except in the wing, and that was because they were bending over."[3]

Nineteen-twenties' Broadway star Ann Pennington (1892–1971) and 20th Century Fox's nineteen-thirties' child star Shirley Temple (b. 1928) borrowed from the relatively heavier style of buck dancing. Early 20th century black tap dancing stars include King Rastus Brown, Eddie Rector, Jack Wiggins and, most important, Bill "Bojangles" Robinson

(1878–1949), the first black solo dancer to star in white vaudeville circuits. Although steel taps are the overwhelming choice of tap dancers in the 20th and 21st centuries, Bojangles, the most famous of all tappers, wore wooden taps even in his musicals such as "The Hot Mikado" (1939) and "Hot from Harlem" (1941).

Early during the 20th century, the aspects of the Russian ballet and folk dance imports that relied on difficult moves created such a hearty audience response that American entertainers were compelled to include these flashy steps in their own vaudeville routines. The Nicholas Brothers, known for their acrobatic tricks and down-style tapping, were one of many black groups called "flash acts" that included speed and dangerous-looking skills in their routines. Fayard Nicholas (b. 1914) and Harold Nicholas (1921–2000) danced in this tradition through much of the 20th century, although they preferred to refer to themselves as "class acts." They can be seen in Hollywood movies as early as Eddie Cantor's United Artists film "The Kid from Spain" (1932) and as late as Janet Jackson's pop-culture MTV video "Alright" (1990). These great artists mastered the illusion of improvisation and spontaneity with their rich rhythmic content, flair and spellbinding skill.

Both black and white dancers have carried the buck and wing flash tradition along. Sammy Davis Jr. (1925–1990), who started out in a vaudeville revue at age three with his tap dancing father, and Broadway dancer-actor Gregory Hines (b. 1946), who watched the Nicholas Brothers from backstage at Harlem's Apollo Theatre, may also be considered artists in the buck and wing tradition. Presenting relaxed body attitudes and heavier sounds than in the essence or soft-shoe styles, these wonderful performers can be seen together, along with a slew of other old-timers, in challenge dances in the 1989 film "Tap."

The soft-shoe. The essence, or "Virginia essence," filtered down from minstrelsy to vaudeville, but also had its origins in the shuffle of African dances. The essence eventually became known as the *soft-shoe* because it projected style more than sound, making paramount the appearance of ease, grace, sophistication and control. Dan Bryant (1833–1875), of Dan Bryant Minstrels, first perfected the essence, and several performers followed the essence/soft-shoe style up through the 20th century. George Primrose (1852–1919) began in 1867 as a juvenile clog dancer in minstrelsy and remained popular with the next century's vaudeville audiences. He created a style referred to as *picture dancing* because of his concentration on positioning the body.

By 1919, *The New York Times* declared Primrose "the man who invented the soft shoe." Eddie Girard, Billy Kersands (1842–1915), and Eddie Leonard (1875–1941) were somewhat less influential but still important essence dancers. And the world-famous tap dancing of Fred Astaire (1899–1987) and Paul Draper harked back to Primrose's essence and picture style.

Eccentric. Another development under the umbrella of vaudeville perform-ance was an out-of-harmony style called *eccentric* dancing, which generally, but not always, was accompanied by the plated shoes. Eccentric dancing is purposely awkward, even acrobatic, and sometimes takes advantage of a performer's unusual body formations, such as double-jointedness. One famous name associated with eccentric dancing was the actor, director, pro-ducer, playwright and composer George M. Cohan (1878–1942). He is described as having a jerky, bamboo-caned walk and a straw-hatted, bobbing head: "the squarest little shooter who ever did the buck 'n' wing and climbed the proscenium arch."[4] For the film about Cohan produced by Warner Broth-ers studios, the classic "Yankee Doodle Dandy" (1942), white film choreog-rapher Johnny Boyle (1916–1965) taught Cohan's style and routines to James Cagney (1899–1986).

Burlesque. A related form of purely commercial slow dancing to strongly rhythmic and punctuated drum sounds is *burlesque.* Although burlesque has roots that encompass comedy, farce and seedy entertainments played most-ly to men, the form that developed in America and died out by World War II employed many entertainers who later went legitimate. In the late 19th cen-tury, before the form had fallen into complete disrepute, solo entertainers such as Lydia Thompson (1836–1908) and groups such as the Floradora girls gave it some class. But by the 1920s, burlesque dancing mainly highlighted the female body as object, as exemplified in the Ziegfeld Follies and other early Broadway revues, and in early film musicals such as "Glorifying the American Girl" (1929; the only film to have been produced solely by Florenz Ziegfeld [1869–1932]) and "King of Jazz" (1930). The dance portions of bur-lesque were simply meant to be as erotic as possible within the limits of the local laws. Its featured dancers used all sorts of gyrations, especially in their striptease numbers, deliberately focusing on the hips and breasts. The Jule Styne/Stephen Sondheim score to the 1959 Broadway show "Gypsy" (film, 1962) highlights the life of one of the most famous of all burlesque strippers, Gypsy Rose Lee (1914–1970).

Bob Fosse (1927–1987), one of the most celebrated Broadway choreogra-phers, started out as a young tap dance entertainer in the decaying burlesque scene of 1930s Chicago. His provocative style combined the bump and grind of burlesque, an eccentric vocabulary of his own (often including minimalist isolations, angled limbs, hats and gloves), tap, a nearly mechanical simplicity and a rich technical array of many of the elements previously mentioned. Although his choreography in his early Broadway shows such as "The Pajama Game" (1954; film, 1957) and "Damn Yankees" (1955; film, 1958) was outwardly propulsive and flashy, like the more athletic dances of Jack Cole, Jerome Robbins and the Nicholas Brothers, his signature style became highly developed in the latter part of his career, in shows such as "Pippin" (1972), "Chicago" (1975) and "Dancin'" (1978), and spread to the entire world through the movies "Cabaret" (1972) and "All That Jazz" (1979). Fosse's impact continues to be felt decades after his death. He knew the tough, seedy world of burlesque but transformed its sexually charged dynamics into a unique, technically demanding dance style that his aficionados quite confusingly called *jazz dance*. His is but one kind of jazz dance, however.

Black Theater

With the onset of vaudeville, black entertainers survived through the 1920s in their own entertainments, which white audiences saw and heard all over the country. One large syndicate, the Theatre Owners' Booking Association (TOBA, which the performers themselves often wryly and more accurately referred to as "Tough on Black Asses"), promoted black shows in southern, southwestern and some northern cities. The TOBA circuit outlasted white vaudeville by a few years, into the 1930s. Sometimes TOBA entertainers were picked up for the more prestigious black Broadway musicals and white vaudeville tours.

Presentation of black musicals in New York coincided with the disappearance of minstrel shows in the 1890s, and these musicals continued to be produced with varying fervor well into the 1930s. They were primarily "race" shows, the name given to all-black musicals of the time, and they included dancing developed in TOBA shows, honky tonks, dance halls and tenderloin districts. White Broadway revues remained ever ready to include simulations of black dancing.

Black musicals, both revues and musical comedies, eventually helped change the dancers and performers' movement attitudes and, more important, society as a whole. The growth and proliferation of tap dancing, vernacular jazz dance and basic postures and movement dynamics filtered onto the popular stages and ballrooms around the world.

The Blues

Contrasting with the faster dance categories mentioned in the previous sections is a very broad form of slower dance known as *the blues*. The blues is actually a song form that evolved out of 18th and 19th century slave work songs (themselves adaptations of African call-and-response working tunes), field hollers, ring shouts and spirituals.

Dancers have adapted essential characteristics of blues vocal and instrumental music into their expressive dance counterparts. Comprehension of the blues might begin with a visualization of some of its musical properties. In any simple gesture, like reaching for the brim of a hat, one can create and feel the blues elements by:

- Altering the emphasis or energy at each point along the path in a way that reminds us of the sharps and flats of blues chromaticism, or making the path smooth but less direct, such as in a sliding, jazz trombone sound;

- Adding improvised flourishes like the "wa-wa" of a trumpet, with its own "hat wavings";

- Extending or stretching out the arm to its fullest possible range and then drawing it to the brim in a sudden percussive movement, like a rim shot on a snare drum;

- Moving the way that a "holler" might be sung, with extraordinary focus and awareness on the altering of each instant of sound;

- Just getting "down and dirty," as blues practitioners might say, and really "feeling it";

- Stretching, yawning and then tightening one's whole body;

- Indirectly moving a limb as if it were dallying (straying) from its joint;

- Initiating movements from the pelvis, with energy slinking sequentially through the body.

Like blues music, the blues as dance is not primarily meant to entertain, but to express human experience. Some concert dance companies have used the music to great effect at times, such as in the Alvin Ailey American Dance

Theater production of Ailey's own *Blues Suite* (1958), set to traditional blues music, and the Bill T. Jones/Arnie Zane Dance Company's works *Soon* (1988) and *Last Night on Earth* (1992), both with sections set to tunes sung by blues great Bessie Smith (1894–1937).

Later Theatrical Fusion: Broadway

In the 20th century, Broadway dance slowly evolved to include black jazz dance, in what seems to be three phases:

1. *The imitative phase: white Broadway imitates black dance.* Mainstream Broadway, dance or otherwise, was a predominantly white enterprise, but Broadway has also always kept current of what is widely acceptable and what sells. Therefore, whites performed on Broadway the popular, black-influenced social dance forms of the 20th century long before black performers themselves were included. Black-based social dances that had reached the Broadway stage—such as the Charleston, the Lindy hop and the jitterbug—included many borrowed vernacular movements and rhythms. Nevertheless, the spine and soul of African American dancers remained for the most part absent and could be seen only in the few "race" musicals created at the time, such as "Shuffle Along" (1921), "Blackbirds of 1928" (with Bill "Bojangles" Robinson) and "Cabin in the Sky" (1940; film, 1943). Black social dance styles on Broadway usually existed in the form of blackface, by both white and black performers, in shows such as "Shuffle Along, Sinbad" (1918), with Al Jolson (1886–1950) wearing his usual burnt cork look, and "Whoopee" (1928; film, 1930), with Eddie Cantor (1892–1964) in a blackface role.

2. *Black dancers dance for white choreographers.* Concert dance was quicker than the mostly white Broadway and Hollywood to introduce important black personalities. Still, some examples of Broadway productions featuring black artists do exist.

Tapper John W. "Bubbles" Sublett (1902–1986) stole the show in the part of Sportin' Life in the original Broadway production of Gershwin's classic "Porgy and Bess" (1935), directed by Rouben Mamoulian (1898–1987). The 1959 film starred Sammy Davis Jr. in the same role, with choreography by Hermes Pan (1909–1990).

Josephine Baker (1906–1975), the first black woman to be featured in a Ziegfeld revue (five years after Ziegfeld died), and the Nicholas Brothers performed in such numbers as *Island in the West Indies* and *Maharanee* in the 1936 Broadway production "Ziegfeld Follies," choreographed (ostensibly) by Robert Alton (1906–1957) and George Balanchine (1904–1983).

The Nicholas Brothers also performed in several numbers in the Rodgers and Hart show "Babes in Arms" in 1937 with Balanchine as choreographer, particularly in specialty numbers such as the mock-Egyptian ballet *Lee Calhoun's Follies* and *All Dark People.*

Balanchine choreographed and codirected the all-black Broadway musical "Cabin in the Sky" (1940), with the wonderful Katherine Dunham (b. 1909) and her dancers, who also performed alongside the Nicholas Brothers and Cab Calloway (1907–1994) in the all-black film musical "Stormy Weather" (1943), with choreography by Clarence Robinson and Nick Castle (1910–1968) (although Dunham herself clearly choreographed the dance to the title song).

Many of these dances drew on the African- and African American–influenced jazz and tap rhythms of the black performers themselves, so it is difficult to say today where the white choreographers' steps start and where the performers' own input stops. Ironically, white choreographer Helen Tamiris (1905–1966) tried to bring a color-blind dance ethic (and aesthetic) to the concert stage by having her all-white company of women perform to African American songs of protest in the 1937 piece *How Long, Brethren?*

3. *Integration.* The third phase of the inclusion of black dance is characterized by two phenomena: *(a)* white dancers and choreographers no longer had to imitate black dance because they were able to study movements previously considered vernacular or ethnic; and *(b)* black dancers began learning the technical traditions of Western theatrical dance in racially integrated dance classes of modern dance and ballet. African American dance pioneer Katherine Dunham opened a school in 1945 in the Broadway theater district. With her considerable experience in film and Broadway, combined with a doctorate in anthropology, she methodically codified a repertoire of movements and dances from the black diaspora for "primitive" and Afro-Cuban dance classes. Colleague Syvilla Forte (1917–1975) headed Dunham's New York studio, and Forte's husband, Buddy Phillips, taught tap. Charlie Morrison taught jazz dance, a shoeless combination of buck and wing and essence. No longer would mainstream Broadway find it necessary to mimic and appropriate black dance. Instead, dancers of various races could be trained in all the necessary skills.

Credit also must be given to the dance institutions with racially mixed faculty and students, such as the High School of the Performing Arts, Dance Theatre of Harlem, the Juilliard School, the Graham School and the Alvin Ailey School, to name just a few New York institutions. Moreover, multiracial graduates of college and embryonic performing arts high school dance departments from all over the country were now available for work in a slowly integrating Broadway.

Audience approval (i.e., revenue) was really at issue. When the black "race" musicals of the late 19th and early 20th centuries, such as "The Creole Show" (1890), "A Trip to Coontown" (1898) and "Shuffle Along" (1921) were conceived, they were a combination of variety show and book shows straight out of the black minstrelsy tradition and were mounted to appeal directly to the curiosity of white audiences. But by the late 20th century, musicals were created to get black audiences to Broadway shows. The black choreographers of these shows—such as Louis Johnson (b. 1930), Donald McKayle (b. 1930) and George Faison (b. 1945)—were exquisitely trained and superbly skilled dancer-choreographers in the modern dance concert field, with access to both concert and vernacular languages. In this case, the box office finally drove racial changes in the right direction.

Rock

The integration phase of Broadway dance coincided with the development of American rock 'n' roll in the mid- to late 1950s. White rock 'n' roll performers like Elvis Presley (1935–1977) and black performers like Little Richard (b. 1932) were "shakin' it up" in popular entertainments rather than on Broadway. All over the country, as seen on Dick Clark's (b. 1932) national weekly television show "American Bandstand," young people were dancing social dances with a new sense of authenticity that fit the interracial music like a glove. Rock 'n' roll was a fresh approach for everybody. Any shame or societal restrictions previously associated with gyrations of any part of the body or with subtle sexual masquerades were gone. Gone, too, was the earlier coordination with a partner's step patterns. As with some short solo "licks" in previous jazz social dances such as the jitterbug, each person could now improvise and participate in a music-movement ritual that related to everyone at the same party.

Without creating a true dance style, these group rituals unabashedly drew on elements of African dance: shuffles, crouched attitudes, spinal waves, isolations, animal imitations (the monkey, the pony), improvisation, propulsion from the hips, swings, lopes and hard-driving percussive gestures. Several manifestations of this transformation can be seen in Broadway shows such as "Bye Bye Birdie" (1960; film, 1964), "Hair" (1968; film, 1979), "Grease" (1972; film, 1978) and "Hairspray" (2000; film, 1988).

CONCERT DANCE

Ballet that employs vernacular jazz dance styles may seem to be a strange combination, considering their different heritages—one from the courts of Europe and the other from brothels and clubs of America's red light districts. In the case of Russian-born ballet dancer and choreographer George Balanchine, this combination may not have been so strange, given his propensity to go directly to music as a source for many of his inspirations. When he emigrated to the United States in 1933, he fell in love with America's sleek and stylized popular tunes.

One inspiration came from the more popular sounds of composers influenced by the rhythms and off-beat harmonies of jazz: 20th century artists such as Richard Rodgers (1902–1979), Aaron Copland (1900–1990), Morton Gould (1913–1996) and Igor Stravinsky (1882–1971). Balanchine's Broadway and concert choreography was set to Rodgers's *Slaughter on Tenth Avenue* (1936), Stravinsky's *Ragtime for 11 Instruments* (1960, 1966) and Gould's *Derivations for Clarinet and Jazz Band* (1964). Other important ballet choreographers who incorporated jazz include Jerome Robbins (1918–1998), in his 1944 dance *Fancy Free* and the 1957 Broadway show "West Side Story," both set to music by Leonard Bernstein (1918–1990), and Billy Wilson (1935–1994), in his 1982 piece *Concerto in F* for the Alvin Ailey American Dance Theater, set to George Gershwin's 1925 composition of the same name.

In the modern dance field, a premiere company is Hubbard Street Dance Chicago, originally founded by Lou Conte (b. 1942) in 1977. It combines contemporary dance, theatrical jazz, modern dance and classical ballet technique to create a unique artistic style. Jazz dance has been integrated into the company's ethos with the help of international choreographers such as Ohad Naharin (b. 1955) from Israel, Jiří Kylián (b. 1947) from the Czech Republic, Margo Sappington (b. 1947) and Twyla Tharp (b. 1941). The Gus Giordano Company, also based in Chicago, tours the United States with programs of jazz-based concert works that embrace modern dance and serious music. Gus Giordano (b. 1930) still sponsors the annual Jazz Dance World

Congress, bringing together teachers, students and performers in a four-day concentration of classes and performances.

Certain works of politically active choreographer Anna Sokolow (1910–2000) present her views on the tense and alienating conditions of urban life, such as the dance piece *Rooms* (1965), set to a screeching jazz fusion score by Kenyon Hopkins (1912–1983). Twin creative sources of inspiration for Alvin Ailey (1931–1989) were the urban body language of black America and the spirit of the rural churchgoing community in which he was raised, but he also created some very popular, jazz-inflected dances to music by Duke Ellington (*River*, 1970; *The Mooche*, 1975; *Night Creature*, 1975) and Hugh Masekela (*Masekela Langage*, 1969).

Because jazz dance and music are so closely related to black dance and music, it would be easy to say that any predominantly black dance company—such as the Alvin Ailey American Dance Theater, the Lulu Washington Dance Company or the Dance Theater of Harlem—is automatically linked to jazz dance. However, black concert dance is not by definition jazz dance.

Tap dance in concert is not as common as jazz dance, but it isn't new, either. Beginning in the 1930s, Paul Draper made a career of artistic tap in a ballet-ic style to the classical music of Johann Sebastian Bach (1685–1750) and Domenico Scarlatti (1685–1757); he also performed unaccompanied tap toc-cata and "portraits" of characters like "the politician." The creative Draper appeared with virtuoso harmonica player Larry Adler (b. 1914) in the elegant and artistic nightclub scene from the 1930s to 1950s. Danny Daniels (b. 1924) and Michael Dominico (1929–1977) joined Draper's ranks on the symphony circuit, when they toured in the 1952 *Tap Dance Concerto*, composed for Draper by Morton Gould.

The 1980s saw the emergence of a new generation of concert tap dancers, such as those in the Gail Conrad Dance Theatre; the N.Y.C. Tapworks, which specializes in many styles of tap, often with their own original pieces; and Manhattan Tap, founded in 1986, which has been a major force not only in New York City but also in the international tap community. Manhattan Tap is a collection of strong individual dancers who fuse themselves into an electrifying ensemble that blends tap dance with music, choreography, and improvisation. Since 1991, Artistic Director Heather Cornell (b. 1956) has been creating choreography in a style dubbed "visual music." Manhattan Tap continues to work with some of the greatest jazz musicians in the world. Brenda Bufalino's (b. 1937) American Tap Dance Orchestra, also based in

New York City, uses polyrhythms through a dozen or so tap dancers to create a symphony of sounds.

The creative potential of tap keeps returning as many forms of dance generate new ideas through the rich tap vocabulary, tap improvisation and oral history. Dancer-choreographer Savion Glover (b. 1973), for instance, created the Tony-winning Broadway production "Bring in 'Da Noise, Bring in 'Da Funk" (1995), which employed tap dance to chart the history of the black experience in America. A newer company, Tap Dogs, an all-male company under Australian choreographer Dein Perry (b. 1962) makes us take a new look at tap as a concert form that can extol the macho in exuberant and even humorous ways.

JAZZ DANCE AS A TRAINING GROUND

Those who say that they are teaching jazz dance are usually teaching technique to dancers who wish to embrace the many styles of jazz that appear on Broadway, in music videos and in concerts. They must jump, turn, fall, contract, release, extend their limbs, be flexible and dance while standing, sitting, kneeling and lying. The value of these techniques is that they provide a solid technical basis for the execution of the styles of many commercial and some concert choreographers. They are eclectic teaching tools that, when studied with ballet, modern dance and tap, can cover most movement patterns necessary for performance. Studying only jazz dance, however, would lack the broader and proper perspective of contemporary concert choreography.

The Roots of Jazz Dance Technique Today

Vaudeville-Broadway dance director Ned Wayburn (1874–1942) made the first significant attempt to create a Broadway-type school. He combined tap, ballet, acrobatics and some ethnic styles into what he called a "modern American dance technique." His courses sufficed for a 1920s and 1930s Broadway that demanded good looks and showmanship for the mostly girl choruses of thinly plotted musicals and music revues. But, by midcentury, Jack Cole, sometimes known as the father of modern jazz dance, had become the preeminent contributor to film and Broadway. Along with the vernacular, he brought a technically challenging intensity to his singular mixture of ballet, modern dance and various ethnic dance forms.

Although Cole began as a modern dancer with Ted Shawn (1891–1972) and later with Doris Humphrey (1895–1958), his indifference to abstraction led him to find success in Paul Draper's world of elegant nightclubs in an era when dining out, ballroom dancing and sophisticated entertainment were upper-class recreations. Cole seemed to exemplify the teachings of Denishawn (the dance school formed by Ruth St. Denis [1877–1968] and Ted Shawn), where all techniques and styles were considered the rightful heritage of the dance student. The Cole vocabulary of movement can best be described as a delicious pie, with one slice Hindu, one vernacular, one Spanish, one ballet, one modern and one miscellaneous, with a tasty crust made out of jazz music!

Cole's carefully crafted and technically demanding system was made known through teaching assignments that were part of his contractual obligations to Columbia Pictures in the 1940s (for many of Rita Hayworth's films) and to 20th Century Fox in the 1950s (often for Marilyn Monroe films).

Besides his difficult knee work, Cole's dancers learned special thrusting movements, powerful gestures, sparseness of motion and a psychophysical commitment to performance, whether ballet, modern, East Indian, Spanish or black ethnic dance. The strength of his movement language was visible in his swift and precise phrasing as well as in his adagio work. Cole and his followers—such as Carol Haney (1925–1964), Matt Mattox (b. 1921), Buzz Miller (1923–1999) and Gwen Verdon (1925–2000)—channeled their dynamic energy as meticulously as those modern dance personalities who originally influenced Cole. His jazz dance technique was later enlarged and refined by dancer and teacher Matt Mattox, and it provided vocabulary and incentive for other creative jazz choreographers such as Bob Fosse, and teachers Eugene (Luigi) Facciuto and Gus Giordano, who were to develop similar inclusive training methods also called jazz dance.

FUTURES

Both Broadway and concert dance benefited from excellent black modern choreographers and dancers such as Donald McKayle ("Raisin," 1973), Louis Johnson ("Purlie," 1970), George Faison ("The Wiz," 1975; film, 1978), Billy Wilson ("Bubblin' Brown Sugar," 1976) and, of course, Alvin Ailey, whose company has demonstrated many black American styles. By the 1980s, black choreographers and dancers had become so much a part of Broadway that it was no longer necessary to delineate their racial background to understand their contributions.

By the time "Dreamgirls" (1981) appeared, the question of black subject matter of special interest only to black audiences had nearly abated. White choreographer-director Michael Bennett (1943–1987) of "A Chorus Line" fame (1975; film, 1985) and a cast of skilled black dancer-singer-actors deftly created the "Dreamgirls" libretto about a popular black singing group's rise to stardom. For Broadway, integration was mandated by both law and pragmatism, but for the dance world as a whole it brought about a new amalgamation of dance styles.

"Cats" (1981), choreographed by British choreographer Gillian Lynne (b. 1926), used ballet, modern dance and jazz to bring to life its feline characters, and became the longest-running Broadway musical, finally closing in London's West End in 2002. The "Lion King" (1997), another immensely popular Broadway musical, based on the 1994 Disney film, was choreographed by the African-Caribbean American dancer and choreographer Garth Fagan (b. 1940) and won several Tony awards. No less than three homages to Bob Fosse continue to tour U.S. and international theaters sixteen years after his death: "Chicago" (1975), "Dancin'" (1978) and "Fosse" (1999). Choreographer-director Rob Marshall (b. 1960) has created an original and eclectic jazz style in his 2002 film version of Fosse's "Chicago." The vital, dynamic energies of jazz dance will no doubt continue to infuse Broadway, film and concert performances for years to come.

Although jazz dance may be indefinable, it remains pervasive and includes one or more of the following characteristics: it must be traceable to the African continent; it must have soul; it is passionate, sensual and erotic, but not vulgar, narcissistic or cute; it must be at least bicultural, not just African, but certainly not without African-based elements; and it must involve both jazzy movements and jazz or jazzy music.

ENDNOTES

[1] Marshall Stearns and Jean Stearns, *Jazz dance: The story of American vernacular dance* (New York: Macmillan, 1979), p. 23.

[2] Ted Gioia, *The history of jazz* (New York: Oxford University Press, 1997), p. 7.

[3] Paul Draper, personal interview by Myron Howard Nadel, 1978, Pittsburgh, Penn.

[4] Ward Moorehouse, *George M. Cohan* (Westport, Conn.: Greenwood, 1973), p. 47.

CHAPTER EIGHT

introduction

Capturing the tradition of the ballet art form, Carol Pardo tours ballet history from the lavish court dances of the Renaissance to the unadorned 20th century simplicity of ballets in leotards and tights. She traces ballet's original path as it leaves Italy and travels through France, Denmark, Russia, England and the United States, pointing out ballet's greatest pioneers, mainly choreographers and impresarios, along the way. The composition of ballet audiences and developments in theater construction were also important factors in its evolution, as were the education and reputations of the dancers themselves. The next time you see a ballet, ask yourself, What tradition is being presented? Where did its elements originate? More important, what vision of the future does the choreography—and therefore the choreographer—provide?

BALLET: A HISTORY IN BROAD BRUSHSTROKES

Carol Pardo

Any history reflects the history of the discipline in question, as well as the concerns of the time at which that history is written. Looking at the history of ballet from a 21st century perspective, one's view is colored by the concerns of the moment, chief among them being the lack of great choreographers to carry the discipline forward and the need to preserve what remains from the past. In order to exist, ballet needs trained dancers, teachers and choreographers; willing and educated audiences; places to perform; money; and, perhaps before all else, a visionary, someone to whom ballet matters so much that the other requirements fall into place or are made to do so.

WHAT IS BALLET?

Ballet is the oldest form of Western theatrical dancing. That it has a history is one of its defining characteristics. Change takes place within a framework governed by the past. Ballet is a combination of athletics and aesthetics, whose result is rhythm given three dimensions by the human body in motion. Rhythm is generally provided by music. Form is based on the range of motion provided by legs trained to turn out from the hip joint and by the five basic positions of the feet, together with their associated positions of the torso, head and arms. These basic elements are assembled to form geometrical relationships to each other and to the stage space in which they are performed. By these formal means, ballets and ballet dancers communicate with an audience.

BALLET'S BEGINNINGS

The origins of ballet coincide with the arrival of Italian dancing masters at the French court during the late 16th century, where the *ballet de cour*, or court ballet, came into being. The court ballet was a series of danced episodes accompanied by spoken or sung text. Its participants were courtiers for whom dancing, along with classical mythology (a prime source of subject matter during the first two centuries of ballet) and fencing (the source of turnout, or the ninety-degree rotation of the feet from the hip joint to increase a ballet dancer's range of motion), was a component of basic education. However, courtiers were never considered and, given the low place of performers in society, would never consider themselves professional dancers. The scenery, costumes and mechanical effects of the court ballet could be lavish, for the presentation of the power and brilliance of the court was one purpose of the spectacle. The performance took place on the floor with the audience looking down from raised tiers of seats and was designed in patterns whose focus was the person in whose honor the ballet was performed, rather like a drawing utilizing single-point perspective where all lines converge.

The most important participant in court ballets was Louis XIV, king of France (1638–1715). He first set foot on stage at the age of seven and first appeared as a dancer at the age of twelve. He retired from active performance at the age of thirty-two, either because of the weight of affairs of state or because he had grown too portly to cut as attractive a figure as he once had. In the decade before his retirement, the king founded both the Royal Academy of Dancing, an appointed group of thirteen ballet masters whose charge was to reestablish the art of dancing "to its original perfection,"[1] and the Royal Academy of Music. The former would disappear in the havoc wrought by the French Revolution (1789–1799), but the latter has survived countless changes of government and name to become the Paris Opera Ballet. In 1713, the king founded a ballet school attached to the opera, also still extant. Although Louis XIV was not the only monarch to dance, he was the first to use his power and his purse in the service of creating institutions that set standards and permitted ballet to survive and grow. (Until the French Revolution, the cost of the ballet was almost always part of the king's household budget.) By doing so, he set the stage for the preeminence of the Paris Opera. The house would retain its cachet until the mid–19th century.

The importance of royal patronage cannot be overstated. Ballet is expensive. Training dancers requires at least eight years of study, which must be paid for. Producing ballets is costly, particularly if they are accompanied by live music. Ballet needs money and an audience to survive. It is no coincidence that until the end of the 19th century, ballet developed most where it was part of the royal household: in prerevolutionary France, in Denmark until 1849 and in Russia until the fall of the Romanovs in 1917. Such enduring connections to nobility have given rise to the criticism that ballet is elitist, as has the fact that not everyone is born with the body or temperament to endure the many years of training required to form a ballet dancer.

By his departure from the stage around 1670 and his interest in teaching, Louis XIV also opened the door to the next great development in ballet: the professionalization of the dancer. At around the same time, the raised proscenium stage was also adopted, which contributed to the differentiation of dancer and spectator and changed the nature of choreography. The first professional dancers were men; by 1681, women had joined them onstage. However, preeminence in the field belonged to the former, in great part because women's wide, weighty skirts forced them to remain closer to the ground and limited their range of movement.

Developments in technique would separate the amateur and professional even more. By the beginning of the 18th century, turnout and the five positions, neither of which had been necessary to execute court ballets, were established as the technical basis of the art form.

THE BALLET D'ACTION

As technique developed, so too did a new idea of what ballet should be and what it should accomplish. Throughout the history of ballet, there has been continuous tension between the concepts that dance is sufficient unto itself and that dance is a means of expressing something outside itself: technique or virtuosity versus expression. Both are necessary to ballet. What good is emotion without the means to express it? What good is technique that communicates nothing beyond physical effort? But technique and expression are never present in perfect equilibrium.

In the 18th century, a movement began to "drag us out of the childhood in which we are still in the matter of ballets."[2] Although much of the work done in the development of the *ballet d'action*, or dramatic ballet, was carried out by others in London and in Vienna, the concept of the dramatic ballet is most often associated with choreographer Jean-Georges Noverre (1727–1810). Noverre, half French and half Swiss, wanted nothing more than to be the ballet master at the Paris Opera but suffered only disappointment once he obtained the post. He accomplished his best work elsewhere—in London, Stuttgart and Vienna. All of his ballets are lost, but his writings in defense of his beliefs and of the dramatic ballet, first published in 1760, have ensured that his name lives on.

All the proponents of the *ballet d'action* sought legitimacy by finding their narrative inspirations in historical accounts of mime under the ancient Romans. Noverre felt that dance and mime, a form of stylized gesture and movement used to convey emotion or dramatic action, had become separated from each other some time between antiquity and the 18th century, with the result that "dancing is introduced for the mere sake of dance; and it would seem that everything consists [of] the movement of the legs."[3] In his view, the two disciplines needed to be reunited in order to engage an audience's emotions. To achieve this, the subject of the ballet defined everything else, including its length, form and style.

Noverre also wanted to do away with the vaunted concept of theatrical unity: the traditional requirement that drama express one theme that would be resolved within twenty-four hours and enacted before one stage set. He also undertook a campaign to banish masks, wigs, headdresses, heeled shoes and the cumbersome conventional costumes, all of which prevented the face and body from being used to their fullest, most expressive extent. Mime replaced words, spoken or sung, as the means of dramatic expression in the ballet.

A true fusion of mime and dancing would not take place until the 1830s. Reading 18th century accounts of *ballets d'action*, one is hard pressed to discover much about the dance side of the equation; mime certainly predominates.

THE ROMANTIC BALLET

A more balanced relationship between dance and mime would take decades to achieve and is only one of the elements that define the next great movement in the history of ballet. With its taste for the exotic, for emotion displayed rather than reined in and for the supernatural and irrational rather than the rational, romanticism permeated all the arts early in the 19th century. Moreover, theatrical mechanics and the theater's audience had changed. In France, most of the traditional audience from the noble class was dead, exiled or lying low. Its place, both in France and elsewhere, was increasingly taken by new money and the middle class, whose interests did not necessarily include tableaux with mythological subjects or ballets intended to glorify monarchy. Also, by the dawn of the romantic era, the audience had finally been chased off the stage. In London, a royal edict was required before spectators would completely leave the stage to the dancers in 1813.

Practices within theaters also would increase the distance between audiences and performers. The advent of gas lighting permitted performances to take place in darkened auditoriums, with the stage the only source of light. By the end of the 1820s, set changes took place behind a lowered curtain, a new and obvious separation, but one that created more anticipation of the magical transformation to come. But the most amazing change was that created by women strong enough to dance on the tips of their toes and the development of pointe shoes (ballet slippers with reinforced, hardened toes), which helped them do so. By seeming to conquer gravity, the woman became the icon of the romantic ballet. Henceforth, the ballerina was able to meet the male dancer in the air, formerly his element far more than hers.

Male dancers and male dancing suffered accordingly, with one critic going so far as to call the male dancer a monstrosity. A woman in pants danced the "male" lead in *Coppélia* (1870), the last great ballet of the romantic era—certainly a low point in the development of male dancing and an indication of the decline of the primacy of the Paris Opera. The role would not be danced by a man at the Paris Opera until 1952.

AUGUST BOURNONVILLE AND
THE ROMANTIC BALLET IN DENMARK

Happily for ballet history, Denmark experienced its golden age of the arts during the middle of the 19th century. Ballet in particular thrived owing to the presence of a dancer, teacher, choreographer and visionary all in one: August Bournonville (1805–1879). The son of a French dancer and Swedish mother, Bournonville was, by his own reckoning, thoroughly Danish. He studied at the Paris Opera Ballet in the 1820s and then joined the company. The classroom scene in his ballet *Konservatoriet* (1849) is based on his training in Paris and provides the only available glimpse in the entire repertory of the dance style and teaching methods of that time. Bournonville also borrowed the libretto of the Parisian version of *La Sylphide* (1832), the first full-length ballet of the romantic era, then presented his own version with a new score in 1836. It is still in the repertory in Copenhagen.

Bournonville called himself a romantic, but he is one with a difference. With the exception of *La Sylphide*, the irrational does not win in his world. Right triumphs, duty prevails, and the social order is maintained. Nor is Bournonville's exoticism solely the product of his fantasies; many of his "travelogue" ballets have their roots in his own experiences while traveling throughout Europe. His affection for Italy in particular remains tangible in his ballet *Napoli* (1842).

Those of Bournonville's works based on Nordic gods and legends may seem exotic to us, but their original audience must have viewed them as part of a common heritage. None of these mythology-based works survives. That any of his works are performed today is owing to Bournonville's intense desire not to be forgotten. An inveterate observer, he wrote three books and many shorter works on his life, work and art. Near the end of his life, he rehearsed a chosen few of his works to ensure that they and, through them, he would live on. Thanks to the will and memories of many dancers and ballet masters, as well as to the comparative isolation of Copenhagen from other trends in ballet, the largest cache of ballets from the romantic era survives in Denmark. Bournonville's legacy consists of perhaps six full works and as many excerpts or short pieces.

Until he was in his forties, Bournonville danced usually as the lead in his own ballets. This practice guaranteed that the male dancer would not lose face or place at the Royal Danish Ballet. He trained his company to his specifications and campaigned constantly and successfully for dancers to obtain the same respect accorded to other "master craftsmen."

BALLET IN RUSSIA

The focus of ballet began shifting to the east, to Russia, where the Romanovs provided the last monarchical patronage of the ballet. For most of the 19th century, imperial ministers were directed to hire the best ballet masters they could find; they were generally French. That they had been either undervalued or not sought out by their national ballet indicates one of the causes of the decline of the Paris Opera—a lack of choreographers. This is only one of the reasons for the ascendance of St. Petersburg as the center of ballet, the place where ballet history was consolidated and the future was forged, as Paris had been and as New York would be in the decades following World War II.

Teachers and dancers were also imported from Italy, just as they had been summoned to France centuries earlier. Bournonville's aesthetic and training were imported in the person of his Swedish student Christian Johannson (1817–1903), who arrived in Russia in 1841 and was engaged as the first dancer of the imperial theaters. He also taught at the ballet school from 1860 until his death. Before his arrival, an audience for ballet in Russia already existed, some members so rabid about the art form that they boiled a toe shoe belonging to their favorite ballerina and ate it.

The most long lasting of the French transplants was Marius Petipa (1818–1910), who arrived in Russia in 1847 and choreographed his last work for the imperial theaters in 1903. Petipa's long tenure as chief ballet master was not without its ups and downs, but he was fortunate, as he himself knew, in having one particularly supportive boss from 1881 to 1899—Ivan Alexandrovitch Vsevolozhsky (1835–1909). It was Vsevolozhsky who commissioned Peter Ilyich Tchaikovsky (1840–1893) to write the scores for *The Sleeping Beauty* (1890) and *The Nutcracker* (1892), and who proposed the former as a subject for ballet, collaborating with Petipa on its libretto. Vsevolozhsky was also instrumental in importing the Italian ballerinas, who danced the leading roles at the premieres of both ballets. These ballerinas brought with them the fruits of their training—strength, brilliance and a highly developed technique.

The Italian contribution, grafted to the French, Danish and native strains, was the last component necessary to create the Russian technique that would dazzle the world throughout the next century. *The Sleeping Beauty* is now considered to be a great classical ballet, the litmus test of style and technique for any company that produces it. More than a retelling of the famous fairy tale by Charles Perrault (1628–1703), the ballet was also the last of the court ballets made about a court for a court. It was a paean to the benefits of imperial rule and the clearest available example of the basic formula of a Petipa ballet. Petipa's ballets were generally three to five acts long, with solos and duets for the leading man and woman in at least two acts. The classical elements were surrounded by balleticized folk dancing and mime scenes, but the focus of his dances tended to be the ballerina, in particular her legs and pointes.

It is no surprise that there was a reaction to this formula; the surprise is that the reaction originated within the Imperial Ballet itself. The proselytizer for this "new ballet" (his term) was Mikhail (also Michel and, later, Michael) Fokine (1880–1942), one of the most talented dancers to emerge from the Imperial Ballet School. The company engaged Fokine as a soloist, two levels above that at which new graduates usually started out, and hired him as a teacher at its school around the age of twenty-two. Fokine's primary belief was that everything in a ballet—movement, gesture, mime, sets, costumes, music, even the length of the piece—should be dictated by the style, period and subject of the ballet. He envisioned a homogeneous creation, only as long as it needed to be, with *all* of the dancers—the corps as well as the featured dancers—contributing to the whole.

Fokine, like Noverre, looked back to the ancient world as the model for all that was natural and expressive in dance. He also looked back to the romantic era, when, it can be argued, Noverre's ideas really came to fruition. Thereafter, in Fokine's view, expression gave way to virtuosity and then to acrobatics. Fokine had his own strongly held notion of beauty, which dispensed with certain aspects of the language of ballet, most prominently turnout. Nevertheless, it is important to note that he believed unshakably in the foundations of classical ballet, including training in turnout. He himself said that the compliment that pleased him most in his entire career was the one he received in 1906 after the premiere of his first ballet created for professionals: "Dear comrade, [I am] delighted by your new composition; keep it up and you will be a great ballet master."[4] The source of the compliment? Marius Petipa. Fokine's rebellion was never against a person, but against the condition in which he found his chosen art.

Fokine did not successfully implant his reforms at the imperial theaters. All his efforts only brought about a ban on applause during performances. He would find much more fertile soil at the Ballets Russes, under the directorship of the great 20th century impresario Serge Diaghilev (1872–1929). Diaghilev said of himself, "I am a charlatan, moreover with lots of dash; a great charmer; an insolent [dandy]; a man with plenty of logic and few scruples; one in torment seeming to be without talent. [But] I believe I've found my true vocation: artistic patronage. For that I have everything needful, except money—and that will come."[5]

There rarely seems to have been enough money, and Diaghilev spent much of his time seeking it out and wooing an audience, but he was more than just a patron or an impresario. He had a nose for the new, the ability to gather together many of the best talents in dance, music and the visual arts—Stravinsky, Prokofiev, Satie, Picasso and Matisse would work for him—and the skills needed to develop choreographers. When Diaghilev founded his Ballets Russes for a tour to Paris during the dancers' summer holiday in 1909, Michel Fokine was the newest of the new, and he thrived under Diaghilev's eye for as long as he remained "new" to his employer—that is, until 1912. Diaghilev would also be instrumental in the development of some of the most important ballet choreographers of the 20th century, including Vaslav Nijinsky (1890–1950), Bronislava Nijinska (1891–1972), Léonide Massine (1895–1979) and George Balanchine (1904–1983)—all this in twenty years.

Diaghilev's company was not attached to a school, so he also had to recruit and develop dancers. The greatest weakness of the Ballets Russes, however, was the company's dependence on one man. When Diaghilev died unexpectedly in 1929, his company died with him, giving rise to one of the great dispersions of balletic talent.

RUSSIAN BALLET DISPERSED: ENGLAND AND THE UNITED STATES

Several companies, many with the words "Ballets Russes" in their titles, sprang up in the wake of Diaghilev's death, both to keep his accomplishments alive and to keep his dancers and choreographers employed. They were touring companies whose presence became the foundation for major developments in ballet in North and South America, New Zealand and Australia. The tours took ballet everywhere, not just to big cities. Some dancers decided to stay in these countries after the company moved on, and some returned once their performing days were over, creating a network of teachers who would in turn train local talent.

England, London in particular, benefited enormously from this realignment of talent. The Italian ballet master Enrico Cecchetti (1850–1928), chief teacher of the Diaghilev ballet, had already relocated to London. Marie Rambert (1888–1982) and Ninette de Valois (1898–2001)—dancers, company directors and choreographers who had worked for Diaghilev—possessed complementary skills needed to encourage ballet to take root. De Valois had a vision of British ballet, as well as the will, tenacity and energy to pursue it. Her company's repertory would encompass the classics of the 19th century, the best works of the Diaghilev era and new works. Rambert, like Diaghilev, had the ability to unearth and nurture promising choreographers, among them Antony Tudor (1908/1909–1987) and Sir Frederick Ashton (1904–1988). Tudor continued the Fokine line but added Freud and the expression of a character's psychological state to the content of ballet. His works, like Fokine's, do not always look like classical ballet, but they are grounded in its precepts and training. Ashton, on the other hand, was one of Petipa's descendants. When asked why he was sitting through yet another performance of *The Sleeping Beauty*, a ballet he had seen or performed hundreds of times, he replied, "to take a lesson [from Petipa]." He would become the chief choreographer of what is now the Royal Ballet. His style, intensely musical and elegant, with its faith in the primacy of dance as dance, became strongly identified with British ballet as a whole.

In the United States, Ballet Theatre (later American Ballet Theatre, or ABT), founded in 1939, resembled de Valois's model. The company was to consist of a classical wing under dancer and company director Anton Dolin (1904–1983), an English wing under Tudor, a Fokine wing under Fokine and an American wing under Eugene Loring (1914–1982), an American dancer whose performing career had taken place only in America. It would be a community of dancers not based on a star system and would perform both the classics and contemporary works.

An undertaking of this scale, with all of its wings, however, proved to be unaffordable. ABT benefited from the strong centralized leadership of Lucia Chase (1907–1986), an independently wealthy dancer who, from 1945 to 1980, was codirector of the company, along with stage set designer Oliver Smith (1918–1994). As far as repertory was concerned, ABT did keep some of Fokine's ballets, even after the choreographer's death in 1942, but they had all but disappeared by the end of the 20th century. Tudor's ballets—although intimate in scale and requiring sensitive dancer-actors and costly rehearsal time—are still presented periodically.

Currently ABT is most identified with its productions of full-length story ballets, both the 19th century classics and more recent efforts, a genre that has been gaining in popularity with audiences since 1976 or so. The company also has embraced the presence of stars, whether as permanent members of the company or as guest artists. With the exception of one year (1978–1979) spent as a member of the New York City Ballet, the dancer Mikhail Baryshnikov (b. 1948) made ABT his home base from 1974, when he defected from the Soviet Union, until 1989.

ABT has not always had an affiliated school, nor has it been able to retain any choreographers who could give it an identity all its own. Although the careers of Eliot Feld (b. 1942) and Jerome Robbins (1918–1998) were launched at ABT, Feld preferred to establish his own companies. Robbins produced most of his ballets for the New York City Ballet.

Diaghilev's last choreographer, George Balanchine, immigrated to the United States in 1933 at the urging of Lincoln Kirstein (1907–1996), heir to a fortune based on Filene's Department Store. Kirstein had become infected with "the red and gold disease," a fascination with ballet, in his teens and would spend much of his time, energy and assets to build an American ballet based on Balanchine's needs.

Before all else, in 1934, the two men opened a school in New York, the School of American Ballet. After fifteen years of stops and starts, a permanent company, the New York City Ballet, came into being, primarily as an expression of Balanchine's aesthetic, which is based on music as the floor for dancing. In his ballets, Balanchine created an intimate structural affiliation, though not a one-to-one relationship, between step and note, music and choreography. When he was still in Europe, he had said he wanted to go to America, where there were girls like Ginger Rogers. Moreover, he incorporated traits in his choreography that he found to be particularly American: speed, clarity, syncopation and a voracious attitude toward space.

Stories were not a necessary starting point for Balanchine's ballets, although he could certainly devise a work with a story when he wished to. Sets and costumes were secondary, in part because he feared they would obscure the dancing, as he felt they had at the Ballets Russes. In truth, there was not always money to pay for them, anyway, and some of his compositions looked best in the most stripped down of costumes, a leotard and tights. Dancers, listed alphabetically on the company roster, subscribed to a no-star policy. If there was a star, it was Balanchine himself. The dancers' reward was to aspire, if not ascend, to the level of the composer. Ballet could stand on its own, with music as its foundation. Dance for the sake of dance had arrived in America.

The other great development in the history of ballet in the 20th century was the rapprochement between modern dance and ballet. For much of that century, these two branches of dance seemed irreconcilable, each mistrustful, if not disdainful, of the other. Fokine and modern dance pioneer Martha Graham (1894–1991) would disagree publicly and acrimoniously in 1931. Almost thirty years later, in 1959, however, Graham and her company were invited to share the stage and the orchestral music of Anton Webern (1883–1945) with Balanchine and the New York City Ballet. One dancer from each company performed with the other; Graham composed a fully costumed work about Elizabeth I and Mary, Queen of Scots; Balanchine created a storyless work performed in leotards and tights. At the time, this collaboration was a great leap forward.

In 1973, the Joffrey Ballet commissioned the third-generation modern dance choreographer Twyla Tharp (b. 1941) to create *Deuce Coupe*, set to music by the Beach Boys. Its set was graffiti, spray-painted live during the performance. Her company joined the members of the Joffrey on stage, where all but one of the dancers danced in her language. That one dancer executed the steps of the classical canon in alphabetical order. Tharp, having "crossed over" from the world of modern dance to that of ballet, would go on to create more works for ABT than any other choreographer in its history.

At the moment, obviously talented, inspired and even visionary ballet choreographers are lacking, so ballet companies borrow talent where they can find it, usually among modern dance choreographers.

The Future

On January 22, 1904, Marius Petipa wrote in his diary, "My work is reduced to ashes." Petipa could not know that George Balanchine would be born on that day and Frederick Ashton on September 17 of the same year, or that through them his beliefs would survive and develop with the 20th century.

Today, we do not yet know whether any of the choreographers who died at the end of the 20th century left behind such a diary entry, a cry from the heart that may unintentionally indicate the renewal—phoenixlike—of ballet in the 21st century. It is true, however, that the history of ballet is comprised of cycles of action and reaction, novelty, apogee and decline, and that a great choreographer appears at the moment he or she is most needed.

The wait, however, seems terribly long.

ENDNOTES

[1] Régine Astier, "Academie royale de la danse," in *International Encyclopedia of Dance*, edited by Selma Jeane Cohen and George E. Dorris (New York: Oxford University Press, 1998), vol. 1, p. 3.

[2] Deryck Lynham, *The chevalier Noverre* (London: Sylvan, 1950), p. 20.

[3] Jean-Georges Noverre, *Letters on dancing and ballets* (New York: Dance Horizons, 1966), p. 22.

[4] C. W. Beaumont, *Michel Fokine and his ballets* (London: Dance Books, 1996), p. 27.

[5] Lincoln Kirstein, *Movement and metaphor* (New York: Praeger, 1970), p. 182.

CHAPTER NINE

introduction

This chapter deals with current dance forms such as modern dance, modern ballet, postmodern dance, and the avant-garde. It amplifies Carol Pardo's chapter on ballet by more broadly contextualizing the newer forms within the 20th and 21st century worlds of American dance. Although ballet has had a relatively clear and identifiable history since Louis XIV's time and modern dance also has its own lineage, the two styles have mutually influenced each other. Twisting and breaking the old rules while creating new rules, current dance forms continue to shape their "traditions" in both accessible and challenging ways. Dance has become an art form primarily concerned with experimentation to find unique ways to "speak" through movement, with and without technique, but also with a continuing passion, commitment and integrity.

CURRENTS OF 20th AND 21st CENTURY DANCE

Myron Howard Nadel and Marc Raymond Strauss

[I]t is the very unpredictability of dance that keeps it eternally fascinating, forever veering off in unexpected directions.

—Allen Robertson and Donald Hutera, The Dance Handbook

It is a daunting task to define and categorize the many styles of dance that have developed since the 19th century forms of romantic and classical ballet were established. Even as those traditions continued to perpetuate themselves in the 20th century, new forms such as *modern dance, modern ballet, contemporary ballet, postmodern dance* and their many mergers and alternatives burst in and out of fashion with ever-increasing speed. The trends of today are often passé by tomorrow; those called avant-garde may already be more than half a century old.

In fact, the seemingly uncomplicated word *modern* can be quite confusing because it can refer to the impressionistic period of French painting, circa 1870, or be used generically to describe current creations, especially those that depart from established conventions. Nearly as confusing, the modern period of ballet is generally considered to have begun in the 1910s, but its vocabulary and history, along with the related but distinct romantic and classical ballet forms, are still called simply "ballet." Moreover, although seminal works of early 20th century modern dance, such as the 1931 *Primitive Mysteries*, choreographed by modern dance pioneer Martha Graham, may still be highly evocative today, many have been decidedly unmodern for decades.

The recent use of the prefix *post*, meaning "after," as in *postmodern dance*, further challenges labelers and new dance audiences, who already have difficulty pinpointing when anything "modern" is supposed to have occurred. The term *avant-garde*, taken from the French word *vanguard*, meaning "a group of people leading the way in new developments or ideas," may be the best word available for referring to cutting-edge creations of any time period.

Readers and audiences attempting to solidify their own concepts may have discovered that eras and their inclusive philosophies in the arts do not begin and end neatly. In truth, the currents of modern dance, modern ballet and contemporary ballet now exist simultaneously with those currents we refer to as postmodern and avant-garde. This concurrent existence, in fact, may herald the beginning of an era of fusion, where differences may still exist but become irrelevant.

However, 21st century dance audiences who are anxious to understand current transformations persistently called *modern* and *postmodern* and who want to contextualize other contemporary styles need to explore the heritage of concert dance in the 20th century.

REVOLUTIONARY CURRENTS

During the ending decades of the 19th century and the early decades of the 20th century, female revolutionaries created dance recitals outside the sphere of and dissimilar to the conventional ballet genre, lighting the sparks that ignited the flames that became modern dance in this transitional period. They were groundbreakers in an exciting new experiment.

Their works might just as easily be considered postromantic or postclassical as modern. After all, Isadora Duncan (1877–1927), the most famous revolutionary outside of the male-dominated ballet (and those who followed in her footsteps) tended to value the expressivity of romanticism more than the technique and form of the pure or classicist in music and art. In a way, Duncan's art was a true *classic* art, inspired by forms of antiquity (primarily ancient Greece) and the sensibilities of accepted musical masters of the time. She also insisted that her dance was fundamentally American and influenced by nature, which led her to rediscover the unique glory of natural movements, made all the more expressive when untainted by balletic vocabulary and when danced in bare feet.

Duncan performed in relatively unadorned dance recitals in salons, concert halls and humble theaters, accompanied only by a pianist playing, say, the *Revolutionary Étude* by Frédéric Chopin (1810–1849). The recital form was bargain basement chic and truly avant-garde for its time. In contrast, works created during the first modern ballet era, the Ballets Russes years (1909–1929)—such as Michael Fokine's *Schéhérazade* (1910) and Vaslav Nijinsky's *Rite of Spring* (1913)—were grand and expensive, requiring full orchestras, elaborate sets and costumes, large theaters and a wealthy producer to sponsor the event.

Loie Fuller, followed by Ruth St. Denis and their modern heirs such as Martha Graham, grew up during the establishment of the late 19th century classical ballet world, as demonstrated by Marius Petipa's (1818–1910) consummate *The Sleeping Beauty* (1890) and *Swan Lake* (1895). These ballets were exemplary in their displays of technical virtuosity and choreographic patterning, but they provided a limited emotional and intellectual palette for their audience. The early modern dancer-choreographers were equally cognizant of the great ballet revolution simultaneously taking place in Russia and in Europe because of Diaghilev's Ballets Russes. They were primed for change and in many ways led its charge.

Loie Fuller (1862–1928) was primarily an actress and singer who had studied a bit of ballet and then began to perform solo movement pieces in the voluminous skirts she had worn in plays. When she received a large piece of lovely cloth as a gift from a friend, she devised a theatrical movement piece that came to be known as her "serpentine dance." Add the newly developing art of stage lighting at the end of the 19th century to Fuller's skirt and serpentine dances, place her on a glass plate lit from below, and the scene was set for experiments based on the movement of body, fabric, shape, color and light. Similar experiments continue today through the marriage of movements and advanced technology.

The growing awareness of the importance of women in society, beginning with the suffragettes in the 1910s and culminating in the passage of women's right to vote in 1920, gave these revolutionary dance artists a greater position of leadership, at least in the eyes of those dedicated to the burgeoning feminism of the time. Expression of a new self-awareness in all the arts, influenced by religions and philosophies such as Christian Science, Theosophy and spiritualism, further charged their spirit.

Ideas from Eastern philosophies such as naturalism and transcendentalism, professed by American thinkers such as Henry David Thoreau (1817–1862) and Ralph Waldo Emerson (1803–1882), were also influential. Disregarding Victorian standards, female dancers came to relish the compelling notion that the human body was a gift of nature or a divine temple to be extolled instead of hidden in shame.

Modern pioneer Ruth St. Denis (1879–1968) also was willing to promote her art within established commercial theatrical contexts in the early 20th century, such as plays, vaudeville and revues, but in these venues the search for new dance foundations depended ultimately on their audience appeal as defined by producers, who in the world of commercial theater understood little of the spiritual fervor of dance's revolutionary energy. Both producers and audiences, however, enjoyed new subjects, new movement arrangements, new personalities and almost anything with exotic, pseudoerotic appeal. The dance artists were wary that their artistic attempts needed to satisfy large audiences, which increased their need to self-produce concerts where their freedom to experiment could remain a primary concern.

Excerpts from the long-standing repertoire of European ballet companies also fit well within the vaudeville milieu of family audiences, who often enjoyed the shorter early works of modern dance, such as Ruth St. Denis's *Radha* (1906), in their entirety. Being a vaudeville performer meant being one of seven or more independent touring acts—dog trainer, tap dancer, singer, comedian, ventriloquist, contortionist and even opera and ballet performers—all on the same program. Although many choreographers disregarded the entertainment value of the art of dance, many pioneers of modern dance, such as Martha Graham, Doris Humphrey and Charles Weidman (1901–1975), learned valuable lessons about salesmanship and about the rules and regulations of commercial theater from an independent company called Denishawn (founded by Ruth St. Denis and Ted Shawn), which performed on these vaudeville circuits.

Being a commercial draw was also a matter of survival, but the diverse personalities of modern dance cared more about expression, honesty, creativity and even social and political issues. Its leaders wanted to be artists for a people's art and to express some very personal insights about themselves and the world through their unique compositions.

When Ted Shawn (1891–1972) teamed up with and married Ruth St. Denis in 1914, he helped her create dances within the given confines of commercial theater. Their Denishawn school and company lasted from 1915 to 1931. The company's concert tours gave them more leeway for artistic experimentation than the works created for the vaudeville circuit.

Ted Shawn began studying dance to compensate for ill health as a young man. His father was a Methodist minister who encouraged his son's combined interests in spirituality and physical movement. Ruth St. Denis was more a seeker of spiritual truth. Her quest, begun well before their partnership, led her into the field of ethnic dance, where she composed pieces of dual Asian and spiritual origin (the currently politically offensive term *Oriental*, associated with Western imperialism, was used during that time instead of the more accurate term *Asian*). St. Denis attempted to emulate the spiritual impetus and movements of East Indian dance through a sort of self-withdrawn trance state in which she assumed a committed (if mock) "Oriental authenticity." Commercial audiences were not always capable of seeing and appreciating the artistic value embedded in her famous dances, such as the Hindu-inflected *Radha*, the Japanese-inspired *O-Mika* (1913) or the Babylonian ensemble choreography in American director D. W. Griffith's epic silent film "Intolerance" (1916).

Ted Shawn added opportunities for greater commercial success by bringing more theatricalized versions of Asian, Spanish, Aztec, American Indian, ballroom and other dance forms to the Denishawn repertoire. He understood and followed a spiritual view of dance but adapted the company's works to more pragmatic theatrical needs. He could "give them, the public, the divine message of dance, the sublime art, but get the public to accept it by using whatever splashy come-ons were necessary."[1] The prolific Shawn created approximately 190 pieces for Denishawn and his own all-male company in the 1930s, including the popular *Prometheus Bound* (1929) and the macho *Kinetic Molpai* (1935).

Shawn's ideas may be the better guide to the realities of a dance art on commercial stages; St. Denis's are more the dreamer's art. Shawn's focused, hard-driving ebullience gave him the psychic ammunition to pioneer an art form for men that struggled against the use of only pretty, liberated female dancers and a few effeminate-looking men in the impoverished homegrown ballet of his time. Ted Shawn paved the road that thousands of American male dancers have traveled in ballet, modern dance and Broadway.

MOVEMENT SOURCES

Doris Humphrey, Charles Weidman, Martha Graham and Louis Horst (Graham's music director, composer, mentor and accompanist) worked for Ruth St. Denis and Ted Shawn at various times. Hundreds of dancers studied at the Denishawn schools, first in California and then in New York, where Shawn's inspired curriculum included classes in Delsarte, Jaques-Dalcroze Eurythmics, ballet, ballroom and a variety of ethnic forms. This broad training formed the basis for much of the future serious theatrical dance education study in America. In 1933, *New York Times* dance critic John Martin gave these pioneering dances and highly personal movement vocabularies the name *modern dance.*

In 1934, at Bennington College in Bennington, Vermont, under the inspired directorship of pioneer dance educator Martha Hill (1900–1999), the founders of modern dance gathered together and combined their expertise to develop modern dance techniques and composition. Around the same time, Shawn continued to influence the education of American dancers by including ballet training at Jacob's Pillow, his summer school in Lee, Massachusetts.

The theoretical movement substructure of the moderns was originally derived from the teachings of European theorists such as François Delsarte, Émile Jaques-Dalcroze and Rudolf Laban. François Delsarte (1811–1871) was a music teacher and movement analyst who delved into the meanings of various gestures of the body. He believed that the physical, emotional and spiritual planes of the body coexist in time, copenetrate space and cooperate in motion. His concerns for concepts of tension-relaxation, form, force, design and concentric (toward center) and eccentric (from center) movements provided a different focus for creating and studying movement outside the ballet vocabulary. Shawn and other early modern dancers came to embrace these tenets.

Delsartian ideas combining the physical and metaphysical worlds were also an inspiration to women, who felt that this approach was the key to gracefulness and the finest forms of expression for the newly liberated female. During the early part of the 20th century, Delsarte and dance seemed to offer women the promise of a break from the Victorian handicaps of being a woman: binding corsets, total allegiance to motherhood, limited careers, poor pay and a ubiquitous sense of disenfranchisement. Concurrently, although Ted Shawn was an ardent supporter of Delsartian ideas, his all-male dance company from 1933 to 1940 helped reform America's sense that modern dance was only for women.

The work of Frenchman Émile Jaques-Dalcroze (1865–1950), called *Eurythmics*, was a system of physical movements designed for the development of a combined musical and rhythmic logic for musicians. It was also found to have great application for training dancers and choreographers to form deeply felt relationships between the eye, ear, memory and kinesthetic awareness. Jaques-Dalcroze's philosophy was especially influential on Ruth St. Denis, who explored music visualization wherein melodic lines, harmonies and forms of a piece of music were visually translated into corresponding dance movements.

The choreographic potential inherent in the great musical forms influenced the entire generation of American modern dancers after Duncan, St. Denis and Shawn. Doris Humphrey and Martha Graham were often able to use their intimate understanding of and training with music as inspiration for their more sophisticated choreographic arrangements. Jaques-Dalcroze's influence was also felt through the application of his ideas in the modern ballets of the Russians Mikhail Fokine (1880–1942) and Vaslav Nijinsky (1890–1950). To this day, complex and precise kinetic-rhythmic correlations remain performance expectations and prudent choreographic devices for all dance compositions.

Jaques-Dalcroze's contemporary Rudolf Laban (1879–1958) was a dancer-theoretician inspired in part by Delsarte's failure to develop further a means of analyzing and writing movement. His special genius lay in the conceptual analysis of movement in space and time, with its characteristic energies. He first analyzed movement according to the speed, direction and level of the body and its parts within an imaginary twenty-sided combination sphere-cube called an *icosahedron*. His scientific approach provided a clear language for movement in space that gave the work of modern dancers, especially the Germans Mary Wigman and Kurt Jooss, an analytical basis from which to acquire greater sensitivity toward motion in relation to surrounding space. These conceptual foundations are still an integral part of the characteristics of much modern dance.

Mary Wigman (1886–1973) saw space as a force to be used, not just as a necessary environment filled with air. She moved with an awareness of the conceivable qualities that her immediate stage space could have as a partner in motion—cutting through, piercing, pressing and being enveloped by it, as in her famous solo *Witch Dance* (1914). Wigman's interest in space and her knowledge of the German Bauhaus group (founded 1919) of artists and designers who experimented with stage space in relation to masked figures, props, body extensions and furniture inspired her to create some of her group dances, which were concerned substantially with the visual impact of their shapes.

Meanwhile, Kurt Jooss (1901–1979) developed dances that allowed the use of some ballet vocabulary but little of its technical tricks. The moderns considered him to be too close to the ballet theater in temperament, whereas his ballet critics were offended by his use of movements they considered "modern." He created a dance theater where his movement choices, like the traditional ballet, also included pantomime. Ballet companies all over the world still perform his greatest work, *The Green Table* (1932), a biting satire about the futility of war, its political tricks and profiteering.

Wigman's student Hanya Holm (1893–1992) came to the United States in 1932 to open a Wigman school in New York. Her choreography was full of social criticism and spatial effects, especially her early group dances such as *Trend* (1937). Holm also explored German expressionism—the dark, emotional aesthetic within art, literature and drama—in an attempt to find emotional truth in her solo work and support for her interest in space design.

DRAMATIC CURRENTS

Through the prompting of late 19th and early 20th century social theory and philosophies of movement, some dancer-choreographers' analytical and philosophical outlooks were changed to varying degrees. For instance, the philosophy of Karl Marx (1818–1883), centered on a utopian socialist society, had some influence on perceptions of the class and gender hierarchy of stage roles.

The more superficial, cliché-style acting of the 19th century (itself evolving out of pantomime and the earlier Italian commedia dell'arte) became a thing of the past, in part because of the great contributions of Constantin Stanislavsky (1863–1938). He created more genuine and realistic methods for training actors. Many dancers and choreographers were aware of the need to find a more honest acting style, one with which they could enter the emotional core of a character. They were also inspired by the scientific exploration of the psyche in the hypnosis and dream work of Austrian psychiatrist Sigmund Freud (1856–1939). The Freud and Stanislavsky ideas folded into both dramatic modern dance and ballet were a far cry from the overacting common in the romantic and classical ballets inherited from the previous century.

The dramatic dances of Martha Graham (1894–1991) required the Stanislavsky perspective of acting. In the 1940s and 1950s, Graham created emotionally charged choreographic dramas based on characters and situations from Greek plays and the literary canon, such as *Oedipus Rex* and *Saint Joan* (1923, by George Bernard Shaw). Her genius was in abstracting archetypal psychological perspectives about a central character and then placing herself in this dance role, showing the character's psychological struggles, which she envisioned as a partly fragmented dream. For example, she embodied the vengeful Medea in *Cave of the Heart* (1946); Oedipus's mother, Jocasta, in *Night Journey* (1947); and Saint Joan in *Seraphic Dialogue* (1955). Unlike in the old-fashioned, straightforward plots of classical ballet, her chorus dancers were never choreographed to punctuate, enhance or provide diversion from the central action, but rather to add to the theater of a dream state. Graham dug into the physical basis of drama and found movements that captured the emotional essence of each moment.

The search for honesty in acting was also the province of choreographers such as Agnes de Mille (1909–1993) and Antony Tudor (1908/1909–1987), Graham's contemporaries, who functioned within ballet organizations such as England's Ballet Rambert and, later, American Ballet Theatre. They, too, were leaders in defining dramatic dance for the 20th century, creating ballets not radically different from Graham's modern dance inventions in that they tended to use sophisticated nonmimetic gestures in order to delve into a character's inner life and psychology.

Louis Horst (1884–1964) was a musician and Martha Graham's longtime mentor. He saw that choreographers, like composers and visual artists, needed a better understanding of theories about materials, forms and style. Based on his knowledge of composition, theory and style in music and other arts, he became the foremost proponent of an original system for teaching dance composition, thus becoming an important theorist for 20th century dance. His interest in the field was fostered while he was the music director for Denishawn. He later became the dance critic for his own journal, the *Dance Observer*, and taught hundreds of dance students about composition.

Another common subject matter in modern dance was the individual as a social creature cognizant of, responsible for and united with his or her fellow humans, regardless of class, a notion that evolved out of a socialist philosophy in Marx's *Communist Manifesto* (1848). Whereas a social hierarchy of characters marks romantic and classical ballet, a more egalitarian society pervades abstract works in modern dance. For example, the "architectural" dances of choreographers such as Mary Wigman, Hanya Holm and Doris Humphrey were choreographies of uniform groups of people, with sections of solos, duets, trios and larger numbers contributing to a group effect.

The more dramatic dances in both modern ballet and modern dance still tended to personify class levels because tragedy traditionally depends on a character's fall from the height of power—for example, the queen in Graham's *Night Journey* (1947), Lincoln in Charles Weidman's *A House Divided* (1945) or Othello in José Limón's *The Moor's Pavane* (1949).

TECHNICAL CURRENTS

During the pioneering days of modern dance, a dancer's physical skills were not likely to be as fully honed as they are today. Instead, the pioneers possessed the courage, vision and will to make unique, meaningful statements about the human condition, sometimes for hostile audiences and critics who could not understand the stage results of their noble causes. Still, they felt required to organize their vocabularies of movement and to create methods for the dissemination of those vocabularies. New but finite lexicons of movement would come to define and sometimes confine each of the moderns, so much so that the dancers who followed would often be criticized for being derivative if they followed these lexicons.

The most widespread of the defined modern dance training techniques to be passed down remain those of Martha Graham, José Limón, Doris Humphrey, Merce Cunningham and, finally, Lester Horton.

Graham's technique includes falls, suspensions, jumps, lifts and just about any conceivable movement, but her signal gesture of the torso was the *con-*

traction, a sudden upward tilting of the pelvis with its immediate and inevitable tension-flexion of the entire torso. This movement impulse was designed to support her dramatic dances. Each gesture—with varying degrees of tension-release, distance and speed—becomes a propulsive chain of movement. The insistent tension-release sequence can be an emotional, sensual and even sexual means for creating powerfully controlled movements such as falls to the floor, turns and total body gestures. The technical skills that Graham's dancers developed were different from but no less rigorous than the skills needed for classical ballet.

Doris Humphrey (1895–1958) developed the concept of "fall and recovery," just one of her major bequests to modern dance. Her fall is a "letting go" from holding the weight of the arms, head, ribs or torso in the standing position, while allowing the torso or a body part to drop toward the ground with the speed and force of gravity, the legs folding at the same rate. As the bottom of the drop is reached, the energy from the automatic contraction of the fully stretched muscles of the legs or torso provides the power for the next gesture—the rebound. The fall-recovery could be used as a metaphor of biblical proportions, such as death and rebirth, or as a reference to something as simple as the constant pull of and struggle against gravity on all matter. Whereas the movement sequences of romantic and classical ballet seem to defy gravity, Humphrey took advantage of weight and pull to compose shapes and movement patterns into phrases, sections and whole dances. Equally facile with complex, even contrapuntal designs, she was an architect of group movements that involved these regular displacements of weight and their subsequent rebounds.

Humphrey's *Passacaglia and Fugue in C Minor* (1938), based on Johann Sebastian Bach's (1685–1750) organ work, demonstrates her vocabulary and focus. Shapes are formed using the height and position of the dancers' upper arms, flexion of elbows and wrists, rotation of the shoulders, lower arms and the hands. Although the fall-rebound is demanded throughout most of this work, many movements of equal importance are directed by precisely isolated impulses in specific parts of the body.

This dance was constructed to match the number of variations in and the optimistic outlook of Bach's work. It is performed as a dance for a group of thirteen women and five men; although one of the men and one of the women act as leaders, its division of labor provides opportunities for all dancers to be featured in large and small groups. Like the rigorously structured buildup in Bach's music, the dancers' movements on the stage floor and on a construction of simple rectangular blocks of varying size allow for a powerful architectural impact on the audience. Fall-rebound, shape, level, gestural development, symmetry versus asymmetry and closeness to, but not slavish imitation of, the music are evident in this dance and in many of Humphrey's dances.

Doris Humphrey was also a great teacher of composition who articulated her theories in a book released in 1959, *The Art of Making Dances*, which remains a defining text for choreographers the world over. To hundreds of budding choreographers, including her student José Limón, Humphrey imparted a strong sense of architecture and composition, which served as guideposts for solving the unique problems of choosing subject matter and developing movement for making a dance. Humphrey's and Horst's theories would be the 20th century touchstones for dance composition. The postmoderns and alternative generations to come would both respectfully and disrespectfully violate those theories.

José Limón (1908–1972) infused his dances and technique with several important elements, the least being signature gestures. His contribution was in making his dancers see the glory and power of the human spirit in dance on stage as well as in the classroom. For him, as for Humphrey, every gesture needed to have a clear motivation, whether dramatic, emotional or abstract. "Abstract" movements in the art of dance—unlike, say, abstract images in mathematics or music—are, in fact, concrete physical manifestations of the intellect, spirit and body. Limón's powerful physique gave a rich weight and energy to his movements. He talked about the human body as a tangible instrument at least as complex as an orchestra. He felt that the dancer needs to treat all parts of the body as individual instruments that, when "sounded" individually or in sequence, could "play" a symphony of movement for an audience's senses. Limón's dramatic talents as a choreographer and lead dancer in his own works, such as the narrative dance *Emperor Jones* (1956) and abstract pieces like *There Is a Time* (1954), are about humanity and the gift of movement. With no other artist of the modern era did there seem to be such a selfless mission to dignify the field of dance.

REDEFINING CURRENTS

Part of the modern dance heritage, and later amplified by some postmodernists, included a mission to redefine dance as an art form. Initially referred to as unofficial members of the modern dance world, dancer-choreographers such as Erick Hawkins and Merce Cunningham created pieces wholly unlike their predecessors. Although trained in several techniques (Hawkins studied with both George Balanchine (1904–1983) and Martha Graham, among others; Cunningham studied with and performed for Graham and trained in folk, tap and ballroom dance), these mavericks rarely referred to dramatic situations, emotions, the vocabulary of ballet or any of the popular idioms of modern dance.

Erick Hawkins (1909–1994) was a poet of motion deeply influenced by Eastern philosophies. Like Cunningham, he felt that dance needed to be what it is, not something else, so he concentrated on the beauty of human motion in the moment and on the act of moving in the presence of an audience also in that moment. For Hawkins, dance was a transcendental Zen experience for both himself and his audience. The titles of two of his most famous pieces, *Here and Now with Watchers* (1957) and *8 Clear Places* (1960), evoke that numinous sense of peaceful presence.

Merce Cunningham (b. 1919) is similarly philosophical about his work and, at times considered the father of the postmoderns, continues to redefine dance today in his eighties. He constructed his hundreds of dance pieces— such as *Minutiae* (1954), *RainForest* (1968) and *Points in Space* (1986)—in whole or in part by deliberately incorporating chance or randomness into their designs, an approach he has refined more recently through his use of computer programs. His dances do not attempt to fulfill any preconceived poetic sense of natural beauty, but instead express ever-changing spatial centers and random, seemingly chaotic multiple strands of activity. Connections between these strands depend primarily on physics, Eastern philosophies and his audience's natural inclination to make sense out of whatever it is they are experiencing. Cunningham knows that no matter how his dances are structured, each will create a unique atmosphere, and audience members can interpret that atmosphere any way they choose.

Like Graham, Hawkins and Cunningham were closely allied to musician composers: Hawkins to Lucia Dlugoszewski (1931–2000) and Cunningham to the avant-garde John Cage (1912–1992), whose sound and music accompaniment gave atmospheric life to their collaborators' unique philosophies.

A third-generation modern dancer, Paul Taylor (b. 1930) employs a large vocabulary in his style of movement. His dancers are capable of virtuoso feats, but Taylor has not tried to create one particular technique from his style, like his contemporaries, concentrating instead on just making dances. He started as an avant-garde upstart, some dances done in total silence, with very little movement or with absurd anthropomorphic creatures, such as in the quirky *Three Epitaphs* (1956). In his later works, however, he established his own traditions. A large number of his dances are musically sensitive and athletic, yet also quite lyrical, with music ranging from Handel to Beethoven to the Andrews Sisters. We can easily see the bouncy and graceful musicality in many of his signature works, such as *Aureole* (1962), *Esplanade* (1975), *Arden Court* (1981) and *Roses* (1985). His wry sense of humor and ability to symbolize the troubled foibles of our society are evident in works such as *Big Bertha* (1970) and *Company B* (1991), and they have made him the leading old-guard representative of modern dance today.

Audiences often confuse the more grounded lyricism of choreographers such as Taylor and Lar Lubovich (b. 1943) with the mellifluousness of the romantic ballet. They are similar in tone at times, and some of the world's leading ballet companies perform many modern choreographers' works, but it doesn't matter anymore if modern dance looks like ballet. What matters is that the company performing the work captures the work's choreographic style. Audiences today see the styles of individual choreographers who may have the capacity to be lyrical, but who also have enough abandon not to care what genres they resemble. Modern choreographers are not afraid to use movements that carry labels, and they employ the right technique for the best performance. Similarly, being a ballet choreographer today also means embracing the vocabulary appropriate for the style of any particular piece.

It follows that dance works branded as enveloping a jazz style can also find expression in both ballet and modern dance. The dances of choreographer Alvin Ailey (1931–1989) combine elements of modern, jazz and African dance with Ailey's own flamboyant and accessible aesthetic. Well-trained through the broad, physically powerful technique of Californian Lester Horton (1906–1953) and through stints on Broadway and with Graham, Humphrey, Holm and others, Ailey established a New York–based company in 1958 and brought the electricity of Broadway dance to the concert stage. Although his works remain part of the serious modern dance repertoire, well-trained African American and Asian dancers provide the company's commercial attack. Ailey and his successors have brought popular recognition to a company that continues to be in great demand worldwide.

Ailey's most famous work, perhaps the most celebrated and infectious of all the works of modern dance, is *Revelations* (1960), a large, many segmented group testimony to Negro spirituals, as fresh today as it was in 1960. Ailey taught us that theatrical excitement can be generated in serious dance and

126

that we can also demand the highest level of technique from modern dance as from ballet or Broadway. At the Alvin Ailey Dance Center, students perpetuate this vital choreographer's vision through the study of Horton's and Graham's modern techniques, ballet and jazz.

Some of the most celebrated modern dancers and choreographers—such as Martha Graham, José Limón, Charles Weidman, Agnes de Mille, Hanya Holm, Mary Wigman and even Ruth St. Denis and Ted Shawn—were still alive to see Ailey perform. In 1960, there was an attempt to institutionalize the heritage of the many modern dance pioneers. Classically trained modern dance trailblazer Helen Tamiris (1905–1966), one of the few who came from but then renounced the conservative ballet institutions, called for such a company to preserve the diverse dances of the previous thirty-five years. Unfortunately, the idea of a repertory modern dance company at New York's Lincoln Center for the Performing Arts quickly died as individualism took over. Perhaps the highly personalized nature of modern dance makes such institutionalization impossible.

One of the most eccentric individualists of modern dance, Twyla Tharp (b. 1941) has a more eclectic background than her contemporaries, having studied piano, violin, viola, acrobatics, ballet, tap, modern, jazz, drums, baton twirling and even gypsy dancing in her growth as a dancer and choreographer. Her work has embraced a wide range of experimental approaches, including dances performed in silence, dances heard but not seen and dances done to jazz, rock 'n' roll, popular songs, classical music and minimalist scores. One of her most celebrated dances, originally made for the Joffrey Ballet, is *Deuce Coupe* (1973), a quirky picture set to a suite of Beach Boys tunes. Many of her works are in the repertoires of both modern and ballet companies.

These still-working third- and fourth-generation modern dancers and choreographers have mixed and matched the traditions of both ballet and modern dance to create very intriguing pieces, often with potent box office staying power. Cusp choreographers such as Bill T. Jones (b. 1952), Ralph Lemon (b. 1952), Mark Morris, Maguy Marin (b. 1951), Susan Marshall (b. 1958), Twyla Tharp, Merce Cunningham and a host of other independent modern dance descendents are in regular and great demand by the very ballet companies their modern elders' previously bypassed. Until comparably talented, next-generation ballet choreographers burst forth from within the ranks of this group, benefits will continue to accrue for both sides of dance: the modern, postmodern and avant-garde creators will at times exploit the technical

127

skills of the ballet companies, and the ballet companies will use ever new, unpredictable choreographies for their dancers.

DESIGN CURRENTS

Whereas some modern choreographers lean toward athletic movement, lyrical pieces, dramatic themes or even dance as pure experience, others have tended to use the dance to create forms out of the technique and geo-metric suggestions of the body shapes themselves. In modern dance, the visual effects of Hanya Holm's and Doris Humphrey's works embody some of that pure-shape quality, and much of Merce Cunningham's works can be viewed similarly. Pilobolus, a collective company of dancers and gymnasts that started out in 1971, and its offspring MOMIX and ISO, founded in 1980 and 1987, respectively, continue to create complex, visu-ally compelling and humorous mobile-like structures through their dancers' muscular strength and proximity. Androgynous, pure body sculptures and offbeat creations such as *Ocellus* (1972), *Untitled* (1975) and *MOMIX in Orbit* (2002), performed with and without props and clever costuming, continue to surprise audiences around the world. Another company, the Swiss-based Mummenschanz (mask theater), founded in 1972, also embodies this aesthetic, along with the futuristic Blue Man Group, founded in 1987.

Filtered through modern dance choreographer Mary Wigman to Hanya Holm, the Bauhaus ideas also influenced the 20th century master of pure design Alwin Nikolais (1910–1993). Nikolais transformed the natural shapes of his dancers into depersonalized, intergalactic figures and created a wholly new dance theater aesthetic through his use of fabric and body extensions, which he lit colorfully and dramatically. He also created his own electronic audiotapes containing musical sound effects that accented these strange figures' movements, which seemed to gambol about anthropomor-phically all over the stage. His more memorable creations include *Kaleido-scope* (1953), *Vaudeville of the Elements* (1965), *Triad and Styx* (1976) and *Video Games* (choreographed for the 1984 Olympic Games).

Nikolais's world resembles our own often-depersonalized age of technol-ogy, where the visual experience is made more facile through moving lighting instruments, video images and new fabrics that can change their designs in an instant. His nonliteral dances are not to be explained, but simply watched. Although some modern dance choreographers have highlighted spatial designs in their dances, many dramatic ballet and modern dance works also evoke images through the design of movement, sets, costumes and lights.

DEFINING CURRENTS

Like the modernists to the ballet traditionalists, we might consider postmodern dance as another era of innovative experimentation in reaction to its modern antecedents. A new generation of revolutionaries—beginning with the famous, free-of-charge Judson Church performance in New York City's Greenwich Village on July 6, 1962—expanded our consciousness about the very meaning of dance. Audiences had to find their own ways to understand and embrace these new and challenging performances. Most of these works—such as Yvonne Rainer's wholly pedestrian *Trio A* (1966), Steve Paxton's *Backwater: Twosome* (1977), which incorporated the now often-used choreographic tool called contact improvisation, and Michael Clark's anarchic *No Fire Escape in Hell* (1986), among hundreds of others—deliberately tested their audience's comprehension and acceptance. Defying categorization, the postmodern dances were performed at the most unique of times (midnight, early morning, unexpectedly), places (city squares, subway platforms, building tops, lofts) and theaters, with dancers sometimes technically proficient and at other times deliberately untrained.

However, the idea that there might exist a particular postmodern dance technique (except for the iconoclastic Cunningham system) counters some postmoderns' frequent questioning of the use of "traditional" dance technique. In general, postmodern art (including dance)—in an effort to evoke the humanizing truth lying dormant beneath the complexities—is more focused on finding ways to deconstruct, understand and articulate the depersonalizing aspects of today's society through experimental applications of existentialism, intellectualism and commercialism.

The choreography can be created through group efforts, not prioritizing just one person's role or one technique, form, performance space, aesthetic, tradition, culture, style or boundary. What seems contemporary might suddenly incorporate a baroque motif; what looks set in fin de siècle Paris might use late 20ᵗʰ century pop or rock music (as in Baz Luhrmann's 2001 film "Moulin Rouge!"); and what seems experimental might be a Broadway commodity meant to earn money (such as Twyla Tharp's 2002 show *Movin' Out*, set to Billy Joel's pop songs).

By the 1960s, choreographers such as Steve Paxton (b. 1939), David Gordon (b. 1936) and Lucinda Childs (b. 1940) led the postmodern revolution. With nihilistic dance events often called "happenings," they countered the solidifying modern dance philosophies and the increasing theatrical capacities of the modern dancers of the 1950s. They structured these programs so that exact repetition was unlikely and often included untrained dancers, pedestrian movements and improvisation in tandem with visual and musical artists of the same persuasion. These experiments were intellectually challenging and exciting because they threw away the recent past of modern dance while retaining its fervor.

Furthermore, these experimentalists have rightly been recognized for their important, continuing contributions; the term *postmodern dance* became affixed to their artistic endeavors. By then, the term *modern* had already become too closely identified with the earlier modern dance pioneers and with their followers, so its use in reference to these experimentalists could only be more confusing. The term *postmodern dance*, then, although connected philosophically to concurrent aesthetic forms among the other arts, was intended originally and simply to mean choreography done chronologically *after* modern dance. Critics could not have anticipated the bewildering ramifications of their newly coined term.

Just as every part of the process of creating a dance could now be called into question, the very act of presenting a dance could also create a symbiotic experience, where both audiences and performers could self-consciously deconstruct and analyze their own existence. Similar to how we watch and listen to whatever is going on in any event in our lives, postmodern performers passively stand on stage resembling pedestrians watching cars going by, mimic the distracted attentions we often embody when choosing which checkout line to stand in at a supermarket or reflect on their faces our frozen, incredulous fear as we watch skyscrapers implode into rubble.

The related Japanese dance theater known as Butoh addresses similar responses to devastating tragedy. The postmoderns may be given credit for creating dances and events that make us think deeply about our society's condition and where we fit in that society. As Walt Kelly's (1913–1973) comic strip character Pogo used to say, "We have met the enemy, and he is us!" Bill T. Jones (b. 1952), a contemporary dancer-choreographer trained in modern dance, Afro-Caribbean and contact improvisation, incorporates multimedia and spoken text into his gracefully athletic, emotionally provocative dances. His works deal with challenging issues such as homosexuality, gender bias, racism, unfashionable body types and other difficult topics. *Still/Here* (1994) "generated a heated debate in the dance world" through its in-depth, in-your-face investigation of "people dealing with terminal illness."[2] Nondancers "of all ages, classes, races, sexual preferences, and states of health"[3] shared their very real and struggling lives through excerpted large-screen-projection video footage in direct-to-audience narratives, mixed with technically demanding onstage dancing and gesture. How does one label such a work? Jones's interests certainly lie somewhere within the postmodern realms of confrontation, experimentalism and intellectualism, but they also draw on traditional modern dance and modern ballet conventions, such as concert stages, strong technique (his choreography is in the repertory of some ballet companies) and a sophisticated musical sensibility.

German dancer-choreographer Pina Bausch (b. 1940), through her Wuppertal Tanztheater, remains one "of the most influential avant-garde artists on the European dance scene."[4] Studying with the socially conscious Kurt Jooss and the psychologically complex balletic dramatist Antony Tudor, Bausch became the

> *natural heir to the German expressionist dance tradition called Ausdruckstanz[;] her productions stress ideas—usually feelings of alienation, anguish, frustration, and cruelty—rather than the elaboration of pure movement. As Bausch herself has said, she is "not interested in how people move, but in what moves them." Her productions usually avoid a linear narrative logic; speech, props, and costumes play a large role. They are masterpieces of theatrical invention. In* Arien *[1979] she covered the stage with water; in* Viktor *[1986] she placed the action inside a huge earthwork grave; in* Nelken *[1982] she covered the stage with thousands of carnations . . . [and in] her landmark staging of Stravinsky's* Rite of Spring *[1975], she covered the stage with wet earth.*[5]

Bausch's work, like that of so many late 20ᵗʰ and early 21ˢᵗ century choreographers, is proof that the relatively simple across-the-arts experiments of the postmodern movement in the early 1960s have evolved far beyond even the artists' wildest earlier imaginings. Much of today's sophisticated, multi-arts experiments may be challenges to audience expectations and attentions and a harbinger of things to come.

Some of these experiments are one person's poison but another's tasty delight. Some people found Laura Dean's (b. 1945) early whirling dervish dances—such as *Drumming* (1975) and *Song* (1976), set to the hypnotic droning of Steve Reich's (b. 1936) minimalist sounds—wholly fascinating in their geometric, endlessly repetitive designs; others felt physically ill. Meredith Monk (b. 1942), "more interested in choreographing time than in devising steps for dancers,"[6] is likewise an acquired taste. Her *Education of the Girl-child* (1971) included a dance solo for the choreographer herself: "She begins seated on a dais draped in white, an ancient sibyl imparting deep knowledge in a foreign tongue. Gradually, as she moves down from her perch to travel a winding white fabric path, she disposes of her gray wig and glasses and trips back through time to childhood and a state of innocence. Her choreography, with its little steps, hops and spins, has the intentional naivety of folk dance."[7] Although many audience members are entranced by Monk, the staged embodiment of the phrase "ancient sybil imparting deep knowledge in a foreign tongue" could be gibberish for some people, and her "tripping back through time to childhood . . . with little steps, hops, and spins" could have felt pointless and absurd, signifying nothing beyond juvenile displays of facile movement. Yet the postmodern movement and its avant-garde practitioners embrace this wide variety of interpretation: if anything goes on stage, the same is true for an audience's reactions.

People still walk out on Merce Cunningham's dances (a back-handed tribute to his lasting power), in particular first-timers, who often are frustrated in the attempt to identify accessible points and landmarks on the stage. Cunningham keeps his dancers partially hidden, tucked away in corners, flitting here and there onstage and offstage unexpectedly. To challenge his audience (and dancers) further, he almost always commissions composers to create an accompaniment—which includes city street sounds and tree branch rustlings more often than the conventional sounds of music—independently from the choreography, bringing the score and even commissioned sets together as late as opening night. Dancers, audiences, choreographer, composer and visual artists experience the piece together for the first time, pristine in its innocence; the "only commonality between them is that they happen at the same time."[8]

CURRENTLY

Today, one can see dance on stage, on film, on video and on the computer screen, synchronously and asynchronously, all around the world. The excitement of possibility and unpredictability, limited only by the imagination, remains always attractive and saleable. The results, however, are not always interesting enough to bear repeating. New art is always like that. Regardless of the format, it is far better to have been moved, as Bausch says, by that invisible but palpable desire of dancers to "speak" with their movements, than to be stunned into incomprehension. Turning performers' skills into communicative devices that touch our own often inarticulate hearts, minds and spirits remains the goal of the majority of the world's working artists.

Dance works that reflect the currency of a certain period are evocative not because of their *style du mode* but because of their impressive kinetic and visceral imagery. The immortal Russian Anna Pavlova (1881–1931), who became known to Americans through a host of concert dates and vaudeville tours between 1912 and 1925, left us an exquisite memory of the romantic era that remained embedded in the ballet psyche of commercial theater for years to come. *The Dying Swan* (1907) was a solo choreographed for her by Michael Fokine, set to music by Camille St. Saens. For that time, complete solos emphasizing one vibrant image were truly modern and revolutionary.

Eighty years on, popular modern dance choreographer David Parsons (b. 1960) created an equally powerful image that stands apart from any label. *Caught* (1987), a solo in the dark with flashes of light, highlights one dancer who repeatedly jumps and leaps about the stage in aerial poses, remotely controlling a strobe light that illuminates the picture at the pinnacle of each bound. Blinded by the darkness between jumps, the eye is fooled into creating the illusion of sustained human flight. *Caught* takes about the same length of time to elicit gasps of suspended belief from the audience as the swan does to reach her last flutter. From Pavlova to Parsons, modern ballet to current modern dance, breathtaking imagery regardless of category is one of the most appealing and coveted aspects of all theatrical dance performances.

Contemporary explorations require dancers to improve not only their technical virtuosity but also their skills in acting, music and all dance styles, thus erasing the demarcations between the capacities of modern and ballet dancers. In general, all dancers today jump higher, turn more, have more stamina and are stronger, faster and more flexible than their forebears because of their increased knowledge and application of better diets, dietary supplements, injury prevention and therapies and because of more scientific training methods for both athletes and dancers.

Our society also has been overcome with the philosophy that a somehow perfect technical creation, human or otherwise, can be achieved. Many feel that the overwhelming need for technical achievement in a highly competitive market has usurped dancers' passion for dance as an art form. Today's audience member can (and perhaps should) demand both passionate involvement *and* exquisite technique from all dance performers. The similarity developing among so many of today's styles of professional dance training has created a technical homogeneity that, right or wrong, now serves scores of choreographers of various ideologies and styles.

The work of current postmodern, avant-garde and experimental choreographers seems to be about process rather than performance. If true, it may have difficulty flourishing because it all too often deliberately avoids accessible traditions with which to hook audiences.

The modern, postmodern and alternative art forms share a choreographic singularity: the notion that an individual has the right to create whatever she or he wishes. In 1966, dance historian Selma Jean Cohen referred to the field of modern dance as an art of iconoclasts.[9] It still is.

Likewise, contemporary ballet's association with traditional institutions continues to change, making it ever more difficult for new audience members to decide if the company is ballet, modern, postmodern, contemporary, alternative, avant-garde, experimental, in vogue or something else. If dance audiences can initially inhibit their need to label a company's repertory, they should be able to better appreciate an assimilation of the broad diversity of ideas often being presented before them.

The artistic currents flowing since the time of Isadora Duncan embrace whatever style is appropriate for the choreographer's expression. Ballets of the past live on, as ballet companies continually remount traditional, evening-length romantic and classical heirlooms, along with mementos of the one-act traditions begun in the 1910s that might still be called modern ballet. The Alonso King Lines Ballet, Australian Dance Theatre, Les Ballets Africains and many other companies around the globe continue to offer new ballet works in unnamable styles, using everything from classical ballet to hip-hop, modern dance and yoga.

Pioneering choreographers continue to investigate and experiment with many different styles, so to label their works as belonging to any one form does their artistic visions a true disservice. Today's dance world is one of enormous complexity and contradiction, full of competing philosophies that daily test the potentially cohabitable waters of new currents of expression.

ENDNOTES

1 Walter Terry, *Ted Shawn: Father of American dance* (New York: Dial, 1976), p. 96.

2 Debra Craine and Judith Mackrell, eds., *The Oxford dictionary of dance* (Oxford: Oxford University Press, 2000), p. 262.

3 Bill T. Jones, with Peggy Gillespie, *Last night on earth* (New York: Pantheon, 1995), p. 252.

4 Craine and Mackrell, *Oxford dictionary of dance*, p. 53.

5 Ibid., p. 54.

6 Allen Robertson and Donald Hutera, *The dance handbook* (Boston: G. K. Hall, 1988), p. 249.

7 Ibid.

8 Craine and Mackrell, *Oxford dictionary of dance*, p. 121.

9 Selma Jean Cohen, *The modern dance: Seven statements of belief,* 1ˢᵗ ed. (Middletown, Conn.: Wesleyan University Press, 1966).

CHAPTER TEN

introduction

R ituals play meaningful roles in our lives, providing important well-springs for spiritual sustenance. In dance, healthy, formalized routines also can propel the practitioner into a spiritually transcendent kind of euphoria or ecstasy. This feeling is often accompanied by a profound sense of belonging to something much greater than oneself. This chapter focuses on the mind-body-spirit triad evoked through the sensuous and sacred rituals of training for, rehearsing and performing dance.

CONNECTING MIND, BODY AND SPIRIT

Myron Howard Nadel

Many systems of religion, education and psychology disconnect the body from the mind and spirit. Some sects and practices both old and new see the body as a detriment to the everlasting soul, promoting the idea of consciousness as a function of mind or brain unrelated to the body, except in the realm of gross pain and pleasure. Although some Western systems of psychology have recognized the inseparable nature of mind and body, they have not pursued that line of thought to its fulfillment, particularly in relation to dance.

For many dancers and those connected with dance, true spiritual fulfillment means education and religious practices that employ a oneness of the mind-body experience. This belief does not mean that religion needs to incorporate trance dance or possessional shaking, or that education must always be filtered through physical exercises. It does mean, though, that every nerve and muscle be recognized as having a part in all thoughts and that oneness of the conscious mind and the material body is an essential part of learning and living.

Many educational institutions, whatever their reasons, continue to value courses where groups of people must sit still and learn while others lecture to them. Colleges have even developed distance-learning courses where the professors and students communicate via television screens, further separating any possibility of mind-body learning through an illusion of interaction with the projected, two-dimensional professor.

So far, dance has not fallen into the trap of distance learning. In a dance class, the body-mind to body-mind consciousness between students and teacher is palpable. I believe that dance can be a metaphor for consummate learning and for what is spiritually communicative in nature.

Reason and most religions tell us that our bodies are impermanent, but also that something in or about this impermanence—the mind or the soul—is everlasting. But during our finite life cycle, these two seemingly contradictory entities are inseparable. In order to understand the dancer's integration of mind and body, we might see the brain simply as extremely complicated body matter and thus, like the rest of the body, impermanent as well. Then we might see what we call *mind* as an integration of the electrical charges of brain into the matter that we also call body. We might follow this idea by considering what we call *spirit* or the human soul as something transcendent of the mind-body, impermanent but still transmittable culturally and generationally.

To further contribute to our understanding of the spiritual value of dance, we might need to decide what we mean by *consciousness* and *self.* Let us say that we identify ourselves as mind-body. Let us also say, for the sake of argument, that we call our identification with this mind-body the *self.* Some might refer to it as *ego identification.* Most of the time, we are so involved in our daily activities that we do not or cannot see this self. Some philosophers ask how the self can even be seen. Nevertheless, we do try to look at and consider that identification, so we will call that looking *consciousness.* It is our consciousness that tries to "see" and understand our selves and everything that we can know and feel.

In the dance world, the professionally trained dancer daily employs such a consciousness in an attempt to develop the most fruitful mind-body relationship by manipulating or subduing the ego. Such a process may not fulfill all that one's spirit entails, but it does engage the spiritual qualities inherent in dance.

THE BODY AS A TEMPLE

Many cultures and peoples value the body as a temple of the spirit. Hindu and Buddhist philosophies rely heavily on this integration of mind, body and spirit. Prayer and meditation become synonymous with the mind's search for truth and experience through the medium of this body-temple.

Furthermore, the development of the body-temple is not a fixed process. Our bodies change on a daily and even momentary basis depending on what is happening to us in our lives: our rate of growth; the foods we eat; the amount of sleep we get; and our location, injuries, loves, fears, perspectives and beliefs. These changes are sometimes very clear and sometimes quite subtle. So even as the dancer attempts to develop incrementally the physiological parts of his or her body-mind, circumstances occasionally reflect a lack of progress or even impediments to that growth.

Dancers often see their bodies as an unwieldy mass of protoplasm that will not listen to directions from the mind. During the many years that it takes for dancers to develop into artists, they occasionally may glimpse integration between their minds and bodies, when movements seem to be efficient and flow easily from one moment to the other. Conversely, the mind-body relationship can often seem like an internally noisy engine, with the driver's commands being ignored or misunderstood. Coordinating this mind-boggling network of commands is a lifelong struggle for every dancer in every dance class. The same movements can be easier to accomplish on some days and more difficult on other days. Dancers must go through a daily ritual of unifying mind and body to the best of their ability. It can at times be either a frustrating or a joyous experience.

This body temple is observed in action by an audience that expects it to deliver a message, to be energetic, athletic looking, interesting or daring and to fulfill a host of other requirements. Dancers must deliver the results of years of training for the audience's pleasure (and sometimes illumination).

I believe that anyone in pursuit of this spiritually cast mind-body connection can use dance training and performance in the quest. Very few people are required in their work to integrate mind and body to the extent that dancers must. Most people work first and then exercise, work and then meditate. It is within the process of integration between job and life that the seeds of spirituality can germinate. A dancer's occupation demands recognition of the mind-body as a temple that can open the doors to this spiritual connection.

The instrument of dance is the human body—our essential and sacred contact with this world. Training and performing push the body to the utmost extremes, but such exertion must be done in a mindful manner, full of awareness. Achieving a sometimes superhuman state through the body can be a sacred act, for if we have not experienced the fullness of developing our physical potential, have we really experienced the fullness of the sacred gift of life?

Students may learn about spiritual journeys in philosophy or literature classes or through books such as Robert Pirsig's *Zen and the Art of Motorcycle Maintenance* (1974), Hermann Hesse's *Siddhartha* (1922) and Peter Matthissen's *The Snow Leopard* (1978), in which the characters are on a spiritual quest for the meaning of life. After many trials and tribulations, they find meaning in all things and in no one thing. It is my contention that when the dance artist realizes that each class, each rehearsal period and each performance can be a journey for meaning, she or he begins a similar personal spiritual journey that involves an ever-increasing conscious participation in the mind-body.

DANCE AS MEDITATIVE PRACTICE
(THE JOURNEY TO BODY CENTER)

Clergy and other religious people seem to have a genuine peace of mind, at least on the surface. This peace of mind likely is a product of a considerable number of hours devoted to prayer and meditation. Through a similar intensity, great discipline and dedication, serious dance training can develop analogous powers of reflection and meditation, and thus in some cases achieve that same peace of mind. The reality of stiff competition for artistic and commercial success can eclipse the benefits of such a meditative approach. Once a dancer achieves artistry and some degree of financial security, he or she may then feel able to become involved in more serious and reflective daily training through the meditative aspect of dance.

If we look at meditation as a form of deep and continuous concentration or focus on a single sound, image or idea, the dancer, like the religious person, can approach a meditative state both in class and in performance. This state is similar in all the arts and is like the flowing current felt in most situations of deep, focused concentration. Accomplished pianists are in a deeply meditative state when they perform and practice; painters are often similarly immersed as they work in their studios.

Although all artists utilize instruments to varying degrees to practice their art, whether it is their own fingers, a French horn, a voice or a paintbrush, the total body is the instrument for a dancer's movement and the fertile medium within which the meditation can deepen. The potential for one's true wholeness of body-mind-spirit then, is very strong in this fully embodied art form.

Especially for those dancers striving for recognition, concentration upon one's self can become an onanistic exercise. No meditative practice is meant to remain fixated upon the self, but rather should be used as a vehicle to achieve some communicative unity with the universe. The narcissistic hazard of dance is that the reflection is not genuinely internalized, but evident only in the mirrors that cover the studio walls. Instead of an inward searching for a sacred source, concentration on self becomes preening as it attempts to attract attention to the self in a prideful way.

But when the body is looked upon as a channel for the spirit, and the dancer is constantly employing the mind's will to guide the body through the imperfections of the moment in order to improve the instrument, self-transcendence and spiritual fulfillment are possible.

The dancer's conscious search for his or her center or the body's central axis is a never-ending process within a mind-body that seldom lands squarely on one point and is rarely parked there for more than an instant. This search is similar to a mantra that allows one to settle upon a chakra or spot on or within the body as a contemplative focal point. Distractions constantly move us from this journey with the mantra. The more the dancer tries to force an arrival at center, fight off distractions and hold on to the steering wheel of consciousness, the less likely he or she will be able to park the vehicle at that center.

Within some religions, dance historically has been considered the antithesis of spirituality and otherworldly pursuits. Some religious practices, however, especially in Asian and African cultures and in a number of traditional Native American cultures, have allowed and encouraged the search for spiritual integration of the body and mind. For example, in traditional Diné (Navajo) culture, the people's dances, music, regalia, histories and sense of community are tied together within their daily lives. Wealth is measured in the number of songs and dances one knows, not in acquisitions.

In the southern Indian Hindu dance style known as Bharata Natyam, believed to be nearly three thousand years old, the tradition incorporates both dance and drama as a form of prayer. Originally practiced only by temple dancers, the style is demonstrated and performed today around the world. Dance, drama, technique (even each facial movement, including brows, eyes, nose, cheeks, mouth and chin, has meaning) and worship are inseparable from the other and evoke ancient rituals connected to praise of the creator god Brahma. Likewise, the Indian god Shiva represents a number of transcendental energies available to all beings here on earth in his simultaneous embodiment of destruction and dancing, referring to the full cycle of life in death and reproduction.

Viewpoints about the body have ranged from eschewing all but the most functional bodily movements to celebrating movements that tell stories of creation or depict mating practices. Religions on all continents have acknowledged that the act of dancing can be a spiritual ritual. Although Western religions have promoted dance only when its evident goal is sacred, even Christ says, "Whoso danceth not, knoweth not the way of life."[1]

Instead of seeing the body as representing lust and sin, dance artists should view the body as a beautiful expression of the gift of life. It can support their awakening consciousness. Each day, in each class, the dancer attempts to integrate the possibilities of the body with the complicated demands of the choreography or exercises. The body at any one point in time is similar to not one instrument but an entire orchestra, prepared to respond to the demands of the conductor (the mind). Multiply that by the millions of moments of movement, drama, rhythm and stage relationships demanded of a dancer, and you will have some idea of the complex challenges in this art form.

In the effort to create moments of shared beauty and communication with an audience, this employment of the most fundamental material and mental tools can bring about a spiritual transcendence. Beginning dancers and audiences need to believe that such transcendence is possible. Great dance artists, like other great artists, are those who have experienced that transformation as they incorporate artistic and spiritual dimensions into preparation and presentation.

Martha Graham (1894–1991), the grand dame of modern dance, frequently equated her work with religious fervor and potency; the spartan rituals of her *Primitive Mysteries* (1931) and her recurrent mining of Greek myths for their archetypal and transformative evocations certainly reflect her commitment to spiritual exploration and radiance. Graham's student and one-time husband-muse Erick Hawkins (1909–1994), sometimes referred to as "the maverick medicine man of modern dance,"[2] created his own ascetic aesthetic that combined an innocent eroticism with an intense, ritualistic spirituality. In fact, Hawkins often argued that his dances were created so that the performer(s) and audience might share in the power of the performance in a kind of ritualistic synchrony and transference. In the modern dance masterpiece *Revelations* (1960), set to the powerful gospel songs of his rural Texas youth, Alvin Ailey (1931–1989) embodied "the spiritual journey from baptism through religious despair to joyous salvation."[3] Through word and deed, many other dancers and choreographers have likewise articulated the essential spiritual dimension of their vocation.

As in religion, dancers must be committed to certain rituals during their lives as performers. The daily routine of training and maintenance methods are quite formalized, such as the order and length of a ballet class. The preparations for a performance, including the process of final preparations with lighting, costuming and making up, are also ritualistic. Although the particulars vary from company to company and country to country, such conventions are conducted worldwide. When professional dancers take their place at the barre, they can be confident that at other times and somewhere else in the present world, someone else is practicing this same "liturgy," providing for them a communal and spiritual link with the community of world dance.

The rites practiced in ballet classes have been proscribed and so are similar throughout the world, in part because dancers need to warm up and progress in a methodical way. The studios everywhere are also very much alike, with mirrors, barres and a resilient floor made of either wood or some type of artificial surface designed specially for dance classes. Female ballet dancers wear tights, leotards and sometimes a rehearsal skirt and a bit of ribbon in their hair, and the male dancers wear tights, a dance belt and a tight T-shirt. Both wear ballet slippers, with some of the women in pointe shoes. They all stretch on their own before class.

The language spoken during a ballet class is also uniform throughout the world. French terminology is used to describe the movements, and dancers from any country are able to understand the ballet instructor's demands. The accompanist will sit at a piano and play music of the masters, arranged to facilitate the exercises. When an accompanist is not used, the same dance CDs or audiotapes can be heard in all studios.

As many religious people find spiritual peace in the rituals of church and temple, dancers often find solitude, inner peace, health and joy in the rituals of dance. The studio, then, is a magical place where the performing dancer attempts to transform the daily attitude of living into a state of awareness that combines beauty, consciousness and physical practice into a sacred act. The dancer joins a group of like-minded supplicants who realize that they can never perfectly accomplish this art, but can improve on it and maintain the magic with daily practice. Whereas an absence from group religious customs may be overcome quickly by returning to the habit, dancers have to work long and hard to rebound from the detrimental effects of missing training. They must attempt to bring habitual patterns into consciousness and change these patterns for the better within the structure of the class. This is a lifelong process. Most dancers say, "If you miss class for one day, you know it. If you miss class for two days, your teacher knows it, and if you miss class for three days, the audience knows it." Dancers can and should practice alone, too, but they should most often work under the watchful eye of a teacher who methodically unfolds the individual rites, exercises and combinations to guide the dancers in their pursuit of enlightenment.

Participation in a group also tends to motivate each individual through the communal energy emitted as many aspirants practice the same ritual at the same time in the same place, day in and day out. Like-minded dancers help reinforce the special experience of disengagement from the everyday. The dancer senses and feeds into this synchronization with others in a kind of harmonious effort and action that empower each participant. Obviously, individual egos can often create a sense of competition, which is hardly a sacred state. However, the dancer who truly strives to grow into an artist can reduce that competitive drive because he knows that he is in competition with only himself. No matter how famous or wonderful he becomes, he must join the group each and every day for this ritual, the class.

If dancers as performer-creators can promote their own spiritual development through dedication to the rituals necessary for excellence on stage, then the act of performance is a potential staging ground for transference of that spiritual energy to the audience at both conscious and sublime levels. Dance, theater and religious rituals have similar purposes: they aim to attract, communicate with and change (or at least affect) their participants if possible. In dance as well as the other performing arts—where proscribed behaviors, actions, words, movements, dress and a host of other elements make up the rites—these purposes are part of a ceremony called *performance*.

Knowing that acts of theater or musical performance involve rituals allows the audience to engage with the performers in these essential aspects of the artistic experience.

The act of dancing does not have to be solemn, however, as correlation to religious dance rituals, particularly in Western society, might imply; subject matter and viewpoints can embrace the wildly comic and the trivial as well. The cathartic effect of watching exciting physical effects and laughing during a comedy or vicariously experiencing a tragedy can only add to the power of such a transformative experience.

When you are totally immersed in watching a dance work, time will seem to disappear or stop. You will have lost sensation of the place where you are sitting and not be aware of how you feel. But you *will* feel, and later you will be aware of those feelings.

When such a riveting and internally moving experience happens to you during a performance, you will understand the spirit of the dance, for you, the dancers and the dance will be interconnected. It does not always happen, but when it does, you can call it "art."

ENDNOTES

[1] E. Louis Backman, *Religious dances in the Christian church and in popular medicine* (London: George Allen and Unwin, 1952), p. 1.

[2] Allen Robertson and Donald Hutera, *The dance handbook* (Boston: G. K. Hall, 1988), p. 71.

[3] Debra Craine and Judith Mackrell, *The Oxford dictionary of dance* (Oxford, England: Oxford University Press, 2000), p. 393.

SECTION TWO

THE DANCE EXPERIENCE

CHAPTER ELEVEN

introduction

This chapter is designed to inspire you to track down, enjoy and study dance films and videos. It also discusses examples of ballet and modern dance video as well as some commercially available films that feature dance by choreographers sensitive to the uniqueness of the media.

DANCE ON THE SCREEN

Marc Raymond Strauss

Dance on the screen, whether via film, video or computer monitor, is a tricky affair. For the average dance-goer, the cost of viewing concert dance on a stage continues to escalate, making access to live performance—the best way of experiencing dance—a tenuous proposition at best. Such a state encourages people to view dance on the cheap, either through the occasional film in movie theaters (such as the recent "Chicago," "Center Stage" or "Billy Elliot") or on video or digital video discs (DVD). Nevertheless, seeing the art of dance on film—especially those dances made with the art of the camera in mind—is not a bad second choice; in fact, such an experience can offer the viewer sights and sounds that are unavailable and even unthinkable on a stage.

Film and video (DVD, VHS and other formats) are independent art forms distinct from dance. They have their own rules, their own vocabulary and language and their own sense of aesthetics, criticism, history and innovation. For example, film does not have to be edited synchronously, with one moment followed by the next, as in everyday life or on a stage. In innumerable ways and for varying lengths of time, yesterday's activities can be spliced onto tomorrow's performances, actions and thoughts. Quick-cut editing, slow motion, fast motion, close-ups, reverse angles, fades, washes, segues and a host of other cinematic tricks exploit the mind's ability to sustain an image in the eye for one-tenth of a second, thereby fooling us (with our permission) into thinking a sense of continuity exists.

Whenever artists work to bring more than one art form together, however, whether in successful collaboration or not, complexities skyrocket as each offers the other new possibilities.

Dance traditionally has made its way onto film or video through two general approaches, although a third fairly recent one has been gaining disciples over the past several decades: (1) straightforward recording of live action from a frontal perspective; (2) dances made for film or with film firmly in mind; and (3) video dance.

STRAIGHTFORWARD RECORDING

Straightforward recording of live action from a frontal perspective—say, with the camera set up at the back of a house auditorium pointed straight toward the stage—with little or no added production values, although "true" to the actual movements, cannot capture the feeling of "being there" during a performance. This is especially true if, in an effort to get all the action, the zoom function on the camera is not used at all, and the dancers appear as small, impersonal figures in the distance. Most of the dances in early film musicals, such as MGM's 1929 "The Broadway Melody" and Goldwyn's "Whoopee!" (1930), were shot in this way. With the addition of sound onto films in 1927 (with Warner Brothers' part-talkie "The Jazz Singer"), filmmakers were thrilled just to be able to put images with voices onto the screen at all.

This unembellished recording technique was also used for many of the films taken of America's modern dance and ballet pioneers in the early to mid-20th century, such as "The Dance Works of Doris Humphrey: *With My Red Fires* and *New Dance*" (1972), which shows both of those dances, performed in 1936 and 1935, respectively. They are nearly impossible to watch, not because they are not interesting or important archives of Humphrey's early work, but because they provide no sense of actual presence from the camera's distant vantage point; the dancers are just too indistinct on the screen. Among hundreds of others like it, the 1956 black-and-white film "Swan Lake," with commentary by Maria Tallchief and Nicolas Magallanes, is a ballet example that fares just as badly.

DANCE MADE FOR FILM

Thanks primarily to some thoughtful mortals such as Busby Berkeley, Fred Astaire, Gene Kelly, Jack Cole, Bob Fosse and Michael Kidd, and to television programs such as the Dance in America series made by the Public Broadcasting System (PBS), we do have an exceptional number of quality dances on film and video that continue to reward repeat viewings. The burgeoning production values of film musicals from the 1930s provided choreographer-directors with the resources necessary to embody so many of their extraordinary visions onscreen. Dances filmed for television by PBS, the Bravo network and the Arts & Entertainment (A&E) channel had the right producers working for them. These people knew that dance on the television screen could be improved with better lights, more cameras (and angles), wooden sprung floors (as opposed to the injury-inducing concrete ones used until the early 1970s) and other dance- and dancer-friendly considerations.

Busby Berkeley

Busby Berkeley (1895–1976) was a truly talented man, even if he did over-objectify and idealize women (who begged to be in his films; they needed the work during the Great Depression). He exploited women's curves, lines and beauty even more than the great revue impresario Florenz Ziegfeld (1869–1932) did in his risqué Follies shows. In fact, Berkeley cut his choreographic teeth working in a number of Follies-type productions throughout the late 1920s. From 1930 (soon after the birth of the talkies) to 1963 (long past the heyday of film musicals), and in no less than fifty-three films in those thirty-three years, he created some of the most indelible dancing images still on the screen today—and his best work was made *for the camera, not the dancers.*

Choreographer—or dance director, as he was actually called—of seminal films such as "Whoopee!" (Goldwyn, 1930), "42nd Street" (Warner Brothers, 1933), "Gold Diggers of 1933" (Warner Brothers, 1933), "Gold Diggers of 1935" (Warner Brothers, 1935), "For Me and My Gal" (MGM, 1942) and "The Gang's All Here" (20th Century Fox, 1943), Berkeley was unparalleled when it came to making his camera literally waltz and swing above (far above, as from a crane), under (legs and water) and through his ever-evolving patterns of hordes of dancers—mainly women—onscreen. In fact, he became so famous for his kaleidoscopic effects of bodies en masse, often shot from his highly mobile camera, that the 1952 *American Thesaurus of Slang* listed a "Busby Berkeley" as "a very elaborate dance number."

Some of Berkeley's greatest creations for the screen are still available on film, video and DVD:

- His dizzying, almost MTV-like edits of the dramatic "naughty and bawdy" title number *42nd Street*, from the film of the same name (1933);

- The pre–Production Code *Pettin' in the Park* number from "Gold Diggers of 1933" (1933), with its display of rain-soaked chorus girls naked in silhouette;

- The simultaneously erotic and abstract, snakelike patterns of his half-nude bathers (all female) cavorting in a giant pool in *By a Waterfall*, from "Footlight Parade" (1933);

- The jaunty tap duet by a very young Jimmy Cagney (dancing much better and almost ten years before his George M. Cohan impression in Warner Brothers' "Yankee Doodle Dandy" in 1942) and Ruby Keeler in the stereotypical *Shanghai Lil*, also from "Footlight Parade";

- The unforgettable, Technicolor spectacle of bananas, strawberries and chorus girls in Carmen Miranda's *Lady in the Tutti-Frutti Hat*, from "The Gang's All Here" (1943)

Not only could Berkeley choreograph the camera's movements in sophisticated ways, but his much-too-modest appraisal of his own dance choreography—in spite of the fact that he never actually took a dance class—was clearly nullified by his most celebrated work, *The Lullabye of Broadway*, from the classic "Gold Diggers of 1935" (1935). With the catchy, immediately recognizable tune by composer Harry Warren and lyricist Al Dubin, stalwarts of most of the Warner Brothers musicals in the early 1930s, the sultry main character Wini Shaw beckons us ("C'mon along and listen to / the lullabye of Broadway!") into the most surrealistically recorded stage space ever created for a filmed dance number up to and perhaps since that time. More than one hundred dancers boom out their series of eerie and ominous taps in perfect unison as Dick Powell and night-clubber Wini get whipped up into a maelstrom of frenzied partying, which ends in Wini's horrible tumble to her death from a balcony outside the dance hall. All the hoped for, unrestrained excesses denied to depression-era audiences culminate in and are shattered by this single ten-minute dance number. During one four-measure section alone, Berkeley's camera jump cuts from high above the dancers to several shots of a row of men tapping like mad—first from the right side, then from the left side and finally from below them, looking up through a glass ceiling at the soles of their shoes. This is choreography in two art forms, film and dance, at its unparalleled finest.

Berkeley understood that the camera had its own laws, which he had to keep in mind if someone were going to enjoy his dances on film. Among so many other aspects of the art, he understood exactly how two of the most basic tools of cinema worked—*montage*, or the craft of piecing separate pieces of film together in unique ways, and *mise-en-scène*, the compositional skill of filling each rectangle of a screen's frame with interesting objects, designs, people and relationships. Through Berkeley's unique merger of two art forms, the camera became the performers' dancing partner.

Fred Astaire

Another important film choreographer was Fred Astaire (1899–1987). We are fortunate to have on video and DVD all thirty-one of his film musicals, from his introduction to film audiences in MGM's "Dancing Lady" (1933) through to his role as the title character in the charming "Finian's Rainbow" (Warner Seven Arts, 1968). A number of extraordinarily talented writers have devoted reams of notable analyses to describing, interpreting and evaluating Astaire's cinematic contributions to the dance world. John Mueller's nearly exhaustive 1985 book *Astaire Dancing* includes an in-depth analysis of all the films and of Astaire's more than two hundred dances, as well as literally thousands of small print stills from the films. Dance novices and connoisseurs alike can compare and contrast dances, scenes and even phrases of movement in each film with Mueller's concise descriptions and evaluations.

Astaire was even more self-effacing about his talents than Berkeley, but there was nothing simple, unplanned or unprofessional about any of his dances. Small mistakes are simply impossible to find. Like Berkeley, he was extremely popular and successful because he, too, thoroughly understood both of the art mediums in which he worked. One of Astaire's primary cinematic tenets—and it became almost a rule unto itself for years to come—was always to keep his dancers' bodies in full-figure throughout the routine. Also, in a partial dig to Berkeley's approach, he said, "either the camera will dance, or I will."[1] In a 1987 biography on Astaire, author Bill Adler states:

> To [Astaire], a dance was an artistic statement made by the body of a dancer. To be right, it must progress from one moment to the next, in an unbroken flow. The image of the dancer must be seen at all times, in its entirety, with no visual break. Thus, in filmic terms, any dance must be filmed from beginning to end with no breaks—or, at most, a minimum of such breaks—cuts, inserts, or moving the camera away from the dancer to feature someone or something else.[2]

To see this artistic directive at work, one need only watch Astaire's choreography (frequently in collaboration with the often unheralded Hermes Pan [1910–1990]) for himself and some lucky, talented costar in numbers such as *Night and Day* (with Ginger Rogers) from "The Gay Divorcee" (RKO, 1934), *Cheek to Cheek* (also with Rogers) from "Top Hat" (RKO, 1935), *Begin the Beguine* (with Eleanor Powell) from "Broadway Melody of 1940" (MGM, 1940) or *Dancing in the Dark* (with Cyd Charisse) from "The Band Wagon" (MGM, 1953). Astaire could not have appropriated, evolved or reversed Berkeley's approach to camera movement had he not also fully understood the principles of montage, mise-en-scène, dolly and pan. Gene Kelly's, Michael Kidd's and Bob Fosse's cinematic innovations, likewise, could never have occurred without such an understanding. Each successive dance artist learned his lessons well from his predecessors.

Gene Kelly

In "Cover Girl" (Columbia, 1944), Gene Kelly (1912–1996) choreographed a duet for his main character and for a superimposed version of his unconscious self in the *Alter Ego Dance*. Here, we see the two opposing forces in Kelly's character at war as they pirouette, leap, wrestle and generally try to outdo each other in an effort to come to some conclusion about his quandary over Rita Hayworth's character. For "Anchors Aweigh" (MGM, 1945), Kelly created a duet for himself and Jerry the Mouse, Hanna Barbera's animated creation, in *The King Who Couldn't Dance/The Worry Song*, another typical action-filled tour de force. And in "On the Town" (MGM, 1949), dance and song are filmed for the first time in a big-city location in the title number *New York, New York*, on top of the Empire State Building and all around other important New York City landmarks such as the Statue of Liberty and Radio

City Music Hall. The dances are boisterous and cheerful, reflecting just what one would imagine three sailors with a twenty-four-hour leave might feel, and are complemented perfectly by the palpable reality of codirector Kelly's placement of cameras out in the real world.

Ballet, Jazz and Modern Dance Choreographers on Film

Michael Kidd (b. 1919). In MGM's "Seven Brides for Seven Brothers" (1954), Michael Kidd choreographed the *Barn-Raising Number* with extremely athletic ballet dancers competing for brides as the camera zooms and spins around their dancing and acrobatics. In "Hello, Dolly!" (TCF/Chenault,1969), his *Waiter's Gavotte* is actually a multicut, fast-edit minimusical of dancers scurrying about in a restaurant, predating MTV's similar style by thirteen years.

Bob Fosse (1927–1987). In "All That Jazz" (COL/TCF, 1979), the sexuality, steaminess, partial nudity, camera zooms and quick-cut edits of *Take Off with Us/Airotica* outdo anything MTV or commercials have done since.

George Balanchine (1904–1983). For the revuelike film "The Goldwyn Follies" (MGM, 1938), Balanchine choreographed the *Water Nymph Ballet*, in which his then wife Vera Zorina (b. 1917) rises out of a fountain and a corps (group) of dancers perform ensemble lifts and patterns around her in a mock Greek arena. Though seeming like weak classical dancing to us today, the ballet is still an important visual marker for the quality of technique at that time in America.

Eugene Loring (1914–1982). The 1953 Columbia film "The 5,000 Fingers of Dr. T" was largely ignored, but it is one of Hollywood's great fantasies (based on a story by Dr. Seuss). In it, a boy has a scary dream about a cruel piano teacher who rules over a land where kidnapped children are forced to practice the piano. Eugene Loring's *Dungeon Dance* can be described as one of the funniest and most bizarre dancing orchestras one could ever hope to witness, as the poor child runs frightened around a cave filled with nightmarish instruments parodying classical ballet steps.

Roland Petit (b. 1924). Mikhail Baryshnikov (b. 1948) performs the brilliantly despairing *Le jeune homme et la morte* (The young man and death), originally choreographed by Roland Petit in 1946, in the opening of the disappointing but popular 1985 Taylor Hackford's Columbia film "White

Nights" (with Gregory Hines). The dance is a tale of hopeless love, with Baryshnikov's character compelled to partner beautiful Death herself, who literally leaves him hanging. Petit's choreography for Goldwyn's "Hans Christian Andersen" (1952), in particular his *Dream Fantasy* for his then wife Zizi Jeanmaire and *The Little Mermaid Ballet*, with Petit himself dancing as the Prince, are wildly surrealistic, with that Technicolor-drenched 1950s look. Petit's work successfully wed his classical ballet training with a rich knowledge of dance as theatrical entertainment on both the screen and stage.

Hanya Holm (1893–1992). Popular modern dancer Hanya Holm's choreography shows up in the rarely seen 1956 Paramount film "The Vagabond King," about the poet-scoundrel François Villon, directed by the usually drama-oriented Michael Curtiz and starring the opera-based Kathryn Grayson and a very young Rita Moreno, soon to be showcased in Jerome Robbins's "West Side Story" (1957; film, United Artists, 1961). The dancers cavort in Holm's exuberantly boisterous and bawdy *Vive la You*, a happy mix of modern dance and musical comedy, and in *Watch Out for the Devil*, a serious parody of the Adam-Eve-snake fable. In the latter, Holm's space-focused training with the German innovator Mary Wigman (1886–1973) was happily merged with her own creative explorations of American speed and energized rhythms; the number is surrealistically corny and bizarre as it humorously yet faithfully parodies the biblical story with goofy lyrics and expressionistic costumes.

Directors

The possibilities of dance on film and video were not lost on directors, either. Michael Powell (1905–1990) and Emeric Pressburger's (1902–1988) still stunning, Oscar-winning 1948 British dance film "The Red Shoes" (GFD/The Archers) is a superbly stylized and dramatic fairy tale of a young ballerina torn between two creative and possessive men. The film's tragic danced climax—with choreography by one of Serge Diaghilev's (1872–1929) last great choreographers, Léonide Massine (1895–1979), and performed by Massine, Robert Helpmann (1909–1986) and Moira Shearer (b. 1926) in her film debut—remains powerful drama. Owing to its integration of dance in storytelling, it is also an important recorded resource, much like Agnes de Mille's (1909–1993) ballet in the 1955 film version (Magna) of the 1943 Broadway show "Oklahoma!"

Television

Television was bringing dance to audiences as early as 1936 in England, when the BBC presented dances from Marie Rambert's (1888–1982) British company. But it was not until the mid-1970s, especially through the PBS series *Dance in America*, that dance on the screen really became available and popular for the general public. The series began to present works by the great choreographers of the 20th century at the height of the ballet boom, in 1976. Funded in part by the National Endowment for the Arts, the Exxon Corporation and the Corporation for Public Broadcasting, WNET/Thirteen Television in New York City led the way for public television stations to "[t]ranslate dances by major dance companies without massive changes or video effects or glitzy attempts at popularization. It seemed a conservative goal by some standards, but for prime-time television it was revolutionary."[3]

The *Dance in America* series continues to represent our country's best efforts at archiving some of the finest dances our choreographers have created and re-created beginning in the 20th century. The list of companies and choreographers represented in this esteemed program reads like a *Who's Who* in Western (primarily American) theatrical dance: the Joffrey Ballet, Twyla Tharp, Martha Graham, the Pennsylvania Ballet, George Balanchine, American Ballet Theatre, New York City Ballet, Dance Theatre of Harlem, Merce Cunningham, Pilobolus Dance Theatre, the San Francisco Ballet, the Feld Ballet, Jerome Robbins, Peter Martins, Trisha Brown, David Gordon, Steve Paxton, Vaslav Nijinsky and Paul Taylor.

Although the dances for the most part are presented without any extra glitz or effects, they are also treated with reverence and are filmed in studios or on stages constructed for dancing, in tasteful lighting and with just the occasional quick-cut edit.

VIDEO DANCE

Video dance, a mostly recent phenomenon, includes choreography not just for the camera as recorder, but for the camera as codancer.

By the 1980s, choreographers no longer felt compelled to lock the camera onto a solid object. They took Berkeley's approach to the next level. Dancers themselves carried small and more mobile cameras on their backs, in their hands or on their clothes, on and off the stage.

The still experimenting Merce Cunningham (b. 1919) is often given credit for popularizing the computer program LifeForms®, which allows simulated movements to be choreographed in a semirealistic manner on the computer. The choreography is then reapplied to live bodies onstage, thereby innovatively appropriating the freedom of imaginatively created movement from the computer program and applying it to the improvisationally tinged energies of the Cunningham-trained dancers. As early as the 1960s, Cunningham and others, such as Birgit Cullberg (1908–1999), were experimenting with choreography for the camera by using a variety of monitors onstage, as exemplified in Cunningham's 1978 video film "Fractions 1." A number of postmodern choreographers have also embraced film and video in unique ways. In 1998, Wayne McGregor used what he calls an asynchronous transfer mode (ATM) to explore modern dance and choreography that features audiences and performers around the globe dancing in different time zones *at the same time*, watching and reacting to each other in a live/virtual dance experience (see "53 Bytes in a Movement" in "Video/Film Resources" listings for this chapter).

Once other art forms are added, the dance becomes something more than just itself. Bob Lockyer, BBC director of dance in London, choreographed dance with film and video solely at the forefront of his thinking in his two-volume set "Video Dance" (1991–1992). As far back as 1980, Twyla Tharp created the television dance program "Twyla Tharp: Making Television Dance," which explored the freedoms of time, space and proximity that video embodies. This unique multiarts creation explored both connotations of the phrase "making television dance." Tharp continues to experiment with forms and styles.

There is no substitute for viewing live performance, but when the choreography is intended for the two-dimensional flat screen, or the camera and dancers are choreographed in concert, the argument over whether it is live or canned becomes moot. Artistry is artistry, and new, unnamed or freshly named forms of "video dance" have already begun to establish a new kind of dance-related art.

ENDNOTES

[1] Bill Adler, *Fred Astaire: A wonderful life* (New York: Carroll and Graf, 1987), p. 112.

[2] Ibid.

[3] Robert Coe, *Dance in America* (New York: E. P. Dutton, 1985), p. 7.

CHAPTER TWELVE

introduction

In this chapter, Janice LaPointe-Crump points out that gender is one of the first things viewers notice when a dance begins—so clearly obvious, and replete with connotation. She discusses specific gender issues and stereo-typical gender-based behaviors in ballet, ethnic and social dance, musical the-ater, film dance, and even MTV dance. Such issues relate to the overall themes, subject matter, movement choices and intentions of any choreographer's work within a specific era.

OF DAINTY GORILLAS AND MACHO SYLPHS: DANCE AND GENDER

Janice LaPointe-Crump

All the gestures are signs of things, and the dance is called rational, because it aptly signifies and displays something over and above the pleas-ure of the senses.

—attributed to St. Augustine

The Pink Ladies are draped over Marty's bed, ogling pictures of Troy Don-ahue and Fabian at a typical 1950s teenage slumber party. The scene is Marty's fluffy pink bedroom, where four girls paint their nails and listen to the newest rock 'n' roll sensation on the radio, while practicing Frenchy's smoking technique, sipping on cheap wine and nibbling Twinkies. They drool over Marty's newest pen pal, Freddie, a marine stationed in Korea, who sent her the Japanese kimono she models. About him, Marty sings a sugary ode, "Freddy, My Love." Fade out.

The next scene finds us in a dilapidated garage where the guys, poring over and under a beat-up jalopy, merge their hormone-driven dream worlds—hot

159

cars and willing girls. "I don't know why I brought this tire iron! I culd'a yanked these babies off with my bare hands," gloats Danny Zuko. Their song, "Greased Lightning," quotes the driving guitar sound of the 1950s, while Kenickie envisions his hunk of junk transformed into a gleaming mountain of carburetors, shocks and taillights. Black out.

Patricia Birch's choreography for the 1972 Broadway hit "Grease" (Paramount film, 1978) dominates the show. She builds up the cartoon stereotypes of that lost era by separating the male and female identities and their nearly empty spheres of influence and empowerment. The girls lounge on Marty's bed dreaming of movie stars and trinkets, but the boys' world, although equally useless, is active and dynamic. Critics of this musical, such as Michael Feingold in his introduction to the Broadway script, insist that "Grease" simply waves good-bye to the obsolescent youth of the 1950s with snappy scenes and a predictable story.[1] Feingold misses the gender ironies so obvious in these back-to-back scenes. In "Grease," sexual imagery, dividing masculine and feminine roles, pumps vitality into the thin plot. We visualize the imagery directly through the body—its posture, attitude and movement.

"Nothing is more revealing than movement," wrote Martha Graham.[2] Never neutral, movement excites our imagination. As others have pointed out, "The body as the means of dance performance is not governed by the same narrative conventions that are found in theatre or literature."[3] If the dancer speaks or sings, it is the body that connects the dancer with the viewer. We share in the pulse of the heart, feel the stretch of the limbs, know the making of a fist and recognize the emotions. Dance is a complete aesthetic that conveys physical, emotional, intellectual and social meanings through movement imagery.

Besides being pleasurable entertainment, what do the songs and dances reveal in these two scenes from "Grease"? Because "gender casts a shadow over the moving body,"[4] the two scenes define gender difference through characterization, gestures and movement. Gender inscribes the body, and the gendered body inscribes the dance.

The aim of this chapter is to explore the vital role that gender plays in identifying and understanding the dance experience. Let us begin with a simple definition. As applied here, *gender is an analytical category that makes sense of a wide variety of biological, historical and cultural considerations that construct, then identify, the world as systematically divided between masculine and feminine characteristics.*

One key to finding meaning in dance movements is to question and reflect after sensitive and discerning observation. What makes a handshake hearty? Why is a glance electrifying or a leap lyrical? What kind of power is implied when a group of men jump onto the hood of a shiny car? What is funny about the image of a hulking gorilla moving lightly or of a transparent sylph crash landing like a two-ton brick? The answers reside in the gender knowledge ingrained in our bodies. The visual and physical humor of gorilla and sylph is apparent because we understand the codes whereby gender fixes certain attributes of physicality, grace, power, authority and beauty.

The four basic avenues for male and female identity within dance imagery explored in this chapter are biological differences and identities, cultural and ethnic constructions, historical presence and choreographic form.

BIOLOGICAL DIFFERENCES AND IDENTITIES

Dancers come to embody an encoded formal representation of gender as part of their training, helping them to define space, rhythm, energy and shape. In an advanced ballet class, for example, the traditions of technique are quite different for women and men. Women tend to develop a subtle musicality that relates rhythm to personality. They typically dance in pointe shoes, command high leg extensions and work diligently on fluidly coordinating the upper body and arm gestures to imbue their dancing with idealized femininity and grace. On the other hand, male ballet dancers traditionally have not been expected to move with subtlety and grace. Instead, they tend to take charge of the space by encircling the stage with high, warriorlike jumps and performing with aggressive strength, while tempering their commanding presence with compassion and protectiveness toward their partner.

Contrast this training with the traditional modern dance class, which often incorporates Martha Graham's "contractions and releases" of the spine and Doris Humphrey's "falls and recoveries" of the body's center, metaphorically associated with giving birth and grappling with the forces of gravity, respectively. Some consider Graham's movements to be anatomically inappropriate and artistically unappealing for men.

There are, after all, physical differences between the sexes, among them (generally) a wider pelvis and greater torso flexibility in women and greater height and upper body strength in men. Women usually are associated with the more subjective, intuitive modes of thinking and behavior; men with objective, rule-governed modes. Thus, conventional choreographies often automatically reflect these easily identifiable gender correlations.

From birth, girls and boys learn about the physical differences that mark them as females and males of the species. These differences are also powerful cultural indicators that influence how they learn to move, think and be in the world. Sexuality is a matter of biology, whereas gender, according to psychologist Carol Gilligan, is a coding or labeling learned from family and society.

A gendered worldview begins to form at the toddler age, with a dawning awareness of feminine and masculine differences. Babies are intuitive observers. They mimic unquestioningly, absorbing sanctioned feminine and masculine distinctions. The ways children are held, guided, corrected and coached become unconscious texts for sexuality. As applied to movement, gendered texts are manifest through behaviors, gestures, postures, clothing choices, music and speech patterns—all active expressions charged with information derived from and influencing the body.

Throughout childhood, boys and girls absorb and mediate the texts of their elders, community and peers. Through mimicking, experimenting and receiving feedback, children gradually shape their identities. By the time they reach adulthood, American culture can accommodate whatever changes in these socialized gender standards they wish to make through subversion or through creation of different ones. Freedom to create or play with the traditions of gender coding is greater today than ever before. But when we dance, we are first and foremost a woman or a man dancing. When we view dance, we see females and males onstage. Dancers in particular are artists who are acutely aware of the physical identities and gender codes embodied in their selves and situated in the roles they are dancing.

In the 19th century and through much of the 20th century, dance was thought to symbolize the feminine. The professional male dancer was marginalized and labeled effeminate or homosexual. To counteract this perception, overpowering displays of virility and power customarily underlie many dances involving men.

One of the founders of American modern dance, Ted Shawn (1891–1972), provides a good example of this vaunted male virility. The Ted Shawn and His Male Dancers company toured the United States almost continually from 1933 to 1940. Shawn created images of sanctioned maleness with whom few could argue. To amazed audiences, in works such as *Kinetic Molpai*

(1935) he and his troupe displayed themselves in heroic, bare-chested, classical Greek poses and in imposing warrior dances. Inspired by a Greek ritual of death and resurrection, the choreography counterpoints fighting gestures and pure displays of strength with oppositional and parallel linear formations, typical ballet *grand allegro* (large and quick jumps and turns) and cascading sequential falls.

Film dancer-choreographer-director Gene Kelly (1912–1996) presented another brand of idealized dance heroism. Rather than likening the male dancer to a demigod, he elevated the ordinary man, the working stiff, to the heights of mythic hero. In MGM films such as "Anchors Aweigh" (1945), "On the Town" (1949) and "Singin' in the Rain" (1952), among a host of others, his bold, strong dances expressed uncomplicated emotions with the dynamic sureness of a top athlete.

Film choreography opens a pathway into viewers' hearts and minds by linking biological traits with movement images that have broad cultural appeal and acceptance. After dancing a festive reel with the ladies in the film musical "Seven Brides for Seven Brothers" (1954), choreographed by Michael Kidd (b. 1919), the men career flamboyantly over rolling logs and split jump fences to compete for top honors and win the ladies' affections. So, too, the men's dances in "Grease" adhere to the same cultural maxim, and we discern the familiar macho imagery. This maxim is seen also in the male's sexual dominance in the controversial *Afternoon of a Faun* (1912) by Vaslav Nijinsky (1890–1950). "One explanation of the macho male display dance," asserts Ramsay Burt, "is . . . that dancers are trying to show that they are not effeminate, where 'effeminate' is a code word for homosexual."[5]

Because today's society generally accepts a greater diversity of lifestyles than previous societies, not all male dancers (or female dancers, for that matter) mirror accepted expressions of biological gender difference. Within even traditional gender roles lie questions that may lead to parody and subversion of standard gendered profiles. Choreographers frequently will introduce unconventional gendered identities and relationships onstage that may jar, confuse and even shock us upon first encounter.

One cannot experience Mark Morris's (b. 1956) *The Hard Nut* (1991), a sardonic version of Marius Petipa (1818–1910) and Lev Ivanov's (1834–1901) Christmas classic *The Nutcracker* (1892),[6] without questioning cultural portrayals of femaleness and maleness. In Act One, the permissive lifestyle attributed to the late 1960s and 1970s is satirized by naughty kids, bratty teenagers and tipsy grown-ups revved up by the male French maid and male momma. Later, Herr Drosselmeier's duet with his nephew sharpens our awareness of male sensuality, revising the conventions of how males may display tenderness, intimacy and love. Shortly thereafter, the music sweeps us into the land of the Snow Queen and a strangely beautiful snowstorm of men and women dancers dressed alike in tutu skirts, pointe shoes and Dairy Queen headdresses. Morris questions the association of certain imagery with women in ballet, such as the habit of enacting beauty solely from the perspective of some feminine ideal. Why must women be privileged over men in portraying beauty and love? *The Hard Nut* presents a startling alternate view of traditional gender constructs, while using humor to raise serious questions of identity and agency.

What happens when male dancers appropriate female attributes? Les Ballets Trockadero de Monte Carlo (founded in 1974), known affectionately by its fans as "the Trocks," is an all-male company that performs cross-dressed excerpts of classic ballets, such as Act Two of Petipa and Ivanov's *Swan Lake* (1895), and of equally respected 20th century ballet and modern works. The men perform the pas de deux (duets), ensemble and solo dances decked out in tutus and pointe shoes, with a little over-the-top comedic inflection. Their witty and spicy humor, with their male characteristics not always completely disguised, is grounded within a reverent and faithful approach to these ballets.

Bill T. Jones (b. 1952) and Arnie Zane's (1947–1988) *Ritual Ruckus (How to Walk an Elephant)* (1985) similarly dissolves traditional aesthetic boundaries by including movement motifs quoted directly from George Balanchine's (1904–1983) dreamily feminine *Serenade* (1934). The male dancers, rather than the female, perform the motifs. Jones insists that their intention was not parody but confrontation against and resistance to traditional male-female aesthetic norms. By changing the gender, he and Zane, like Morris, wanted to affirm the male as a legitimate symbol of beauty.

The themes of dances choreographed by women often ask psychological questions involving mentoring, nurture and community versus status, individuality and personal liberation. The early modern dances of Isadora Duncan (1877–1927), Doris Humphrey (1895–1958) and Martha Graham (1894–1991) are particularly rich in examples of the "new woman" archetype of the 20th century. Drawing together in communities dominated by women, these dancers strived for empowerment and authority in piercing solo and ensemble dances. In their works, the lone female dancer symbolizes women's courage and dynamic independence, set within an all-female ensemble representing the unity and harmony of a single-gendered community.[7] Doris Humphrey's quintet in *Air for the G String* (1928) depicts the world of women as communal, supportive and responsive.

With her leg hitched up on a fencelike set piece, Martha Graham peers westward, spearing the air at the outset of *Frontier* (1935). She is both the driven woman carving up space with a succession of *grand battements* (large kicks) and the toiling woman representing the noble pioneer. *Cry* (1972), by Alvin Ailey (1931–1989), includes a female solo that follows in the Humphrey and Graham tradition, enacting semifictional portraits of the modern heroine. *Cry* is a moving yet unsentimental dance tightly linked to the issues of the civil rights movement, critiquing the condition of black women in particular.

Johanna Boyce and Meredith Monk (b. 1942) are two of many early 21st century American choreographer-performers who continue to examine gender ideology. Boyce maintains the singular theme of women absorbed by the unique issues of an all-female company, choreographing works that explore womanliness wholly outside of a male context. Her *Kinscope/Coming of Age* (1982) was inspired by girls' playfulness and "sportswomanship," without reference to boys' competitive athleticism.

Meredith Monk, in questioning her feminine identity and place in the family matriarchy, frequently is inspired to interface her biological attributes with her Jewish heritage. *Education of the Girl Child* (1973) is a loosely organized autobiographical allegory about her role within a Jewish sisterhood of women. Regressing from great-grandmother to grandmother to mother and finally to herself as daughter, Monk singularly embodies the cycle of life in archetypal American female roles. In much of their work, Boyce and Monk, like Morris, Jones and the Trocks, are guided by their gendered views to envision the possibilities for change in dance storytelling—for example, through their semiautobiographical "her-story" approaches.

When women create dances, their position in the world and their identities are generally the focus of attention. Conventional dance forms, in contrast, tend to validate and even exaggerate patriarchal traditions. Contemporary dances find men and women questioning their places in the world and accounting for personal and gendered transformations when a level of independence from cultural constructs is attained.

Three fascinating dance films explore men on mythlike journeys in which they question coded stereotypes, seek personal renewal and achieve an enriched identity often in opposition to cultural norms. The transformation process enfolds dance as a central metaphor and is the very substance of the stories. In a romantic model reminiscent of the 19th century classic *La Sylphide* (1832), the Japanese film "Shall We Dance?" (1996) is about a man's midlife quest for a seemingly unattainable dream. Learning the intricacies of Western ballroom dance and resisting conservative Japanese mores form the spine of the plot. The British film "Billy Elliot" (2000) concerns a coal miner's son who, through his study of ballet dancing, discovers self-identity and self-worth. And the American film "Dance with Me" (1998) focuses on a Cuban emigrant's resistance to the commercialism and politics of joyless American dance competitions. His search for community and family is symbolized by a natural salsa dancing style that is contrasted with the cold, overly stylized dance sport version he encounters at a Texas dance studio. In all three films, dance is defined as a potent form of expression, conveying universal cultural texts, revealing biological and personal identities and introducing transformed viewpoints.

CULTURAL AND ETHNIC CONSTRUCTIONS

Ethnic and folk dances unquestionably direct our attention to the dominant beliefs and cultural structures of their communities. Imprinted in the designs of the dances are coded patterns of everyday life contextualized by a particular society. From the steps, posture, uses of space and rhythm, costumes and props, dancers learn symbolized values and practices. Only the choreography depicts ideologies and practical occupations. Traditional partnering techniques in many of these dances express the dualisms of male masculinity and female femininity.

In traditional folk dances, men's movements are usually more imposing and spacious, physically bold, daringly gutsy and strenuously technical, with a strong sense of shape and linear design. In women's dances, even the energetic ones, the movements emphasize precisely detailed footwork and hand gestures, an opening outward and folding inward to the body's center, spiral and curved shapes, contrasting circular and linear patterns and a grounded relationship to the earth.

Such a contrast is apparent in the sublime spirituality of the women's dances and in the exciting acrobatics of the men's dances from the former Soviet Republic of Georgia. Women glide effortlessly and soundlessly through complex curving patterns, heads covered, gazes quietly lowered, arms folded with hands hidden beneath long sleeves. Merging energy, shape and timing, the Georgian women reveal their spheres of influence as peacemakers and express the serene solidarity of the female community. The men's dances, in contrast, stress bombastic physical agency, unflagging courage and prowess. Sometimes dressed as warriors, the men run on the toes of their soft leather boots to leap and tumble in thrilling solo aerial tricks. The Georgian women and men dancers share and preserve a unique cultural identity and dignity through these gendered dances.

Conversely, the Greek American *miserlou* is a mixed social dance performed in unison that circles and curls around the room in an open formation. Together, the men and women twist back and forth performing the same steps in a community more homogeneous than the Georgians', spiraling around the space lightly connected by their hooked little fingers. Still, the physical differences between men and women in this dance, seen in the size of the steps, the costumes and the dancers' postures, help us discern how the Greek American men differ in their dancing from the women.

Within a ceremonial tradition, dance often epitomizes a union of thought and action, the mythic balance of female and male energies and functions. Of deep religious significance are African women's ritual dance offerings to the water goddess Oshun. Their footwork beats the earth, but their upper bodies show undulating arm movements, fluent gestures and swaying hips.[8] How different the women's grounded, earth-connected movements are in comparison with the sudden high jumps, threatening stomps, deep lunges and spearing actions found in many African warrior dances, performed by men only.

In China, we also see mythic differences in the choreography and performance of gendered dances. Compared with the abrupt changes in direction and thrusting or jabbing actions of a large metal fan in the men's martial arts dance, the Chinese woman's ribbon dance is a poem of harmonious, circular designs, with light, leaping steps. The continuous lyricism of the woman's entire body manipulates the twenty-five-foot-long satin ribbon.

In many Native American intertribal ceremonials and powwows, dances exemplify formal and carefully performed gender attributes, suggested by the construction of memory through "rituals and bodily actions of posture, patterned movement . . . and verbal and gestural repetition."[9] In fact, gender play is one of the most obvious of elements in many Native American dances. In the Diné (Navajo) tradition, for example, the opposition of male and female behavior and qualities is considered natural. Depicted through dances and songs, natural contrasts between women and men are essential to balancing cosmological, oppositional forces, ensuring a "continuous, dynamic change that allows [certain affinities] to perpetuate themselves," such as the changing seasons, birth and death, and female and male.[10]

HISTORICAL PRESENCE

In Western social and ballroom couple dancing, the patterns of behavior have less to do with biological differences or individual performing ability than with social convention and historical precedent. First set forth as a demonstration of courtly manners or etiquette, couple dancing was scrutinized, and the intimacy of the couple carefully controlled.

Beginning with the late medieval period, ballroom dance choreography mirrored and enforced restricted interaction between the sexes. Ideally, men were gallant: they removed their hats in a lady's presence and never coughed in their faces. Refined ladies, directed by their partners, curtsied demurely and walked with small, mincing steps, eyes averted.

When performing a dance choreographed to depict other cultures and eras—such as a Renaissance pavan, an 18th century minuet, a 19th century waltz, a late 20th century Cuban salsa or a ballet pas de deux from any era—we accept certain social practices as culturally valid and as part of the aesthetic of the dances. We also value the dances because of their unique, formal properties.

CHOREOGRAPHIC FORM

The pas de deux is a scintillating formal courtship dance originally associated with 19th century romantic ballet. Although generally fixed in its form, the pas de deux distills gender values of the past, but in ways that have evolved over time. Its antecedents are the aristocratic and elaborate court duets of the 17th and 18th centuries. Ornate gestures and clothing differentiated the sexes, but the choreography for dances such as the minuet, the allemande and the bourrée equalized differences between men and women in their symmetrically geometric figures or patterns.

This was not the case throughout the 19th century, when ballet couples enacted an idealized love consummated in the aroused passions of the romantic hero and heroine. By the 1880s, men resumed the archetypal role of the noble and courtly knight, whose physical prowess and careful leading safeguarded and directed his lady. The women, on the other hand, were left to flirt coquettishly to gain attention and favor. Formalized courtship rituals and contrasting piercing pointe technique with small, delicately precise steps were expected. Ballerinas wore short tutus designed to reveal the idealized body and to display the line of the leg and foot. Aided by the pointe shoe, the ballerina achieved both femininity and physical dominion. In contrast, the princely danseur's movements, both spacious and airborne, were designed to balance bravura physicality with courtly self-control and support.

Imagine this generic pas de deux. The danseur extends his upturned hand to the ballerina. She accepts and, pressing down on it, poises delicately on one pointe, then slowly performs a *développé* into a deep *arabesque penché*.[11] Sustaining the arabesque, the danseur promenades his ballerina, controlling her balance effortlessly with one hand. Because the ballerina is supported and directed throughout the pivot, her spatial freedom and turning ability are enlarged. The danseur ensures a lyrical fineness in the conclusion of the adagio portion of the pas de deux, when the ballerina leaps lightly into a swooping "fish" dive, breathlessly close to the floor. In the subsequent solo variations for each dancer, the ballerina and her cavalier display romanticized feminine and masculine qualities in the movement, rhythms, musicality, spaciousness and technical superiority of their classical dances. Each dancer is a virtuoso, toughly scrutinized by the viewer's gaze. In the concluding coda, the female dancer challenges her male partner to turn more quickly and leap more grandly until, in a crescendo of energy, she is tamed by her partner in the climactic lifted pose. Thundering applause.

When we view a 21st century version of a 19th century pas de deux, which embodies many of the elements and qualities just listed, we can observe the ways cultural ideology reinforce our perceptions of the dance aesthetic. Gallantry and formal etiquette are made vivid through the dancer's focus, arm and head movements, literal and abstract gestures, entrances and exits, and the formality established between the dancers and the stage space.

This partnering model, instilled in the leader-follower relationship that remains the basis for much Westernized couple duets in ballet, has far from died out in other styles. It is retained in contemporary choreography such as Paul Taylor's (b. 1930) *Esplanade* (1975), Twyla Tharp's (b. 1941) *Sinatra Suite* (1984; winnowed down from *Nine Sinatra Songs*, 1982) and many forms of current social dances. Couple dancing still includes the firm, sure lead of a powerful man and the subdued sensuality and disguised athleticism of the woman.

Not all duet forms have retained courtly chivalry. Before World War II (1939–1945), the Lindy, swing and tango were social dances that disrupted traditional leader-follower partnering. In swing dancing, a two-handed grip freed the female dancer to achieve greater independence, and the spins, tosses and acrobatic lifts required the muscularity of both partners. The ballroom image of the delicate female and the controlling male was subverted. Also popular in the 1930s, the Argentine tango dramatized the sexual combativeness of partnering, while preserving the closed ballroom dance position. Sharp angles and abrupt changes in direction and focus "dramatized complex social conflicts in sexual terms" and created an impression of female resistance and equality to the male leader's control.[12]

The role of women in swing and tango reflected the historical reality of the 20th century. The energy and tension between the partners in these dances remains palpable today as the dancers share weight and responsibility, investing their emotions equally.

In ballet, musical comedy, modern dance and cultural dances, certain movement phrases continue to adhere to historical stereotypes about women and men. Full-bodied split jumps, multiple pirouettes and overhead lifting are movements still generally reserved for men, whereas high arabesques, quick jumps, sweeping and embracing arm gestures and a supple use of the spine privilege women. The male dancer usually pursues the female dancer, who, although countering his aggression, is more interested in establishing a sensual rather than an overtly sexual encounter.

Compare, however, the casual androgyny of postmodern dance to the explicit gendered "Grease" characters munching Twinkies in Marty's bedroom or overhauling a V-8 engine in the greasy garage. Differences in gender conceptions began to melt with Merce Cunningham (b. 1919) and his quirky dances in the 1950s. His choreography, performed by a mixed-gender company dressed in unitards, eliminated the romance factor, replacing sexual excitement with austere chance procedures that disbursed expected relationships. For Cunningham, "dancing has a continuity of its own. . . . Its force of feeling lies in the physical image, fleeting or static. It can and does evoke all sorts of individual responses in the single spectator."[13]

By the early 1960s, the postmoderns costumed their dancers in even less-conspicuous pajama-like pants and tops. "No to spectacle," raged Yvonne Rainer (b. 1934), so dancers completely denied gender difference in experiments, applying contact partnering in rhythmically rich phrases founded upon ordinary or vernacular movement vocabulary, basic locomotor skills, democratic relationships and asexual imagery. Dancers sought to represent a neutral, natural body. Maleness and femaleness may have been the undisguised context, but they were not the subject of dance. Of the neutral body, Rainer writes, "I love the body—its actual weight, mass, and unenhanced physicality. . . . [M]y body remains the enduring reality."[14]

Rainer's *Trio A* (1968) was not conceived as a feminist exercise per se but was intended as a "clean-scrubbed" dance to emphasize a nongendered, natural body. Without focusing directly on the audience, Rainer unraveled a continuous skein of unrepeated movements.

By the 1970s, a time that saw the passage of Title IX, which demanded equal opportunities for women in the educational systems, choreographers were depicting a "new age" equality and community, as in Twyla Tharp's *Eight Jelly Rolls* (1971), Paul Taylor's *Esplanade* (1975) and David Parsons's *Nascimento* (1992). Both men and women skip, slouch, slide, leap, strut and sweep in complex clumps. Dancers join up then dissolve into new groups, only to reform into quick duets and solos.

Today, etiquette and formal female-male partnering no longer serve as markers for biological, historical or cultural aesthetic conventions any more than traditional rules serve to determine who drives the bus or serves in combat. Weight sharing and lifting, leading and following, and community solidarity characterize contemporary experiments, which are often improvisational or collaborative or both. Movement, enacted for its own sake, now blends various cultural and artistic dance techniques with a total body-mind approach to creativity and performance. Dancers purposely may bend expected gender associations or dismantle traditions of courtship by appropriating the coded attributes of the opposite gender. Thus, men may float, tilt and represent a sensitive spiritual essence (the dainty gorilla), and women may aggressively appropriate the weight-bearing role from their male partners (the macho sylph). Because the body is inscribed as a cultural, social and historical construction, we always dance who we are and what we aspire to be.

ENDNOTES

[1] Martin Feingold, Introduction, in *Grease*, by Jim Jacobs and Warren Casey (New York: Winter House, 1972), pp. 1–4.

[2] Nolini Barletto, The role of Martha Graham's notebooks in her creative process, *Martha Graham: Choreography and dance* 2 (1999), p. 54.

[3] Johanna Boyce, Ann Daly, Bill T. Jones, and Carol Martin, Movement and gender, *Drama Review* (winter 1988), p. 83.

[4] Ibid., p. 84.

[5] Ramsay Burt, The trouble with the male dancer . . . , in *Moving histories/dancing cultures*, edited by Ann Dils and Ann Cooper Albright (Middletown, Conn.: Wesleyan University Press, 2001), p. 44.

[6] In Morris's version, Herr Drosselmeier's gift of a nutcracker to Clara is sharply changed from the Petipa and Ivanov Christmas classic. Even so, Clara's relationship with the nutcracker-turned-prince reveals much about the expectations for 19th century middle-class girls to enjoy romantic dreams—to fall in love with the hero, who demonstrates his ability to kill dangerous enemies, such as the seven-headed mouse.

[7] See video documentaries of Isadora Duncan, and view such works as Humphrey's *Two Ecstatic Themes: Circular Descent, Pointed Ascent, Water Study* and *With My Red Fires*, as well as Graham's *Primitive Mysteries, Cave of the Heart* and *Appalachian Spring.*

[8] Oshun is one of the four divinities of the Brazilian African Indian Macumba religion. She is derived from the goddess of the Niger River in Africa and is the consort of the thunder god, Chango. Similar to the Greek goddess Aphrodite, she rules love, beauty and flirtation.

[9] Ann Axtmann, A diaspora of native American dance. In *Congress on Research in Dance Conference Proceedings* (New York: CORD, 2001), p. 311.

[10] Richard Anderson, *Calliope's sisters: A comparative study of philosophies of art* (Englewood Cliffs, N.J.: Prentice Hall, 1990), p. 102.

[11] Because ballet was codified in France, all dance terminology around the world is given in French.

[12] Marta Savigliano, *Tango and the political economy of passion* (Boulder, Colo.: Westview, 1995), p. 47.

[13] Quoted in Jack Anderson, *Art without boundaries* (Iowa City: University of Iowa Press, 1997), p. 206.

[14] Yvonne Rainer, qtd. in Sally Banes, *Women dancing* (New York: Routledge, 1998), p. 224.

CHAPTER THIRTEEN

introduction

This chapter presents a brief history of the turbulent 20th century marriage of two seemingly compatible areas—dance and physical education—within the U.S. educational system. On the surface, both disciplines involve the study and training of the body as an instrument for growth and knowledge. Although the instrument remains the same, their purposes have evolved along two distinctly different paths: dance toward artistry, and physical education toward a healthy lifestyle.

A FAILED MARRIAGE: DANCE AND PHYSICAL EDUCATION

Myron Howard Nadel

The biographies of performers in the printed programs of professional modern dance companies today clearly indicate that dancers rarely come to their professional career via the field of physical education. A half-century earlier it was more likely. In the ballet arena, it has never been likely.

More and more dancers are being trained in departments of dance (or theater and dance, or even music) under the aegis of schools or colleges of the arts and, of course, in private dance academies such as the School of American Ballet in New York. In our global arts community, we also see dancers who were trained in state-supported schools in Latin America, Australia, western and eastern Europe, Russia, Asia, Japan and Israel. We may also find the rare dancer who began studying in high school physical education classes and then transferred to one of these other institutions. Most commonly now, young Americans who want to be professional dancers study in an arts magnet school or a private precollege conservatory or dance studio, then follow that preparation with either professional conservatory training or university dance arts education. There are still many physical education dance courses in universities, however, and dance in high schools is still likely to be under the administration of the physical education unit.

This chapter is concerned with the long-term relationship between two distinct and invaluable educational fields: dance and physical education. Because of their unique ideals and potential in education, it might benefit those interested in dance to know how and why these two fields were wed, what they accomplished together, why they separated and how they might cooperate effectively in new opportunities in the future.

BEFORE THE BREAKUP

Certain historical conditions affected the confluence of physical education and dance. In the late 1800s, as public school systems in the United States were growing, the field of physical education was borne out of a need for physical training as wholesome exercise and as a way to handle and direct thousands of working-class and immigrant children. To us today, the physical curricula for this 19th century compulsory system of free education look strangely like military drills. The predominantly male teachers taught forms of gymnastics or calisthenics, but did not teach the art of dance because dance was a maligned profession even in the arts at the time.

In the first years of the 20th century, increasing numbers of women's colleges introduced physical education, particularly in New England, and their graduates began filtering into the public schools as teachers. Again, the physical education curriculum taught by these teachers was more like rhythmic calisthenics, although sometimes with musical accompaniment. The classes were fashioned on European models such as Swedish gymnastics and the French form of aesthetic calisthenics espoused by François Delsarte (1811–1871). Originally developed for expressive physical training in drama and opera, Delsarte's theories were joined with rhythmic calisthenics, the influence of famous turn-of-the-century dance revolutionary Isadora Duncan (1877–1927) and the public penchant for exotic influences from Asia and the Middle East. These confluences developed into movement forms called *aesthetic*, or *natural*, dance.

Men and boys rejected such an approach, however, judging it to be physically unchallenging and unmasculine, especially for a nation facing World War I in 1914. The field of physical education, already separated into classes for men or women, was divided philosophically as well. As team sports took over men's physical education, universal principles of physical education were opening the doors to dance education for women. At the University of Wisconsin, women's physical education director Blanche Trilling (1876–1964) promoted courses "designed to secure a high degree of organic power, harmonious physical development and a reasonable degree of skill and grace."[1]

In 1916, Trilling encouraged one of her most promising young teachers, Margaret H'Doubler (1889–1982), to go to New York for a year to study aesthetics and philosophy, which Trilling believed would undoubtedly strengthen the Wisconsin program. H'Doubler had been familiar with Delsarte movement and some folk dance, but she had little interest in the cutting-edge work of Isadora Duncan or Ruth St. Denis (1879–1968) or in what she saw as the empty routines of the ballet classes of the day. Instead, she was drawn to the ideas about creative dance and dance education based on anatomical principles currently used by Gertrude Colby at Columbia University Teachers College, Bird Larson at Barnard and Alys Bentley (1868–1951), who taught creative music and movement classes at Carnegie Hall.

H'Doubler believed that the educational philosophy of Columbia University's premier educational philosopher John Dewey (1859–1952) and her experiences with Colby, Larson and Bentley could be combined into a valuable and meaningful movement education. Trilling had already scheduled H'Doubler to teach a dance class at Wisconsin upon her return from New York, so H'Doubler was given the opportunity to allow her fresh ideas to flower into a philosophy of educational dance for women. The Wisconsin program was the first of its kind in the nation, and H'Doubler subsequently established the first university dance major there in 1926. The popularity and success of this new educational dance existed in part because it represented and fostered American women's burgeoning demands for opportunities for creative expression, individuality and greater freedom at that time. H'Doubler's intelligent and imaginative program included the performances of a students' modern dance group, Orchesis. In Orchesis and in the many groups that followed in the image of the Wisconsin original, the process of creation, cooperation and learning held sway over the more authoritarian choreographic precedents, which were generally necessary in the professional theater.

Although H'Doubler's students received an abundance of scientific and creative technical dance training as they strove to become skilled dancer-teachers, her new philosophy of dance education circumvented the undeniably grueling, time-consuming and all-encompassing requirements of

175

preparing a dancer for the professional stage. Ballet and some of the more rigidly defined techniques associated with the new theater dance, soon to be named *modern dance* by *The New York Times* dance critic John Martin (1893–1985), were not suited to the kind of progressive, nontheatrical education to which H'Doubler was committed.

Because of leaders such as Blanche Trilling, who, following the Dewey school of thought, believed that young people needed vital movement experiences, women physical educators embraced—or at least tolerated— the goals and interests of H'Doubler's philosophy. They believed that movement skills were a basis for knowing, imagining, creating and executing in life, as well as a stimulus to self-initiated activity and creative communication. Such cutting-edge ideas preceded by three-quarters of a century the theories of Harvard professor Howard Gardner (b. 1943), who today espouses a bodily/kinesthetic intelligence as part of his theory of "multiple intelligences."

The women physical education dance pioneers valued creative movement activities the most because they felt that such activities integrated the capabilities of mind, body and spirit and increased aesthetic and artistic potential. Understanding the science of movement also seemed crucial considering that the basic instrument of athletics and dance is the human body. They agreed that dance helped develop a sense of "the beautiful," as did gymnastics and ice skating, and that all children are entitled to experience the joy of movement. They also agreed that whether or not students intended to become professional dancers or athletes, they should study the pivots, runs, jumps, stretches, falls and kicks used in sports or dance. These objectives and others provided a rationale for including modern dance in the physical education curricula of colleges.[2]

In stark contrast stood the predominant attitudes of the male-dominated physical education field overall, where individual and group achievement through aggressive competition was highly valued. Prejudice against all forms of theatrical dance and against the involvement of men in dance reinforced the thinking that dance could flourish only for women. The essential movement philosophy of leading women physical educators quickly became embodied in modern dance—physical education's own art form—and the collective image of modern educational dance within physical education for women seemed set in stone.

The antimale bias in dance continued to fester in three ways. First, it was rooted in a time when the image of a servile and immoral European male—

the antithesis of the athletic hero—was associated with theater and dance, especially ballet. Second, dance had little appeal for men in the 1920s and 1930s. Third, men had little interest in joining the female-dominated dance education profession. Unfortunately, this bias has defined modern educational dance as being about women and for the primary benefit of women.

Although some male administrators of physical education programs agreed with the philosophical bases of educational dance, some also saw modern dance as a way to handle and be credited with large numbers of female students in what they considered a harmless, even enlightened, way. Dance also seemed like an economical way to increase the administrative cache of (mostly) male physical educators with the least expenditure of funds for equipment, uniforms and space. Today's Title IX efforts for equality still struggle with these attitudes and practices.

A separation between dance education and the male-dominated field of physical education was inevitable, for professional dance was also making its way onto the college scene. Wisconsin alumni began to head many successful dance programs at women's physical education units around the country, in such institutions as Mills College, the University of California and Ohio State University. Wisconsin graduates went off to work in major modern dance companies. Moreover, in competition with H'Doubler's summer programs, modern dance masters such as Martha Graham (1894–1991), Hanya Holm (1893–1992), Doris Humphrey (1895–1958) and Charles Weidman (1901–1975) were instrumental in creating a vibrant summer program of dance at Bennington College in Vermont beginning in 1934. This program drew together students and teachers from many college programs to experience the excitement, technique and creativity of professional modern dance. These summer session students in turn would inevitably influence other educational dance programs.

The director of the Bennington program, Martha Hill (1900–1995), had been one of Gertrude Colby's students, a former Graham dancer and a teacher at New York University.[3] After nurturing the strong professional summer dance programs at Bennington College for many years, Hill proposed to composer William Schuman, president of the famous Juilliard School of Music in New York City, that Juilliard form a year-round dance school. In 1951, she became the founding director of the Juilliard Dance Division. Her genius was in bringing together many of the seminal dance pioneers of the 20th century, such as José Limón (1900–1972), Doris Humphrey, Martha Graham, Antony Tudor (1908/1909–1987), Margaret

Craske (1882–1990) and Louis Horst (1884–1964), from both ballet and modern dance. In her dance curricula, Hill connected dance techniques with a strong academic program of music theory, dance history and criticism, composition, anatomy and notation. Also included was a full spectrum of liberal arts studies as she created a conservatory dance education in which talented and bright male and female students could also earn a college degree. Hill's tenure lasted more than forty years. In that time, most major dance programs around the United States developed from her conservatory model or moved from physical education departments into schools of fine arts. Her profession-based philosophy provided an enlightened academic model that signaled to other like-minded dance educators the coming break of dance away from physical education.

Seeing the benefits of creating a more catholic dance experience based on the Hill model, important dance educators in the country led the fight to separate dance education from women's physical education and to make it an independent and equal entity alongside art, music and theater. In the 1960s and 1970s, dollars could be found to support such moves because both modern dance and ballet were playing to larger audiences all over the world. Many university schools of fine arts created dance departments to respond to the demand for dance degrees and professional training.

One of the many effects of this migration is that the number of men in both professional dance companies and higher education for dance has increased significantly in the last quarter century. This increase may also be attributed to the ability of coeducational dance departments to attract men, the outstanding dance seen on public television, the presence of men from diverse cultural backgrounds who are interested in dance and the encouraging example of excellent male dance role models throughout much of the 20th century, such as Fred Astaire, Mikhail Baryshnikov, Jacques D'Amboise, Rennie Harris, Bill T. Jones, Gene Kelly, and Edward Villella.

AN INHERITANCE DIVIDED

The physical education and dance education components subsequently took two distinct paths, both of which continue to this day. Physical education responds primarily to the goals of health and wellness, fitness, recreation, kinesiology, sports psychology and coaching. Jazzercise and folk, square, social or ballroom and aerobic dance are among the subjects still taught frequently in physical education programs. Some programs also include the presentational aspects of cheerleading and popular dancing, which are often expanded into team competitions seen by millions of people at high school, college and professional sporting events around the country. Their musical counterparts are the marching and pep bands, providing recreational and group musical experiences for even more students.

In support of the dance-related aspects of physical education, the National Dance Association (NDA) was established in 1932, becoming an integral part of the American Alliance of Health, Physical Education, Recreation, and Dance (AAHPERD) in 1974. Its mission was (and still is) "[t]o increase knowledge, improve skills, and encourage sound professional practices in dance education while promoting and supporting creative and healthy lifestyles through high quality dance programs."[4]

In contrast, the National Dance Education Organization (NDEO) was established in 1998 to "[advance] dance education centered in the arts." The NDEO: (1) promotes dance as an artistic process that broadens and deepens human experience; (2) strengthens the national voice in articulating and implementing a vision for dance education; and (3) weaves dance into the complete fabric of learning.[5]

Both the NDA and the NDEO continue to work hard to bring the value of dance to the country's youth at all levels of the educational system. In particular, the creation and growth of the NDEO after the breakup of dance education and physical education in the United States reinforced the value of treating dance as a wholly autonomous and equal art alongside its sibling disciplines in the educational system. As of this writing, unfortunately, dance as an art form is still taught in only a few high schools and in even fewer elementary schools.

Elementary Schools

Not surprisingly, the elementary school is the place where dance and the arts would provide the best outlet for expression and creativity, before children become jaded and overly self-conscious. Dance and the arts have been discovered to be viable, enjoyable and stimulating tools for learning, not just something more to learn. Patterns, symbols and problem solving are all an integral part of dance and the arts, and their practice helps develop mathematical perception, reading ability, social skills, cultural literacy, historical understanding, language acquisition and a host of other traditional education forms. Elementary school educational systems cry out for the H'Doubler model, and artistically talented children cry out to be discovered.

Too many school districts cannot afford to hire arts specialists, however, and so the arts in elementary education are left to classroom teachers untrained in them. Some elementary schools do offer their students opportunities to enjoy classroom experiences with itinerant teachers from the various arts. Many of these teachers are certified to teach an art form at all levels, from kindergarten to twelfth grade, but few of them teach theater/drama and dance. Physical education specialists attached to several elementary schools sometimes have legitimate credentials to teach some forms of dance. Folk forms are best suited to these situations, unless the certified K–12 physical education instructor is comfortable with and understands the methods and reasons for creative activity and aesthetic expression.

In a few locations in the country, classroom teachers are beginning to receive a small amount of training to use all the arts for teaching other subjects. New national standards (see note 5 for Web sites) are beginning to be applied to studies in art, music and drama from the lowest levels to the twelfth grade and in dance from the fifth grade.

High Schools

The best situations for dance in K–12 public education at the beginning of the 21st century are in the arts magnet schools. In cities such as Houston, Louisville, Philadelphia, Cincinnati, Pittsburgh, Buffalo, Miami and especially New York, dance majors at these magnet schools spend a good portion of their day studying their craft in a professional atmosphere. These principals have taken the initiative to hire professional dancer-teachers who can teach even though they may not be credentialed in the very same manner as most high school teachers.

Like any trade school, the arts magnets often find that their greatest problem is to maintain the standards of their state-required comprehensive academic program while providing training and education for the arts professions. Nevertheless, most of these schools have excellent records for getting their graduates into universities and into various careers in many fields, not just the arts, because their students' total education is demanding, and those students who complete their programs demonstrate discipline, intelligence and dedication.

Sadly, if dance exists at all in typical comprehensive high schools, it is not valued equally with other core studies. Students are tracked into curricula that are supposed to open doors to colleges and to prepare them for "more important" careers. In many subject areas, skilled teachers bring their students to a high level of accomplishment, but only in the magnet schools can we even imagine that high school teachers are training concert artists or painters.

The most forward-looking comprehensive schools do use the arts to support a well-rounded education. When they do offer the visual arts, dance, drama and music, both boys and girls are required to choose at least one art form to study. Administrations and school boards fortunately are stating more and more frequently that these subjects are important for all students. Still, dance is often taught through the women's physical education component, thus perhaps inadvertently saying that dance is an activity solely for girls and women.

Even when dance teachers from the physical education or pure dance components set up after-school dance clubs, they have a difficult time recruiting boys. In addition, if dance groups are formed, the administration encourages dance performances that are cute, commercial, sexy, flashy and applause worthy. These dance groups are sometimes called "teams" that compete with other dance teams from other schools. This competitive element sometimes brings in a few males, who might lift the girls and add some athleticism, but it also further encourages gender-based stereotypes. One occasionally may find a choreographic work of substance on a high school dance concert program, however.

It will undoubtedly take years to implement the current National Standards for the Arts and even longer to see any benefits for dance. The standards include student knowledge and skills in the arts that are just now being deemed essential in a core curriculum. For dance to gain a meaningful foothold in the high schools, credentialed dance teachers must be found, nurtured and put to work in coeducational settings that foster the National Dance Standards.

This will be a monumental task, even where dance is already taught in comprehensive high schools. Although high school choirs attempt to sing Handel, orchestras take a shot at Beethoven, drama clubs tackle Shakespeare, and music theater groups produce Rodgers and Hammerstein, high school dancers usually perform their own or their teachers' choreography because they lack a truly sophisticated dance canon.

Dance is not necessarily the career specialty or even the educational choice of the teacher who teaches dance at a comprehensive high school. It is sometimes not even one of his or her fields of interest. However, the spread of excellent dance education in university schools of fine arts has broadened the pool of available, skilled and dedicated dance teachers that high schools should be willing to hire. Some high schools now have enough class sections of dance to make a full teaching load for one or more faculty.

A bright spot that highlights the art of dance in high schools is the National High School Dance Festival (NHSDF). The sixth annual NHSDF was held in Miami in 2002, and more than one thousand comprehensive and magnet school students from all over the United States, Canada and Australia attended in order to study and perform in a professional atmosphere.

Similarly, the American College Dance Festival Association (ACDFA) has been hosting regional and national festivals since 1973 for the same purpose, providing workshops, master classes, panel discussions and other hands-on opportunities for university students and faculty to present their choreography alongside their peers'. Nationally recognized dance artists judge and discuss the performances and choreography in open and constructive forums. Although some awards are granted, the main reward is the opportunity for young and established artists to receive and share feedback on their unique visions and artistic endeavors.

RECONCILIATION: IS IT POSSIBLE?

If dance is to be incorporated into coeducational physical education programs, some guidelines should be followed: the teachers should be well educated in dance; dance should not be considered a sideline to other major activities; the students and faculty should be provided with adequate dance studios and adequate time for each class and rehearsal; performances should be presented in a theater, and they should be considered artistic endeavors, not contests. Following all of these guidelines is sometimes feasible in colleges, but rarely in comprehensive high schools.

The field of physical education became a better discipline when it relinquished dance and began to concentrate on disciplines such as movement analysis and wellness. Many physical education departments are now called kinesiology departments. In addition, there can now be an extremely beneficial relationship between dance and kinesiology because of mutual interests in movement analysis and wellness. Dancers need help with wellness, including dietary concerns and with injury prevention, rehabilitation treatment and therapeutic body modalities, as well as with the development of a life-long appreciation of recreation, health and exercise.

Dance forms that serve primarily health, recreational or social purposes are perfectly suited as teaching subjects in these reformed departments. Appropriate subjects include folk dance, square dance, ballroom dance, aerobics and dance therapy. Because the number of hours of dance training for physical educators is still low, the basic skills required in one or more of these forms can be learned within their time constraints and then taught to others as part of an arsenal of teaching skills.

Given that it will take time to integrate the National Dance Standards fully into the public education curricula, it is more important than ever for both physical education and fine arts specialists to have the ability to provide physical, creative and aesthetic dimensions of dance to boys and girls in kindergarten through the middle grades. Future teachers can learn these dimensions and proper perspectives within independent, coeducational dance, drama and physical education departments.

All in all, dance education and physical education are much better off apart because although their relationship had benefits for the field of women's movement education, it had little interest or benefit for men. Also, women's dance education overall was incompatible with most of the ideals of the professionally trained conservatory dancers, who struggled to become artists first. Yet it would be nice if some way could be found to utilize H'Doubler's ideas for a meaningful movement education practice for young people in the schools.

ENDNOTES

[1] Janice Ross, *Moving lessons: Margaret H'Doubler and the beginning of dance in American education* (Madison: University of Wisconsin Press, 2000), p. 81.

[2] Howard Gardner, *Frames of mind: The theory of multiple intelligences* (New York: Basic, 1983).

[3] Ross, *Moving lessons*, p. 203.

[4] Information about the NDA is available at: www.aahperd.org/nda. October 15, 2002. The address for AAHPERD is 1900 Association Drive, Reston, Virginia 20191-1598.

[5] Information about the NDEO is available at: www.ndeo.net. October 15, 2002. The address for the NDEO is 4948 St. Elmo Avenue, Suite 301, Bethesda, Maryland 20814. The National Standards for the Arts in Education may be viewed at: http://artsedge.kennedy-center.org/professional_resources/standards/natstandards/standards.html. Information about the American College Dance Festival may be viewed at: www.fsu.edu/~acdfa/.

CHAPTER FOURTEEN

introduction

It may seem obvious, but a dancer's physical instrument is not a piano, paint-brush or pile of clay, but a body. Right from the start, there is little room for distance or objectivity—the dancer *is* the dance, from the inside out. Nevertheless, he or she must treat his or her body with the same intense mix of subjectivity and dispassion as that pianist, painter and potter treats a piano, canvas and clay. Who dancers are is integrally tied up not only in their bodies but also in their hearts, minds and spirits. How dancers achieve skill or tech-nique through that emotionally, spiritually and intellectually charged physi-cal instrument is the topic of this chapter. A clearer sense of what constitutes technique for dance, regardless of the style, comes through knowing both the vocabulary needed to discuss a performance and the connection between that vocabulary and the actual physical feelings experienced in dancing.

TECHNIQUE: THE CRAFT OF DANCING

Myron Howard Nadel

Each and every craft involves various methods in creating the desired prod-uct. With skill, some methods may result in a product more durable, lighter, cheaper or beautiful. Less skill may cause the product to break, tear or oth-erwise serve the producer or consumer improperly. Dancing is a craft, and, like all craftsmen, dancers attempt to create the best product possible with-in their means. An old saying attributed to inventor Thomas Edison is that genius is "one percent inspiration and ninety-nine percent perspiration." This truism more than applies to the art of dance, too.

In Western culture, the main difference between the crafts of choreography, painting or musical composition and the crafts of furniture or teapot mak-ing is that the end product of the artistic practice is not likely to be useful in an obvious utilitarian sense. Designing the teapot or furniture or door chimes to be visually and sonically interesting and to evoke an aesthetic response can help functional objects become works of art, though.

Many of the methods used to create paintings, songs, dances or written works are traditional—that is, quasi-formulaic or technical in their practice. The formulas seem tried and true because they are based on consensually agreed upon methods that have worked well repeatedly across eras. These conventional methods allow for a generally stable framework within which to practice creative endeavors. Sometimes the methods used are nontraditional, however, created on the spur of the moment for developing and organizing the contents of a specific work of art in a specific context.

In the visual arts, we might describe technique as the craft of creating a complete work that is presentable to a viewer. In the performing arts, artists similarly use specific techniques for creating the structure of a play, musical or dance, but the final work is never complete until it is actually performed. Then it is gone.

In both the performing and visual arts, *technique* usually refers to an artist's mastery. Some audiences appreciate the technique of a painter, such as the 19th century Frenchman Jean-Baptiste-Camille Corot (1796–1875), who seemed to reproduce reality on a canvas. Opera audiences enjoyed the way early 20th century singer Enrico Caruso (1873–1921) held his high notes, and many theater audiences appreciated the mellifluous voice of the mid-20th century actor Richard Burton (1925–1984). A performer's ability to control his or her instrument should be a part of the audience's concern, but focusing only on the painter's brush strokes, the singer's high notes, the actor's voice or the dancer's body mechanics will not necessarily help viewers gain the richest meaning from that aesthetic, nonfunctional experience. Nevertheless, technique is an essential access point for that understanding.

Technique for any artist is the ability to create or perform a work of art so that the audience can see beyond the moment of execution into its true character or essence. This sense of the completeness of a work is often called its *gestalt*, a German word meaning "an organized whole that is perceived as more than the sum of its parts." Audiences may certainly recognize technique for its contribution to the entirety of a product or performance, but they must also strive to see *through* the technique to the substance of a work, its total expression. The performing artist must be able to use his or her developed technical ability to create a presentation that conveys the work's clearest and deepest significance to the audience.

When a dance piece is about how well the dancers jump and turn or stay together, that is not art; it is spectacle. It can be pleasurable and even breathtaking. But when technique stands alone as nothing more than a display of physical skill, it is no more meaningful than a weight lifter showing off his or her muscles. A dancer with great technique and no expression is not a dance artist. Technique and expression are symbiotic and inextricable within the arts.

Like singers, professional dancers work constantly to maintain and improve their instruments with their teachers' guidance. They strive to master technical skills that are never to be owned once accomplished. Without a routine of practice and daily exercise, the body will quickly lose strength, flexibility and a general sense of itself. Although different dance styles may feature various body types, choreographers tend to hire the dancers who appear to be at the highest state of physical fitness and body tone. Audience tolerance for the unfit at costly professional dance events is unlikely.

The body-mind-spirit is the dancer's instrument, and she or he must care for it with exercise, diet, adequate rest and intellectual stimulation. Besides a lifetime of disciplined eating and personal habits, a career in dance means daily classes where the dancer religiously practices routines that maintain and improve skills. As exercises are continued, these skills are always in a state of development with greater expectations. Injuries should be avoided, but if they occur and do not require complete rest, they must be worked with as a form of therapy within the setting of the daily class. Unlike the singer, who often practices alone, the dancer must practice with other dancers, who are all under the professional tutelage of a master teacher. Like no other artists, dancers are dedicated to technical development within a group setting. The attention and involvement of the mind and spirit are crucial in these exercise rituals in order to make the body a well-honed instrument for expression.

When dancers are in their preprofessional years, their classes can often seem overly competitive. Competition can be a great motivator as well as a producer of tension. In a professional company class, however, the atmosphere and the dancers' good sense should lead to a more reflective, internalized and focused environment, but this is not always the case. In her film "A Dancer's World" (1973), famed 20th century choreographer Martha Graham (1894–1991) said that the soloist must return daily to the studio to become one of many. No other artists have so little choice about how to maintain and improve their chances to be expressive artists.

No matter how much the dancer attempts to be expressive, only the most exquisite physical skills can allow any breadth or depth of articulation. A dancer who must hold her leg at a 120-degree angle or balance on pointe or leap into a split position because the choreography is designed that way will not accomplish the choreographer's intentions if her skills will not allow her to do those things. A dancer who must fall to his knees, wrap himself up like a pretzel and cartwheel to standing must do the tasks clearly, or the meaning of the phrase will be overshadowed by his lack of skill. Dancers must keep themselves at a generally heightened technical level to be able to perform a wide range of movements in a wide variety of styles and to be able to add specific skills for new choreographies at any moment.

The ultimate goal is to perform any given movement with the greatest accuracy and the least amount of energy necessary. The dancer must have tremendous strength, flexibility, endurance and musicality. That is skill. A movement that does not begin or end where or when the choreographer intends will communicate something other than that intention. A jump that is supposed to carry the performer to considerable height or a kick that is supposed to be higher than the head or a long, demanding phrase where the dancer must increase his energy for the climax or a soft slow movement that needs to capture a unique musical phrasing can never be eloquent or masterly without strength, flexibility, endurance and musicality.

TECHNIQUE AND THE AUDIENCE

As you watch dancers in performance, you are observing their technique as they execute choreographed movements, positions, dynamics and rhythm in relation to other dancers, often with dramatic content. It is not always possible to observe technique, though. Beginning in the 1960s, improvisation began to be featured in some works, taking audience attention away from design and technique and moving it toward the unexpected: a pedestrian aimlessly walking or turtles moving around with flashlights tied to their shells.

Sometimes an audience is fed only technique, devoid of substantial expression. Some choreography even features pyrotechnics, or fiery movements meant to evoke only applause. The applause reward goes to the performer who accomplishes the flashy or hard-to-do movements, such as high jumps in rapid succession or multiple successive pirouettes on the same leg with the gesture leg never touching the ground. For the sake of variety on a program, a dash of pyrotechnics in an appropriate setting may be acceptable and exciting.

However, the audiences new to dance should not be ready to applaud every feat that looks difficult, however much fun and striking such actions may be at the moment. Concert dance is not circus. In the styles of 19th century opera and ballet and continued in many Broadway and film musicals, some moments are singled out as "showstoppers," but, overall, individual movements and moments in the serious concert dance of the past hundred years or so are not performed just to garner cheers.

I clearly remember the embarrassment I felt as an audience member in a discomfiting mismatch of choreographic intention and audience perception of technique. The powerful 20th century dancer José Limón (1908–1972), and his company performed at the Chicago Lyric Opera House in the mid-1960s. The work was *Missa Brevis* (1958), set to music by the Hungarian composer Zoltan Kodaly (1882–1967). It confronted the horrors of war through an abstract dance staged in a set resembling a burned-out cathedral after World War II. At one point, the lead character, danced by Mr. Limón, is on his knees, then quickly "runs" sideways across the stage remaining in this low position. At this powerful theatrical moment, colored by Limón's great passion, the audience began to applaud as if Limón were performing a trick. The audience was on the lookout for tricks, thinking that this master choreographer of 20th century modern dance had included pyrotechnics to cull their favor, when in fact the choreographer-performer was employing his extraordinary technique in the service of a harrowing image.

On the other hand, when a dance piece is in the style of 19th century classical ballet or is emotionally lightweight and purports to be physically thrilling, then applauding great skill is part of the fun of watching. Generally, however, noticing technique involves a bit more subtlety.

When you want to evaluate honestly the quality or level of a dancer's technique, think hard about the level of expectation and the features of execution connected with the given style, subject matter and accepted traditions of the form before you. You then will be better able to judge the *quality* of the dancing—in other words, how the dancers' proficiency faithfully renders the choreographer's intention.

FUNDAMENTAL MOVEMENT PRINCIPLES
OF CONCERT DANCE

In this section, I offer some very general principles and prescriptions for dance movement on concert stages that might help any audience member know what to expect technically from dance performers. These prescriptions will not work well for many world dance forms, but they do provide some mainstream values of good dance teaching and learning in Western theatrical dance. Most professional dancers and choreographers employ them not because they are formulas for good technique, but because dancers who command these ideas can accomplish amazing feats.

Traditional Principles of Concert Dance Technique

The dancer should perform all movements with the greatest ease and efficiency, unless specifically asked to be awkward or inefficient. Efficiency is the ability to create any movement with the least amount of necessary energy. It is not synonymous with a lackadaisical attitude or effortlessness, however. Good technique allows the dancer to develop a working method and artistic expression that have at their core ease and efficiency, but that simultaneously allow the dancer the freedom to explore resistance, power, high energy and tension.

Dancers must move with precision. Even when they are attempting to appear awkward and inefficient or to move with high tension, only those body parts that are supposed to appear undefined or inefficient should be so.

The dancer's athletic body should show the results of a life of discipline and hard work. (The exceptions, of course, occur where choreographers want to highlight performers who represent a certain population or certain cultural norms.)

The torso should seem integrated with the movements of all limbs. When an arm or leg is moved, the torso should seem to remain quiet and efficiently maintain its shape. Look for this integration of the torso especially in kicks *(battements)*. When a dancer raises an arm or leg, the torso should still retain its basic shape. Such integration should seem to occur without effort, which takes years of practice.

The dancer's feet should be fully stretched when a limb is lifted off the floor or both limbs are off the floor in a jump. (This is not true in many ethnic forms, but mostly true in Western theatrical dance.)

The legs should be either stretched or clearly bent. Loose-looking limbs are generally reserved for comical or very specific dramatic intentions. The amount of stretch of the limbs must be (and look) predetermined.

190

The dancer should be able to hold a position in the air momentarily during a jump (this is known as *ballon*).

The dancer should be able to isolate areas of the body so that only that part seems to be (or actually is) moving.

The dancer should be able to turn on one leg and end that turn on balance before stepping into the next gesture.

The dancer should be able to lead movements with different parts of the body so that it seems as though the rest of the body follows willingly and in a connected fashion. Examples of leading gestures are the hips leading into a falling motion or a knee lifting to lead the rest of the body into a turn.

The dancer should have "extension"—that is, the strength and ability to keep a leg high off the ground for more than a brief moment.

A dancer should be able to touch, lift and support a partner without fumbling.

A dancer should be able to crouch and move close to the ground with efficiency. This is especially relevant in African, jazz and some forms of contemporary contact improvisation.

Dancers should be able to control their falling to the floor, in all directions and at all speeds, without hurting themselves.

A dancer should be able to rise onto high *relevé* (arched feet) without bending the legs.

The dancer should seem to be musical—that is, involved in some relation with the music (when there is such accompaniment). He or she may not be on the beat, but still must be musically sensitive to the accompaniment according to the choreographer's requirements.

The dancer's movements should be well defined at both the slowest and quickest speeds.

Throughout the work, the dancer should be able to perform all movements with energy, clarity and expressiveness.

A dancer should use only the degree of energy necessary to stand erect. Excess energy is necessary only for playing a specific character or for creating a specific style or mood.

The dancer should have flexibility, the optimal movement in joints allowed by their structure, with the least restrictions from habitual muscle tightness.

This flexibility will allow the extension and flexion of the legs, flowing movements of the arms and a full range of movement in the torso for bending in all directions. Not all well-trained dancers are equally flexible. Audience members might notice the degree of flexibility according to their expectations of the capability of a given body.

The dance artist should display a wide lexicon of dynamic movements, ranging from the strongest to the weakest, with a host of qualities attached to those moves. The audience should be able to sense this expressive range through the amount of purposeful muscular resistance to movement, resulting in either greater or lesser amounts of tension.

The audience should be able to understand exactly what direction the dancer is facing and where the dancer's eyes are focused. Sometimes one or more body parts are choreographed to face different directions at the same time, and various choreographic or dramatic intentions call for different levels of intensity for eye focus. An audience can judge whether the focus fits and serves the choreographic intention.

The dancer's eyes should be expressive and reveal the movement's intention rather than wander about to see if he or she is in the right place at the right time. Dancers train their use of peripheral vision, sense of location in space and sound markers in the music to free their eyes to reveal what they are imagining.

The dancer should seem focused on the content of the choreography, not on how well he or she is doing.

The dancer should be able to draw the audience into his or her focus.

Describing Movement

There are no good or bad movements other than ones that will hurt a dancer's body. There is no hierarchy of movements that make some worth more than others. We cannot say that a slow gesture of the head is worth less in a choreographic work than a triple turn followed by a daring somersault. It depends on the choreographic intention. Instead, the best we can do when speaking of the techniques used in a dance work is to describe what we see and then assess how well the action fulfilled the dancer's and choreographer's objectives. A basic vocabulary can be used to associate technique (the "how") with any specific gesture (the "what").

Uncomplicated Gestures

A gesture is a simple movement that lasts for a variable amount of time and incorporates a variety of energies. It can be a simple shift of weight or a complex, disjointed movement of any or all parts of the body. It can be as quick as a pointing of the finger at someone or a slow, labored rising from the floor to a standing position.

In describing movement, begin by pinpointing *what* part of the body moved: the arm, the leg, the foot or several parts at the same time? Then describe from *where* and to where the part moved. For example, "In the thematic gesture, the right hand moved from touching the dancer's left knee, up along the left leg and then along the left side of the body, until it stopped at the left shoulder." Then describe *how* the body part was moved: slowly, abruptly, fragmentally, smoothly, rigidly or some combination of these actions? Describe the *qualities* of the movement as well—sensual, deliberate, thoughtful, careless and so forth—and the relationship between the components of the movement. Did parts begin moving and end moving at the same moment, or were they initiated or ended at different times?

COMMON VOCABULARY OF WESTERN THEATRICAL DANCE

This chapter presents only some of the words for the movements and attitudes commonly seen in ballet, modern dance and jazz. Unfortunately, this short list cannot even begin to indicate the multitude of variations available in the use of these movements. It also does not address motivation. Even if I were to include notes about the most functional way to perform these movements, they may not be accurate because choreographers are likely to alter the vocabulary for expressive or stylistic reasons.

General

Adagio: Slow movements, or a name for a slow partnered section of a classical pas de deux (duet).

Allegro: Fast movements, or a name for a quick partnered section of a classical duet.

Petit allegro: Quick movements, especially used in ballet for fast movements of the feet and small jumps.

Grand allegro: Used especially in ballet to describe big jumps and leaps. In most other forms, it is more fitting to use the English words *jumps, leaps, runs, skips* and *hops.*

Ballon: This is the quality of "bounce." A dancer who seems to land and spring off again like a rubber ball is said to have ballon. It creates the illusion that the dancer temporarily stays in the air for a second. Mikhail Baryshnikov (b. 1948) and Vaslav Nijinsky (1890–1950) were two classical ballet dancers who had incredible ballon.

Barre: A railing that surrounds most dance studios. It is meant to be used gently to stabilize a dancer's balance as he or she works on a variety of exercises. While the dancer exercises the right leg, he or she lightly touches the barre with the left hand, and vice versa. Barre exercises also include stretches and *port de bras* ("carriage of the arms") at varying speeds. Although ballet dancers seem to be "born at the barre," most contemporary dancers use it as well. The word *barre* also relates to the first part of ballet class. Choreographies, films and theater pieces have used the barre as a primary image for the training of a dancer and for the dancer's daily life.

Battement: Refers to kicks, low or high. In *battements* of any height, there should be minimal distortion of the torso other than for dramatic effect or choreographic design. Dancers work for years to be able to thrust a gesture leg off the ground without destroying the integration of the torso and therefore the quiet balance of the entire body on the standing leg. The term *grand battement* is widely used in ballet, modern and jazz dance to mean a very large, "grand" kick.

Petit battement tendu: From a closed position, a movement to or at the *tendu* position (pointed toe on the floor).

Petit battement dégagé: A movement to just above the *tendu* position, slightly off the floor from a closed position.

Bourrée: A very rapid succession of small steps performed on pointe in place or while moving. The tips of the feet seem to press down or trammel the earth below. The *bourrée* historically has been performed by women in ballet and can be used for both agitated and serene effects depending on the degree of calm in the torso and face.

Character: The role a dancer plays in a dramatic work. It can also refer to the dancer's own persona behind the dance steps and is a name for ballet steps and whole ballets *(caractère)*, usually based on folk dances originating mostly from European sources, such as the czardas from Hungary and the polonaise from Poland.

Combination: A series of steps linked together, usually as an exercise in a dance class. One or two dance phrases may also be called a combination. The term *phrase* is used more often when discussing a dance piece.

Contraction/release: These terms describe a way of moving in many 20th century dance works. There is no one position or series of positions for the contraction/release. It is movement that seems to be initiated with a rather propulsive and tense forward titling of the pelvis, quickly followed by a subtle upward flexion of the remainder of the torso, resulting in a bound (tight and held) position. The release refers to the release of this bound energy, which initiates a return to a centered, more efficient position and on to the next movement.

Développé: The foot of the gesture leg is first drawn up to the height of the knee of the supporting leg into the *retiré* or *passé* position, and then the leg straightens smoothly to a gesture at varying heights, often parallel to the floor. This is a common movement in almost all forms of dance. Reversing the process is called an enveloppé.

Dunham wave: A wavelike sequence of flexion and extension beginning at the pelvis and then moving through each vertebra to the skull. Before the flexion or extension sequence has ended, the reverse direction begins, creating the illusion of a spinal wave. One could simply call it a "body wave," but I choose to honor Katherine Dunham (b. 1909), who has provided Western theatrical dance world with a codified vocabulary of African and African-inflected gestures.

Dynamics: The vocabulary of dynamics or changes of energy is a complex combination of efforts: flow, force and timing. Flow can be bound or free—that is, with varying amounts of resistance. When resistance is greater, the movement is more bound, and when it is lesser, the movement seems freer. The amount of force or energy applied to a movement allow us to describe it as *strong* or *light*. The effort can be accomplished *suddenly* or *gradually*, and the length of time of an effort can be *quick* or *sustained*. This construct for discussing dynamics is a very quick overview of the language of effort handed down by Hungarian dancer and theorist Rudolf Laban (1879–1958). Movements that punch, glide, squeeze, wring, toss, tap, stroke, strike, dart and press are some combination of these efforts.

En face: A good way to describe a dancer when he is facing the audience.

En l'aire: Describes a gesture leg that remains off the ground for the duration of the movement, or a dancer who is actually in the air.

Épaulement: Refers to the isolated axial movements of the torso, shoulders and head that characterize balletic poses and movements. In the 20th century technique of Martha Graham, the rotating torso often initiated movements of the whole body.

Feet, positions of: There are five basic positions of the two feet while standing in ballet, but only four of them have relevance to a new audience. In classical ballet technique, both the hips and legs are turned out, whereas in modern dance and jazz they can be rotated to varying degrees. Classical ballet technique demands a turnout of the legs, but dancers in all forms of concert dance refer to these relationships of the feet as first, second, fourth and fifth, whether turned out or not. Obviously, because of turnout and possible directional relationships, many positions are not named at all.

First position: a "closed" position with the heels together, feet turned out (usually to a natural position), and both legs directly under the torso.

Second position: an "open" position with the legs side to

side, separated by the length of a dancer's foot in ballet and wider in some other dance forms.

Fourth position: an "open" position with the relation of the legs described as one *forward* and the other *backward*. The stride or width is approximately the length of a dancer's foot in ballet and wider in some other forms.

Fifth position: A "closed" position, with one foot crossed in front or in back of the other. The degree of overlap varies among the styles of ballet.

Isolation: When a dancer is able to draw a viewer's attention to the movement of one part or section of his body—such as the ribs, head, hips or fingers—and the rest of his body seems not to move, the dancer has "isolated " a body part. A special sort of isolation, called *part leading,* occurs when the viewer's attention is drawn to a particular part of the anatomy as the dancer seems to lead or initiate a movement from that section or part, and the rest of the body follows passively or in some kind of response to the initiated movement.

Penché: A tilting of the body in positions begun on one leg, while the other leg is lifting at a considerable height, at least 90 degrees. Upon completion of the lift, the body then tilts back toward its original position. The *arabesque penché* is the most common, beginning with the dancer's leg in arabesque (90 degrees or higher to the front, side or back). The torso usually maintains its relation to the gesture leg during the tilt, but the angle between both legs opens considerably. In some ballet or modern dance companies, *penchés* greater that 180 degrees are used. Choreographers can use *penchés* or tilts to the side and to the back, and even with the leg to the side and the body tilting forward.

Plié: Refers to a "bending of the knees," but is better described as a lowering of the entire torso by means of flexing the thigh joints, knees and ankles. In most ballets, it is performed with the legs turned outward, but a *plié* is still a *plié* at other degrees of turnout. In positions where the legs are closed or in a forward-back relationship (first, fifth or fourth), the bend normally is complete before the heels must lift off the ground in order

197

to accommodate the limits of bending or flexion of the ankle joint *(demi plié)*. At that point, the weight is transferred to the ground via the balls of the feet, and the body lowers farther *(grand plié)*. The *demi plié* refers to the depth of a *plié* before the moment where the heels would have to lift from the floor, at which point the *grand plié* begins. In the second position, where the legs are open in a side-to-side relationship *(à la seconde)*, the heels do not leave the floor at any depth of the *plié*, and the weight remains transferred through the whole foot, both heels and toes.

Pointe, point work, toe: In many ballets, female dancers traditionally dance on their toes *(sur les pointes)* in pointe shoes, or toe shoes, which have a hard, built-in box that allows them to support their entire body weight. The dancer on pointe in a ballet must be able to balance on this box with the aid of a partner or by herself. Rising or stepping quickly to pointe or rising slowly to pointe takes great strength. The audience should expect that if a ballet is danced on pointe, the dancers have the capacity to rise fully onto and to descend smoothly from the pointes.

Port de bras: Like the word *plié*, the term *port de bras* refers to the act of moving or "carrying" the arms in ballet, though other dance forms might name positions and patterns of the arms quite differently. In ballet, the positions of the arms are numbered. Not all ballet systems are exactly alike, but these few positions are most common. Four of the two-arm positions occur regularly:

> **First position:** arms forward, elbows rounded, middle finger tips touching in front of the waist.

> **Second position:** arms opened sideward, sloping downward, elbows slightly rounded, with the fingertips at about the level of the navel. In most styles, the arms will be slightly ahead of the torso. It will nearly always be safe to describe arms to the side as being "in second position."

> **Fifth position *en haute:*** arms slightly rounded above the head, middle finger tips nearly touching.

> **Fifth position *en bas:*** Arms slightly rounded, hanging

downward with fingers about a hand's length away from each other, and the little fingers nearly touching the tops of the thighs. This position can also be called *bras bas* ("low arms").

Relevé: The dancer rises from the standing position in which the whole soles of the feet contact the floor to a position in which the heels are raised off the floor. These raises can be performed at various tempi and to varying heights. If the feet are "arched" with the weight of the body on the balls of the feet, that is usually called three-quarter point. The dancer who is on full point in pointshoes is also in *relevé*. It is standard for the knees to be stretched along with the *relevé*. Dancers work hard to be able to have both a fully flexible and a strong arch. There is nothing more amateur looking than a relevé that is supposed to be on a fully stretched leg but is not.

Retiré: A movement in which the gesture foot is drawn toward the knee of the supporting leg. The position of the foot at the height of the knee of the standing leg is also called *retiré*. The word *passé* is also commonly used for the *retiré* position as it passes through that position. Many pirouettes are performed in *retiré*, and the position is nearly as common for positions standing on one leg, either turned in or turned out, as is the *plié*. In a pure *retiré*, the dancer's hips should clearly establish "front" (*en face*), and the torso should not change its shape whether the *retiré* is turned out or in.

Rond de jambe: A circular movement pattern of the entire gesture leg, at various heights with various degrees of flexion. The gesture is usually straight in ballet, but can also be in *attitude* (bent). In anatomical terms, it is a circumduction, but to the audience it appears like a fanning of the leg, depending on the speed and the height of the movement. The standing leg can be in *plié*, straight, in *relevé*, on pointe or at changing levels. It is called a *grand rond de jambe* when it is executed at a 90-degree height.

Temps lié: Describes a linking of standing ballet positions through the use of a *plié* while moving between the positions. Therefore, the *temps lié* will seem like a sinking movement when traveling between these positions. Although this is a ballet term, the use of the linking *plié* is of utmost importance in any dance that demands these changes, which are, of course, regular requirements in most dances.

Terre-à-terre: Describes when a dancer performs quick steps, maintaining contact with the ground, and excludes jumps. Literally it means "earth to earth."

Turnout: Refers to the amount or degree of rotation in a dancer's legs. Although ballet dancers use a greater degree of turnout than dancers in other styles, most dancers today can turn out or in whenever called upon to do so. The typical classical ballet stance or movement of the legs employs turnout.

Turns

Turns, like all movements, should fit into individual choreographies and are not always alike in their dynamics, starting positions, ending positions or number. The great dance composition teacher Louis Horst (1884–1964) would sarcastically say to budding choreographers, "When in doubt, turn!" The body and its dynamics should be clearly shaped in a turn.

Chaîné: A series of quick turns that move across the floor alternating weight between feet, making one full turn after every two changes of weight. The head will usually spot sharply in ballet.

Pirouettes: Turning balances on one leg. Turns or pirouettes are most commonly seen with the gesture leg in *retiré, attitude* (forward or back) or arabesque at various heights, but any position can be used. In ballet, the torso will most likely be erect, but in jazz or modern dance it can be distorted for dramatic effect. Especially in ballet, the dancer often spins more than once, although a single pirouette that ends on balance before the dancer moves on to the next step is more technically demanding than a double turn that ends falling away from the balance point. Many dancers can fool an audience into thinking that multiple turns are more demanding than a well-ended single. The participation of the arms should contribute to the turn but not use more energy than is necessary to keep with the dramatic atmosphere of a work.

Spotting: This is a technique of focusing the eyes toward one spot while turning. As the body turns and the head can no longer twist to accommodate the focus point, the dancer's head releases quickly, joins the action of the turn, and the eyes quickly refocus on the same spot. It looks as if the body begins the turn, and then the head follows and completes the turn before the body. It is a technique that helps a dancer avoid becoming dizzy during multiple turns and that gives clarity and precision to the direction from which a turn begins and ends.

Tour en l'air: A turn in the air.

Jumps

There are five basic kinds of jumps: those that begin and end on two feet (generic *sautés*); those that begin on two feet and end on one *(sissonne)*; those that begin on one foot and end on two *(assemblé)*; those that begin on one foot and end on the same foot *(temps levé,* or hop); and those that begin on one foot and end on the other *(jeté,* or leap). All jumps, aside from some comical or character jumps, will begin and end in *plié.* Jumps also may be done turning in the air and with all sorts of body and leg variations.

As in turns, the body and its dynamics need to contribute to the execution of the jump and to be shaped to fit the expression of the choreography. In all concert dance, we can expect that the feet have pointed fully to enable the dancer to reach his desired height. We should expect that the torso and arms reflect the expression of the dance work and not the effort of lifting many pounds of bones and muscles off the floor.

Assemblé: A jump that begins on one leg and ends on two legs. A common balletic variation of the *assemblé* includes an "assembling" of the legs while in the air before landing in fifth position.

Changements: Used mostly in classical ballet, these jumps begin on two feet in fifth position and land on two feet after their

201

relative forward/back positions have changed during the jump. If the right leg is in front at the start, it will end in back. If the legs exchange two or three times in the air, it is called an *entrechat quatre* or *entrechat six,* respectively. *Entrechats* are not common in dance forms other than ballet.

Échappé: A jump that begins in fifth position plié and lands in second position. *Échappé* may also begin in fifth or first position plié and slide, without a jump, and end in second position *relevé* (usually done by the ballerina in pointe shoes).

Grand jeté: The dancer takes off from one leg and lands on the other in a big leap that starts with a kick or *battement.* Leaps can travel in any direction, although forward and sideways are most common, in that order. The dancer often opens or "splits" the legs in the midst of the flight for extra excitement or dramatic flavor.

Temps levé: A hop of varying heights in a variety of positions. A *grand temps levé* is a hop in arabesque, sometimes called a *grand sauté arabesque.* Good dancers are able to seem to pose the *temps levé* in the air (*ballon*) in positions such as arabesque, *à la seconde* and *retiré.* In modern dance and jazz, it is better to call this movement a hop or a skip.

Gesture Leg Positions

When a limb does not transfer weight into the floor, it becomes a gesture. Each of the following positions is normally performed with minimal distortion of the torso, but the distortion tends to increase with increased height of the gesture leg. Dancers may use positions with the tips of the toes of the gesture leg touching the ground or lifted to the height of the ears. They may have their legs straight or bent. In all of the positions listed here, no weight is transferred to the floor through the gesture leg.

Arabesque: Also known as *à la quatrième derrière,* or "at the fourth in back." The imaginary centerline of the torso presents itself in a C-shaped curve, with the skull centered on the uppermost vertebrae. Many different variations of accompanying arm positions are possible. The audience can expect arabesques to have a smooth, C-shape centerline and for the skull to be minimally distorted.

Attitude: Refers to a pose with the gesture leg clearly rounded or bent at varying degrees and held at various heights, especially parallel to the ground and higher.

Dégagé: Indicates a pointed or stretched leg (and foot) where the toes appear to be barely off the floor or on up to 45 degrees off the floor.

Quatrième devant, à la: Means "at the fourth in front." The leg gesture points to the front of the body.

Seconde, à la: Means "to the second." Just as when feet or arms open side to side in standing position means second position, when one leg functions as a gesture to the side, it is also in second position, or "*à la seconde.*"

Tendu, or *pointe tendu:* Indicates a pointed or stretched foot (and leg) where the toes appear to be in contact with the floor to the front, side or back, but the weight of the body is held on the standing leg.

CHAPTER FIFTEEN

introduction

Because the dancer *is* the dance—literally the *embodiment* of the choreography—it is easy to mistake the dancer for the choreographer (although sometimes she or he is). Sometimes the dancers have collaborated so closely with the choreographer that they may deserve to be listed in the program as choreographers. In order to discern the difference between the dancer and the dance—where the dancer as person-artist starts and where and how the choreography adheres to the dancer's body—one must see a great deal of dance, in both performance and rehearsal if possible. The word *choreography* comes from the ancient Greek word *khoreia*, meaning "to dance in unison," which in turn originated with the Greek word *khoros*, meaning "chorus." In ballet, there is still the "chorus" of the *corps de ballet*, but choreography today embodies so much more.

SEEING CHOREOGRAPHY: SEPARATING THE DANCE FROM THE DANCER

Myron Howard Nadel

After a dance performance, dance audiences will sometimes say, "That was great choreography," when what they really mean is that the dancers' performances of the steps pleased them. Others might say, "That choreography was difficult," but what they really mean is that the steps were difficult to perform, which is not necessarily an important part of a dance composition. Describing the dancers' performances or the relative difficulty of the steps does not tackle the issue of the choreography. If a dance is truly engrossing and the audience is enabled to become one with the moments of performance, a successful confluence of the choreography with the dance probably took place. The audience might subsequently review how that successful integration occurred. If the audience finds that the dancers seemed proficient, yet their communication to them seemed dysfunctional, then, too, the composition might need to be examined.

Separating the impact of the performed dance—that is, its visual and performance elements—from the blueprint or choreography of that dance is one of the most daunting and rewarding tasks for audiences both new to dance and accustomed to it. It is the first step, however, in being able to discuss choreography and to reach beyond initial responses.

THE CHOREOGRAPHER

Working with dancers in creating a dance is a long and tedious process, where respect and patience from both parties are crucial. The actual labors of choreography are carried out in a rather public setting—a dance studio. It takes years of experience to know how to approach dancers, for each new piece is a new idea, each dancer is different, and each dancer may feel different each day. A choreographer's task is the equivalent of both a playwright's and a director's, with the actors waiting for their dialogue and preparing the work for a performance at the same time. Building a dance calls for creativity, knowledge of psychology and group dynamics, teaching skills and, most of all, close human interaction.

A choreographer's talent may be a gift, but the craft is learned. Like any artist, the choreographer, whether consciously or unconsciously, creates from the sum of her or his experiences. These experiences begin in two ways: with direct observation of established choreographers as they create both successful and unsuccessful works, and in the more structured university programs that teach courses in choreography.

In the 1930s, Louis Horst (1884–1964), Martha Graham's mentor, guide and musical director, began teaching dance composition to young dancers and actors. Although Horst was a musician, not a dancer, his deep knowledge of musical composition, artistic styles and theatrical dance informed his methods as he led dancers from the world of pure inspiration to one that combined passion with the tools of logic. His ideas were never meant to be or taken as recipes for good dances. Instead, he taught budding choreographers the concepts of form and style that were taught to composers, playwrights and visual artists. Horst believed that once choreographers were informed about a fairly long list of extant methods of structuring in time and space, borrowed from the other arts, they would be able to break the molds and create new structures for the dance. He felt that choreography could rarely rise to the level of art if it were based only on looking good or feeling good, without such understanding.

Choreographers begin their adventure by needing two things: dancers and ideas. The first may be acquired by simply asking a few dancers and other choreographers if they would like to contribute to a rather sparsely produced workshop performance. The second is much more difficult. Creating a dance can be an inspired activity or merely a task. For instance, the idea for a dance might occur in a dream or might be forced upon the choreographer because a concert date must be met. The idea for a dance might come from the conditions of a character in literature or from the human condition itself, a human relationship, a love of animals or plant life, a deep anger or concern about an event or social problem, a dancer's own potential for movement or idiosyncratic designs, a pure interest in the feel and shape of movement or a special love for a piece of music that seems to generate movement. Complicated plots, grandiose subjects such as a war or political philosophy and other themes that need explanation or development outside the dance world are probably not good sources for dance ideas. The core idea for a dance must be the physical expression of an internal state. Just about any inspiration for a dance, however, can be credible if its focus is physical expression.

THE CHOREOGRAPHY

The choreographic process may begin with the creation of short bundles of one or more gestures, which are then combined together into longer bundles of movement patterns until the end of a section or even the entire dance. Recognizing the patterns of the movement bundles and then seeing how they are linked or arranged into a composition are the first steps to analyzing or actualizing a dance creation.

Skill in choreography, as in any creative endeavor, is the ability to analyze the possibilities; the art is in the proper selection of those possibilities.

Whatever the source of inspiration that holds a piece together, the choreographer will develop movement patterns that we call a *theme* or *core movement bundle*. A long, complicated work often has more than one of these themes. All movements, no matter how simply they are used, and all bundles, no matter how intricate their manipulation and development, will always fall into the three broad categories of space, time and energy. In other words, no movement can exist, let alone be danced, without filling space, spending time and using energy.

Several good texts on composition are available, although they may be somewhat dogmatic for a novice. If a choreographer studies all points of view and learns the rules for the sake of finding her own way, then the texts and especially the theories in them are useful. If she takes the rules or theories too literally, however, she may never find her own way and may wind up a crafty but uninspired artist. Choreographers in training must respect rules until the rules are a part of their unconscious. Only then will they be able consciously to form unique styles.

Every dance either starts with or includes at some point one or more movements or gestures that are the crux of the composition. All movements in a dance are connected to all other movements. Those few crucial gestures and their connections are the keys to the map of a composition.

LOOKING AT THE CHOREOGRAPHY

If a dance has had some success in seizing our attention, we may have carried away one or many more unique visual images of various durations from what may seem like a still photograph to a series of movements. As we try to re-create the images in our minds as well as we can, we can use a short list of starter questions (not all at once, of course) initially to help us to describe the spatial features of a core gesture bundle and then to form perspectives about those images that might support our notions about the choreography of a dance work.

How many dancers are involved?

Which body part or parts move?

What are the geometric relationships of the body parts?

What is the range of movements? If large, how large?

In what direction are the dancer's eyes focused?

Where is the dancer in the performing space?

Which body part seems to lead?

What shape does the body carve in space?

At what level is the movement or position? Is the dancer on the floor, lying, sitting, standing, jumping, falling? Does the body change levels?

Does the body stay in one place, or does it travel?

What is the locus or path of the center of gravity of the bodies as the dancers travel from one place to another?

Do the images create some sort of connection to what we know, have felt or have seen previously, either in reality or in our minds?

Other questions lead us into a description of time or rhythmic elements of the theme or core bundle:

Can we sound out or clap out any of the rhythmic images of the patterns of movement?

How much time does the movement take? One second? Five seconds?

Do the motions of more than one dancer or more than one part of the dancer's body occur simultaneously?

Where is the impulse located? With which dancer? In what part of the body?

What are the reactions to the impulse or impulses that follow? Are they in quick succession, or are there pauses? How long are the pauses? Are there a quick series of movement reactions?

Is there an underlying pulse? Is the pulse regular or irregular? If it is irregular, how much time is there between the irregularly recurring pulses?

Do the movements seem to mimic the music? Are they totally independent, or do they work in tandem, with effective convergences in time?

Are the energy patterns involved in the visual and rhythmic images full of contrast and dynamics? (For example, lack of contrasting energy patterns can either be monotonous or create a tension of its own.)

We probably will not be able to answer all these questions to our satisfaction, but whatever decisions we make about what we think we saw, then we should ask, "Do my explorations tell me anything about the overall mood(s), movement expressions or symbols that the work might be trying to provide?" For example, if the movements seem jerky, quick and indirect, and the title of the work is *Life in the Fast Lane,* we might conclude that, at least, the choice of movements is appropriate for the subject matter. If the movements are strong and slow, with circular arm designs performed while the dancer is kneeling on the floor, we might want to see if some alternative perspective on "life in the fast lane" is calling out to us.

After the core bundle or theme is analyzed, the next challenge is to determine how the gestures and movement bundles were linked, without necessarily being exact about where a gesture or gesture bundle actually began and ended. This is a theoretical problem that has never been solved or defined satisfactorily to me. For the sake of argument, most dancers and audience members seem to "know" kinesthetically where and when a movement ends. The point is that after the most complete analysis of the core gesture or bundle (which in the finished dance may occur anywhere or multiple times), an analysis of the possible interrelationships of movements can begin.

Repetition

The choreographer's most important tool, like the musical composer's, is repetition. Repetition is the key to unifying a work in time. *Exact repetition* is only one form of repetition, but it still allows time and energy patterns to be varied. Its effective and subtle use can keep an audience hooked because they now know something about the individual bundle when they see it repeated in various guises.

The overuse of exact repetition without substantial reason will obviously become monotonous. The audience can discover that the time in between the repeated movements can change as well as the overall tempo of a group of repeated movements or bundles. Clever choreographers use exact repetition in one or more dimensions while manipulating the other dimensions, and they deal with the time between movements as if it were one of the elements of the choreography.

Other forms of repetition include *reverse repetition,* in which the movement begins where the core movement ended and traces itself back along the same spatial track until the beginning. In *body part repetition,* the general spatial pattern is repeated by another body part. If an arm twists in a certain way, perhaps that twist can be repeated exactly by the other arm or modified for the head or both. *Divided repetition* takes part of a gesture and repeats only that part. *Spatial repetition* involves performing a certain gesture in one position and then repeating it in another position. These forms of exact repetition can be combined and repeated as well, which is the simplest basis of developing movement through manipulation.

Other types of repetition include: *variation of duration,* where the duration of the repeated movement is either elongated or shortened; and *expansion* or *diminution repetition,* where a gesture that first appears small expands until it is larger (a small circling of the foot becomes a grand swinging leg movement), and vice versa (a large back bend diminishes to a tiny nod of the head).

The choices a choreographer makes must have a logical basis for controlling the information presented in any piece, for the moment that two gestures or two movement bundles are created, a relationship exists between the two. If we call the first movement A, the other movement could be B if it seems different enough. It could be similar enough to be called A prime. The choreographer must also consider the time between the movements. How long is that pause? Is the pause significant enough to develop as an add-on to one or the other movements?

As more of the dance is created, the choreographer must control, organize and arrange the increasingly complex collections of movement. This conscious arrangement of the content requires the recognition of *form.* Of course, it also requires the ability to know when to stop. As renowned dancer-choreographer Doris Humphrey (1895–1958) reminds us, all dances are too long!

Form

In order to comprehend the craft of composing movements, we need a good working definition of *form:* it is quite simply the arrangement of parts. It is the way that gestures or movement bundles are arranged in one section, but it is also the distribution of all the parts of the entire work.

Form in choreography entails placing the parts of the dance into some order or planned relationship. This relationship is repeatable, meaning that in both its micro- and its macrocircumstances it will remain the same each time the piece is performed. The form or blueprint of the piece will unfold according to a plan. Although there are no rules for what form a piece should take, we might want to remember the familiar principle "form follows function." In our case, the choreographer needs to arrange or systematically order the individual parts into larger parts, called *sections,* and compose the sections into a whole work that functions successfully in some fashion.

A very common whole form is called the *telic form*, literally meaning "tending toward an end." Ups and downs as well as increases and releases build toward an eventual climax and end. A sort of telic time arrow holds together most works in the Western performing arts. It is the theatrical way. The friction of the phrasing heightens an experience, allowing us to rest momentarily at times, but then building up to an ending. Most good stories or films do the same. Even if played down, the denouement is commonly a return to the tone set out at the beginning of a work. Without the forward pressure of the telic arrow, Western audiences find themselves losing concentration. Dances or whole programs of dances with many sections are programmed to build to a climax.

Sophisticated audiences can also enjoy works that seem to ramble or avoid climactic ends. Not all dances come to an end button or conclusion. An ending that does not actually stop (dancers continue to move as the curtain comes down, for example) often illustrates a statement about the formal telic process, wherein the choreographer might be saying, "See, I have taken you to the end, but there is no end."

The most common formal arrangement is the *ternary form:* a beginning form, a middle form and a return to the beginning form—a kind of birth, life and death cycle. Most audiences find this three-part form satisfying because of its familiarity to humans in our daily lives. Presenting an integrated section A, contrasting that with B and then returning to the original A idea gives an audience a sense of connection and completion. Most forms of Western dance and music, including those based on chronological stories, employ either simple or complicated variations of the ternary form.

The following questions regarding the structure of the dance can help determine if the formal design is rational and clear:

> What kinds of repetition are used in the dance?

> Are movements organized into clear phrases, some of which end and some of which seem to end? Is it similar to a composition that has phrases, long and short, and endings in sentences?

> If the structure seems similar to a sentence structure, has the choreographer kept like ideas together and then gone on to new ideas in new paragraphs, or does the entire dance seem to occur in one ongoing section?

Does the dance seem to be in sections: ABA, AABA, ABACAD, or some other variation of the ABA form? The ABACAD form is called a *rondo*, a variation of the ternary form. It consists of a "home" section, then ventures to a new theme and development, returns to home for a while, then ventures out again and returns until the composer's or choreographer's ideas are completed. Dances, movies, plays and musical pieces often start in one place with one idea, tell their story or offer variations in alternating sections and then return "home" in the intervals between contrasting sections.

Does the form of the dance, its sections and structure, match that of the accompaniment? If so, has the choreographer become the slave to the music, or do the dance and the music have an interesting relationship?

Does the formal arrangement of the parts make sense with regard to the overall subject matter?

Style

Style combines all elements of a dance (movement content, design in time, subject matter, images, music and form) to create the *character* of a work. It is not possible for a dance to lack style any more than it can lack form. It just may be difficult for an audience member to nail down one simple word to describe that overall style.

The style of a dance most often should be consistent, but it can be inconsistent if the subject matter requires it to be so. Style as an approach can refer to a certain period in history; a philosophy; a religious practice; a local, ethnic or national idea; another artist's output or a subset of movement ideas. The word *style* has a kind of mystique about it in that it can be used to describe whole categories of similar works, the character of a very simple unit in one work or merely personal mannerisms.

Elements of style tend to reappear within the artistic works of individual artists, cultures, or time periods, and these reappearing traits, qualities or features may be grouped into style categories. In dance, style categories reflect unique uses of space, time, energy motivation, form, subject matter and historical and cultural references. Styles can be grouped to help us perceive apparently unrelated features that reappear in multiple works, so we can talk about, study and ultimately understand comparisons between works, artists, time periods and cultures.

For example, the romantic ballet was an extremely popular dance style during the 1830s and 1840s in Europe and was characterized by a fascination with the supernatural and exotic, usually involving ethereal and idealized spirits of women, as in *La Sylphide* (1832) and *Giselle* (1841). These works can still be seen in the repertory of many companies.

Oppositional concepts of style also can be helpful tools in describing and comparing the manner of works, from ancient history to the present: Apollonian/Dionysian, concrete/abstract and intellectual/sensual.

Contemporary naming of Apollonian and Dionysian stylistic perspectives is credited to philosopher Friedrich Wilhelm Nietzsche (1844–1900). *Apollonian* refers to the ancient Greek sun god, Apollo, who represents the straightforward, serious, upright, noble and universally tragic. His character celebrates the intellect and vision. In opposition is the *Dionysian*, referring to Dionysus, the Greek god of wine, who represents the wild, frivolous, emotionally charged, passionate and personally tragic. The neoclassicist George Balanchine (1904–1983) choreographed a dance in 1928 called *Apollo* (originally, *Apollon Musagète*), still in the repertory of the New York City Ballet and other companies, which includes numerous overt images embodying the sun god's inherently focused nature as he directs his muses about the stage. The very next year Balanchine choreographed *Prodigal Son*, which includes a Dionysian revelry scene full of drunken characters who savagely strip the hero of all his worldly possessions. In their works, many choreographers have included allusions both overt and subtle to these two powerful oppositional forces.

The *abstract*, with its sense of exaggeration, distortion, substitution and symbolism, is often contrasted with the *concrete*, or whatever is realistic, tangible and definite. Even though dance involves the very real presence of bodies, it is by its very nature inherently abstract. Like other arts, it often tends toward the sensual rather than the intellectual. The sensual in the dance world appeals directly to humans' animal senses and may even refer to sexuality, but it still maintains a decorum, distance and conscious abstraction. Merce Cunningham's (b. 1919) dances invariably feel abstract because they rarely use narratives, single points of reference on stage or any recognizable coordination of accompaniment to the movements. On the other hand, Marius Petipa's (1818–1910) *The Nutcracker* (1892) is universally recognized in the West as the penultimate story ballet and is a very concrete and straightforward dance for audiences to experience. Cunningham's abstractions often appear in realistic and tangible ways, too, if only because his male and female bodies move in space with their strongly sculpted technique on display; his distinctions between abstract and concrete opposition are quite clear. And *The Nutcracker,* as accessible and linear a story as it is, certainly has its sensual, fantastic side in the mice-soldier battle, the snow scene and the Land of the Sweets variations, culminating in the romantic *grand pas de deux* (grand duet) between the cavalier and his princess. The point is, oppositional styles make for richly charged experiences onstage and contribute greatly to the pleasurable energies and tensions in choreography.

If we were to examine the output of a choreographer over a lifetime or through single works, we might be able to determine a very personal style. Twyla Tharp's (b. 1941) work tends to have a quirky, spontaneous-looking, vernacular mix of classical, modern and jazzy vocabularies, often with a humorous edge, as seen in such pieces as *Deuce Coupe* (1973) and *Push Comes to Shove* (1976). George Balanchine could be funny, too, with his playful, jazz-inflected, adopted American sensibility, but he also developed his own Apollonian, neoclassical formality clearly connected to the Petipa tradition of technical sophistication. An individual's psychological, cultural, educational, social, political and personal experiences both consciously and unconsciously influence elements of his or her style.

Styles rooted in a particular location-time are called *period styles.* A few examples of Western period styles are the medieval, the baroque, the classical, the impressionist and the modern. The Eastern world also has its period styles, and a choreographer might refer to many other established categories of styles, such as primitive, jazz, Americana, cerebral, folk, sacred and pop.

Style is an important field of study that encompasses the arts and cultures of all historical periods. In order to define a style, it may be easiest to describe all the elements of a dance: title, subject matter, use of space, rhythm, use of energy, music, lights, costumes, props and set pieces. Because style includes all the elements of a dance, we have begun to describe it simply by identifying those elements.

Many obstacles will interfere with an audience member's ability to separate the choreography from the performance. A dancer's exemplary technique can disguise poorly organized movement; conversely, well-constructed compositions can be buried within a distractingly poor performance. Viewers new to dance may be influenced easily by loud and extended applause or "bravos" directed solely toward one dancer, which may distract them from both the craft and choreography behind the dance.

The only way to master being able to separate the choreography (movement, form and style) from the performance is to watch a great deal of dance so that you can discuss either the dancers or the dance accurately and intelligently—but also perhaps poetically and passionately.

CHAPTER SIXTEEN

introduction

Imagine the exasperation of musicians trying to learn a string quartet from a CD, or actors and directors mounting a play while relying on the memory of actors who had been in the play only once before. Without a notated repertory of works, dance is in a similar situation. Representing human movement on paper or on the computer is a complex task because the dimensions of space, time and energy need to be considered if any measure of accuracy is to be accomplished. Nevertheless, such a system is necessary for dance to have a literature that can be analyzed, studied and re-created.

Recording dance for future production has been a concern of dance makers for centuries. Transcribing movements onto paper is exceedingly difficult because bodies are three-dimensional objects that perform multiple and simultaneous movements using more than two hundred joints or fulcrums of motion. Sometimes bodies move in tandem with other bodies, perform dissimilar patterns, interweave together in intricate designs, change levels of energy and relate differently to rhythmic and tonal conditions of musical accompaniment. These complexities have made interpretations and imitations more common than reconstructions, which provide the clearest approximations of the original dance.

Today, dance companies hire notators and reconstructors to record dances that they wish to preserve or to reconstruct dances that are already recorded. The notation system must be as accurate as necessary to make reconstruction possible years after a dance has faded from the muscle memory of the choreographer or company members. Of course, a degree of interpretation is expected. Without a dance score, though, each succeeding revival is but a rougher and rougher imitation of the original work.

During earlier centuries, various notation systems have served the parochial needs of the particular forms and styles of their time. The ability to reconstruct a dance accurately was all that was required. From the Renaissance to the early 20th century, the idea of recording dance for academic analysis and understanding was antithetical to dance as entertainment or recreation. Even so, after the invention of the printing press (c. 1450), many dance masters concocted systems that others could decipher, including such tools as recorded words, illustrations, track drawings, stick figures and a variety of symbols. These methods were not wholly reliable, however, especially for the dance forms that were to follow in the centuries ahead.

The Beauchamps/Feuillet notation system (1700) is one of many examples of a system that served its purpose very well for its time. It used track drawings coordinated with music and pictorial signs, which the educated participants were able to decipher easily because of the limited vocabulary of the dances being performed or practiced for recreation. Scholars today have a wealth of information about baroque dance from the Beauchamps/Feuillet system.

The Maryinsky dancer Vladimir Stepanov (1866–1896) published another workable system in 1892 in Paris. Many famous ballets of that era—including those by Marius Petipa (1818–1910), such as *The Sleeping Beauty* (1890) and *Swan Lake* (1895)—were recorded with this method. The Stepanov system employed the common element of musical notes to indicate duration of movements; the notes were then adapted to indicate anatomical body parts and written on a musical staff.

Two important methods of human movement notation that enabled dance to forge respectability in the arts and education of the 20th century were (1) Labanotation (formerly called Kinetography Laban), developed in 1928 and named after its European creator Rudolf Laban (1879–1958), and (2) Benesh Movement Notation, developed in 1955 and named after Joan Benesh (b. 1920) and Rudolf Benesh (1916–1975), and sometimes referred to as Choreology. Both Labanotation and Choreology answer to the issue of validity because they can be either as easy or as complex to use as necessary.

These processes of analyzing, coding and decoding movement were not only about constructing a written literature for the art of dance, but also about creating a symbolic language to represent movements that a choreographer could accurately teach to his dancers, who needed to be able to understand details about movements, positions, rhythms and energies.

Because the Benesh system is known to be the most facile for notating ballet and Labanotation for being a bit more complex but also more accurate, the former has become popular within ballet companies, especially those associated with the United Kingdom, and the latter with American modern dance companies. Keeping up with breakthroughs in computer technology, the actual writing and manipulation of the symbols can now be managed with software programs written especially for the two systems: Laban-Writer® and Benesh Notation Writer®. Moreover, when the symbols are connected with a program called LifeForms®, the notation results can be seen on a monitor as fleshed-out, semirealistic figures. In combination with digital video imaging, systems of notation can also contribute to the study of dance history, world culture and experimentation in creative possibilities between humans and machine (see the Ohio State University Web site www.dance.ohio-state.edu/ for more information).

Still, television and computer monitors cannot fully satisfy dancers' practical need to learn either a reconstructed or a new dance from a teacher or ballet master. Dance is three-dimensional movement, whereas video is only two-dimensional imagery.

Both Labanotation and Benesh Movement Notation maintain the symmetry of the human form: the former within a left-right divided vertical staff with columns representing parts of the body, and the latter within frames placed on a horizontal staff appearing much like a music staff. These frames are similar to a series of pictures in a left-to-right movement flow. In Labanotation, time flows vertically up the page as passing beats. Both the Benesh system and Labanotation place symbols within their respective frames or columns to represent adequate details about the motions of the various parts of the body, including directions in three dimensions. Signs are added as needed to represent the many movement points of information required by the situation.

Labanotation scores, as well as a more limited number of scores from other systems, are available from the Dance Notation Bureau in New York City, and Benesh scores are held at the Benesh Institute in London. Both institutions insist that their certified experts supervise the reconstructions of dances. Videotapes of specific performances and information about costuming, settings, lighting and the history of the dance are also available. For the choreographer, these organizations provide a way to copyright, own, receive royalties for and protect a work from unapproved performances.

The signs and symbols used in Labanotation are the building blocks for yet another system of notation, the Language of Dance® (LOD), which Ann Hutchinson Guest presents in this chapter. Guest makes a strong case for a less complicated version of Labanotation through her "Movement Alphabet®," a system that can accommodate the use of ambiguity while targeting what the notator believes to be crucial elements of the dance. Although her system will require comprehensive details for notating and reconstructing professional theater dance, Guest provides what appears to be a more facile system of notation for the complexities faced by today's dancers, choreographers, educators, anthropologists, psychologists, critics and efficiency experts.

WHAT IS DANCE NOTATION?

Ann Hutchinson Guest

Do you want to remember something? Write it down. Do you need information? Go to where it is written down. Do you want to jot down ideas? Organize them? Then use the tools at hand that allow your ideas to take shape, perhaps first in a general way and later in more specific detail. Our focus here is on recording movement, but with special reference to dance.

We specifically are concerned with dance notation, the recording of dance on paper through the use of symbols. In many respects, such a process is comparable to music notation, which had a long gestation period. We do not know exactly when dance notation first appeared or who first thought to put signs on paper to represent steps, but we do know that the earliest known manuscript that is dance notation lies in the Municipal Archives in Cervera, Spain; it is from the mid–15th century and indicates the limited number of steps used and arranged in different sequences to compose dances of that time. You could learn that notation system in two minutes, but it would take you quite a bit longer to master a correct performance of the steps.

Through the centuries, more than eighty-five dance notation systems have been invented for the needs of specific time periods. It is a fascinating study to look at the devices used (track drawings, stick figures, music notes, modified word notes and abstract signs) in relation to the forms of dance they sought to record. Although the development of dance notation systems is closely linked to the evolution of Western theatrical dance, in this chapter we are not concerned so much with history, but with the present. Today, dance is highly developed, and we are interested not only in dances of different cultures around the world but also in gymnastics, athletics and movement in a wide range of disciplines. How can one notation system cope with all that is being demanded of it by practitioners worldwide?

Words, the common currency of communication, have been used to describe dances, but words fail because they are not precise or practical. Arguments among dance historians have arisen because word descriptions can be interpreted differently. What exactly did the writer mean? We are grateful to those people who did describe dances in words, for such information is better than nothing, but the art of dance requires, indeed deserves, a much better method of recording.

A study of notation systems reveals the inherent limitations of those based on a particular movement style. What is required of a universally based system? Consider the flexibility of our language and its alphabet. So few letters, but they serve to produce many millions of words. Such a familiar fact points to the desirability of having a movement notation system that operates in a similar way—that is, like an alphabet, providing the means of spelling out thousands of movements. Such a system need not have any limitations.

LABANOTATION

In his first book, *Choreographie* (1926), Rudolf Laban (1874–1958) utilized a simple device to record his Space-Harmony patterns. Two years later, in his 1928 book *Schrifttanz* (Written dance), he presented an early, somewhat primitive version of what is in use today. He was clearly striving to evolve a system that would be applicable to all movement. Although a good start, it incorporated elements derived from his particular approach to movement, a focus on spatial designs. Giving his system to the world in the early 1930s, Laban then focused on other ideas. In the decades that followed, contributions by others, in particular Albrecht Knust (1896–1978), further developed the Laban system. I wrote the first definitive book on Labanotation (as the system came to be called), which was published in 1954. To meet the needs of the time, the book was based mainly on European folk and theater dance.

In the 1950s and 1960s, with the challenge of notating works by different choreographers and encountering new, sometimes radically different views of movement, the New York Dance Notation Bureau, the focal point of Labanotation teaching in the United States, had to break new ground. Was the system flexible enough? Where and how did it need further development to be free of cultural bias and restrictions? Focus until then had been on the framework of the movement, the outer structure—the skin, so to speak—of established, clearly defined movement patterns in dance techniques and choreography. But what about the inner intent, the concept, the origin of the movement, the inner flesh and blood? Notators had to get to the heart of the movement.

221

The need to consider these aspects became more and more evident as choreographers broke away from traditional movement materials and sought fresh approaches, such as improvisation. Where previously the Labanotation system had sought to be more and more specific in describing movement, Labanotators now faced the need, required by the choreographer, to be *less* specific, to provide more open, general statements that would allow greater leeway for interpretation on the part of the reader-performer.

INVESTIGATING PRIMARY SOURCES

No matter how well trained Labanotation specialists may be, to get "inside" an unfamiliar movement style they need to work closely with exponents of that style—that is, with people for whom that style is part of their heritage. How do they experience the movement? View it? Explain it? From such questions comes a more intimate understanding of where the emphasis for a particular dance style lies. Working closely with African dance exponents, Spanish dance experts, Bharatya Natyam specialists or Japanese Noh performers, notators need to include movement descriptions not provided through standard Labanotation descriptions. The image the performer has in mind can affect the rendition of any movement.

Can such a personal image be accommodated in the notated movement description? The basic facts of movement, its space-time-body dynamic, may not be enough, so motivational concepts—or, as one might say, the "movement's imagination"—need to be added to the notation to equip the dancer with a means toward a more enriching performance. Developing this aspect of movement notation makes it possible to indicate the inner feelings and attitudes toward the movement, in addition to the standard description of its patterns or gestures.

INVESTIGATING THE PHENOMENON OF MOVEMENT

It is not enough to learn a system of notation or to be familiar with particular dance forms. One needs to know the very nature of movement, of what it is made. A cordon bleu chef does not work with prepared packages; he or she deals with the raw material of each ingredient. In a comparable way, the movement specialist draws on the store cupboard of movement possibilities. What dancer does not want to know these possibilities? Yes, of course, physical technique is important for the dancer, and it has to be developed and fine-tuned, but there is more to dancing than that. Awareness of the possibilities of movement and understanding how such knowledge can be used contribute not only to the act of performance but also to the task of gaining a high level of technique. How and when can gaining such an understanding begin?

Children learn their ABCs of language when young, so why should not young dance students also learn the ABCs of movement, or what I have named the Movement Alphabet®? "The Movement Alphabet?" you ask. "Is that generally known?" Not until now! But every person interested in and involved with movement should have knowledge of the basic elements of movement as part of their basic equipment. If we are going to "speak" what anthropologists term the movement languages of dance found in cultures around the world, if we are going to record movement sequences in their terms, we need to know the movement universals applicable to all styles and all movement disciplines—hence, the Movement Alphabet®.

Hearing of the "Seven Movements in Dancing" as taught in the Cecchetti Classical Ballet Method, I noted both duplications and omissions of movements. In his 1831 book on dance movement vocabulary, E. A. Théleur (1817–c.1844) provided an interesting but also incomplete list. Laban's list of basic actions was also not satisfactory to me. I researched contemporary dance sources such as that provided by the seminal dance educator Margaret H'Doubler (1889–1982). Where was the definitive list? Why had dancers grown up not knowing such a list? The ABCs of movement, which I codified in 1967, became an integral part of the Language of Dance® (LOD) movement exploration.

In the LOD method, focus is on exploring the physical experience through each basic movement element. What better way to start an understanding of movement than through exploration at an early age of the wonderful world of movement? Older students, teachers and choreographers are amazed at the degree to which they are enriched when they explore movement from such a basic perspective. Freed from habitual patterns and ways of thinking and moving, all can find new avenues to creativity and a deeper understanding of their current movement involvement. Linking the basic possibilities provides the beginnings of composition, which later leads to choreography. To clarify differences and to act as a visual and a memory aid, as well as a means of preserving dance creations, a symbol on paper represents each basic movement—a simple use of notation called Motif Notation, which is related to Labanotation. This introduction to symbols provides the beginning of movement literacy.

223

THE MOVEMENT ALPHABET

The prime actions and concepts of which movement is comprised are as follows:

Presence or Absence of Movement

1.		**Any Action**	Movement of some kind, a change
2.	Ŏ	**Stillness**	Suspension of motion, sustainment of an arrested activity

* * * * * * * * * * * * * * * * *

An action may be concerned with or may focus on:

Anatomical Possibilities

3.		**Flexion**	Contracting, folding, closing in, making smaller, narrowing
4.		**Extension**	Lengthening, reaching out, enlarging, opening out, elongating, unfolding
5.		**Rotation**	Any revolution, rotation of the body as a whole, or of parts of the body

Movement Ideas or Concentrations

6.		**Travelling**	Any path (straight, circular, meandering or curving) moving from one place to another
7.		**Direction**	Movement into different directions such as up, down, to the right, left, forward, backward
8.		**Support**	An action ending in a new support, transference of weight
9.		**A Spring**	Any aerial step; leaving the ground and returning to it
10.		**Balance**	Equilibrium, centre of weight vertically over a moving or static support
11.		**Falling**	Not in balance: centre of weight moves beyond point of support; loss of balance results.

* * * * * * * * * * * * * * * * *

Specific or Relative Description

12.		**Destination**	Statement of an ending situation, position or state to be reached
13.		**Motion Toward**	Approaching a person, object, direction, or state; a gesture toward oneself
14.		**Motion Away**	Leaving, withdrawing from a person, object, direction, or state; a gesture away from oneself

224

Why the Name "Language of Dance"?

The term *Language of Dance* was chosen with care and thought. Anthropologists speak of the various languages of dance inherent in different cultures around the world. In the language of one such culture, foot stamping is featured; in another, the intricate use of the hands; in yet another, the free interplay between parts of the torso. These differences are important. They are significant individual uses of the universal LOD.

All languages have parts of speech. So does movement. In LOD, the movements and the actions are the verbs, and how these actions are performed (the timing and dynamics used) are the adverbs. The nouns are the parts of the body, a partner, an object or parts of the room. How the movement sentence is constructed can change its meaning, as well as its impact. How movement sentences are combined reveal individual styles. What is important? What is the main thrust? What is merely a linking passage? These differences need to be understood physically and cognitively.

Those who are introduced early to LOD and Motif Notation symbols, and those who continue to a more advanced level, where the transition to the structured Labanotation system can take place, discover that they gain a wealth of advantages.

Labanotation Libraries

Since the 1930s, notators throughout Western society—primarily in Europe, the United States and Australia—have recorded many different dance styles and choreographic forms. In more recent years, they and their Asian counterparts have added scores of Asian dance forms and choreographies. The result is an impressive collection of scores suitable for research about performance all over the world, housed in such places as the Dance Notation Bureau in New York, the Ohio State University, the Centre national d'ecriture du mouvement (in France) and the Laban Centre London. (For a more complete listing, see the references at the end of this chapter.) In comparison with our vast heritage of music scores, the notated dance heritage is admittedly small, but its value far outweighs its size.

Many choreographic works have been notated by those who performed in the piece or by a notator present at the creation of the work. Of particular value are works notated by the choreographer, a prime example being Vaslav

Nijinsky's (1890–1950) 1912 ballet *L'après-midi d'un faune* (Afternoon of a Faun), published in the Labanotation transcription and thus available for degree studies as well as performance. The libraries of notated works provide rich sources for comparative research. For example, how did the choreographer relate movement to the music? How was a particular dramatic effect achieved? What compositional devices were used? How was the thematic material developed? These and many more aspects of movement can be studied through the notated score. Dance forms as varied as the Bournonville School, Spanish dance and modern dance, to name just three, have been recorded and explained through Labanotation.

The best time to learn any language is, of course, when one is very young. This is true for the language of movement, too. Whatever a person's later interest in movement—be it athletics, gymnastics, skating, swimming or dance—an introduction to the universal terminology for movement and its information in notated form can provide an invaluable basis for later specialization. This language can pave the way to a deeper understanding of any movement or dance form encountered in one's life because the same movement factors apply in all forms.

REFERENCES

BOOKS ON OTHER SYSTEMS OF NOTATION

Guest, Ann Hutchinson. *Choreo-graphics.* London: Gordon and Breach, 1989. [Offers a close comparison of identical movements analyzed and written in fourteen different systems, including contemporary methods.]

———. *Dance notation: The process of recording movement on paper.* London: Dance Books, 1984. [Answers the questions "What is it?" "Why is it needed?" "When did it start?" "How is it used?" Offers practical and historical information.]

ORGANIZATIONS HOUSING LIBRARIES AND COLLECTIONS OF LABANOTATION SCORES AND MATERIALS

Language of Dance Centre (United Kingdom)

Dance Notation Bureau (United States)

New York Public Library

Ohio State University Libraries

Dance Notation Bureau Extension, Ohio State University

Labanotation Institute/National Resource Centre, University of Surrey (United Kingdom)

Laban Centre London

University of Hawaii Archives of Ethnic Music and Dance

Centre national d'ecriture du mouvement (France)

Institute of Musicology (Hungary)

Hong Kong Academy of the Performing Arts

Folkwang Hochschule, Essen (Germany)

Sigurd Leeder School of Dance (Switzerland)

Centre for Dance Studies, Jersey (United Kingdom)

CHAPTER SEVENTEEN

introduction

This chapter focuses on the dance experience as both a visual and a movement art form. Collaborations between the visual arts and dance have pleased and challenged audiences around the world. Although patterns of human movement on a "bare" stage are indeed visual, the work of visual artists can enhance the lived experience of dance and be enhanced in return. Backdrops, small stage sets, large movie sets, props and even painting on costumes take their place alongside the arts of costume, lighting design and, of course, movement in contributing to the rich delight of so many dance experiences.

COLLABORATION AMONG THE ARTS

Marc Raymond Strauss

I love watching dances by the prolific Russian American choreographer George Balanchine (1904–1983), mainly because of their neoclassical clarity. Much of his choreography celebrates the human body in motion while dressed only in practice clothes: black or pink tights and leotards for the women, black tights and tight white T-shirts for the men, ballet slippers for everyone and little if nothing else on stage. Stripped down to the barest essentials—simple lighting, few if any sets, bare designs on a back cyclorama and no props—the neoclassical ballet vocabulary is revealed naked before me in a Balanchine dance. His spare use of the related arts feels like a traditional Japanese landscape rendered in calligraphy, full of clarity, openness and suggestion.

I am fascinated with his intricate and ever-evolving designs, his mutating groups of clearly etched bodies always morphing into new and surprising patterns. His intelligent musicality and the evocative sounds of Stravinsky, Tchaikovsky or Bach are always presented in clever harmony or counterpoint. Balanchine's dances give me the feeling of an improvisational and

229

kinesthetic jazz riff (not surprisingly, he was greatly influenced by African American vernacular dance). Among his masterpieces, *Serenade* (1934), *Concerto Barocco* (1941), *The Four Temperaments* (1946), *Theme and Variations* (1947), *Agon* (1957) and *Jewels* (1967) are just some of my favorites.

Perhaps my infatuation comes from an early love of mathematics. Balanchine's work is nothing if not geometrically complex—all those wonderful chains of dancers moving around, under and through each other's linked arms. Permutations of triangles, parallelograms, diagonals and spirals continually merge into each other and then reemerge in new and startling ways. His dances are best seen from a balcony, many believe, for that is the perfect spot to apprehend fully his firework figures blazing up from below. There are no better practitioners of the classical and neoclassical vocabulary than his now second- and third-generation dancers at New York City Ballet, Miami City Ballet and other companies around the globe. All-American speed, sleekness and artistry rolled into one explosive confection.

Because of an almost fanatical love for the paradox of Balanchine's very rich but unadorned purity, it took me a long time to realize that concert dance could also function quite well in conjunction with other arts. Of course, Balanchine used lighting, costuming, sets and a variety of other production values, too; he just tended to stress the dance. Successful artistic collaborations between dance and the visual arts both honor the individual artists and create something greater than the sum of their separate parts. It was another choreographer working in a wholly different dance style who initially opened my eyes to the collaborative potential of the visual arts with dance.

Martha Graham (1894–1991), the 20th century modern dance pioneer, developed her own unique technique and aesthetic, performing well into her seventies and choreographing until she died at the age of ninety-six. She was a deeply thoughtful and driven choreographer, and she often chose to use symbolically evocative props and décor in her pieces—in particular sculpture. From the 1940s through the 1960s—her darkly psychological, mythic Greek period—Graham developed a particularly rich collaborative relationship with the Japanese American sculptor Isamu Noguchi (1904–1988). Noguchi constructed a number of abstract yet evocative sculptures that challenged Graham's audience not only to determine the identity and significance of her dances, but also to interpret the relationship between the dancers and their stone and wood allies.

For *Errand into the Maze* (1947), for example, Noguchi sculpted an eight-foot tall piece that looked like a large wishbone, which the principal dancer (often

Graham herself, in those days) alternately walked through and around, hugged, caressed and used to protect herself. The dance was the choreographer's interpretation of the Ariadne and Minotaur legend. Was the sculpture symbolic of a woman's (or Graham's own) pelvic bone, embodying her burgeoning sexuality, fears, hopes and struggles? The suggestive yet troubling beauty of Noguchi's works and their tactile, solid presence next to the dancers continue to draw viewers to Graham's dances decades after they were first presented.

The Noguchi-Graham collaboration *Cave of the Heart* (1946) is a nasty ballet about the original scorned woman, the vengeful Medea (from the Euripides tragedy), set to Samuel Barber's music. The dance uses a strangely exotic, prickly "wire dress" that Noguchi made for Graham and a blood red rope that she slowly regurgitates and then swallows. Many viewers see the rope as Medea's literal guts coming up and the sparkling reflections on the costume as her all-consuming, jealous hatred.

Night Journey, also from 1947, is Graham's dance-theater study of the "incestuous Oedipus myth recounted from the viewpoint of Jocasta."[1] This work, too, has a literal and metaphorical rope in it (Graham liked the multiple symbols associated with ropes). The dance

> begins at the drama's climax—the moment before Jocasta's suicide—and then travels back in time to explore the events which have led up to this point. . . . The rope, which Jocasta is about to use as her noose, becomes a web that ensnares husband and wife, and is simultaneously an umbilical cord tying mother to son. This is echoed in movement where (from the audience's point of view) ecstasy takes on maternal overtones. Oedipus's swaggering seduction of the older woman is akin to a boastful son showing off for his watching mother, while the couple's later lovemaking is laced with movements that replicate a mother's cradling of her child. Graham's use of movement as double-edged metaphor is at its most acute in this primal horror story. . . . The set of Night Journey is dominated by Isamu Noguchi's raised and tilted platform supporting a bone-like structure. Suggestively pelvic, it functions as bed, throne and bier [coffin] in turn.[2]

Graham never shied away from tackling disturbing, even taboo topics in her dances. Many new audiences have had difficulty with the challenges of her themes and with her somewhat stiff-bodied technique. (This is true for her early and middle periods. Graham's later work from the 1980s on is surprisingly lyrical and balletlike.) The Graham-Noguchi works that spanned

231

the middle three decades of the 20th century, however, are important land-marks in the history of collaborative art-making between a choreographer and sculptor, particularly in their evocation of the still relevant, psycholog-ically disturbing Greek dramas.

Modern dance experimentalist (some say the father of postmodernism) Merce Cunningham (b. 1919) collaborated with visual artists as diverse as antiart pop artist Andy Warhol (1930–1987), ready-made collagist Robert Rauschenberg (b. 1925) and assembler-sculpture-painter Jasper Johns (b. 1930). For his 1968 piece *RainForest*, Cunningham borrowed Warhol's silver Mylar balloons from an exhibition and asked Johns to cut holes in the dancers' nude-looking unitards. He then created a strangely beautiful char-acter study for an androgynous, homeless "community" of six dancers:

I saw Andy Warhol's pillows in an exhibition and I thought they were mar-velous, and asked him about the possibility of having them as a set and he agreed. They are silver in color and filled with helium: each of those at the back of the stage is tied to a fishing line with a weight on the floor to keep it from disappearing into the flies, and the ones that are loose are only half filled with helium, sometimes they go up anyway, but they can move freely and not necessarily disappear. We like them to give as much as possible the sense of moving; they need not stay still. In fact, it's like a landscape. In a rain forest, there is always something over your head, the sense of something up there from which the rain is dripping. There are rain forests in the northwest [where Cunningham grew up]. I thought that the pillows would give a sense of space since they're not fixed. For the costumes, Andy had no idea except nudity. That was not possible for the vigorous movement I had choreographed. So I said to Jasper, "As if skin were torn," and Jasper cut small jagged holes in our flesh-colored leotards while we were wearing them. Carolyn [Brown] said that she wanted Jasper to do hers so that she would have an original Jasper Johns.[3]

Visual artistry painted on costumes that ripped into tatters while on the dancers, helium balloons that look like huge silver pillows hovering about the stage, some tied down, others free-floating, with bodies occasionally displacing them—a tour de force potpourri was what I saw in *RainForest*, as balletic Cunningham legs worked with stiff-armed, Graham-like upper bodies in virtuosic and challenging juxtaposition. The combination of these disciplines, interacting with composer David Tudor's collage accompani-ment—birds chirping, machines squeaking and the occasional toilet dripping—conspired to create a modern-day world of bleakness and hope, technology and tranquility anxiously coexisting on someone's curious notion of a planet. The visual arts thus provide collaborative opportunities for choreographers like Cunningham.

Perhaps no greater artistic collaborations among a wide and talented pool of visual and performing artists occurred than when the singular impresario Serge Diaghilev (1872–1929) coordinated their skills in his Ballets Russes from 1909 until his premature death twenty years later. As dance historian Lynn Garafola states in the preface to her comprehensive and eminently readable *Diaghilev's Ballets Russes* (1989), the company

> *created the first of this century's classics:* Les Sylphides, Firebird, Petrouchka, L'Après-midi d'un Faune, Le Sacre du Printemps, Parade, Les Noces, Les Biches, Apollo, *and* Prodigal Son, *all of which continue to be performed today. It nurtured several of the century's outstanding choreographers—Michel Fokine, Vaslav Nijinsky, Léonide Massine, Bronislava Nijinska, and George Balanchine—and through them influenced the direction of choreography until the 1970s. It brokered the century's most remarkable marriages between dance and the other arts, partnerships involving composers such as Igor Stravinsky, Claude Debussy, Maurice Ravel, and Serge Prokofiev, and painters like Pablo Picasso, Natalia Gontcharova, André Derain, and Henri Matisse.*[4]

Some of these collaborations—with Pablo Picasso (1881–1973) on *Parade* (1917) and *Pulcinella* (1920), with Henri Matisse (1869–1954) on *Le chant du Rossignol* (1920), with Natalia Gontcharova (1881–1962) on *Le coq d'or* (1914) and with Maurice Utrillo (1883–1955) on *Barabau* (1925)—included brightly painted original sets, costumes and decor by the original artists themselves. For *Parade*, Pablo Picasso contributed cubist-futurist designs and costumes; Léonide Massine (1895–1979) choreographed quaint and festive steps; and Erik Satie (1866–1925) wrote a jaunty contemporary score. All of these elements reflected the upbeat big-city life and impersonal chaos that began during World War I.[5] Audiences loved it and were greatly enamored by its radical, avant-garde energies.

Nicholas Roerich's (1874–1947) primitivist sets and designs for Vaslav Nijinsky's (1890–1950) riot-inducing *Sacré du printemps* (Rite of Spring) (1913) contributed an alien sense of otherworldliness to the fantasized Russian pagan sacrifice of a virginal Chosen Maiden who dances herself to death in support of her tribe's celebration of spring. The so-called sophisticates of Paris were not quite ready for the dance revolution taking shape before their eyes that night, but Diaghilev's twenty-year promotion of groundbreaking artistic collaborations continue to resound more than three-quarters of a century later.

Perhaps the most popular and accessible marriage of the visual arts to dance (as well as to film, music, costuming and many other production arts) was created by no less a luminary than the musical theater and film musical performer-choreographer-actor-innovator Gene Kelly (1912–1996), in his Oscar-winning film "An American in Paris" (1951). Academy Awards for best picture, art direction, musical direction and costumes, and a special choreography award for Kelly, among many others, were more than deserved.

Costing nearly $3 million to make, with more than half a million dollars for the ballet alone, the movie grossed more than $8 million, unheard of numbers for the time. Audiences can still scarcely register the magnitude of the sets, especially in the *American in Paris* ballet. Gene Kelly's electrifying choreography for the fifty-odd dancers careening all over the sound stage to the driving musical pulse is just too pleasurably distracting.

Kelly pulled out all the choreographic stops in this extraordinary collaborative undertaking. The best film musicals, of course, are true collaborations, with the magical whole so much greater than the sum of its singular parts. Alfred Gilks (1891–1970) and John Alton (1901–1996) won Academy Awards for the lush pastels of their Technicolor cinematography (camera work), which drenched Kelly's dancers in brilliant light. Walter Plunkett (1902–1982) and Orry Kelly (1897–1964) also received Academy Awards for the more than two hundred period costumes they created for the film, imaginatively transporting the audience to the highly stylized neighborhoods of a fantasy-filled fin de siècle dance-driven Paris. Irene Sharaff's (1910–1993) Academy Award–winning art direction should also catch our eye, as her seamless incorporation of the huge impressionist and postimpressionist backdrops subtly reinforce our sense of superabundance up on the screen.

The film peaks with Kelly's seventeen-minute ballet, *American in Paris*, set to George Gershwin's (1898–1937) jazz-inflected score. The work of six world-famous visual artists was spectacularly represented in the six distinct sections of this extravaganza:

¤ Fastidious Parisian painter Raoul Dufy's (1877–1953) oilscape *Place de la Concorde* is rendered as a 40-by-150-foot backdrop that fills MGM's largest sound stage;

- Pierre Renoir's (1841–1919) bright blues, reds, yellows, pinks and greens explode off the screen in the mist-filled Flower Market pas de deux (duet);
- Maurice Utrillo's work is on display in his picture-postcard, atmospheric rendering of Parisian side streets in all their crumbling stucco glory;
- Henri Rousseau's (1844–1910) "direct, simple and hauntingly naïve vision [of an] elaborately fanciful and picturesquely exotic"[6] fairground appears in the carnival scene;
- Vincent Van Gogh's (1853–1890) rendition of an open-air café on the *Place de l'opéra*—reminiscent of the synthesist movement, during which time the artist employed a "greater simplification of his forms and . . . less modulated color" than in the "writhing, flame-like forms"[7] of some of his more well-known works—shows up in the fifth section of the number. If you did not know it is Van Gogh, you would never recognize the backdrop.
- Henri Toulouse-Lautrec's (1864–1901) *Moulin Rouge* scene is a rather mild (for Henri) mix of live and cut-out figures from the famous dance hall, around which Kelly, as the character Du Chocolat, wriggles and swaggers. A brief can-can is de rigueur in such a scene.

Novice and experienced dance students alike must see "An American in Paris." Rarely recorded with such sensitivity and attention to detail, artistic collaborations like this one are excellent resources for repeat study and enjoyment.

George Balanchine, in spite of his propensity for pared down neoclassical works, also occasionally engaged the visual arts. Ironically, he commissioned sculptor Isamu Noguchi to create both the decor and costumes for his interpretation of the Greek myth of Orpheus in the Underworld, entitled simply *Orpheus* (1948), presented at the first performance of his newly formed New York City Ballet. The prolific 20th century composer Igor Stravinsky (1882–1971) wrote the score for the ballet and conducted the orchestra on opening night.

For *Orpheus,* Noguchi came up with a "sense of space and airiness" that "seemed absolutely right to Balanchine and Stravinsky, as well as [to Lincoln] Kirstein [1907–1999]. The setting was an archaic yet timeless world. The costumes, of embroidered wool, seemed to Kirstein suggestive of ritual tattoos. The props and other objects—the masks, bones, the lyre—were like sculptured carvings, imbued with ritual or magical import."[8]

In a passage from his book *A Sculptor's World* (1968) (excerpted in *Tributes* [1998], New York City Ballet's recent celebration of fifty years of artistry), Noguchi offers an assessment of the collaborative process of putting *Orpheus* together—the magical power of specialized artists working in tandem on one project:

> We breathe in, we breathe out, inward turning, alone, or outgoing, working with others, for an experience that is cumulative through collaboration. Theater is the latter kind. My interest is the stage where it is possible to realize in a hypothetical way those projections of the imagination into environmental space which are denied us in actuality. The theater of the dance in particular adds the movement of bodies, in relation to form and space, together with music. There is joy in seeing sculpture come to life on the stage in its own world of timeless time. Then the very air becomes charged with meaning and emotion, and form plays its integral part in the re-enactment of a ritual. Theater is a ceremonial; the performance is a rite. Sculpture in daily life should or could be like this. In the meantime, the theater gives me its poetic, exalted equivalent.[9]

According to Lincoln Kirstein, Balanchine's proponent and benefactor, *Orpheus* was "a triangulated collaboration in which music, sculpture, and dancing were lightly and tenderly balanced."[10] The performance was apparently so riveting that dance critic Edwin Denby was "so overwhelmed that he stayed slumped in his seat during intermission, arousing solicitude from the ushers."[11] Reactions such as these reflect moments of wonder that move one's being in profound ways. Such is the welcome result of artistic visions that succeed in bringing distinct artistic disciplines together.

The esteemed Wellesley College professor and dance critic Robert Garis, known as a lover of Balanchine's work, hated *Orpheus*, however, calling aspects of Noguchi's decor "dinosaur eggs." For some, the magic works; for some, it does not.

Dance and visual arts collaborations will challenge your own assumptions and understanding as you try to figure out whether the performance is just a bunch of art objects and subjects thrown together or an evocative and persuasive totality much greater than the sum of its parts.

You most likely will have witnessed a successful collaborative performance if you experienced any one or more of the following:

¤ The loss of a sense of time because you have been imaginatively transported *into* the dance for several minutes or more. This feeling is sometimes referred to as being captivated, enthralled, drawn into, entranced by, transfixed, mesmerized or held spellbound by an experience so that you are temporarily unaware of your self or your surroundings;

¤ A semiconscious or conscious awareness that something very special is going on;

¤ The ability to identify both the individual artistic elements and the cohesive *gestalt* of the artwork, either simultaneously or alternately, resulting in a deeply satisfying and pleasurable sensation in your heart, mind and spirit.

ENDNOTES

[1] Allen Robertson and Donald Hutera, *The dance handbook* (Boston: G. K. Hall, 1988), p. 69.

[2] Ibid.

[3] Merce Cunningham, *The dancer and the dance* (New York: Marion Boyars, 1985), p. 113.

[4] Lynn Garafola, *Diaghilev's Ballets Russes* (New York: Oxford University Press, 1989), p. vii.

[5] See, among many others: Richard H. Axsom, *"Parade": Cubism as theater* (New York: Garland, 1979); Nancy Van Norman Baer, ed., *The art of enchantment: Diaghilev's Ballets Russes, 1909–1929* (San Francisco: Fine Arts Museums of San Francisco, 1988); Nathalie Gontcharova, Michel Larionov and Pierre Vorms, *Les Ballets Russes: Serge Diaghilew et la décoration théâtrale*, rev. ed. (Belvès Dordogne, France: Pierre Vorms, 1955).

[6] Peter Murray and Linda Murray, *The Penguin dictionary of art and artists* (London: Penguin, 1991), p. 368.

[7] Ibid., pp. 171–172.

[8] Bernard Taper, *Balanchine: A biography* (New York: Times Books, 1984), p. 222.

[9] Christopher Ramsey, ed., *Tributes: Celebrating fifty years of New York City Ballet* (New York: Alfred A. Knopf, 1998), p. 92.

[10] Lincoln Kirstein, *Thirty years: Lincoln Kirstein's the New York City Ballet* (New York: Alfred A. Knopf, 1978), p. 100.

[11] Taper, *Balanchine*, p. 225.

CHAPTER EIGHTEEN

introduction

I n this chapter, Catherine Norgren, an accomplished costume designer for dance, provides personalized and illuminating insights into the skills and sensitivities necessary *backstage* in order to present the choreographer's dressed vision accurately *onstage.*

SEEING FEELINGS: COSTUME DESIGN AND DANCE

Catherine F. Norgren

Costume designers are storytellers. They work in conjunction with the other designers—of scenery, lighting and sound—to make the audience feel something. Costumes are clothes for characters. Costumes are always real on real bodies made of real fabric, even if that fabric is plastic garbage bags. And costumes are always abstract, meaning they are extensions of bodies that move through space and time. Regardless of whether they are used for theater or dance, they are one small part of a great whole. They work in conjunction with the other arts in the context of a production, the text of a play or the music of a choreographed work. Costumes are clothes, and they are art. They make invisible ideas visible. As Christopher Bowen put it, "Traditionally, ballet was considered a composite art of dance, music, libretto, and design."[1]

Costume design does not exist or function by itself. It is affected and made effective by its context and its synergy with music, motion, scenery and lighting. Whether for dance or theater, costumes and lighting coexist in an environment and are mutually complementary; they provide both mood and atmosphere. In dance, costumes are also abstract extensions of the dancers' bodies. The lighting, although atmospheric, seems the more concrete because it is as palpable in dance as scenery. Whatever the parts, they are put together through conscious choice, and such careful selection is what constitutes the art of design.

COSTUMES AS PROCESS

The design process is about listening and asking questions. It is about dialogue. It is about making choices. Designers start by listening to the music or soundscape (which may include the spoken word or even silence). I ask myself questions about the sound: How does it feel? I prefer answers that evoke visual adjectives—*gentle and flowing* or *staccato and delicate*, for example—because these words are useful to me for making pictures. I can imagine colors, shapes, patterns and textures that elicit those words rather than a general word such as *romantic*. I don't know what romantic looks like! I know what the stereotypical symbols for romantic are, but they may be too obvious and trite: the word *roses* may not connect to the feeling of music or story as effectively as *seductive* and *thorny*.

I talk to the choreographer. How does he or she interpret the music? What story does he or she imagine telling? Then, *romantic* may be more helpful and important. What style of dance are we doing? What kinds of movement? Athletic floor work? Intricate footwork? Partnering? Do we need to emphasize hands, torso, head, feet? How do I help the dancers most effectively? What do the costumes need to evoke, a sad love story or a happy one? Does the piece feel calm and then frantic? What ideas should I work with, and which ones should I punctuate by working against? Do we want to predict the outcome of the story or to let it be an unexpected surprise? Which does the music evoke?

I must know the style of dance, the expectations of convention (ballet and pointe shoes? modern dance and bare feet? jitterbug and the 1930s?) and what the fabrics' weight, texture and shape will do to and on the body in motion. I consider how the clothes will move—With or away from the body? Will this movement contribute to the choreography and the music by reiterating the dancer's movement (circle skirts continuing to swirl after the dancer changes direction or comes to a stop)? Will the choices (appropriately) exaggerate the movement, or will they reveal the movement in new and exciting ways, or both? Do they juxtapose movement, (consciously) eliciting humor, surprise or discovery? The designer might reveal contrasts in the music so that the audience can make visual discoveries: curves against angular movement or harsh shiny textures against liquid moves. Color is often the last element I consider. It is complex and provocative; it can be personal, limiting and overly symbolic; like line and texture, it can reveal contrasts or with a single hue unify everything.

Design is about idea and craft, and their execution is part of my process. I have to help build functional clothes that fit active dancers, dye and paint those clothes, construct masks and headdresses, dress wigs, set hair, choose makeup and even play cobbler—I once managed to put taps on sneakers.

I have to keep talking to the choreographer! That person's idea drives the production. It is his or her "story" the designers help to communicate. In 1995, when Matthew Bourne (b. 1960) choreographed a revival of *Swan Lake*, originally choreographed by Marius Petipa (1818–1910) in 1895, his idea was "to replace the female corps of leggy, tutued swans" because "[t]here is something about the shape of the wing that is much more like a male musculature."[2] So costume designer Lez Brotherston designed "a flock of bare-chested blokes in feathery leggings."[3] The "feathery leggings" ended at the knee, with all exposed skin as white as the feathers, whiteness that extended into encrusted, slicked-back hair. They had black, beaklike points on their foreheads, which emphasized black-ringed eyes. They were strong, powerful, menacing and beautiful. Just like swans.

But the conversation between designer and choreographer cannot stop there. Such an idea has to be coherent. The path has to follow to a logical conclusion: "Set in some fantasy British Fifties-land, this 'Swan Lake' presents The Prince . . . as a pawn of the establishment, in a court where meaningless ceremony has replaced familial affection, and the swans of Bourne's imagination represent the freedom and love that The Prince craves."[4] Brotherston clothed the other characters in elegant but stiff formal wear, much of it covering skin from neck to wrist and ankle, much of it black or red leather and velvet—completely in contrast to the conventionally natural, "naked," organic, "free" swans of the original.

COSTUMES AS ART

Costume design uses the language of art to convey information visually. The parts that make up a work of art are often referred to as a vocabulary and a grammar, which together produce a decipherable language—an analogy also used in dance and in music. The interaction and integration of these languages in choreography and design are directed toward the same goal of telling a story, revealing a mood or idea or commenting on the music. These languages can elevate a prosaic dance from a series of arbitrary movements to an exceptional piece that touches us somehow, even if we are not (yet) able to articulate how or why. Perhaps this happens subliminally, but I think it is more accurate to say that we notice it working on us.

It is difficult to ignore visual stimuli. We do it everyday when we choose what to wear (and what statement we want to make with that choice), when we choose a friend or partner (because of the color of someone's eyes or the shape of her face or the rock band logo emblazoned on his T-shirt), or even when we pick a brand of cereal to buy in the grocery store. In each case, the elements of design, presented through the use of the principles of design, join together to create a visual statement that evokes a mood in us. There are some cereals I just will not try—I don't care how tasty they might be—if the packaging is too loud or too bland. I have discovered great musical artists because an album cover was too visually poetic to leave behind! But beware: this is not an excuse to be close-minded (someone once said a mind is like a parachute—it is useless when it is not open). Note that I know why I won't buy the cereal.

Costumes as art are expressively abstract; they help the audience see and understand something more.

> A ballet has to stand up under steady scrutiny almost as an easel painting does. At first sight it tells a story, it has local color or period interest or shock value. But then it starts to change the way a picture in a museum does as you look at it attentively for five or ten minutes. The shapes and colors, lines and textures in the set and costumes will act as they would in a picture, they will seem to push and pull, rise and fall, advance and retreat with or against their representational weight. . . . A good ballet decor, like a good painting, does different and opposite things decisively; like a painting, it presents a bold equilibrium of pictorial forces.[5]

Costumes support and expand what we hear in the music (or in the silence or in the text being used as music). They are figurative and metaphoric, evoking in us an expansive response, with poetic and emotional echoes:

> Trisha Brown wears shot silk in Opal Loop/Cloud Installation #72503. You see her glinting blue; the next moment the blue has disappeared and she's in mauve; scarcely have you formulated this thought when puddles of the blue reappear along the folds. The silk was an inspired choice by costume designer Judith Shea; it's a dandy metaphor both for Brown's dancing and her current compositional processes. Now you see it, now you don't. Watch it under a new light before it ducks, twists, and slips shining into another current.

> . . . and Glacial Decoy . . . drifted ravishingly in front of its changing array of black-and-white slides by Robert Rauschenberg. . . . This time, I even liked

Rauschenberg's pleated white tent dresses with bells for sleeves. [Beverly] Emmon's lighting rendered them lighter and more transparent, and the combination of their prettiness with the gentle rambunctiousness of the movement became quite engaging. I remembered being sent off to birthday parties in my organdy dress and coming home with rips in it because I'd tried to follow the boys over the fence.[6]

Deborah Jowitt reviews more than one piece in this article, but notice how her writing weaves together the visual elements. Although not specifically mentioned in the first paragraph, Emmon's lighting design is as important to Jowitt's awareness of Shea's costumes as it is later to her new view (unveiled by Emmon's illumination) of Rauschenberg's costumes. It is the sensitivity of the lights working with the fabrics that so eloquently reveals the duality of the dancer-choreographer and Shea's costumes.

We can give and receive visually many bits of information at once. Sometimes the visual information is concrete, identifying character attributes such as socioeconomic status, occupation, time of year or a specific activity (think clubbing—you wouldn't go in your pajamas, would you?). The information is always emotional. Visual design has the magic ability to layer parallel tracks of information simultaneously—just like the multiple tracks of music recorded on an album. The artist cannot actually sing all those parts at once, but you can hear them harmonizing together at the same time that your ear and brain separate them.

The fact that information is emotional is the most abstract aspect of design. It is also the challenge and the delight of the art of costuming. To some extent, regardless of what the designer does, the audience will react emotionally: "Design in the theatre is the creation of atmosphere. It is either representational atmosphere, such as in the naturalistic theatre of accurately placed suns and moons, or it is the abstract arrangement of an environment that creates an atmosphere right for the dramatic intention."[7]

In order to appreciate costumes and their design, we must analyze the pieces to discover the details of those choices. How do they help us see the music? How do they contribute to our understanding of a story? How do they reveal the themes that support the storytelling or mood(s) or both? Once we have identified the component elements and principles, we can put them back together and see them more fully as a successful whole.

So what are these elements and principles? Most of us know already, but we need to develop a specific vocabulary to express what they are.

ELEMENTS OF DESIGN

The notion "costumes as art" involves the two-dimensional elements of design—line, shape, value, texture and color—the words or vocabulary with which costumers build their sentences. It is safe to say that dancers and choreographers have the three-dimensional elements—space, time and motion—all sewn up (pun intended). However, designers cannot ignore how the costumes occupy and move in space. Their art addresses how best to draw attention to the dancer expressively moving through that space.

Line

Swiss painter Paul Klee (1879–1940) defined *line* as "a dot out for a walk." Line can be an internal gesture or an external silhouette. In either case, the line of any costume has to acknowledge the body that it is on. Costumes may disguise the body in a bag or try to make it look like a box, but they cannot ignore the body and the dynamic of its movement through space. The line of the dancer and how much space he or she takes up, illuminated and colored by the lighting, is as important as the space in which the dancer and costume exist and as the speed, rhythm or path they take to move through that space.

Shape

Shape includes *form*, *volume* and *mass*, all of which are related to space. To purists, shape refers only to two-dimensional geometry (circle, rectangle, triangle), whereas form refers to the three-dimensional counterpart of shape (sphere, parallelogram, pyramid). Costumes are sculptural. They are totally three dimensional. But I find it limiting to remove *circle*, *rectangle* and *triangle* from my vocabulary; after all, there are such things as circle skirts, rectangular necklines or triangular sleeves.

Volume, like form, has three-dimensional connotations (but not exclusively) and refers to the mass or bulk of a shape—how much space it takes up. Thinking in scientific terms, we can be even more specific about the distinction between volume and mass: volume is about air (or weightlessness), the space contained within an object (costume), whereas mass is about weight and force, the necessary energy to move an object (costume) through space.

244

We might ask, "How big is the costume?" as well as "What is its overall shape?" and "How heavy is the fabric?"

Value

Value is the lightness or darkness of an object. It is a component of color, but is not the color itself. In light, value is additive—white is the presence of all color, and black is the absence of all color. In pigment (paint), value is subtractive—white is the absence of all color, but black is the presence of all color. Imagine a scale with white at one end and black at the other, with an infinite number of grays tilting in between. The range of values is as important as the value itself. Are the costumes all light toned? Is there a scale from light to dark? Are the costumes a limited range of grays, or are they contrasting values of dark and light? In *Swan Lake*, the black swan is not like the white ones. How do the contrasting color values make us feel as the black swan tries to seduce or join in with the others?

Texture

Texture is the tactile response evoked by visual information. It can involve a pattern on fabric as well as the visible weave of the fabric itself. Decoration also counts as texture: fringe, feathers, beads and rhinestones can create texture. All of these elements contribute to the movement and how we see it. Think of the flappers of the 1920s, drawing attention to their shockingly bare knees and the freedom of their bodies, all that fringe moving right along with them. Fabric and lighting can play together to reveal or hide the form through texture: the sheer tulle of romantic tutus or the shiny, reflective unitards of the late 20th century, emphasizing the curves and angles of the body and its muscles.

Color

Color consists of *hues* (red, yellow, blue, green, orange, purple or a mixture of these colors), *values* (pink is actually light red) and *intensity*—the brightness or dullness of the hue (dusty rose is a duller light red than bright pink, and brick is a darker dull red). Color is obnoxiously emotional, personal and symbolic. Designers (and audiences) need to look at color from that standpoint, but also more abstractly. Red can mean anger or love, or it can simply be the brightest event on stage, indicating nothing other than its difference. Is that important to the story? Is the dance about isolation and belonging? Do the colors help us see that? Do the clothes make that discovery a delightful surprise?

In summary, then, how does the designer decide what lines, shapes, values, textures and colors to use? No element is used or seen in isolation to any other. Choosing how the design vocabulary supports and comments on the accompaniment and the choreography is the very essence of design. Putting the elements together in grammatical combinations means employing the principles of design.

PRINCIPLES OF DESIGN

The principles of design are a bit more complicated than the vocabulary (isn't grammar always like that?). Despite the grammatical analogy, they are complicated because no one can agree on the exact labels or on a hard and fast set of rules for using them. To me, the principles exist in pairs: repetition and variety, emphasis and rhythm, scale and proportion, unity and balance. They help explain context and always function in relation to one another.

Repetition and Variety

Too much repetition produces a boring, static effect. Too much variation can be confusing. A tiny variation draws attention to the repetition and its variant. The reverse is also true. Any of the elements can be repeated or varied to express relationships between characters (three dancers in heavy, roughly textured fabrics, juxtaposed with two others in sheer, lightweight ones). They can clarify the choreographer's concept or story (two dancers wearing the same color and other dancers wearing "clashing" colors might tell us who is sympathetic to one another, antagonistic or "family").

Emphasis and Rhythm

Emphasis and rhythm are about focus and contrast. *Where* do we look? At what speed do we do that? Do our eyes "bounce" or "flow" at the same pace as the music or choreography? How does the designer create focus (often contrasting with repetition and variety) so that we know who is the soloist and who are the chorus? We must watch the use of color, value (a lighter pink in the midst of dark reds and oranges), texture (fuzzy, contrasting sequins or satin; stripes among a sea of polka dots; one patterned unitard surrounded by solid-colored ones) or shape (trousers among skirts; sleeveless leotards contrasted by two with long sleeves; scooped necklines revealing skin versus a turtleneck).

Scale and Proportion

Scale and proportion are about ratio and degree. They refer to the size of one costume in relation to another. They also refer to the size of one part of the costume. For instance, do headdresses cover the entire body? Are hairstyles as sleek and close to the body as the costumes? They refer as well to the proportion of elements such as color: Is everything blue? What about the range of values (the proportion of light to middle to dark) and intensities (degree of bright blues to dull blues)? Is there a range of hues: green blues, blue blues, purple blues?

Unity and Balance

Together, the principles and elements of design elicit an emotional response in the audience. They exist in every visual work. How do all of these parts come together to create a single whole, however? Are the proportions of repetition and variety balanced (not necessarily equal or symmetrical, just balanced)? As long as the result is aesthetically pleasing; works with the accompaniment, choreography, scenery and lighting; evokes the response the designers hope for; and conveys the information they need it to, they have achieved unity and balance. But how do they recognize success? It is in many ways a purely instinctive awareness: "The sole and essential function of [design is] the creation of visual poetry."[8]

STYLE DICTATES CLOTHES

In the beginning, the designer's aspiration is always the same—to create a visual atmosphere that will support the dramatic intention and reveal an emotional story. But in the end, the product will be different for a drama, a ballet, an opera, a modern dance, a cakewalk or a music video. The style called *ballet* is easily recognizable—shoes and tutus are usually the unequivocal clues. The men's clothes tend to match the women's light colors and tight-fitting bodices, but the men never (well, rarely) go *en pointe* in the classical or romantic ballets. Any variations on these conventions are clear signals of a style other than ballet.

With one such style you have as much experience as anyone. You know more about social dance than you probably realize. With two photographs in front of you, could you tell the difference between an 8th grade dance and a senior prom? Could you tell the difference between your senior prom and your parents'? Of course you could. Although they might have formal ingredients in common, they have different period styles. Check out the clues: not just the cut (bow tie dimensions, skirt length), but also the color of shirts, jackets, dresses, as well as hair and makeup styles—oh, and the shoes again!

"A dazzling fantasy is created by lace and chiffon, brocade and lamé, ribbons and paillettes."[9] This quote by fashion designer Diana Vreeland (1906–1989) may refer to a specific period, but it does not matter which because the essence of a formal dance and the dresses worn there are the same in any decade or century. Of course, the knowledge that lamé is shiny metallic fabric and that paillettes are great big sequins the size of a dime helps fulfill the conventional expectation that ball gowns are shiny, sparkly, decorated and special.

Social dance can easily cross over into ethnic or folk dance. Some styles or genres of dance are more familiar than others; most styles can be identified as easily by the clothing worn as by the movements of the dance or by the music. Many of the clothing styles have evolved because of different movement styles during particular eras. The visual clues of the clothes can be overt or subtle.

Think flamenco: men in long-legged trousers, the length of which is exaggerated by a very high waistline, emphasized in turn by a sash and a short jacket; women in tight, elongated bodices stretching over the curves of breast and buttocks, exploding into cascades of ruffles. Flamenco is a very seductive style of dance and involves competition between men and women in a kind of courting ritual. The music of flamenco is also competitive: guitar playing against castanets in fast, complex and precise sounds. The dancers' feet beat rhythms that are sometimes in their own voice, sometimes in counterpoint to the music and sometimes in concert with it. The differences between the muscular male and sinuous female are emphasized: he usually wears dark, solid colors, and she is in brightly colored garments, sometimes with contrasting trim or petticoats and often made of patterned fabrics. The long clean lines of his clothes draw attention to his emotional control; visually, they bring the focus to his feet, which speak to her in rhythmic patterns. Often, she has to lift her skirts to deliver the rapid replies of her feet without tripping. She thus reveals her legs, so obviously an intentional sexual tease. The layers of ruffles on her skirt are also seductive; they echo her rounded figure and swirling movements, and they make visual the fluid sounds of her castanets.

Or think tango: a seductive dance of a different sort. Although also using primarily guitar music, tango is as different in sound quality from flamenco as the movement and clothing are different. Rather than frantic and crisp, tango is smoother, more languorous and more streamlined. Dancers are already paired, and the dance seems to be a public display of a more private enterprise! Clothing for the tango can be anything from jeans to evening wear, but it is invariably form revealing and slender. The dancers wrap around each other and often look as though they are a single unit, so the less fabric and frills the better. Women frequently wear really high heels and long, narrow skirts, which make them appear tall and willowy. Their skirts must have vents, or slits, from hem to hip joint to allow their legs to stretch or lift and wrap around their partner's waist.

A BRIEF HISTORY

"[A] stage costume . . . is created to enhance the particular quality of a special occasion. . . . [I]t is an organic and necessary part of the drama in which it appears."[10] It helps to know something about the history of dance and its designs to watch dance intelligently because that history offers a sense of context. Bourne's *Swan Lake* is more effective if we understand what it is not doing (convention) so that we can appreciate the freshness of his vision.

The name or names of the first costume designers will probably never be known because they were not yet known as "designers." Peasants, queens, famous artists, fashion designers and trained stage designers have designed costumes over the years. Designer Robert Edmond Jones (1887–1954) tells us that any clothes chosen to suit a particular need or purpose is a stage costume. Therefore, we might consider Catherine de Medici (1519–1589) to be one of the first costume designers and perhaps also the first producer. Like Serge Diaghilev (1872–1929) of the Ballets Russes and Lincoln Kirstein (1907–1996) of the New York City Ballet some 350 years later, Catherine de Medici had a talent for making things happen. In 1581, she imported the idea of Italian masqued balls, huge spectacles involving hundreds of people, to the

249

French court for her son Henri III. The *Ballet comique de la reine* was staged and choreographed by Balthasar de Beaujoyeulx (b. early 16th century, d. c.1587). The music was precise and measured, almost mathematical; the dance steps small, specific and formal. The massive, heavy, stiff clothes of the period emphasized the feet and enhanced the slow, measured specificity of the dance steps. The costumes for the court ladies and gentlemen who were to appear in the entertainment were an integral and elaborate part of the spectacle. Undoubtedly, the queen was demanding and specific with her designs. Those employed to make the clothes were the best court dressmakers and tailors of the time, and they worked long hours stitching real jewels onto heavily embroidered and brocaded fabrics to please Her Majesty.

In the next century, Louis XIV (1638–1715) took the idea of masqued balls as theatrical entertainment to new heights and may have been responsible for the earliest collaboration of lighting and costumes. Surely the jewels and metallic threads of embroidery that encrusted the clothing of the period were designed and executed to make their wearers more visible under the candlelit chandeliers in the mirrored great hall of Versailles.

But dance has maintained its piecemeal relationship with costume designers; today, just as in 1581, few designers are household names. Conversely, the history of design for dance can also be read as a list of an era's premier painters, sculptors, choreographers and producers!

For the Ballets Russes, Serge Diaghilev used famous artists such as Pablo Picasso (1881–1973), Marc Chagall (1887–1985) and Henri Matisse (1869–1954), as well as stage designers, to create lavish backdrops and gorgeous costumes. Alexander Benois (1870–1960) and Léon Bakst (1866–1924) fit both categories: trained as architect and painter respectively, they made their reputations not in the studio arts in which they had their antecedents, but as two of the most successful stage designers for the Ballet Russes. Diaghilev himself seems to have dictated the lighting designs most of the time. Lighting was not firmly established as a design art until Jean Rosenthal (1912–1969) made it so in the middle part of the 20th century. Diaghilev also used preeminent fashion designers of his time: Coco Chanel (1883–1971) designed the costumes for *Le train bleu* (1924).

Martha Graham (1894–1991), recognized as an important pioneer of modern dance, also worked with fine artists. But as often as she worked with sculptor Isamu Noguchi (1904–1988) or stage designer Edythe Gilfond (d. 1989), she also frequently designed her own clothes for a piece. Gilfond designed the costumes for Graham's *Letter to the World* (1940), which probably provides the quintessential photographic image of Graham, but Graham herself designed her solo *Lamentation* (1930), the other "visual icon" of her career. Many choreographers still design their own costumes, but others work with well-recognized studio artists or fashion designers. Merce Cunningham (b. 1919) has strong collaborative relationships with artists Frank Stella (b. 1936) and Robert Rauschenberg (b. 1925). Mark Morris (b. 1956) had current fashion guru Isaac Mizrahi (b. 1961) design the costumes for his 2001 premier of *Gong*.

COSTUMES AS CLOTHES

As clothing, costumes give the audience much information. The dancers are wearing ball gowns, but it is somehow clear that they are going to a picnic. You need to ask yourself, "Why?" Such a design choice should be very intentional: to make you laugh or at least to make you consider the statement such a juxtaposition makes. The cowboy hats of Saul Bolasni's (b. 1923) designs for Agnes de Mille's (1909–1993) *Rodeo* (1942) leave us without questions. By using the unambiguously iconographic imagery of a particular type of hat, Bolasni informs you of locale and occupation: you know where you are (the American West), who the dance is about (cowboys) and what the characters do for a living (work on a ranch).

Clothing can also delineate period. Tie-dyed T-shirts and heavily decorated blue jeans have become iconographic of the 1960s; straight bangs, short-cropped hair (bobbed) and knee-length dresses covered in beads or fringe have come to represent the flapper of the 1920s. The more you know about the specifics of art history, the history of clothes or of period styles in general and the history of dance, the more you will understand and appreciate the visual clues that a costume designer provides you.

Conventions establish iconographic expectations. If you see a bunch of white tutus, it is likely that you are at the ballet. If the dancers are wearing corsets and leather pants, you are probably not at the ballet, so you might want to check out some other details, find other traditional clues. Try asking, "What do their shoes tell me?" Soft leather shoes might identify a jazz dance piece. Wooden clogs or tap shoes help you to expect a completely different style of movement and a different type of music. Satin pointe shoes return you to the ballet, but those leather pants make it more modern than classical.

What aspect of the music does each visual evoke? Be specific: notice color. Color completely alters how a piece feels. Imagine how the dance would change if the corsets were pink polka-dotted satin (color, pattern and texture), the leather pants lime green and the satin pointe shoes red. Is the music playful (fast, happy, utilizing a variety of instruments)? Loud? Bright (brass instruments versus strings)? Does the dance make you laugh?

How would you react to an image entirely in black: velvet corsets, leather pants and satin shoes? What could the music be? Jazz saxophone? Hard rock? How would the meaning change by simply altering the textures to make corsets and shoes leather like the pants? What if the shoes are pink, and everything else remains black? The possibilities and the combinations are endless.

How do designers go about deciding which choices to make? All of their choices must function in the context of style and genre.

EXPERIENCING THE ART OF COSTUMES

Robert Edmond Jones points out, "Many people confuse imagination with ingenuity, with inventiveness. But imagination is not this thing at all. It is the peculiar power of seeing with the eye of the mind."[11] Your imagination is as important as that of the composer, choreographer or designer. You, too, should always be an active participant in the process. Be open-minded, feel, think. Have a sense of expectation. You will enjoy any evening in the live theater more fully if you engage with the performers on stage. Dance is a temporal art: it takes place in time and is shared uniquely at each performance. Ask mental questions. Do not sit back and wait to be told how to feel. If you don't feel anything, it may well be that you are not participating, but it as easily may be that you know something you don't want to admit—you are bored and unengaged (perhaps because the performers are or the designers were). But before you are lazy, mean-spirited or petty-minded in your thoughts and reactions, be honest about how much effort *you yourself* put into watching the performance. It is okay to love or hate something *if you can explain why.* If you can put your response within an appropriate context, it will be a clearly stated opinion rather than a rude or dismissive comment.

Your response to all cultural activities is in some way always judgmental. Making judgments is not pejorative by definition; it means to make choices that emphasize one element over another in order to create order and focus. The question is, How do you shape those judgments? It is helpful to find ways to move beyond "I like it" or "I don't like it" and "the clothes were pretty" (or "ugly" or "pink").

As an audience member, you cannot second-guess the designer. You can only do as the designer does: trust your taste and instincts, make informed judgments and base them on specific observations and choices. Be aware of the context and style of what you are viewing. Are you seeing a classical ballet or a Broadway musical? Know if you are going to see a professional company: Is it conventional or avant-garde? Read something about the history and conventions of the genre before you go.

Take this snatch from a review by dance critic Clive Barnes: "Fascinatingly, in its lovely scenery and glamorous costumes by Yolanda Sonnabend [b. 1935], instead of placing the ballet in some Gothic never-never land, this version plonks it down in a Ruritanian Russia around, yes, 1895!"[12] Barnes is talking about yet another production of *Swan Lake*. Anthony Dowell (b. 1943) choreographed this version in 1987, but Marius Petipa and Lev Ivanov (1834–1901) made the most famous early version of the ballet in Russia in 1895. Barnes's knowledge allows him to compliment the clever design reference to the ballet's origins.

Be willing to entertain new ideas in spite of your expectations. Weigh what you know and that which you have seen previously against the new and the thought provoking. Art makes us expand our horizons—we recognize comfortable old thoughts, but we can think and feel in new ways, too. Let what you are hearing and seeing inspire you to think and feel differently. Perhaps you will discover enjoyment in an upside-down or sideways or downside-up perspective!

The most effective method of judging costume designs is to develop a meaningful visual vocabulary. Start slowly. Try looking at one element at a time. Go to more than one performance of the same work. Describe line, shape, value, texture and color. Connect each to the dance. What is the movement like? What texture does it have? What lines and shapes? Do the lines and shapes of the costumes feel similar to the sounds of the music, or are they in counterpoint to it? How is the space filled? Is it about unfilled space? How do the elements interact? What is repeated, and what is not? What is focal to your eyes, and how do you notice that? Does the dance feel balanced and whole? If not, why not? Do you think that is intentional? What clues tell you so?

The more clearly you understand how the elements and principles of costume design work on you subliminally and emotionally, the more you will appreciate dance as a whole.

ENDNOTES

[1] Christopher Bowen, qtd. in Matthew Bourne, Giving the classical a shot of irony, *Dance Magazine* (May 1997), p. 52.

[2] Ibid.

[3] Ibid.

[4] Ibid.

[5] Robert Cornfield, ed. *Dance writings and poetry: Edwin Denby* (New Haven, Conn.: Yale University Press, 1998), p. 142.

[6] Deborah Jowitt, *The dance in mind: Profiles and reviews 1976–1983* (Boston: David R. Godine, 1985), pp. 72, 74.

[7] Jean Rosenthal and Lael Wertenbaker, *The magic of light* (Boston: Little, Brown and Company, 1972), p. 34.

[8] Bowen, qtd. in Bourne, Giving the classical, p. 23.

[9] Carol McDonagh Wallace, Don McDonagh, Jean L. Druesedow, Laurence Libin and Constance Old, *Dance: A very social history* (New York: Rizzoli and the Metropolitan Museum of Art, 1986), p. 7.

[10] Robert Edmond Jones, *The dramatic imagination* (New York: Theatre Art Books, 1980), p. 93.

[11] Ibid., p. 90.

[12] Clive Barnes, Swains, swans get Royal, *Dance Magazine* (September 2001), p. 94.

CHAPTER NINETEEN

introduction

L ighting designer Rick Yeatman rightly notes that you have to see the dance clearly first in order to experience it. Then the magic of lighting design— its pools of color, washes, specials, fades and other atmospheric flavors— appropriately helps create and heighten mood, image and theme in highly effective ways.

"AS A FISH LIVES IN WATER, A DANCER LIVES IN LIGHT"

Rick Yeatman

Designed light is not a new phenomenon, but specialized theatrical lighting designers are.[1] Performances have always involved decisions about light. The earliest outdoor dramatized rituals were positioned to take optimal advantage of natural light, and early theater buildings were also sited with regard to the trajectory of the sun. Since the time of the very first indoor theaters, the positioning of every lamp, whether candle, oil, gas or electric, has involved a design decision. Just as there has always been designed light, there have always been people responsible for designing it. They may not have been called *lighting designers*, but they were always there, making design decisions, usually as one of many duties in a combined role. However, the second half of the 20th century saw the emergence of a specialist who, within the creative team, assumed design responsibilities for the lighting alone.

Why have a specialist make the lighting decisions? Why not the director or the choreographer or the scenic designer or all of them together in a joint operation? The need for a specialist arises in part out of the size of the typical workload for contemporary productions and in part from a general desire to develop the role of light by taking advantage of new possibilities offered by rapidly advancing technology. Lighting has become a bigger and bigger operation as we have sought to do more with light by using equipment installations, which have become larger and increasingly complex. The history books are full of theater designers whose lighting ambitions far exceeded the technology available to them. The situation today is reversed: any failure of the light to support a stage production is more likely to arise from a lack of imagination and organization than from any deficiencies in the available technology.

Stage lighting stands at the crossroads of art and science, yet detailed technical knowledge is not essential for it. Indeed, too much technological background may inhibit imagination rather than stimulate it. For a lighting designer, the science tends to be simpler than the art. Handling the technology is the easy part: the core skills of a lighting designer are coordinating that technology with all of the associated people and their ideas. In conjunction with the rest of the production team, lighting designers take the lead in the concept and development of the lighting style. They establish where light is required and where it is not required—its qualities, color and quantity. Then they devise the means of implementing these decisions as to which types of instruments and color filters to use, where to position them and how to focus them. This drawing-board process has evolved into today's computer-based drafting technology. Like an iceberg, the greater proportion of the work is hidden from view, not under the sea but away from the stage.

The lighting designer then supervises all the preparations in association with colleagues who have other technological responsibilities. He or she visits the rehearsal spaces as much as possible to absorb the action and to continue discussions with the director, choreographer(s) and other members of the production team. Then he or she implements the design during the technical and dress rehearsals, working according to the prepared plan but keeping a flexible approach in anticipation of inevitable developments and changes throughout the process. This implementation can involve personal and professional group agonizing, which is often at the heart of all creative processes.

The most important thing to remember when discussing theatrical lighting is that the main function of the lighting designer is to light the dancers' or actors' bodies and faces for optimal clarity of physical and facial expression. Because of the performing styles used in modern theatrical productions, it is of principal importance for the audience to be able to discern the smallest changes in physical and facial expressions in order to make the production fully understandable. Dance lighting, in particular, is designed to concentrate light on the whole human form so that the greatest amount of plasticity, meaning of gesture and emotional impact may be transferred to an audience.

Early Stage Lighting

Stage lighting design is probably as old as formalized theater. The early
Greeks built their theaters as open air spaces and orientated them in relation
to the sun, presenting their plays at different times of the day to take advantage of the different types of natural lighting. This approach was quite possibly the earliest form of theatrical lighting design. The Theater of Dionysus
(Athens, c. 330 B.C.E.) and the theater at Epidaurus (c. 340 B.C.E.) are examples of these early public theater facilities.

Lighting for the theater developed over many centuries, using both natural
and artificial sources. Sunlight, candlelight, torchlight and oil, gas, electric
arc and lime lighting have had their place in early stage lighting. In Italy
during the Renaissance, many of the principles of modern lighting design
were firmly established and codified by people such as Nicola Sabbattini
(1574–1654). Sabbattini was an architect, theater designer and painter at the
court of Urbino, Italy. His famous *Practica*, or "how to" books on theatrical
devices, published in two volumes (1637 and 1638), were the first written
handbooks on the art of scenography for the practicing theater technician.
Sabbattini describes a number of techniques related to lighting, illumination,
scenery and special effects, writing in detail about the need and placement of
footlights and the arrangement of other lighting around the stage and auditorium. In a drawing in the 1638 volume, he even shows a mechanical
method of lowering cylindrical metal hoods around burning candles, caus-
ing them to dim.[2] The publication of these texts represented a significant step
in the awareness, use and evolution of light in the theater.

Until the invention of controllable gas lighting in the early 19th century, candles and oil lamps were the most common method of theatrical illumination
in the theater. In the gas lighting era, complex stage lighting finally became
possible but was limited by its bulky, smelly and dangerous nature. During
this period, fires destroyed a great number of theaters. On the night of
December 5, 1876, more than three hundred people who had come to see the
popular actress Kate Claxton in *The Two Orphans* died, along with some of the
actors, in a fire that engulfed the Brooklyn Theatre in Brooklyn, New York.
This L-shaped theater, built in 1871, occupied a large portion of the Johnson
Street blockfront. Started by a spilled kerosene lamp, the fire swept up the
ceiling and turned the auditorium into an inferno. The theater had no fire
escapes and only five narrow exits. Unidentified bodies were buried in a
common grave in Greenwood Cemetery, and a monument was erected to the

257

victims of one of the worst fires in recorded history.[3] The installation of electric lighting and modern fire prevention in public places resulted in part from this and other tragedies.

Modern stage lighting design began to flourish with the development of the incandescent lamp in the late 1800s. This invention allowed for the development of small, safe and portable lighting fixtures that could be placed anywhere around the stage and then controlled by a remote electrical dimmer system. As stage lighting continued to develop into the early 1900s, certain parallel industries evolved from the many basic principles of the growing field of stage lighting design, such as architectural and industrial lighting design. Today's modern technologies of display, photographic, film and television lighting design have evolved from these fundamental roots of early stage lighting design. Stage lighting design is now recognized as an exciting and rich discipline in its own right, merging science with art.

The history of modern dance and the history of electric lighting in the theater are one such parallel occurrence. In the history of theater technology, it is interesting to note that the first group of artists to experiment with electric lighting were dancers. An early modern dance precursor, Loie Fuller (1862–1928), was one of the first performance artists to recognize the creative possibilities of electric lighting as an element of design. In 1892, Fuller was the first American to present her unique form of nontraditional dance on the concert stage. Raised in a theatrical family, she discovered dance by improvising "deliriumlike" movements in early experimental performances. As she continued to build on these experiments, her primary interest was in creating theatrical effects by illuminating the fabric of her costumes with electric light. Although Fuller did not develop a technique or start a school, her great contribution to the development of modern dance was to "set an example of theatre magic arrived at through the use of lighting and deft manipulation of costume material": "Suddenly the stage is darkened, and Loie Fuller appears in a white light which makes her radiant, and a white robe which surrounds her like a cloud. She floats around the stage, her figure now revealed, now concealed by the exquisite drapery which takes forms of its own and seems indistinct with her life."[4]

At the 1900 Paris International Exhibition in the Palace of Electricity, Fuller's piece began on a darkened stage. Then series of tableaux appeared, derived from the manipulations of drapery and combined with the effects of colored light and shadow. The tableaux were named after the forms that Fuller's drapery seemed to resemble—large flowers, the surf, a spider web, a butterfly—and each was separated by a return to the darkness into which the dancer disappeared. This dance employed very little of the rhythm and movements found in traditional choreography, offering instead a constantly transforming series of formal effects on the fabrics and visual pyrotechnics created by the colored and sharply focused light and shadows. The swirling surfaces of Fuller's silks acted as a screen for the projection of an equally protean succession of colors.

Fuller was an inventor and stagecraft innovator who held many patents for stage lighting, including the first chemical mixes for gels and slides, and was the first to use luminescent salts to create lighting effects. She was also an early innovator in lighting design and was the first to mix colors and explore new angles. She clearly understood the contribution that artificial lighting could have on performance art.

THE FIRST PROFESSIONAL LIGHTING DESIGNERS

In the history of contemporary theater, the lighting designer has been the newest member to join the visual design team. Although a few scenic designers enjoyed lighting their own scenery, the lighting of most professional productions in the first half of the 20th century was relatively neglected and became, by default, one of the innumerable duties of the stage manager or stage electrician. It was inevitable that lighting specialists would eventually move into this gap in order to develop the full range of possibilities for electric lighting.[5] Many 21st century lighting designers are still inspired by two of the most important and influential pioneers in the field, Stanley McCandless and Jean Rosenthal.

Stanley McCandless

In the 1920s, Stanley McCandless (1897–1967) was one of the first designers to envision an entire system for lighting the stage, giving performers greater plasticity by revealing their form. To McCandless, plasticity meant that the performers should appear three dimensional and naturally lit, as though stage lighting was a controllable and flattering sun. In experimenting with colored light, he deduced that two front lights were the most desirable, with the beam of one spotlight directed at a forty-five-degree angle above and to the right of the performer, and a second spotlight directed forty-five degrees above and to the left. One light would have a warm color, such as amber or pink, and the other light would be a cool color, such as blue or lavender, combining on the performer in a pleasing, natural effect. He named the warm light the *key* and the cool light the *fill*, with the key light representing the apparent direction of a light source striking the performer.

In what became known as the "McCandless theory," the process of lighting the performer became divided into six basic parts in order to achieve this "plastic" effect:[6]

1. Divide the stage into six areas. Three areas cover the downstage edge, and three areas cover upstage;

2. Make sure these areas are between eight to ten feet in diameter;

3. Use two spotlights per area;

4. Make one spotlight a warm color and the other a cool color;

5. Hang each of the two spotlights at a forty-five-degree angle above the edge of the stage and forty-five degrees off center;

6. Use colored toning striplights above the performers to set mood and time of day.

McCandless published his lighting theories while a professor at Yale University in the late 1920s. Although lighting equipment at the time was still in its infancy, the use of his techniques gave both a clear indication of the performers' facial structure and a variety of moods.[7] With today's sophisticated equipment, McCandless's ideas now seem crude and garish, but his principles remain philosophically correct. Through a clear understanding of these six basic techniques, the beginning lighting designer can easily achieve plasticity, and more seasoned designers can adapt them for richer and more dramatic lighting schemes.

Whereas McCandless focused his attentions primarily on lighting for actors, the other important pioneer, Jean Rosenthal, modified the McCandless theory in the service of dance.

Jean Rosenthal

A student of Stanley McCandless at Yale, Jean Rosenthal (1912–1969) described lighting the stage as an attempt to make the dancer or actor appear "jewel-like." She achieved this effect by enveloping the performer in light, often creating the impression of "light and shade on a stage that contained no shadows."[8] Her major contributions to modern lighting design theory were the addition of deeply colored washes of back and side light to the designer's vocabulary and an organized approach to lighting dance.

Rosenthal introduced back light and side light to drama and dance in the late 1930s, while she was working with the well-known American modern dance choreographer Martha Graham (1894–1991): "My system required fixed lighting booms along the side at every entrance as a basis for flexibility and for lighting the whole stage. That made the ballets look different, which rousted the European choreographers and designers for Ballet International in 1944."[9]

In addition to her extensive use of side light, Rosenthal often used "down lights" coming from directly above the stage to form pools of light on the stage floor and "back lights" coming down along a back cyclorama screen to silhouette the dancers. She seldom used front light because of its "flattening" effect (a two-dimensional look), usually reserving this position for "color wash" lighting.

According to Rosenthal theories, side lighting techniques require a vertical lighting boom (a tall, solidly grounded pipe) in each "leg" or entrance from the side wings; four to six booms are often required on each side. Each boom has one or more lighting fixtures, but usually three to five. The lighting fixtures are focused straight across the stage in order to wrap the performers in light. A typical three-fixture boom might have fixtures mounted at ten-foot, eight-foot and one-foot positions above the floor. Their fixtures are often referred to as being in a *top, mid* or *shin* position. The top and mid fixtures are usually used for general side lighting and often have different colored filters. The bottom lamp, called the *shin* or *shin buster,* for obviously painful reasons, was traditionally used to light the legs of the ballet dancer and to provide light through and under a tutu. Modern dance designers often use the shins as the principal source for an unnatural angle of light, often with strong color(s). If the light is properly shuttered, the dancer appears to "float" across the floor.[10] This effect can be very dramatic, particularly with opposing colors from opposite sides.

Jean Rosenthal was a pioneer in the art and craft of lighting design. Her ideas for lighting the various types of theatrical presentations—plays, opera, musicals and especially dance—are as valid and vital today as they were when she first demonstrated them in the 1930s.

THE TOOLS OF STAGE LIGHTING

Adolphe Appia (1862–1928), a Swiss scenic designer of the early 20th century, was one of the first people to see the vast aesthetic possibilities of electric lighting in the theater. He wrote: "Light is to the production what music is to the score; expressive elements in opposition to the literal signs. And, like music, light can express only what belongs to the essence of all visions' vision."[11] Appia's contemporary, Edward Gordon Craig (1872–1966), a designer of some note who was passionately involved with Isadora Duncan (1877–1927) at one point, spoke of "painting with light."[12]

The lighting designer can indeed "paint with light," but far more is possible, of course. On the deepest sensual and symbolic level, the lighting designer can convey something of the feeling and even the substance of a performance piece. In order to go from mere illumination to an aesthetically pleasing and functionally practical lighting design, a designer must seriously consider and understand certain guidelines.

THE FUNCTIONS AND OBJECTIVES OF STAGE LIGHTING

"Stage lighting may be defined as the use of light to create a sense of visibility, naturalism, composition and mood." So begins a chapter in the 1933 text *A Syllabus of Stage Lighting*, by Stanley McCandless. Most comprehensive lighting texts since that time also tend to discuss the artistic objectives or functions of lighting in these terms.

McCandless recognized that a number of qualities do not exist independently of each other, but instead overlap. According to McCandless, the six functions of stage lighting are:

1. *Providing visibility*. The chief practical function of lighting is, of course, visibility. First and foremost, we must be able to see at some visual level the performers' actions. Occasionally, lighting designers, carried away with the atmospheric possibilities of light, will make a portion of a dance piece so dark that we cannot see what is happening. Mood is important, but seeing the performers is obviously more important. At times, the mood of a particular sequence does call for the lights to dim; in a suspense-filled sequence, for instance, the lights in a haunted house might go out. But

these are exceptions. Ordinarily, if we cannot see the performers, the lighting designer has not carried out his or her assignment.

2. *Establishing time and place.* The color, shade and intensity of lighting can suggest various times of the day, giving us the pale light of dawn, the bright light of midday, the vivid colors of sunset or the muted light of evening. Lighting can also indicate the season of the year because the sun strikes objects at very different angles in winter and summer. Lighting can also suggest place—indoor or outdoor light, for instance.

3. *Creating mood.* Light, together with scenery and costumes, can help create a certain general mood. Rarely, however, can lighting alone create a specific mood. For example, if a stage is filled with blue light, it might be inviting, romantic moonlight, but it could also be a cold, dark, evil setting. In dance, when action, scenery and music are combined with light, they tell us *exactly* what the mood is. In general, a happy, carefree piece calls for bright, warm colors, such as yellows, oranges and pinks. A more somber piece will lean toward blues, blue greens and muted tones.

4. *Reinforcing style.* With regard to style, lighting can indicate whether a dance piece is realistic or nonrealistic. In a dance that leans toward realism, the lighting can simulate the effect of ordinary sources, such as table lamps and sunlight. In a nonrealistic production, the designer can be more imaginative: shafts of light can cut through the dark, sculpturing performers onstage; a glowing red light can envelop a choreographer's vision of damnation; a ghostly green light can cast a spell over a nightmare scene.

5. *Providing focus and composition.* In photography, the focus has to do with adjusting the lens of a camera so that the picture recorded on the film is sharp and clear. In dance lighting, focus means that beams of light are aimed at, or "focused on," a particular area. *Focus* in lighting directs our attention to one part of the stage—generally the part where the important action is occurring—and away from other areas. Lights should illuminate the dancing or playing area, not the scenery. Obviously, if more light is on the scenery than on the performers, the audience's attention will be drawn to the scenery and away from the performers. Therefore, the first objective of focus is to aim the light at the right place. A good example of the use of focus occurs when there is a split stage, with half the action on one side and half on the other. The lights can direct our attention from side to side as they go down in one area and come up in another. *Composition* is the way lighted areas are arranged onstage in rela-

tionship to one another—which areas are dimmed, which are brightly lit—and what the *overall* stage effect is with regard to light. By means of focus, light can create a series of visual compositions onstage, much like a montage of scenes in a film. The effects can vary from turning the stage into one large area to creating small, isolated areas.

6. *Establishing rhythm.* Because changes in light occur over a time continuum, successive lighting changes often establish a succession of rhythms that run through a production. Abrupt, staccato changes with stark blackouts convey one rhythm; languid, slow fades or gradual cross-fades another. Lighting changes are (usually) timed in coordination with scene changes, with mood and tempo changes in the music and with the message that the piece is trying to convey to the audience at any particular point in the production. Directors and designers recognize the importance of these coordinated efforts, and they take great care to "choreograph" shifts in light and scenery with the movements of dancers.

The Qualities of Light

Once light is created, whether from an artificial or a natural source, it has certain inherent qualities that become characteristic of the medium itself:

1. *Intensity (the brightness of the light).* Impression of brightness is subjective. Compare the brightness of the sun to the brightness of car headlights at night. The latter *appear* more blinding. In the theater, brightness is determined by the number of instruments used, the size of each light source, dimmer use, gel (color medium) use and set and costume color schemes.

The point to remember is not how bright the light is, but how bright it *appears to be.* For example, a single candle on a dark stage may appear bright, whereas a 1,000-watt spot may appear dim on a brightly lit stage; eight lights striking a white set will look brighter than the same lights striking a black set.

> *Adaptation:* A bright scene will appear even brighter, by contrast, if it follows a dim one. For example, prior to a dim scene, the houselights are slowly dimmed, allowing the audience to adjust more easily.

Visual fatigue: Too much or too little light or too many rapid changes of intensity may prove tiring to the observer.

Visual perception: The amount of illumination needed to allow an object to be clearly seen depends on its color, reflective quality, contrast, size and distance from the observer.

Intensity and mood: Bright light makes an audience more alert. For example, bright light is often used for comedy.

2. *Color.* On stage, color is the product of the color of the light and the color of every object. This can be understood easily by observing the effect of two different gels on the same set of walls or a screen.

Visual perception: People see more clearly in the yellow-green zones of the middle spectrum than at the red-blue end zones.

Color and mood: People more generally associate warm colors with a happy mood. It is a well-established psychological fact that they feel more comfortable viewing warm, naturalistic and highly visible scenes, and generally associate these images with a positive mood. They more generally associate cool colors with an unhappy mood or with their instinctive fear of the dark.

It is important to understand the inherent psychological nature of light, but it is relatively simple to modify these examples to achieve other effects. For example, warm colors onstage can be modified to achieve an effect such as "the calm before the storm." Likewise, cool colors can be modified to create a "loving, romantic" feeling.

3. *Distribution.* All light has form and direction, ranging from a soft, shadowless diffusion to a stark and direct shaft of light. Control of direction gives highlight, shade and shadow to the composition. Compare and contrast strong overhead light to backlight, side light from different angles and front light from different angles. The eye is invariably attracted to the brightest object in the field of vision.

4. *Movement.* Each of the three properties of light (intensity, color and distribution) may be changed either quickly or slowly: a room may grow darker, or a setting sun may slowly change color. Intensity, color, distribution and movement are controllable properties of light. How they are controlled is determined by what is to be achieved on the stage.

Special Effects

Special effects are out of the ordinary or unique effects used in a given production. They usually do not fall within a given design area without discussion among the production team.

In many cases, special lighting effects are the difference between a successful production and the merely ordinary. Except for special effects, lighting design generally strives to be unobtrusive. Just as in set design, however, the skillful use of color, intensity and distribution can have a subliminal effect on the spectators' perceptions. The lighting designer is often responsible for projections and other special visual effects, such as still or moving images that substitute for or enhance painted and constructed scenery, stars or moonlight and written legends for the identification of scenes. Images can be projected from the audience side of the stage onto opaque surfaces or from the rear of the stage onto specially designed rear-projection screens. Similar projections are often used on *scrims* (semitransparent curtains stretched across the stage) or on a *cyclorama* (opaque curtains stretched across the stage), often called the "cyc" (pronounced "sike").

The most common type of special effect of lighting design involves the use of a *gobo*, a piece of cut metal or glass that is inserted into a theatrical lighting instrument in order to shape the light output. Gobo lighting effects and some other common special effects that fall into the lighting designer's purview include:

- ¤ *Creating a moon onstage.* This effect can be achieved by using a gobo pattern on a cyclorama, by using a projected slide image on the cyclorama or by using a shadow box that simulates the effect of moonlight filtering through trees or other objects.

- ¤ *Creating stars onstage.* This effect can be achieved by using a gobo pattern on a cyclorama, using a fiber optic curtain or attaching Christmas tree lights to a black scrim.

- ¤ *Creating lightning onstage.* This effect can be achieved by photo floods, camera strobes or shadow boxes.

- ¤ *Creating a water effect onstage.* This effect can be achieved by bouncing light off actual water or combining projections

with a gobo rotator (an electrical device that spins one or
more gobos inside the lighting instrument).

¤ *Creating a fire effect onstage.* This effect can be achieved by
projections with gobo rotators, a stylized, rolling log covered
with aluminum foil and lit with red and amber light or
standard lighting equipment with random chase effects of
red and amber light.

Special effects have helped the designer to achieve heightened visual images,
but in the history of stage lighting no one lighting fixture has revolutionized
the art more than the invention of the automated lighting fixture. Throughout all of recorded history and up until the 1970s, all stage lighting fixtures
had one thing in common: they were static. They provided a single color and
a single focus and were useful only for single lighting applications. It was
only a matter of time before someone decided to try and automate a lighting fixture. Early designs in the 1970s included motors to pan and tilt the
fixtures in real time, much as when a human operator manipulates a fol-
lowspot (a spotlight that can be manually directed to follow a performer).
Although rather primitive at first, the automated lighting fixture was indeed
born then.

During the 1980s and 1990s, the technology continued to develop. Companies such as Vari*Lite™, Clay Paky™, Hi-End Systems™ and Martin™ started
to produce automated fixtures. Some fixtures actually moved, whereas others remained static and a moving mirror directed the light beam. As fixtures
developed, they became known as "intelligent" fixtures. Today, the modern
automated lighting fixture is a technological wonder. Controlled by computer and using modern light sources, they move, change color, dim, project
patterns and images, provide strobe effects and do much more.

Automated fixtures are available in two basic types: *moving fixture* or *moving mirror.* Each has its advantages and disadvantages, and each is suited for
specific lighting applications. Fixtures generally are designed for color wash
lighting (wide angle) or area lighting and imaging effects (narrow angle).
Automated fixtures can be and are used for all lighting applications, depending on the design of the particular fixture.

Many current automated fixtures are still quite noisy in operation, mainly
because a fan is required to cool the lamp. This fact and their general overall expense and poor record of reliability have kept the automated luminaire
from replacing conventional fixtures for most stage lighting applications. As

these fixtures become quieter and more reliable, they certainly will be in greater demand for theater, dance and opera.

THE PROCESS OF LIGHTING DESIGN

Communication

Craftwise, lighting designers must be able to visualize their proposed design in three dimensions. Further, they must have the necessary skills to verbalize or describe the proposed design in words and visual images. Finally, they must be able to document the proposed design on paper and direct the design in practice.

The art of stage lighting relies also on communication, however. It really does not matter how designers communicate the technical aspects of their design intentions to others, just as long as they do it clearly and effectively. In professional situations, certain design conventions and expectations have been established over the years. Crews expect clear, concise and detailed information so that they can work efficiently and within time constraints. The lighting designer must ensure that the lighting crews receive the necessary direction and information so that all details of the lighting installation are absolutely clear. The use of renderings (formal or informal drawn lighting plots) often helps.

Once the designer has a full understanding of all the ingredients, he or she usually prepares a rough "lighting concept" drawing for each scene. These sketches summarize the stage pictures and provide other important lighting details, including mood, atmosphere, time of day and indication of any natural or artificial light sources.

Lighting Concept

At some point prior to producing the actual lighting design, the designer must form a lighting concept, typically a statement of what he or she hopes to achieve with the lighting design and how he or she hopes to achieve it. This statement may be written or verbal, but the concept must exist, at the very least, in the designer's mind.

This concept should be extremely fundamental. It should capture the intrinsic qualities of the dance or play and relate and describe them in terms of light. If properly developed, the concept will assist the designer with every step of the lighting design process. The designer will use it constantly to justify his or her choice of style; lighting methods; directions of light; use of intensity, distribution and color; and movement.

The lighting concept may become clear after the first meeting with the choreographer or director and the other designers, or it may develop slowly over a period of weeks, not becoming evident until the designer has had the opportunity to watch several rehearsals. The lighting concept is generally based on the emotional qualities of the piece being lit. The choreographer and the other designers' interpretations of the music and themes of the piece also will influence the concept. Everyone must be on the same page at the same time when it comes to the design concept.

The lighting concept sometimes may be as simple as, "Provide a feeling of warm, muted sunlight over the entire stage, with a strong dramatic sense of motivation from stage left." The concept is often far less simplistic and relates to a specific dance on various emotional or metaphorical levels. As the designer analyzes the piece, he or she often finds contrasts, conflicts, juxtapositions, metaphors, symbols, ironies and other dramatic devices that must be considered in the design. How he or she relates these images to the kinesthetic requirements of the dance is an important part of the design process and is usually defined as part of the concept.

For example, a stylized dance about two people who are diametrically opposed to each other and are always fighting might be seen as a "cat and mouse game," so the designer will use "cat and mouse colors" (maybe pink from one side, and bluish gray from the other). The designer may show the contrast between the two characters with contrast in the lighting. The "cat" may be illuminated with sharp, threatening lighting, whereas the "mouse" may be sympathetically illuminated with soft, warm light. Everything regarding choice of intensity, color, direction and movement of light can be justified by this concept.

Good lighting can and often does exist without a concept. However, the lighting designer who takes time to develop a strong overall concept is ultimately better equipped to make rapid design decisions, for there must always be complete justification and direction for all of his or her choices.

ENDNOTES

[1] The title for this chapter is taken from Jean Rosenthal and Lael Wertenbaker, *The magic of light* (Boston: Little, Brown, 1972), p. 43.

[2] Bill Williams, *Stage lighting design,* available at: www.escape.ca/~williams/sld/sld-100.html

[3] Ibid.

[4] Richard Current and Marcia Current, *Loie Fuller: Goddess of light* (Chicago: Northwestern University Press, 1997), p. 31.

[5] Oren W. Parker and Craig R. Wolf, *Scene design and stage lighting,* 7th ed. (New York: Thomson, 1996).

[6] Stanley McCandless, *A method of lighting the stage,* 4th ed. (New York: Theatre Arts Books, 1958), pp. 19–22.

[7] Parker and Wolf, *Scene design,* p. 103.

[8] Rosenthal and Wertenbaker, *The magic of light,* p. 66.

[9] Ibid., p. 67.

[10] Ibid.

[11] Adolphe Appia, *Music and the art of the theatre,* edited by Bernard Hewitt (Miami: University of Miami Press, 1981), p. 96.

[12] Edward Gordon Craig, *Index to the story of my days* (London: Hulton, 1957), p. 47.

CHAPTER TWENTY

introduction

This chapter makes a strong argument for movement as the fundamental requirement in all the performing arts. Performing artists by their very nature must start with the body as their instrument and then work inward to work outward. The editors of this book believe dance is the most interesting, challenging and spiritually profound art form on earth. Many artists feel the same way about their chosen enterprise. Those of us passionately engaged with our art processes often say that the form picked us, not the other way around. We *have to* dance, choreograph, paint, sing, act, direct, write, weave or sculpt in order to live; these activities are inseparable from our beings.

DANCE, MUSIC AND THEATER IN THEORY AND PRACTICE

Myron Howard Nadel

As you sit in a theater waiting for the curtain to rise at your first dance performance, you may not notice any difference in atmosphere than if you were waiting for the beginning of a play or musical. In fact, from the moment you first heard about the dance event until this moment of expectation, there was very little difference. The duties of putting on any theatrical production are the same: managing stage, house and box office; conducting and playing music; operating light boards; organizing, cleaning and repairing costumes; maintaining lighting instruments and sound equipment; and adjusting the level and quality of sound.

The checklist for the performance and the contributing personnel are also similar, but for the audience the performance itself will be a different experience. You may have imagined dance as merely theater without words, but when the curtain goes up, you will detect highly developed visual and musical components, too. Dance performances are very rich and complete theatrical, musical and visual experiences.

MOVEMENT: THE BASIS FOR DANCE AND ALL THE ARTS

Movement is the most primordial and vital source for all the arts. The human body in motion is their fundamental instrument, and paintbrushes, clay, trumpets, piano keys, voices, pens and props are their secondary instruments. However, dance, in contrast to most of the other arts, can be limited solely to the medium of the entire body and its movements, requiring no secondary instrument or means.

Of course, a singer's or actor's primary instrument is also the human body, and the performer's vigorous voice and actions are also within, not separate from, the body. Like dancers, these artists do not require a secondary instrument, although secondary media such as sounds, poetry and language are commonly part of their actions. Moreover, singers, musicians and actors also experience intense physical demands on their primary instrument during practice and performance. Although dancers may use their voices, stamp and clap out rhythms and use the movement of costumes and props as extensions of their bodies, their actions are by definition body centered and are more likely to focus on the creation of signs and symbols emanating from movement of the body alone.

TIME: THE DISTINCTIVE DIMENSION OF THE PERFORMING ARTS

The performing arts happen sequentially over time. They are planned, sometimes sketched on paper or on a computer, taught, learned and then made to occur. Audiences for the performing arts are always *in the midst* of an experience. The moment a shape, sound or action is seen, heard or felt, it is over, and the next shape, sound or action comes into the moment called "now." The performing arts, then, are forms *being made.* The visual arts are humanity's deepest emotions made concrete through paintings, sculptures, jewelry and buildings, but the performing arts are similar to life itself—impermanent, fleeting and illusory.

As part of the illusion of the performing arts, time itself is a commodity to be controlled. As the "nows" come into and out of our awareness, they can be manipulated to give us a sense of relative time within the context of the play, opera or dance. Movements or actions in the performing arts are causes that create effects, which in turn cause the next effect, and so forth. This continuum of action-reaction creates a structure in time called a *form*, one that can be understood best as a totality only after the experience has ended. Whether the form of a dance is related to a scenario or contrived purely around abstract movement sequences, the development over the whole length of a dance is based mostly on units of visual-kinesthetic time patterns; in other words, their duration, repetitions, similarities, contrasts and relationships are revealed over time. This control of time and rhythm is similar to the process of musical composition. Scenarios can be the inspiration, but movement composition is the matter.

Although the performing arts take place in the perpetual present tense, in a scenario-driven dramatic work such as a story ballet, opera or play, present time can be made to pass as if it were happening at another time in another era. The illusion of time past can also be created with the aid of a narrator, program notes, costume design and lighting effects. The audience must cooperate in a self-deceiving exercise called *suspension of disbelief*, giving stories on stage an imagined but meaningful realism.

Dissecting the word *performing* can offer a better sense of the importance of time to the performing arts. The prefix *per-* means "through," "all over," "by means of" and "during." It refers to the actions of movements over time. *Form* is the structure or shape of something—its literal figure and embodiment. The suffix *-ing* conveys the progressive process of an action, as in "I am talking" or "she is dancing." A performing art is thus a form in the making, witnessed by an immediate viewer. Once a performance has been videotaped or audiotaped, though, it is no longer a true performing art because it is not being formed in the immediate present.

Like the visual arts, the performing arts take time to plan and prepare, and the result of that planning is both expressive and communicative. The end product of the time spent preparing a work of visual art is called an *artifact*, a tangible object worthy of our time and attention. The performing arts are artifacts, however, *only as they are performed* in sequential moments of "the now." The performance of an entire dance is comparable to an art object, but it is a virtual, not an actual, product. It no longer exists after it has been performed, except in one's memory.

THE VIRTUAL NATURE OF THE PERFORMING ARTS

Music and Movement

The art world is generally not considered part of the "real" or concretely useful world. It is part of our play, spiritual, aesthetic and therapeutic worlds. Yet humans have created art for almost as long as they have existed, indicating that the experience of art is as useful and essential to us as the fulfillment of any other need. An imaginative and communicative expression is at the heart of every work of art.

I have always been drawn to the idea that the essence of communication in dance, theater or musical performance may not be movement, action or sound, but feeling. Philosopher Suzanne Langer (1895–1985) pointed to dance as a "virtual power"[1] that impressed its energies onto audiences in inarticulate but definite ways. Not minimizing the feelings evoked by the kinesthetic and visual aspects of the dance, the virtual power that emerges from dance as human movement is *felt* on a variety of dynamic levels. The audience senses these shapes and energies as an infectious and vicarious communicative experience.

Performed music is the power of sound waves striking our ears and bodies. Choreographers, dancers and audiences react to the energy of these sounds in virtual space: up, down, fall, rebound, around, through, on or under. Our kinesthetic reaction to the shape of music's time and energy in virtual space frequently inspires all of us.

Unfortunately, the complementary relationship between music's described shapes in virtual space and the kinesthetic excitement that results from these shapes can sometimes lead choreographers to enslave dance to the music. Skilled choreographers, instead of making the dance into an imitative art, design the merger of energy, shape and sound into something that the viewer-listener can enjoy and view critically.

Dance and Drama

Langer pointed out that the audience is a part of the virtual reality of a drama. We participate in our own deception, knowing full well that the actors are performing a tangible yet projected illusion of real or imagined events. The basic abstraction of performed drama is an "act" springing from past, future or imagined experiences. With or without the spoken word, the essence of the dramatic thrust of all acts involves relationships in contrast or conflict. Each argument, difference or tension begs for resolution, which in turn leads to the next conflict. We might think, then, that dramatic dance based on a story line, with dance characters representing real-life events, is very similar to a play without words. It is not.

Dance drama is *dance*; the basic abstraction of dance is movement, not the act, the story or virtual reality. The story or characters are but an inspiration to create an expressive work of music-dance-drama constructed and composed in the dimensions of space, time, energy and motivation. If a choreographer wants to emphasize the story, he or she should write a poem, play or book instead.

There are two basic forms of dance drama: the *chronological drama* and the *psychological drama*. The chronological form is common in traditional ballet, opera and musicals. Dancers represent a character from the originating story, which could have been a play, novel or even dramatic poem. Then, in chronological order, the major events of the story unfold though pantomimic actions. People will flirt, woo, fight and carry out all sorts of actions that can be "read" in an instant. We know the bad guys and the good guys, the lovers and the warriors. Famous late 19th century scenario classical dance dramas such as *The Sleeping Beauty* (1890), *The Nutcracker* (1892) and *Swan Lake* (1895) follow an obvious chronological structure.

The psychological dance drama, made popular by choreographer Martha Graham (1894–1991) in the mid–20th century, was focused more on the movement expression of the subconscious psyche of her characters. With dramatic movement, she commented on great literary themes as in the stories of Oedipus Rex and Medea in the dances *Night Journey* (1947) and *Cave of the Heart* (1946), respectively.

Choreographer and teacher Doris Humphrey (1895–1958) felt that all movement must be motivated by an idea.[2] She strongly believed that the dimensions of dance had to include motivation, along with space, time and energy. Thus, dancers in both dramatic and abstract dances need to immerse themselves so intensely that they, like actors, draw on their own life experiences. Even abstract dance includes a sense of the dramatic at some level.

SYMBOLS AND SIGNS

The *symbol* is a key element in all the arts. Its parallel communicative device is the *sign*. A sign is a word, logo, sound or movement with a direct and clear meaning in a specific culture. For example, a bent elbow and a hand clutched with thumb pointing backward are generally taken to mean, "I'm hitchhiking; please give me a ride." Most spoken language is full of signs that we use as explanation and signifier. Objects such as stop signs and even sounds such as a foghorn or a telephone ring can accurately represent ideas.

Symbols are nonliteral expressions that represent deeper, more universal truths than signs. They can mean one thing to one person but have a much different meaning to someone else. The musical phrases of Ludwig Von Beethoven's (1770–1827) *Moonlight Sonata* (1801), the dialogue lines of Arthur Miller's (b. 1915) *Death of a Salesman* (1949), the shapes and colors of Pablo Picasso's (1881–1973) *Guernica* (1939) and Antony Tudor's (1908/1909–1987) ballet *Echoing of Trumpets* (1963) are full of symbolism through which we glimpse the glory and folly of humanity. Not only do they have different meanings for different people, but they have different meanings to us at different times, places or states of mind. Works that concentrate on signs devoid of symbolic interest tend to change less over the years.

A sign is meant to represent what it stands for, but it sometimes can also be a symbol. Nearly every one who sees the American flag realizes that it stands not only for the nation between Canada and Mexico, but also for a wealth of ideas and ideals. All artists must use signs to some degree because signs are our basic form of communication and give the artists' work a point of view.

In dance, audiences are often confused by the symbolic nature of human movement. In everyday life, however, we understand it easily: we jump for joy, we point to indicate a direction, and we clutch ourselves when we hunger for affection. Our bodies are familiar instruments that use signs to communicate directly or indirectly in reaction to emotional states. The choreographer uses the body as well as sets, lights and costumes as symbolic tools, and the audience must enter into that world of full possibility for human movement as both symbol and sign.

The ballet essays written by the French symbolist poet and critic Stéphane Mallarmé (1842–1898) advance the notion that dance can literally be the embodiment of poetry, which communicates past the limits of signs and includes levels of meaning beneath the words, syllables and rhythms:

[T]he ballerina is not a girl dancing; that, considering the juxtaposition
of those group motifs, she is not a girl, but rather a metaphor which symbolizes some elemental aspect of earthly form: sword, cup, flower, etc., and
that she does not dance but rather, with miraculous lunges and abbrevi-
ations, writing with her body, she suggests things which the written work
could express only in several paragraphs of dialogue or descriptive prose.
Her poem is written without the writer's tools.[3]

In general, commercial art uses signs because there is less doubt about what
is meant by them. It will not attempt to be poetic but may use some rather
superficial level of symbolic communication to make the message appealing.
The clearest example of the commercial art approach is the equation of auto-
mobiles or bottles of perfume with male or female bodies as sexual objects.

It is the viewer who senses the depth or shallowness of dance works. The
more educated, open and sensitive an audience is, the greater depth of meaning it will seek and find. You sense depth on an emotional level first: the work
makes you laugh, amazes you, intrigues you or turns you on in some way.
That may be deep enough for most people, but some degree of analysis of
the symbolic nature of the work may help you know whether it is worth
seeing again. If you think you understand the work right away, it may not
be as wonderful as you think. If it attracted you in some way, and you think
that it has more there than meets the eye, you will be drawn back to it again.
Then you may begin to sense the difference between sign and symbol and
begin to enjoy the underlying layers of works that you may eventually
decide to call art.

CREATORS AND INTERPRETERS

Unlike in the visual arts, where the artistic work can be distinguished easily
from an interpretation of that work, in dance it is difficult to ferret out content that uniquely belongs to the originator—even if one has outstanding
skill in reading a dance score. As music is not a musical score and plays are
not scripts, a dance is not dance notation. Plays, dances and musical compositions require performers, directors and designers acting as interpreters to
create and embody the art.

Plans written or merely passed down by memory are not the art, either, but
rather the blueprint for a performance. If performances are mixtures of creation and interpretation, why would anyone need or want to separate the

plan from the performance, however? Audiences may be applauding only for a dancer, but they should also consider the contribution of the choreographer, the ballet master-director, the lighting director and the costumer.

When looking at a classical ballet, an audience member might want to determine if the choreographer is protecting one of the traditional versions of a ballet or creating an original concept inspired by the tradition. Today's versions of the classics more commonly include rechoreographed parts of the ballet to suit the dancers' abilities. Is the rechoreographer a creator, an interpreter or an imitator? In my opinion, although his task can be as time consuming, demanding and creative as that of the originator, he is more of an interpreter, his function similar to that of a play director, a symphony conductor or an opera director.

The Creator's Creative Process

Choreographers, composers and playwrights have unique skills with movement, music and words, as well as the passion to create and communicate. Serious, committed creators carry around in their heads a sort of a breeding ground for the performing arts. Playwrights are noted for seeing characters and dramatic situations in their minds, composers for hearing tunes and sound combinations. Choreographers are more in touch with their kinesthetic response to themselves, to others and to their environment. Perhaps the propensity to think kinesthetically or imagine characters or sounds may be a talent, but only with the skills to shape those impulses will that talent be noticed or even matter.

The most obvious difference between choreographers and other creators is that movement, not text or sound, is their core material. Playwrights, painters and designers do much of their work privately, but choreographers work with the dancers standing right in front of them as they create and present movement sequences for the dancers to attempt. The dancers try to perform the sequences as directed, and their imperfections and idiosyncrasies may also become material for the choreographers to mold. It is an interactive, interpersonal process.

Choreographic skills include a keen awareness of the intent, spatial results, rhythms and effort levels of gestures and patterns of movement. Choreographers possess a large vocabulary of movement from their years of dance study of various forms. They must be cognizant of how their movement choices are derivative or different from those they have learned.

Choreographers might be inspired by dramatic situations, emotional out-pourings, paintings, books or just about anything, but they eventually must translate their inspiration into a movement poem. Like the compos-er who arranges sound into a musical composition, and like the sculptor who can pattern the visual results of kinesthetic inspiration, choreogra-phers must invent movements and arrange them into a visual structure in time. Although they are sometimes interested in dramatic and emotional situations, they spend more time patterning the rhythmic and visual effects of movement. They rarely worry about creating a work of art as they mold and shape their blueprint for the interpreters (the dancers, the designers) who will join in the common aim of attracting and perhaps igniting their audiences.

The Interpreter's Creative Process

Interpreters—dancers, actors and musicians—are expected to have great skills that they are ready to adapt to the needs of the creator's plan. Musi-cians are not generally expected to remember the notes in a musical score, but actors and dancers must commit all parts of their performance, includ-ing their special interpretation, to memory. Dancers learn the music (if there is any) to the point that they can hear every note in their heads. After learn-ing a new physical vocabulary for each new dance, they find the right accents and qualities for certain movements and practice until they can accomplish them with excitement, physicality, musicality and precision. They seek out and discover spatial and energy relationships between them-selves and other dancers, and they cooperate in the execution of phrases that demand careful partnering and lifts. If dancing a dramatic role, the dance interpreter, like the actor, also will study the background of the character.

The processes of interpreting a work of drama, music or dance are quite sim-ilar. In some cases, when an actor or musician has a physically challenging work to perform, she may feel like a dancer in preparation; a dancer who must create a controlled dramatic expression may feel like an actor.

The degree of instruction from the creator to the interpreter varies in each performing art and from artist to artist. Composers suggest dynamics with words such as *accelerando, pianissimo* and *marcato* in the musical score, or they indicate speed and tempo with pulses-per-minute markings. Play-wrights often provide stage directions in an attempt to eliminate ambiguity. Some choreographers provide detailed instructions for the movements of the little fingers or for the eyes in an almost dictatorial way, but some allow for input from the dancer, providing very little direction and encouraging a nearly improvisational exchange.

Choreographers often draw upon their own reservoir of movement patterns for their choreographies. For example, they may include many jumps in their works or short sequences of what seem like erratic motions or unadorned, classical, clean movements, perhaps contractions or falls and rebounds. Great dancers, like great actors, develop a facility to neutralize their personal mannerisms and adapt to the needs of an individual choreographer and work. Each body type, of course, has a unique muscular tone, yet the greatest performers exhibit the greatest range of muscular control from the most neutral of neuromuscular patterns.

On the other hand, sometimes unique movement patterns can be the stylistic "glue" that provides consistency to a work of art. To create the most successful work possible, the creator or choreographer must respect each dancer's potential.

The Choreographer as a Team Member

In concert dance, the choreographer is the director and makes the final decisions about the variety of production and musical elements. In opera and musicals, the choreographer is but one part of a team of creators and interpreters, and the dancing may be relegated to a pure entertainment role or may be used as an interlude loosely related to the primary work.

The dancing in some older musicals, operas and operettas provided a sort of intermission (intermezzo or entr'acte) to rejuvenate the audience's attention. This role for dance was common before the 1940s in North America and Europe. In such settings, a choreographer may have great authority over the content of the ballet as a separate entity.

In the musical comedies of the first half of the 20th century, the choreographer was known as the "dance director," who needed much more commercial stage savvy than knowledge of the principles of dance composition as he devised entertainments within a larger work. In the late 1930s and 1940s, a new phenomenon occurred as talented and many-faceted ballet choreographers such as George Balanchine (1904–1983) and Agnes de Mille (1909–1993) were hired as choreographers, not dance directors, for Broadway musicals. At this time, a new genre of musical was beginning—the musical play. Scripts were adapted from books and plays such as *Green Grow the Lilacs* (1931) and *Liliom* (1921), and the respective musicals "Oklahoma!" (1943) and "Carousel" (1945) were born. In the musical play, character development became important, demanding that the music be written for the needs of the script, now called a "book," and that it be more specific to the characters and their times. Dance, like lyrics and music, became an important element to help flesh out plot and character, sometimes supplanting dialogue when it could reveal the emotional basis of the situation. Adding to the importance of dance in the musical play were the many dancers who were recruited from ballet and modern dance companies.

The next phase of dance in the music theater began when choreographers took on the dual interpretive roles of choreographer and director as well as the originator roles of writer or creator. The control of the musicals then switched to the dance-trained choreographers, with much success. For the 1957 "West Side Story," ballet choreographer Jerome Robbins (1918–1998) asked that the program credits read, "conceived, choreographed and directed by Jerome Robbins." Over the next forty or more years, box office success brought choreographer-directed shows by Gower Champion ("42nd Street," 1980), Michael Bennett ("A Chorus Line," 1975), Lynne Taylor-Corbett ("Cats," 1982) and Bob Fosse ("Pippin," 1972). In fact, shows such as "Dancin'" (1978), "Jerome Robbins' Broadway" (1989) and "Contact" (1999) brought full evenings of dance and music to Broadway audiences. The authority of the Broadway choreographer and the demands of the actor-singer-dancer increased exponentially in the 20th century. Today, dance-driven musicals make teamwork even more important for the choreographer and demand that each performer be a skilled combination of actor, singer and dancer.

COMBINING ART AND ENTERTAINMENT

Dance, like the other performing and visual arts, can involve aesthetic or commercial dimensions depending on the purpose of the work. It is more usual for works of art to have both commercial and "pure" art elements, and less likely for commercial works to have elements of art. For example, a dance work created for a college dance concert normally falls under the category of art dance, whereas a dance created for a television commercial will be just that, commercial. However, the commercial works that best communicate with us follow common principles of composition and may even contain a layer of symbolism and meaning beyond the need for pure salesmanship. Conversely, the works of art that most successfully communicate to an audience take into account theatrical or entertainment values, even showmanship, that attract audience interest so the communication can take place. In a commercial piece, attracting the audience is paramount for something to be sold, such as a new car, computer or clothing. In an artistic piece, the communication itself is being "sold."

Successful artistic choreographers take into account that audiences need to be sold on their work, so they incorporate elements often associated with the commercial world, such as humor, surprise, suspense, innuendo and danger. Works of art that are too personal and too introspective, performed by a creator for his or her own expressive needs, can become neurotic or narcissistic and turn off an audience. In contrast, very personal works that take into account standard theatrical elements can be among the most moving of artistic experiences. Choreographers like Alvin Ailey (1931–1989), Martha Graham and Vaslav Nijinsky (1890–1950) created exciting dances that communicated deeply self-reflective subjects by including showmanship as well.

Comprehending differences between crass commercialism and artistic expression is important because it can lead to understanding the intent behind a performance of music, dance or drama. Some works, however, utilize a commercial style or setting as a gateway to some less obvious revelation: for example, Andy Warhol's (1930–1987) paintings of Brillo boxes and Campbell soup cans, composer Duke Ellington's (1899–1974) soundtrack for the 1959 film "Anatomy of a Murder" and choreographer Twyla Tharp's (b. 1941) *Nine Sinatra Songs* (1982; *Sinatra Suite*, created in 1984, was a distillation of the original). Each of these pieces feels popular but can lead us to new and deeper perspectives about art and life.

The commercial arts are limited to answering questions such as, "Will the audience buy what we are selling, keep buying it and recommend it to others to buy?" For artistic creators and interpreters, the questions are: "Who will come to see my work? What can I do to keep their attention? How can I give them a unique and rich experience?" Unless they ask these questions, they will fail, no matter how personal or clever their work may be. They must attract enough audience members to keep their art alive.

The greatest Broadway shows that have sold tickets for years and made a return on their investments with considerable profits, such as the dance-filled "West Side Story" (1957; film, 1961), successfully blended the commercial with the artistic in compelling new ways. Art and commercialism can work beautifully together. Norman Rockwell's (1894–1978) paintings were as poignant and eye-catching on the cover of *Life* magazine as they are today in major art museums. Wolfgang Amadeus Mozart (1756–1791) and William Shakespeare (1564–1616) created popular operas and plays that all classes of people could enjoy. The greatest and most successful artistic works offer both delight and depth.

It is rare that an artist can avoid the audience's predilections, and a patron paying the bills can dictate the level and type of expression. History is full of examples of artists who had to please a patron. For example, when the French baroque court hired musicians, choreographers and playwrights, they had to provide spectacular entertainments worthy of a great court, or they were sent packing.

During the 1960s and 1970s, two major sponsors helped create an atmosphere that brought the arts to more places and people in the United States than ever before. The federally funded National Endowment for the Arts provided substantial grants to dance companies and other arts groups for touring and creating new works. The Ford Foundation, an arm of the Ford Motor Company, supported the growth of ballet companies influenced by George Balanchine.

At the same time, the nation's universities were developing dance major programs at both the undergraduate and graduate level in schools of the arts, with an accompanying increase of faculty members and talented students who would create works for various audiences.

THEATERS

The performing arts are presented in a variety of venues, so the dance audience can expect varied levels of intimacy depending on a theater's features and primary use. Some concert halls are built for the best sound conduction possible, whereas other auditoriums and stadiums are built primarily for lectures or sporting events. Some universities will mount dance concerts in an auditorium designed for large-scale musicals, operas and touring Broadway shows. The stage is usually raised several feet above the base of the auditorium floor, and the auditorium seating is angled so that each row is higher than the one in front of it. These types of theaters also have an orchestra pit, further separating audience from stage. Such outsized theaters can hold up to several thousand people and accommodate a large dance company. They offer excellent opportunities for people to attend an event for various prices. With good lighting and sound, a dance experience in this setting can be exciting.

Attaching dance to a musical recital or symphony concert creates work for dancers and helps sell dance to music audiences, but the audience must understand that dance concerts themselves are very different in terms of their production aspects. Concert halls are designed for musical recitals, but music concert halls do not provide the kind of aesthetic separation needed for the greatest enjoyment of dance because they normally do not have a full complement of theatrical lighting boards or proper stage masking.

Some dance concerts will be staged in fully equipped proscenium/thrust (or apron) drama theaters. Stages that thrust out into the auditorium configure audience seating in a semicircular pattern, although temporary seats may be placed in the space for the aprons, which can be removed when a production calls for a proscenium-only presentation. Of course, dances can be choreographed for the thrust or with an audience surrounding the performers (in-the-round), but most professional touring dance companies will fit their works best on the proscenium stage. In these theaters, a three hundred to six hundred seat capacity is likely. The lighting can be very striking, and the distance from dancer to audience promotes the kind of kinesthetic audience participation that helps make a dance experience personal and exciting.

If dance is part of a musical, an opera or a symphony concert, the focus of the event dictates the dance space. If a dance is in a musical, play or opera, the sets must be considered as part of the dance rather than as a barrier to the dance.

If you are fortunate enough to see dance on a stage with expressive and related lighting, an adequate performance space, an auditorium with good sight lines and seating in comfortable proximity to the stage, it will not matter to what other performing arts the theater space responds.

MUSIC AND DANCE, A SPECIAL RELATIONSHIP

A choreographer's choice of music is very important to the character of the final work. Audiences should be aware of the relationship of music and dance. Sometimes choreographers choose music previously written. Although experimental choreography has been created without musical accompaniment, most choreographers find great inspiration in music.

If the choreographer uses music previously written, he or she must masterfully marry the music and the dance into a whole work, but the music must always serve the intentions of the choreography. Simply "dancing to the music" as a sort of visualized response may work well at times, especially with the complex compositions of composers such as Johann Sebastian Bach (1685–1750). Some choreographers, such as Ruth St. Denis (1879–1968) and Doris Humphrey, can be masters at music visualization, but if choreographers allow the music to dominate the movement, they have made their art a mere supplement. Skilled choreographers use music as one of their main tools and compose movement patterns fully cognizant of the interplay between the perceived motion of the sounds and their dances.

At other times, a choreographer works in tandem with a musical composer. This dual creative process is challenging on both the concert and musical stages. In original musicals, a composer or "dance arranger" will work with the choreographer. The difference is that in musicals the director is the final arbiter, but in concert work the choreographer assumes final responsibility for the collaboration. The commissioned composer may be able to create a musical score that is completely autonomous and that may later fit nicely into a musical concert, but its first purpose is for the dance. For example, composer Aaron Copland (1900–1990) created the score *Appalachian Spring* for a piece with the same title by Martha Graham in 1944. The music and the ballet were successful together, but the musical work stands on its own, like much ballet music heard in concert or on the radio. Sometimes the choreographer will suggest, "Write a five-minute work, and I'll choreograph a five-minute work, and we'll put them together opening night." Merce Cunningham (b. 1919) and composer John Cage (1912–1992) frequently worked in that way during their long association.

Conversely, composers sometimes set previously choreographed dances to music—similar to the process in which a film composer creates a film score after the film editor's work has been completed. When choreographer Marius Petipa (1818–1910) approached late 19th century Russian composer Peter Tchaikovsky (1840–1893) about a score for *The Sleeping Beauty* (sometimes referred to as "The Sleeping Princess"), he had mapped out the entire four-act ballet measure by measure.

Though all the performing and visual arts are closely related in theory and practice, music is the closest ally to dance. In some cultures, it is inseparable.

ENDNOTES

[1] Suzanne K. Langer, *Feeling and form: A theory of art* (New York: Scribner, 1953).

[2] Doris Humphrey, *The art of making dances* (New York: Grove, 1959).

[3] Stéphane Mallarmé, Ballets, in *What is dance? Readings in theory and criticism,* edited by Roger Copeland and Marshall Cohen (Oxford: Oxford University Press, 1983), pp. 111–112.

CHAPTER TWENTY-ONE

introduction

The meaning of the word *criticism* is "coming to understand." That is what both audience and critic of a performance are trying to do. We expect that a professional critic, through an incisive use of words, will clear up misinformed theories about the dance in question and describe, contextualize, interpret and evaluate that work in an interesting and engaging manner. The critic tries to arrest on paper an experience that by its very nature is fleeting and thus to create a useful document of evidence, however subjective it might be. Understanding a dance work is more profound than explaining the meaning of that work. Criticism by the best writers is valuable because it shows how they understand dance works, providing you with an excellent model for discussing your own dance experiences.

The quotes in this chapter introduce you to some influential dance critics. Unfortunately, outside of reviews in one of the primary dance journals such as *Dance Magazine* or *DanceView*, popular literary journals such as *The New Yorker* or *The New Republic*, a leading newspaper such as *The New York Times* or some of the excellent available compilations of dance criticism, it is more likely that you will read basic reports, not insightful critiques. Reviews in many newspapers or even on local arts news programs are usually little more than a rehash of material from printed concert programs. Dance reviews in *The New York Times* represent the highest caliber of thoughtful and engaging criticism, and they can be accessed on-line at www.nytimes.com/pages/arts/dance/index.html.

DANCE CRITICISM

Marc Raymond Strauss

A dance critic tries to train the memory as well as the organs of sense [so he can] make the afterimage that appears in his writing match the performance. But often it doesn't match literally because the senses are assimilating impressions and not recording facts.

—*Arlene Croce*, Afterimages

After attending a dance concert, our first (and last) response all too often is, "I liked it" or "I didn't like it." But experiencing a dance concert involves more reaction than just a thumbs up or a thumbs down, even if such a response is our final word on the subject. This chapter deals with all the information that may be hiding beneath the surface of our own thoughts and feelings and within the dance itself—information that influences our reactions in both obvious and subtle ways.

Some questions to consider as you read this chapter are: What made me say what I said about that dance performance? What specific qualities about the dance contributed to my understanding of it? How might I support, defend or argue the position I am taking? What might allow me to change my opinion over time?

EVALUATION

Starting with a positive or negative assessment of a performance is natural —*everyone* has an opinion. Opinions are very human judgments, so there is never a short supply of them. Critics who write about the visual and performing arts include judgment as an integral part of their critiques. As reviewers (after the event) or previewers (before the fact), they play an important role for their readership; assessment of the value of the event itself—whether it is an art exhibit, theater production, music recital or dance concert—is often what helps us decide to attend or not. Will we attend a showing of the next "Harry Potter" or "Star Wars" or "Spider-Man" movie if the previewer doesn't state why we might benefit from experiencing it? Critics can wield extraordinary influence.

Evaluation is an integral part of our critical thinking skills. The challenge with such judgments, which are almost always immediate, is to flesh them out a bit, dig into *why* we are reacting a certain way and into what reasons we have for saying something was good or bad. A statement of value and worth is just that—a surface assessment with no supportive commentary or documentation to back it up. Figuring out what went on quietly beneath our consciousness in *determining* that opinion can open up our thinking and discussions with others in many interesting ways.

As an audience member, you do not usually have one of the artistic, musical or choreographic directors handy to provide you with detailed information and insight into a dance concert—all the more reason why you should develop your own critical thinking skills as a student of dance, whether for class discussion or in everyday conversation.

In addition to evaluation, at least three other general categories of criticism can help you respond intelligently to a performance: description, interpretation and contextualization.

DESCRIPTION

The act of *description* involves providing a detailed and accurate account of an action or object with which most if not all viewers can agree. Originating in the scientific community, the descriptive process is often called *analysis*, which involves the dissection of a whole subject into its constituent parts for subsequent study. Scientists and critics literally and figuratively break down complete objects into their basic elements in order to understand better the relationships of those elements to each other (quantitative or proportional analysis) and the object's genuine nature (qualitative analysis). The trick with descriptive analysis is to be objective enough so that the descriptions are just that: consensual accounts of obvious content as free from bias as possible.

A perfect example of nearly pure descriptions in the dance world runs throughout John Mueller's 1985 book *Astaire Dancing*, which presents step-by-step descriptions of all 212 musical dance numbers from Fred Astaire's thirty-one film musicals. Routine after routine, Mueller clearly describes the actions that occur, allowing the readers to imagine and decide for themselves the significance and value of these song-and-dance routines. Perhaps one of the reasons Mueller's book speaks so well from the descriptive perspective is that Astaire's meanings are so clear (comic-romantic entanglements) and his excellence so consistent (rhythmic complexity, insouciance, seeming spontaneity).

In a primarily descriptive passage of the song-and-dance number *Pick Yourself Up*, from the 1936 RKO film "Swing Time," Mueller writes (the parenthetical identifications refer to still frames in the book):

> *"Pick Yourself Up" is one of the very greatest of Astaire's playful duets: boundlessly joyous, endlessly re-seeable. The dancers open out into a pose in which Astaire adopts a casual, shrugging, look-ma-no-hands demeanor (B7) while Rogers, following along, glances down in astonishment at his suddenly educated feet (B8). Inserted here are a couple of reaction shots of the*

289

incredulous Blore (B9), after which the dance is recorded in a single shot. A cascade of tap scamperings around the floor shows Rogers ever looser and more spirited as she frolics with Astaire, who once again gives his wry shrug (B10). A neat joke about contrasts follows when a marked, swaying part-nered figure (B11) changes abruptly into a casual linked-arm stroll (B12). This idea is varied with tap barrages that include some impertinent little kicks (B13). Next comes a splendid Astaire double-helix maneuver: the dancers make separate and independent circles, emerging smoothly into a partnered pose (B14–19).[1]

With mainly description alone, Mueller transfers an accurate account of this scene into the reader's imagination. Thoughtful, well-chosen adjectives describing what you saw in a dance is an essential starting point for all later commentary. Of course, it is not possible to present your comments about a dance (or art work) with description alone, for discussions among human beings are necessarily colored by their own experiences, feelings and thoughts at particular times and places. For example, although words such as *playful, casual, incredulous* and *wry* may be taken as purely descriptive terms, Mueller's use of adjectives such as *impertinent, neat* and the uninformative exclamation *greatest* are clearly much closer in tone to either interpretation (meaning) or evaluation (judgment). Nevertheless, by trying to speak only descriptively, without your prejudices toward, evaluations of and guesses at the work's meaning coming out of your mouth first, you begin to separate—and understand—the various elements involved with true critical thought. Keep in mind, too, that your feelings and thoughts may also change over time and from place to place, even in the space of a day, an hour or a few moments.

How can you clearly describe dances, then? What words can you use in accurately identifying and discussing what you see?

Fortunately, a vocabulary of descriptive terms has developed over many years, drawn from a variety of styles such as ballet, jazz, tap, modern and contemporary dance. This vocabulary provides a common language that most people in the dance world generally understand. Although far from exhaustive, chapter fourteen, "Dance Technique: The Craft of Dancing," offers the dance reader and viewer approximately twenty-four traditional principles of technique to draw on in describing dances of all styles, as well as more than fifty definitions of common words used in a variety of those styles. You also should refer to chapter fifteen, "Seeing Choreography: Separating the Dance from the Dancer," for a brief list of "starter" questions that can help you in describing some of the basic elements of what occurs onstage.

Dance has also borrowed descriptors of many kinds from music, such as *adagio* (slow movements) and *allegro* (fast movements). A host of other terms such as *theme, variation, canon, coda, tempo, rhythm, riff, bridge, break, repetition, cadenza, divertissement* and *suite* provide shorthand information for describing elements, sections and qualities of whole dances in useful ways for both professional and novice critics alike.

Descriptions facilitate understanding. They provide a way for a viewer to observe, account for and discuss a dance or any art form with some degree of accuracy.

INTERPRETATION

Interpretation is the process of explaining the meaning or significance of something. The word comes from the Latin root *interpretatio,* meaning "explanation" or "translation."

In the quoted excerpt from Mueller's book, his use of the phrases "bound-lessly joyous," "glances down in astonishment," and "wry shrug" are more than just descriptive—they are interpretive statements about certain states of emotion that Mueller is claiming exist at various points during the dance between Fred Astaire and Ginger Rogers. Mueller's meanings, however, are bound up in their association with his accurate description of specific movements and gestures that we all can see and agree on thanks to the existence of these wonderful film recordings. We believe him because we can see these movements and meanings for ourselves. Nearly everyone who views the song-and-dance routine *Pick Yourself Up,* even if it is excerpted out of context from the rest of the film, will probably experience a boundless, repeatable joy, just as Rogers does during the dance—that mixed sense of spontaneous wonder and awe when Astaire starts to tap. We probably will laugh along with him during his recurring "wry shrugs" to the camera and also vicariously feel both Blore's and Rogers's incredulity as they marvel at Astaire's "sudden" dancing skills that all of us know are far from sudden. Astaire's art is that apparent and infectious.

Is Mueller telling us how and what to feel by his descriptions? If he is, the combination of freeze frames and exhaustive detail of the movements occurring before and after those shots is compelling. He can make such interpretive assertions *because* he provides clear, detailed descriptions of his subject. The lesson here for budding dance critics is to go beyond just an opinion; enrich your commentary with plenty of accurate descriptive references so that your interpretations will be plausible.

Which comes first, description or interpretation? It does not matter, but certainly one cannot be presented without the other. They are often interwoven.

Determining the meaning of a dance is often simultaneously maddening and joyous. If something is too easy to figure out, what fun is that? Conversely, if you have no clue about a dance's meaning because it is too obscure or self-referential, you will not be engaged at all. The choreographer wants you to make up an interpretation, and he or she is often pleased to hear your conjectures. Regardless, the meanings of a dance cannot exist in a vacuum of empty assertion; they must be grounded in references to elemental descriptions of the dance.

Can you interpret a dance described to you on paper through a review or in a book? The written words are once removed from the original dance. It is certainly worth the effort to read through a critic's impression of a dance, however, especially if you go to see the same dance. You may then be in the position of evaluating the critic's review (a practice known as *metacriticism*).

Remember that critics most assuredly have biases. It is unlikely, for instance, that Maurice Béjart's Lausanne-based company will soon perform in the United States again after receiving adverse reviews in the summer of 2002. Likewise, in the autumn of that same year, New York City radio critic Francis Mason said that the San Francisco Ballet's new works "should never have been brought to New York." And, right or wrong, the phrase "crucified by Croce" (Arlene Croce [b. 1934] was the dance critic for *The New Yorker* magazine from the early 1970s to the early 1990s) was common parlance in the dance world. So a certain amount of metacriticism is necessary for the budding critic to uncover why professional critics have their own prejudices.

For example, note Croce's critique of Vyacheslav Gordeyev (b. 1948), a great (judgment word) male classical dancer (description) who performed with the Russian Bolshoi Ballet in the 1970s:

> *Gordeyev reminds me of Martha Graham's phrase "divine normal." He has strength, virile beauty, perfection of style, and also the gift of appearing utterly genuine on the stage—not frozen into a picture. Classical dancing is a language he speaks naturally and with astonishing poetic flair. He can assemble*

elements of classical syntax in new and surprising formations, as when his
passé leg in a multiple pirouette sweeps through rond de jambe en l'air into
the opening battement of a series of grands jetés en tournant. And those jumps
are thrillingly strong, not only in the forward battement but in the feath-
ery freedom of the back leg. Another typical Gordeyev multiple-pirouette
sequence (he commonly does five or six) evolves through développé into rond
de jambe to end in a huge, still arabesque penchée. Bolshoi technique has
always seemed to me much more handsome for men than for women—more
developed, too. But not until Gordeyev has it seemed a sensitive style.²

Although some background in ballet terminology might be necessary to imagine what Croce is describing here (you may want to review the "Common Vocabulary" section of chapter fourteen), you nevertheless can get a strong sense of Croce's descriptions and interpretations of this Bolshoi dancer by simply trying to picture what a "genuine" and "natural" feeling of "divine normal" might look like onstage during the presentation of what to Croce was an extraordinary technical demonstration of classical ballet. You also might try to imagine the thrilling power of the forward and backward movements of Gordeyev's legs in action as he repeatedly pirouettes, especially during his juxtaposition of multiple pirouettes that finally pause in a still *arabesque penché* (a held balance on that same turning leg).

What kind of talent, both technical and artistic, permits a person to do something like that? Croce speaks of Gordeyev's "virile beauty" and "sensitive" yet "handsome" style. How can such seemingly disparate qualities merge together in one person? It would be quite something to see such a performer, and Croce's descriptions, wedded to intimations of meaning and value, stimulate us into going to see for ourselves, or at least into more clearly envisioning such a performance.

In the next excerpt, Edwin Denby (1903–1983)—a distinguished poet, dance critic and mentor to Arlene Croce—offers a discussion about a dance that is still performed regularly by a variety of companies and is available on video. If you see this dance, compare your own afterimages and interpretations with Denby's.

Fancy Free deals with three sailors on shore leave who come into a bar. They
pick up one girl who happens by, then a second girl. That makes two girls
for the three sailors. The three sailors first show off, and then they fight: result,
they lose both girls. Now, too late, a third girl shows up. They decide it isn't
worth getting into another fight about her. And then comes a tag line, so

to speak, and a blackout. If you want to be technical you can find in the steps all sorts of references to our normal dance-hall steps, as they are done from Roseland to the Savoy: trucking, the boogie, knee drops, even a round-the-back done in slow motion. But the details aren't called to your attention. Or when each of the sailors to show off does a specialty number you may take John Kriza's turn (the second) as a Tudor parody and Jerome Robbins's rhumba as a dig at Massine mannerisms. But they are just as effective without an extra implication. Most effective of them was the first dance of the three, Harold Lang's brilliant acrobatic turn, with splits like those of the Berry Brothers. It was in this number that the house took fire, and from there on the ballet was a smash.[3]

Where are Denby's purely descriptive passages, if they exist alone? When does the critic bring his own meanings (interpretations) to those descriptors, and when does he offer an evaluation (judgment)?

CONTEXTUALIZATION

Contextualization merely means placing an event within a specific context or in specific circumstances. Contextualizing a work provides even more information and knowledge that audiences can use to understand and discuss a dance work's details and meanings. The context of a dance can include a wide variety of settings and situations—spatial, temporal, philosophical, historical, sexual, social and thematic.

One obvious context is where the performance or event actually takes place—in a theater, in the open air, in the round on a stage—in other words, its venue. Among its many production requirements, the mass-formation choreography of Marius Petipa's (1818–1910) ballet *The Sleeping Beauty* (1890) must have a stage large enough to accommodate large numbers of dancers. Such a venue is wholly different from the purposes of the usually outdoor dances and songs of the Kwakiutl tribe's pow-wows in the northwestern United States. In both cases, the venue and the performers' experiences are integrally connected, and those places significantly color the descriptions, significance and value of the events.

Another important context worth considering is the choreographer's and dancers' biographies. Who are these people, what are their backgrounds, and what events influenced and brought them to this place at this particular time? The childhood experiences of modern dancer and choreographer Alvin Ailey

(1931–1989) in the rural churchgoing community of Rogers, Texas, strongly contributed to the creation of his signature work *Revelations* (1960), a powerfully danced evocation of southern gospel life. Vastly different were the early experiences of George Balanchine (1904–1993) in America as a Russian immigrant enamored with the speed and excitement of urban New York in the 1930s and 1940s, which led in no small part to his neoclassical ballet technique—sharp, clean and jazzified lines combined with the swift and intricate Petipa-inspired patterns from Balanchine's Russian background.

The time period when the original choreography was created also provides context for any production. Was the work made during a particular era in response to current events or interests? Does the current context affect performances of works created in the past? In the 1980s, in an effort to bring to life past masterpieces and to pay homage to the Ballets Russes history, the Joffrey Ballet painstakingly reconstructed the lost choreography of Vaslav Nijinsky's (1890–1950) *Rite of Spring* (1913) and *Afternoon of a Faun* (1912) so that contemporary audiences might get a better sense of what those dances might have been like at the time of their premieres. Still, it is impossible to know exactly what those dances were like then, for we always look backward with the eyes of today.

Knowledge of a particular trend, time period and background helps contextualize the dance work for an audience or readership and provides an important source of information for discussions about its meaning and value.

In his autobiography *Private Domain*, modern dance choreographer Paul Taylor (b. 1930) reveals this awareness of various contexts at work during his choreographic process:

> No craft, however finely honed, can disguise a passionless base—that is, if the dance doesn't come from a particular and vivid place, my craft can't rescue it. Strangely enough, the best places that new dances take me can usually be traced back to things in the past that have already left an imprint and are being revisited, continuations of paths or patterns that started in childhood, or maybe even much earlier, and which repeat themselves in different forms without me realizing it until later.[4]

The reflective Mr. Taylor clearly acknowledges the essential value that passionate and "vivid" contexts play in his work, regardless of their source.

Most critics do not consciously separate the four tools of criticism—evaluation, description, interpretation and contextualization—into their constituent parts in their writing. A critique is a confluence of these elements and the writer's style, its goal to evoke in the reader a particular awareness and understanding of the dance in question. It is only through an artificial dissection of the critique, however, that we can scrutinize these elements as they appear before us.

In a final excerpt, note how dancer-choreographer-teacher turned writer Deborah Jowitt (b. 1934), from the distance afforded her by reflection, seamlessly mixes all four elements in her brief discussion of Martha Graham's *Night Journey* (1947):

> Martha Graham's Night Journey *can't be reduced to a synopsis claiming it as the tragedy of Oedipus told from Jocasta's point of view, any more than it can be explained only by an analysis of the huge, angular, percussive moves that wrench the dancers' bodies and psyches around the stage. Ceremonious processions give it immense formality; like a Noh actor, the protagonist moves from remembering action to re-entering it. So her hobbled advance—hands lifting to frame silent calls for help, while Oedipus reaches from behind to touch her breasts, her belly—affects us in a complex way: we see a woman fleeing impending rape and a woman in the act of remembering that moment, her gestures polished and restrained by the passage of time (in itself an artistic illusion). And we see a creature stalked by an intruder (we feel the disruption in our own senses), her every step forward blocked by a new impediment hooking around her, invisible until it touches her.*[5]

If Jowitt's writing does its job well, you will want to track down some of the historical references (context) and try to see the dance in order to compare your own descriptions, evaluations and understandings of meaning to Jowitt's. Working with the four elements of criticism, alone or in tandem, can be a rewarding and useful exercise for the budding dance critic.

ENDNOTES

[1] John Mueller, *Astaire dancing* (New York: Alfred A. Knopf, 1985), p. 105.

[2] Arlene Croce, *Afterimages* (New York: Alfred A. Knopf, 1978), p. 152.

[3] Edwin Denby, *Dance writings* (1944, reprint, New York: Knopf, 1986), pp. 218–219.

[4] Paul Taylor, *Private domain* (New York: Knopf, 1987), p. 360.

[5] Deborah Jowitt, Beyond description: Writing beneath the surface, in *Moving history/dancing cultures: A dance history reader,* edited by Ann Dils and Ann Cooper Albright (Middletown, Conn.: Wesleyan University Press, 2001), pp. 7–8.

CONCLUSION

YOUR DANCE EXPERIENCE

Marc Raymond Strauss

The word *experience* means to have practical contact with and observation of facts or events, as well as the knowledge or skill acquired by such means over a period of time. Experiences through books do not count because they are virtual and imaginary, exercising just one part of your entire being.

If you have tried the experience of taking a dance class, what was it like? Fun? Strange? Easy? More difficult than you thought? Not as bad as you had feared? Exhilarating? We hope for the latter.

If you haven't taken a class, in reading this book you will have glimpsed certain areas of the dance world from a closer vantage point.

As you look at a dance in concert or in the studio, we hope the experience stimulates your thoughts and spirits in pleasurable and surprising ways. Concerts or dance classes might confront you with your own mortality, give you a workout, hit you on the head with a revelation, introduce you to interesting people or simply turn you on to the intrinsic and powerful energy inside of yourself that you may not have believed existed.

You may now want to travel to Japan or Africa or Europe to see for yourself some of the places, peoples and dances discussed in this book. Remember, the dance experience is about *your* experience. You might start by watching a touring dance company and taking a class in your own town or university. The initial investment is small: fifty cents for the local or regional paper or next to nothing to get on the Web and surf around.

We also hope that you have begun to realize that dance is not just about movement alone, bereft of thoughts, feelings, senses, spirituality and a host of other qualities. When you approach this art form, you immediately engage intellectual and emotional faculties o various levels.

How can dance be only about dancing when it requires one's memory to learn steps and exercises; one's spirit and sense of community; one's ideas about war, death, sickness, hope, love, sex, God, gods; and one's sense of sexuality and sensuality, gender, class, age and ability in all types of movement?

297

You perhaps are still asking yourself, "Why should I have a dance experience or try to understand better the value of dance in my life?" We did not write this book to convince you of the worth of dance. But if you choose to engage yourself with the dance world, we promise that you will almost always have a fresh and bracing experience to add to your understanding of yourself, of others and of various aspects of this planet.

Your dance experience can be as broad or as focused as you wish it to be. Just a quick glance at a list of where our contributors live provides you with some idea of the breadth of experience and cultural influences brought to bear in their writings. Our authors hail from places as distinct and distant from each other as: Sierra Leone, Milwaukee, Tanzania, Denton and El Paso, Daytona and Miami, London, Geneseo, Brooklyn, Buffalo, New York, Ohio, New Mexico, Ciudad Juárez, British Columbia, Maryland, Massachusetts, Missouri, Paris, Copenhagen, Washington, D.C., Tokyo, Hong Kong, and the Universities of Hawaii, Kentucky, Mississippi, Tennessee and Utah.

We believe that the book has provided you with a number of evocative vistas onto landscapes of dance experiences. We believe that each of our contributors has articulated valuable and varying insights into these worlds for your consideration, for they remain passionate artists engaged in their own ever-evolving dance experiences. Which vistas you pursue and how close you get to an actual dance experience is up to you.

APPENDIX

VIDEO, FILM, AND INTERNET RESOURCES

Marc Raymond Strauss

More videos, digital video discs (DVDs) and films on dance are available now than ever before. Of course, such a surfeit of choices makes finding exactly what one wants alternately quicker and more confusing. This videography reflects our efforts to ease these search challenges by focusing primarily on the content of the contributors' chapters and listing the most pertinent dance video and on-line resources. Whenever possible, the videography identifies one or more videos or films on those topics that are the easiest to borrow, rent or buy. A short commentary usually accompanies each reference, summarizing that resource and offering ideas or queries to stimulate your curiosity and interest. At times, we also have included resources that support extended investigations into either the subject or related areas. If we think a video resource may be of value to other chapters in the book, we have placed a cross-reference to the number and title of that chapter in brackets (for example: [Use also with chapter six, "Social Dance: A Portrait of People at Play"]).

Please keep in mind that the list of videos and Web sites in this appendix is based on the information available as of early 2003. Films, videos and DVDs are constantly going in and out of print. If you find errors or have suggestions for other sources, please direct comments to the appropriate Web sites.

WEB SITES

This brief list of Web sites provides further options for the avid dance video, DVD and film explorer. By typing in "dance videos" on your computer search engine, you will be confronted with more than 750,000 choices (mainly of the instructional dance variety), an impossible number to wade through. Refining your search to "performing arts videos" (or www.performingartsvideos.net) lowers that number to a relatively modest 200,000! We recommend, though, that you start with our suggested sites and then, if interested, branch out.

www.dancehorizons.com: Princeton Book Company/Dance Horizons, specialists in dance books and videos for more than twenty-five years, has one of the most comprehensive listings of primarily ballet and modern dance videos in the world. Its catalog of dance titles is listed alphabetically, followed by the title of the video, which often includes the choreographer's name.

www.insight-media.com: Probably the best source for up-to-date, quality dance videos, particularly in world and ethnic dances, but also one of the most expensive. The dance videos available at Princeton Book Company/Dance Horizons are often also available at Insight Media.

www.kulturvideo.com: A more generalized resource than Dance Horizons, Kultur Video has a huge selection that includes dances from around the globe, with two category areas devoted specifically to ballet and dance.

www.multiculturalmedia.com: Also a generalized but extensive catalog, Multicultural Media focuses on world and ethnic dances from all seven continents.

www.amazon.com: A worldwide retail outlet that has a surprising number of popular and occasionally obscure dance videos, in categories as diverse as ballet, jazz, musicals and Broadway, among many others. Amazon.com also sells new and used films from the major Hollywood studios such as MGM, Warner Brothers, Universal, Columbia, 20th Century Fox and many others. If you cannot find the Hollywood film you are seeking at Amazon.com, please check the individual studio's Web site (mgmua.com, warnerbros.com, paramount.com, tcfhe.com, disney.com, etc.).

www.facets.org: Similar to Amazon.com, except that it tends toward the more purely artistic films of all types, dance or otherwise. Offers a huge selection of classics, especially from the silent era through the 1930s and 1940s.

PBS.com: *The* source for all Dance in America, Public Broadcasting Service (PBS) videos and films mentioned in this appendix. Go to its "Theatre and Dance" Web page. These videos are also available via toll-free phone: 1-800-336-1917. Many of the PBS films come in and out of availability, however.

www.adfvideo.com/adfv.html: The American Dance Festival video store site for purchasing videos of performances that have graced this primarily modern dance–oriented, annual North Carolina festival.

www.dancefilmsassn.org: This Dance Films Association site is relatively new and is dedicated to disseminating information on dance films around the globe. Its listings include many other Web site links that can help with your searches.

www.danceonvideo.com: Another recent Web resource, with extensive listings and links for dance on video.

www.art-books.com: Lists a number of dance categories, including dance-related forms such as art, theater and film.

www.artslynx.org/dance/video.htm and **www.dancer.com/dance-links/misc.htm:** Two farther-reaching Web sites that provide excellent links to the dance world on a global scale.

RESOURCES BY CHAPTER

CHAPTER ONE: THROUGH WORLD EYES   CARL WOLZ

"Dancing: The Pleasure, Power, and Art of Movement." *Jonas, Gerald.* Princeton Book Company/Dance Horizons, 1992. Eight-part video series. Thirteen/WNET, in association with RM Arts and Great Britain's BBC-TV. A book by the same name accompanies the videos and is noted in Carl Wolz's list of references. All eight videos are excellent one-hour introductory overviews on particular styles in the world of dance. Of special note in connection with Professor Wolz's chapter are: Part I, "The Power of Dance," with references to the dances of Cambodia, Indonesia, the South Pacific (in particular Hawaii and other Polynesian islands), India (in particular Kathakali) and Native America; Part II, "Lord of the Dance," similarly cross-cultural in tone and content, but uses various religions around the globe to present dance as a sacred activity, from such diverse countries as India and Nigeria, such time periods as the Greek and Roman eras to the Renaissance and such religious groups as the Christians, Jews, Shakers and Hindus; Part V, "Classical Dance Theater," with an interesting comparison between Western culture's classical ballet tradition and the classical Japanese dances of Kabuki and Noh theater [use also with chapter five, "Piercing the Mask of Japanese Dance Theater"]; Part VI, "New Worlds, New Forms," with a focus on the European and African diaspora, including ballroom dances (the waltz and other couple dances), African American influences in the United States (the cakewalk, the jitterbug and the Charleston), as well as Brazilian dances such as *candomblé* [use also with chapter six, "Social Dance: A Portrait of People at Play"].

"JVC/Smithsonian Folkways Video Anthology of Music and Dance." Six-part series. JVC, Victor Company of Japan, 1988; Rounder Records, 1996. This collection was originally a thirty-video series with a reduced, more accessible (and reasonably priced) six-part video series released in 1996. Dance references throughout this book are based on the smaller six-video package, available through Multicultural Media.

This set is an extraordinarily detailed series of videos that demonstrate a wide variety of specific songs and dances from around the globe. The dances involve indigenous peoples in their local communities, representing specific regions and across regions, in performance and demonstration. In relation to chapter one, particular attention should be paid to: Tape 1, "Canada—Native, Francophone, and Anglophone Traditions," as well as "USA—African American Secular and Sacred Traditions," especially the field hollers, work songs and game songs from the pre-Emancipation period (1600s to 1865); the blues, ragtime, boogie woogie, jazz and big band dances and songs from the post-Emancipation period (1865 to 1945); and the soul, bebop, Motown, funk, disco, rap and hip-hop dance styles from the post–World War II period (since 1945) [use also with chapter six, "Social Dance," and chapter seven, "And 'All That Jazz' Dance"]. Tape 2, "Africa," from Nigeria "The Praise Song" and "Juju" are of especial value. Tape 4, "The Caribbean," island countries such as Barbados, Cuba, Curaçao and Haiti are represented [use also with chapter six, "Social Dance"]. Tape 5, "Central and South America," continues along the lines of tape 4, with countries such as Brazil, Colombia, Chile and Guatemala represented, especially dances such as the samba, capoeira and *candomblé* from Brazil [use also with chapter six, "Social Dance"].

CHAPTER TWO. DANCE IN EARLY GREEK SOCIETY   MARC RAYMOND STRAUSS

"Early dance: From the Greeks to the Renaissance." Princeton Book Company/Dance Horizons, 1995. Traces the history of dance from the Greek theater to Elizabethan masques and involves explanations of dance in ancient Greece, with reference to visual arts renderings, as well as demonstrations of the pavan, galliard and volta, among others.

"Isadora." Directed by Karel Reisz, Universal, 1968. Starring Vanessa Redgrave (in the title role of Isadora Duncan), James Fox and Jason Robards. A gripping study of the choreographer, the performer, the most prominent free-thinker of her time and the first of the modern dancers. Sticking close to her life story, director Reisz brings his actors to Greece and revisits many of the sites that inspired Duncan.

"Isadora Duncan Dance." Princeton Book Company/Dance Horizons, 1994. Demonstrations of Duncan's technique and eighteen original reconstructed Duncan dances arranged chronologically.

"Isadora Duncan: Movement from the Soul." Insight Media, 1994. Duncan drew much of her inspiration from the ancient Greeks—their perspectives on nature, classicism, spirituality and posture. This video profiles the modern dance pioneer's flamboyant life and how she used her choreography to rouse political and social conscience.

"Prodigal Son/Chaconne." Dance in America series, PBS; Princeton Book Company/Dance Horizons, 1978. Includes the dances *Chaconne* and *Prodigal Son*. A strong example of Aristotelian catharsis as borne out through great struggle, Balanchine's 1929 version of the biblical story of the prodigal son returning home to the unconditional love of his father, despite his carousing and loss of all money and pride, is rendered powerfully through the classical ballet idiom in this presentation by New York City Ballet. Starring Mikhail Baryshnikov, who embodies both the youthful abandon and sorrowful humility of the title character's evolution. [Use also with chapter eight, "Ballet: A History in Broad Strokes."]

CHAPTER THREE. AFRICAN DANCE: DIVINE MOTION   FERNE YANGYEITIE CAULKER

World Dance Videos

"Caribbean Crucible." Repercussions series. Home Vision/Third Eye Productions, 1984.

"Cuban Rumba." Insight Media, 1984. Rumba originated in the barrios and streets of Havana and Matanzas, Cuba, in the mid-1800s and was influenced by both African and Spanish dance. In turn, rumba would influence the development of the *son* and salsa dances.

"Divine Horsemen: The Living Gods of Haiti." Filmed and directed by Maya Deren. Princeton Book Company/Dance Horizons, 1997. A Voudoun initiate, Deren was able to film this rarely seen sacred dance.

"JVC/Smithsonian Folkways Video Anthology of Music and Dance." Six-part series. JVC, Victor Company of Japan, 1988; Rounder Records, 1996. See tape 2, dances of Africa, demonstrations of many dances mentioned in this chapter: numbers 2-4, "bukE mOE-nu tOmbO" (Hunters' Dance), 2-7 "maa tOmbO" (Competitive Dance), and 2-8 "Ngele" (Communal Dance), among many others, by the Vai Musicians and Dancers of Liberia; numbers 2-16 to 2-29, a variety of songs and dances from Ghana; numbers 2-30 to 2-33, a variety of songs and dances from Nigeria, especially "Highlife" by the Oriental Brothers from eastern Nigeria and "Juju" by King Sunny Ade, both popular forms especially among the Yoruba people. Both songs and dances involve core features such as the call-and-response and leader-and-chorus singing. These features closely correspond to many African American songs and dances from the 17th through the 21st centuries in the United States, including ring shouts, call-and-response songs, the blues, Gospel singing and many other styles. [Use also with chapter seven, "And 'All That Jazz' Dance."] See also tape 5, the dances of Central and South America, in which you should take a close look at number 5-4, the *candomblé* religious possession dance from Salvador, Brazil.

"Out of Africa." Portrait of the Caribbean series, BBC/Turner Broadcasting System, distributed by Ambrose Video Publishing, 1991.

"Rennie Harris Puremovement." Insight Media, 1997. The essence and spirit of hip-hop dance as conceived by this Philadelphia-based dance company, which merges hip-hop with ancient African music and choreography.

"UNESCO/Banyan Caribbean Eye." UNESCO, 1991. Series of thirteen half-hour video documentaries on Caribbean expressive culture.

Film Musicals

The great tap dancer Bill "Bojangles" Robinson starred in a number of pictures with Shirley Temple, most notably "The Little Colonel" (1935), "The Littlest Rebel" (1935) and "Just Around the Corner" (1938), all at 20th Century Fox studios. These films, usually colorized, are often on the film musical shelves of Hastings and Borders book and video stores. [Use also with chapter eleven, "Dance on the Screen."]

In almost any Eddie Cantor (Goldwyn Studios), Al Jolson (Warner Brothers) or Bing Crosby (Paramount) picture from the 1930s and 1940s, there invariably will be a song-and-dance routine in which white performers wore blackface. However distasteful today, these routines are examples of those in 19th and early 20th century minstrel shows. For example, see: "Palmy Days" (1931, Goldwyn), starring Eddie Cantor in the number *There's Nothing Too Good for My Baby;* "The Kid from Spain" (1932, Goldwyn), starring Eddie Cantor in *What a Perfect Combination;* "Kid Millions" (1934, Goldwyn), starring Eddie Cantor in Irving Berlin's *Mandy,* with the Nicholas Brothers; "Wonder Bar" (1934, Warner Brothers), starring Al Jolson, who wore blackface and surrounded himself with two hundred black children playing angels in *Going to*

Heaven on a Mule; "Holiday Inn" (1942, Paramount), an excellent film costar-ring Fred Astaire and Bing Crosby in blackface. [Use all these films with chapter eleven, "Dance on the Screen."]

Elvis Presley's gyrating hips, which so shocked middle America in the 1950s, are on full display in the *Jailhouse Rock* number from the 1957 MGM film of the same name, his third and possibly most popular of some thirty-odd musicals. Compare how tepid his dancing really is to, say, the Nicholas Broth-ers dancing in the great all-black film musical "Stormy Weather" (1943). Katherine Dunham's wonderful dancers can also be seen at their best in this lat-ter film, in the exquisite *Jumpin' Jive,* sharing the stage with none other than Cab Calloway, Bill Robinson and the Nicholas Brothers.

Josephine Baker (1906–1975) can best be seen in two rare films, both made in France in 1934, "Zouzou" and "La Créole." Beginning her career as a chorus girl in the now famous all-black Broadway musical "Shuffle Along" (1921), Ms. Baker went on to perform in France to great acclaim at the famed Folies Bergère, also becoming an unofficial world ambassador for a group of multiracial orphans over the years. [All of these films may be used with chapter eleven, "Dance on the Screen."]

CHAPTER FOUR. FOLK DANCE: FATHER MUSIC, MOTHER DANCE   ROSA GUERRERO

"Ballet Folklórico: Folkloric Dances of Mexico." Insight Media, 1990. A
   special presentation by the Ballet Folklórico Nacional de Mexico, this
   video presents twelve traditional Mexican dances that represent every
   major geographical region of Mexico.

"Dancetime! 500 Years of Social Dance." Vol. 1, "15th through 19th
   Century." Princeton Book Company/Dance Horizons, 1998.
   Demonstrates quadrilles, minuets, contra dances, polkas, mazurkas,
   waltzes and many other dances.

"Dancetime! 500 Years of Social Dance." Vol. 2, "The Twentieth Century."
   Princeton Book Company/Dance Horizons, 1998. Demonstrates the
   rumba, mambo, tango and many other styles. [Both volumes are particularly valuable in relation to chapter six, "Social Dance."]

"JVC/Smithsonian Folkways Video Anthology of Music and Dance."
   Six-part series. JVC, Victor Company of Japan, 1988; Rounder Records,
   1996. Of particular note are dances from tape 1, "Canada and the
   United States" especially numbers 1-2 "Lancers Quadrille" (5th part),
   demonstrated in Quebec, and 1-10 "French Quadrille," from New
   Brunswick, Canada, both of which first appeared in fashionable French
   and English society in the early 19th century. They are basically reor-

ganized *contredanses* invented in France around 1800 and in turn became the precursors to the "contra dances" (sometimes referred to as "country dancing") of the United States, such as the Virginia reel. See also tape 2, "The United States," including number 2-23 "Polka and Conjunto," from San Antonio, Texas, which is both a German polka and Texas Mexican conjunto medley and is typical of Texas German dances such as the schottische, mazurka and waltz. [Use also in relation to chapter six, "Social Dance."]

"Moiseyev Ballet." Kultur International, 1994. Features famed folk dances from Russia.

"Russian Folk Songs and Dance." Kultur International, 1981. Four different Russian companies sing and dance, including Cossack dances.

"Tapestry II: A Story of Rosa Guerrero." Martin Recording Company, 1998. Write to: 120 West Castellano, El Paso, TX 79912. Or phone: (915) 532-2860.

CHAPTER FIVE. Piercing the Mask of Japanese Dance Theater   Helen Myers

Web Sites

There are many Web sites for information on tracking down videos of traditional Japanese dance theater, as well as videos on contemporary and traditional Japanese life. Several excellent places to start are:

www.cgjsf.org: The Consulate General of Japan office in San Francisco offers a surprising variety of more than three hundred titles for purchase.

www.nhk.or.jp/englishtop/: Features Japan's version of PBS. It is called the NHK Japan Broadcasting Corporation, and its site has a good number of dance videos.

www.jin.jcic.or.jp/today/culture/culture12.html,http://ux01.sonet.ne. jp/~mae/annaie.html and **www.fix.co.jp/kabuki/about/links.html:** Offer information on Japanese theater forms.

www.ux01.so-net.ne.jp/~mae/annaie.html: The home page of the Japanese National Noh Theatre.

www.iijnet.or.jp/NOH-KYOGEN/english/english.html: General information about Noh.

www.fix.co.jp/kabuki/kabuki.html: General information about Kabuki.

www.fix.co.jp/kabuki/biblio.html: A listing of Kabuki bibliographical sources.

www.asahi-net.or.jp/~ab4t-mzht/: The Kazuo Ohno dance studio home page (contains some characters in Japanese).

www.ne.jp/asahi/butoh/itto/hiji/hijikata.htm: Information about Tatsumi Hijikata and his studio, run by his wife.

www.home.earthlink.net/~bdenatale/AboutButoh.html: General information about Butoh and links to other sites.

Videos

"The Art of Kabuki." NHK, Japan Broadcasting Corporation, Films for the Humanities, 1993.

"Butoh: Body on the Edge of Crisis." Insight Media, 1990. Details the fourth and most contemporary style discussed in this chapter.

"Gagaku: An Important Intangible Cultural Property of Japan." Shimonaka Memorial Foundation and Tokyo Cinema, 2000. A video of various Bugaku dances.

"JVC/Smithsonian Folkways Video Anthology of Music and Dance." JVC, Victor Company of Japan, 1988; Rounder Records, 1996. A huge selection of videos on Japanese dance theater, in particular: Bugaku dance theater, tapes 1–7; Kabuki, tapes 8–15. Look under the title "JVC Japanese Classical Performing Arts."

"Kabuki Acting Techniques." Department of Theatre, Instructional Media Center, Michigan State University, 1980.

Libraries

Two university libraries that have extensive Asian dance collections and that permit interlibrary loans are: the Center for Asian Studies, Arizona State University, West Hall, Room 105, Tempe, AZ 85287; and Media Resources Center, Moffitt Library, University of California, Berkeley (searches available through www.lib.berkeley.edu/MRC/).

CHAPTER SIX. SOCIAL DANCE MYRON HOWARD NADEL

"Il Ballarino: The Art of Renaissance Dance." Princeton Book Company/Dance Horizons, 1991. Explores 16th century dance in couples and groups based on the Italian dancing masters Caroso and Negri. You will see authentic costumes and hear authentic music.

"Dancetime! 500 years of Social Dance." Vols. 1 and 2. Princeton Book Company/Dance Horizons, 1997. Features songs and music from the 15th century through the 1990s, including such dances as the *ballo,* volta, galliard, polka, mazurka, waltz, *apache*, tango, Charleston, jitter-bug, rumba, swing, mambo, twist, disco, moonwalk, hip-hop and country western swing.

"Early Dance: The Baroque Era." Princeton Book Company/Dance Horizons, 1995. Demonstrates the development of dance from the entertainments of the French court of Louis XIII to the theatrical art form during the reign of Louis XIV, re-creating spectacles performed at Versailles and dances from the Molière comedies *Le bourgeois gentilhomme* and *Folie d'Espagne.*

"Gotta Dance!" American Movie Classics (AMC), 1995. Fox-trot, waltz, swing, jitterbug, tango and cha-cha are demonstrated to live big band music by everyday folks out for a night of partner dancing.

"How to Dance Through Time: Dances of the Ragtime Era." Princeton Book Company/Dance Horizons, 1999. Presents an historical overview and instruction for more than forty-four step combinations, including animal dances such as the fox-trot, kangaroo hop, chicken scratch and grizzly bear, as well as more elegant dances such as the castle walk, tango, maxixe and hesitation waltz, among others.

"How to Dance Through Time: The Majesty of Renaissance Dance." Princeton Book Company/Dance Horizons, 2000. Featuring period dress and music, this instructional program presents the Italian court dance suite *Nido d'amore,* which is representative of typical Renaissance dance. Basic steps include the galliard and saltarello.

"How to Dance Through Time: The Romance of Mid–19th Century Couple Dances." Princeton Book Company/Dance Horizons, 1998. This video teaches beginners the waltz, gallop, polka, schottische, mazurka and others.

"JVC/Smithsonian Folkways Video Anthology of Music and Dance of the Americas." JVC, Victor Company of Japan, 1988; Rounder Records, 1996. See especially tape 1, "Canada and the United States," and tape 2, "The United States," both of which show numerous examples of contra dances, reels, rags, two-steps, polkas, salsa and others.

"The Maner of Dauncynge." Insight Media, 1980. This program illustrates English dances from the 16th century to the early 18th century, high-lighting two basic steps—the simple and the double—and demonstrating how they are used in a variety of dances.

"Strictly Ballroom." Directed by Baz Luhrmann, Miramax, 1992. The director of "Moulin Rouge!" (2001) puts us into the world of competitive ballroom dancing down under, with examples of tango, cha-cha, rumba, waltzes and other styles.

CHAPTER SEVEN. AND "ALL THAT JAZZ" DANCE   MYRON HOWARD NADEL

General

"Bamboozled." Directed by Spike Lee, Entertainment/New Line/40 Acres and a Mule, 2000. Black minstrelsy and coon songs and dances from the 1890s are updated to a fictionalized television program of the 1990s. Please refer also to the list of video and film resources under chapter three, "African Dance: Divine Motion" for other minstrel examples from "popular" 1930s and 1940s films, as well as for the Shirley Temple and Bill "Bojangles" Robinson films from the same time period.

"The Call of the Jitterbug." Insight Media, 1989. Centered around Harlem's Savoy Ballroom, this documentary features vintage footage and interviews with musicians and dancers discussing and demonstrating the jitterbug (a.k.a. the Lindy hop or swing) from the 1930s.

"Chicago." Directed by Rob Marshall, Miramax, 2002. Filmed version of Bob Fosse's 1975 Broadway show; with Catherine Zeta-Jones, Renée Zellweger and Richard Gere. Songs and dances are based on vaudeville routines of 1920s Chicago.

"The Cotton Club." Directed by Francis Ford Coppola, Zoetrope, 1984. Fictionalized homage to the colorful days of gangsters and the Harlem Renaissance, starring Gregory Hines, Maurice Hines, Charles "Honi" Coles, Richard Gere and others.

"Dance Black America." Princeton Book Company/Dance Horizons, 1983. Brooklyn Academy of Music African American festival celebrating the evolution of black dance from the cakewalk to Alvin Ailey, Mama Lu Parks' Jazz Dancers and Garth Fagan's Bucket Dance Theatre.

"Donald McKayle: Early Work." Insight Media, 1960. This video includes the seminal works *They Called Her Moses*, a dance about Harriet Tubman, and *Rainbow Round My Shoulder*.

"Gregory Hines' Tap Dance in America." Dance in America series, PBS, 1989. Includes a host of vintage and contemporary tappers on stage in rapid succession and together, including Gregory Hines, Sandman Sims, Bunny Briggs, Brenda Bufalino, a teenage Savion Glover and many others.

"Jazz Tap Ensemble U.S.A." Princeton Book Company/Dance Horizons, 1998. Presents this jazz tap company in eight contemporary dances that feature spoons, wood blocks, harmonicas, mouth music, hand clapping, guitar, piano and tap dancing.

"The Jazz Dance of Matt Mattox." Insight Media, 1960. Features rare, early work by dancer, choreographer and teacher Matt Mattox, with groups of dancers demonstrating several of his pieces and exercises.

"Lost in the Shuffle." Insight Media, 1995. Traces the roots of contemporary dance styles back to African tribal dance, Appalachian buck dancing and Irish folk dancing, featuring tap dancer Savion Glover.

"Luigi: The Master Jazz Class." Princeton Book Company/Dance Horizons, 1988. A beginning class of center work in the Luigi style, including pre-warm-up through combinations, by Luigi himself and members of the Luigi Dance Center in New York.

"No Maps on My Taps." Insight Media, 1979. Features reminiscences and documentary street corner challenges of veteran jazz tap dancers Bunny Briggs, Chuck Green and Sandman Sims.

"Paul Draper on Tap." Insight Media, 1980. Portrait of dancer and choreographer Paul Draper demonstrating tap routines, dancing and teaching a tap class; also features commentaries by Lee Theodore and Bob Fosse.

"Steppin'." Insight Media, 1992. Introduces the step show, a dance style popular in many black fraternities and sororities, by examining its roots in African dance, military marching and hip-hop.

"Tap." Directed by Nick Castle, Braveworld/Fox/Morgan Creek/BECO, 1989. Starring Gregory Hines, Savion Glover, Harold Nicholas, Jimmy Slyde, Sandman Sims, Bunny Briggs and Sammy Davis Jr. as "Little Mo" in his last film.

"Tap Dance." Insight Media, 1972. Ralph Brown and Chuck Green, masters of the art, demonstrate single- and double-time steps, the cramp roll, the buck and wing and many other classic tap steps.

Film Musicals

The Nicholas Brothers in action can be seen in the following fairly accessible films, available through video stores, at the studio Web sites and through Amazon.com: "Down Argentine Way" (1940, 20th Century Fox), unbilled, singing the title song in Spanish, then dancing; "Tin Pan Alley" (1940, 20th Century Fox), in *The Sheik of Araby*; "Sun Valley Serenade" (1941, 20th Century Fox), doing the *Chattanooga Choo Choo* number with Dorothy Dandridge; "Orchestra Wives" (1942, 20th Century Fox), wailing in *A-B-C-D-E-F-G-H-I've Got a Gal in Kalamazoo*, with dances staged by Nick Castle; the classic "Stormy Weather" (1943, 20th Century Fox), with Cab Calloway, Lena Horne, Bill "Bojangles" Robinson and the Katherine Dunham dancers in the number *Jumpin' Jive*; and "The Pirate" (1948, MGM), with Gene Kelly in Cole Porter's *Be a Clown*.

Bob Fosse's films, in particular his early ones from the 1950s, are still available at local video stores. The ones that most clearly demonstrate the jazz influences on his choreography are "Kiss Me Kate" (1953, MGM), "My Sister Eileen" (1955, MGM), "The Pajama Game" (1957, Warner Brothers) and "Damn Yankees" (1958, Warner Brothers). "Damn Yankees" includes Fosse's only filmed duet with his wife and longtime collaborator Gwen Verdon in *Who's Got the Pain?*

Jack Cole's choreography is a bit more difficult to track down, but his work can be seen, credited and uncredited, in the following films, among others: the rarely seen "Meet Me after the Show" (1951, 20th Century Fox), in the steamy number *Bettin' on a Man*, with Cole himself partnering Betty Grable, and in the even hotter, testosterone-filled *No Talent Joe*, with both Betty Grable and Gwen Verdon vamping it up; "Gentlemen Prefer Blondes" (1953, 20th Century Fox), starring Marilyn Monroe in the glorious *Diamonds Are a Girl's Best Friend* and in *Ain't There Anyone Here for Love?* with Jane Russell and several dozen male gymnasts (we see Cole's entire jazz warm-up on display in this dance, according to Cole researcher Danny Buraczeski); and "There's No Business Like Show Business" (1954, 20th Century Fox), with Marilyn Monroe again in the hot, hot, hot *Heat Wave* and with Marilyn, Donald O'Connor and Mitzi Gaynor in *Lazy*.

The Arts & Entertainment (A&E) television network is well known for its "Biography" series, with new installments being created every day. Famous choreographers and dancers on their extensive list already include Bill "Bojangles" Robinson, Fred Astaire, the Nicholas Brothers, Gene Kelly, Bob Fosse, Sammy Davis Jr. and George M. Cohan. Visit the A&E Web site for ordering or perusing its lists: **www.AandE.com**.

Early films from 1928 on (just after the beginning of the sound era) recorded almost without change some of Broadway's current revues of the time. Notable films still occasionally on sale or rent at video stores include: "The Hollywood Revue of 1929" (1929, MGM), "The Show of Shows" (1929, Warner Brothers), "King of Jazz" (1930, Universal, in early two-tone Technicolor) and "Paramount on Parade" (1930, Paramount).

CHAPTER EIGHT. Ballet: A History in Broad Brushstrokes   Carol Pardo

General

"Balanchine Lives!" Insight Media, 1998. Through the Balanchine Trust, established four years after he died in 1983, excerpts from rehearsals of Balanchine's ballets are presented with members from numerous companies around the world. In addition to this video, there are many other videos on Balanchine's choreography, particularly through the Nonesuch Dance Collection/The Balanchine Library series from Dance in America/NVC Arts (nine videos), as well as through the PBS Dance in America series.

"How Ballet Began." Insight Media, 1975. Traces the history of ballet from the royal European courts of the mid–17th century through the early 19th century. It includes excerpts from *Ballet de la nuit* (1653), John Weaver's *Loves of Mars and Venus* (1716), Jean-Georges Noverre's *Petits riens* (1778), August Bournonville's *Konservatoriet* (1849), Marius Petipa's *The Sleeping Beauty* (1890) and Kenneth MacMillan's *Concerto* (1966).

"Man Who Dances: Edward Villella." Insight Media, 1974.

"Suzanne Farrell: Elusive Muse." Insight Media, 1997.

"The Video Dictionary of Classical Ballet." Princeton Book Company/Dance Horizons, 1990. Featuring dance greats Merrill Ashley, Denise Jackson, Kevin McKenzie and Georgina Parkinson, this video provides a visual dictionary of every classical ballet movement.

Romantic Ballets

"Baryshnikov at Wolf Trap." Dance in America series, PBS; Princeton Book Company/Dance Horizons, 1976. Includes excerpts with Gelsey Kirkland performing *Coppélia pas de deux*.

"Margot Fonteyn." Princeton Book Company/Dance Horizons, 1989. A Bravo Network documentary on this famous ballerina that includes excerpts from her extraordinary partnership with Rudolf Nureyev in such romantic dances as *Giselle* (from 1962), MacMillan's *Romeo and Juliet* (1966) and Ashton's *Ondine* (1966).

"Nureyev Does Nijinsky." Dance in America series, PBS, 1981. "Paris Does Diaghilev." Princeton Book Company/Dance Horizons, 1990. Both videos feature early 20th century romantic ballet, in particular Michel Fokine's *Spectre de la rose* (1911), but also others.

"La Sylphide." National Video Corporation/Danmarks Radio, 1988. Also included in this video is *Napoli*, by August Bournonville.

Russian Ballet

"The Maryinsky Ballet of St. Petersburg." Bravo Network, 1991. Includes Petipa's *Paquita* and *The Nutcracker*, and Maryinsky resident choreographer Oleg Vinogradov's *Barber's Adagio*.

"Bolshoi Ballet Presents." A&E Network, 1989. Features The Nutcracker.

20th Century Ballets or Choreographers

"American Ballet Theatre." Dance in America series, PBS, 1976. Actor Paul Newman introduces Eugene Loring's seminal ballet *Billy the Kid* (1938).

"American Ballet Theatre." Dance in America series, PBS, 1984. Features *Don Quixote*.

"American Ballet Theatre at the Met." Dance in America series, PBS, 1985. Features *Les Sylphides*, *Triad* and *Paquita*.

"Baryshnikov by Tharp." Dance in America series, PBS; Princeton Book Company/Dance Horizons, 1984. Modern dance choreographer Twyla Tharp works her magic on perhaps the greatest living ballet dancer of the time in *The Little Ballet*, *Sinatra Suite* and *Push Comes to Shove*.

CHAPTER NINE. CURRENTS OF 20TH AND 21ST CENTURY DANCE MYRON HOWARD NADEL AND MARC RAYMOND STRAUSS

"Brooms." Insight Media, 1995. Captures the essence of the New York off-Broadway show *Stomp*, in which brooms, dustpans and trash cans are used in the performance/dance pieces.

"The Dance Works of Doris Humphrey: *With My Red Fires* **and** *New Dance.*" Princeton Book Company/Dance Horizons, 1972. Doris Humphrey's choreography of two works from 1935 and 1936.

"Dancing on the Edge." 4 vols. Insight Media, 1992–1996. Highlights performances by experimental dancers and companies, including Paul Taylor, the Bill T. Jones/Arnie Zane Company, Jin Xing, Reijo Kela, Sukarji Sriman, Pilobolus, Molissa Fenley, Sutki, Ralph Lemon, Ann Carlson, Elizabeth Streb, Eiko and Koma, Laura Dean and many others.

"The Dancing Prophet." Insight Media, 1970. Examines the artistic development of modern dance pioneer Ruth St. Denis and includes interviews with Dame Alicia Markova, Jack Cole and Sir Anton Dolin, as well as excerpts from St. Denis's work.

*"**Dido and Aeneas:** A Danced Opera."* Insight Media, 1995. Mark Morris's critically acclaimed and provocative dance to Henry Purcell's 1689 baroque operatic masterwork.

"Erick Hawkins." Princeton Book Company/Dance Horizons, 1994. The modern dance master discusses his career and collaborations. With excerpts from his dances.

"Hanya, Portrait of a Pioneer." Princeton Book Company/Dance Horizons, 1988. Traces the story of dancer and choreographer Hanya Holm from Germany in the 1920s through her career on Broadway, with vintage footage, as well as interviews with Holm, Alwin Nikolais, Murray Louis and others.

"Isadora." Directed by Karel Reisz, Universal, 1968. Starring Vanessa Redgrave (in the title role), James Fox and Jason Robards. A gripping study of Isadora Duncan, most prominent free-thinker of her time and first of the modern dancers.

"Isadora Duncan Dance." Princeton Book Company/Dance Horizons, 1994. Demonstrations of Duncan's technique through eighteen original dances arranged chronologically.

"Isadora Duncan: Movement from the Soul." Insight Media, 1994. Profiles modern dance pioneer Duncan's flamboyant life and how she used choreography to rouse political and social conscience.

"The José Limón Company." Insight Media, 1956. Presents excerpts of Limón's dancing and company in performance, in works by Limón and Doris Humphrey.

"Making Dances: Seven Post-modern Choreographers." Insight Media, 1980. Contemporary New York choreographers retrace their artistic roots back through Graham and Cunningham, among others.

"Martha Graham: The Dancer Revealed." Princeton Book Company/Dance Horizons, 1994. Film clips show Graham speaking about her art and in performance from *Heretic, Lamentation, Frontier, Appalachian Spring, Primitive Mysteries* and *Night Journey,* among others.

"Murray Louis in Concert: Dance Solos." Princeton Book Company/Dance Horizons, 1972–1988. Excerpts from thirty-five years of Murray Louis's choreography, 1953–1988, featuring interviews with Louis, who worked closely with Alwin Nikolais for many years.

"Paul Taylor Dance Company." Dance in America series, PBS; Princeton Book Company/Dance Horizons, 1978. Features *Esplanade* and *Runes*, two extraordinary works by this modern dance choreographer.

"Pilobolus." Insight Media, 1997. Includes multicamera versions of *Walklyndon*, *Aeros*, *Olympic Dances* and other classic numbers by this highly original gymnastic modern dance company.

"Retracing Steps: American Dance Since Post-modernism." Insight Media, 1988. Nine choreographers including Molissa Fenley and Stephen Petronio were instrumental in leading dance away from the formal austerity of the 1960s and 1970s. This video shows how performances began to incorporate poetry, popular music, character acting and other nondance areas.

"A Tribute to Alvin Ailey." Dance in America series, PBS; Princeton Book Company/Dance Horizons, 1992. Ailey's *For Bird with Love* and Ulysses Dove's *Episodes* are featured.

"Trisha Brown." Insight Media, 1996. Recipient of the MacArthur Foundation Fellowship, Brown speaks with Charles Reinhart about her life in dance.

"Trailblazers of Modern Dance." Dance in America series, PBS, 1977. The definitive, if dated, overview of the history of modern dance in America, including brief histories of Isadora Duncan, Ruth St. Denis, Ted Shawn, Martha Graham and many others.

"The World of Alwin Nikolais." 5 vols. Princeton Book Company/Dance Horizons, 1996. These videos offer a history of the dances and life of experimental modern dance choreographer Alwin Nikolais.

CHAPTER TEN. CONNECTING BODY, MIND AND SPIRIT   MYRON HOWARD NADEL

"Bali: Mask of Rangda." Insight Media, 1975. Traditional Balinese culture involves frequent elaborate religious ceremonies and dramatic performances. Filmed far from places where similar rites are performed for tourists, this video shows such rites as the self-stabbing trance of the Barong-Rangda and the Ketjak trance.

"The Cosmic Dance of Shiva." Insight Media, 1990. This program visits temples dedicated to Shiva, the god of reproduction and destruction. Dancers Raja and Radha Reddy interpret the deity's cosmic dance in accordance with the tenets of Indian classical dance, which strictly govern physical movements used to express emotions and feelings.

"Dance and Trance of Balinese Children." Insight Media, 1996. Combining footage shot by Margaret Mead with more contemporary film, this video explores the tradition of teaching Balinese children to dance in ceremonial dances.

"A Dance the Gods Yearn to Witness." Insight Media, 1997. Hosted by the successor to the legendary Indian dancer Balasaraswati, this video introduces classical Indian temple dancing, tracing the origins of the style back thousands of years and showing how it was given as a gift to humanity by the god Shiva.

"Dancing." Princeton Book Company/Dance Horizons, 1993. Eight-part series. Filmed in eighteen countries on five continents, this set offers a cross-cultural look at dance as art and a vehicle of worship, among other things. Of particular interest in relation to chapter ten is tape 2, "Lord of the Dance," which focuses on the religious and spiritual aspects of dance through Christianity, Buddhism, Hinduism and other sects throughout the world.

"Ecstatic Dance." 3 vols. Insight Media, 2000. Gabrielle Roth is a pioneer of body-based spiritual work. She teaches methods for integrating dance movement with inner awareness to ignite creativity, intuition and energy. This series of three complete dance workouts includes "The Wave," "The Power Wave" and "The Inner Wave."

"Ethnic Dance Around the World." Insight Media, 1983. This program depicts the religious basis of many dances, with examples of festival dances and dances that glorify work, planting, harvesting, courtship and many other cultural acts.

"JVC/Smithsonian Folkways Video Anthology of Music and Dance." Victor Company of Japan, 1988; Rounder Records, 1996. See listing of video and film resources for chapter three, "African Dance: Divine Motion," particularly in relation to *candomblé* and Santería from Brazil and Yoruba dances from Nigeria.

"Kecak Ubud Dance." Insight Media, 1998. Bali's traditional Kecak dance is an ancient ritual that originated to give participants a chance to listen to their god's voice under mass hypnosis. This video shows the excitement of the performance and features more than one hundred men and women in tribal costume.

"*Last Supper at Uncle Tom's Cabin/The Promised Land.*" Dance in America series, PBS; Princeton Book Company/Dance Horizons, 1991. The Bill T. Jones/Arnie Zane Company tackles issues about gays, men, African Americans, rituals and community in this challenging and complicated dance work.

"*Oba Koso:* Nigerian Dance Drama." Insight Media, 1975. This program contains excerpts from the National Theater of Nigeria production of *Oba Koso*, a folkloric Yoruba drama-musical-dance about a wicked man who tries to overthrow a king.

CHAPTER ELEVEN. DANCE ON THE SCREEN   MARC RAYMOND STRAUSS

General

"Blue Studio." Insight Media, 1976. In this "video dance" solo, dancer and choreographer Merce Cunningham emphasizes the body's natural articulation, incorporating ordinary gestures and movements and using abstract space to achieve a synthesis of dance and video in a performance that would be impossible to stage.

"The Broadway Melody." Directed by Harry Beaumont, MGM, 1929. Touted at the time as the first "ALL TALKING! ALL SINGING! ALL DANCING!" release, this film won the Academy Award for Best Picture that year, in spite of its static camera work, particularly on the song-and-dance routines *The Broadway Melody* and *The Wedding of the Painted Doll*, both of which were filmed as they were performed—straight out from a proscenium stage. Worth buying or renting just to see how far we've come since then!

"Changing Steps." Insight Media, 1989. A dance choreographed by Merce Cunningham and featuring his innovative use of camera, editing and design, as well as John Cage's Cartridge Music. This video presents a work that mixes dance and video in challenging ways.

"Dancing on the Edge." 4 vols. Insight Media, 1992–1996. Highlights performances by experimental dancers and companies, including Paul Taylor, the Bill T. Jones/Arnie Zane Company, Jin Xing, Reijo Kela, Sukarji Sriman, Pilobolus, Molissa Fenley, Sutki, Ralph Lemon, Ann Carlson, Elizabeth Streb, Eiko and Koma, Laura Dean and many others. Choreographers such as Streb, Dean, Eiko and Koma, Pilobolus and others are more than willing to challenge the boundaries of performance by including the computer, camera, multiangle shots and unique venues into multimedia performances that use dance as but one aspect of their artistry.

"Fantasia." Supervised by Ben Sharpsteen, Walt Disney Studios, 1940. Unique and at the time controversial attempt to visualize eight concert pieces through the use of cartoon animation. Highlights include Stravinsky's *The Rite of Spring*, Dukas's *The Sorcerer's Apprentice* (with

Mickey Mouse), Ponchielli's *Dance of the Hours* and Mussorgsky's *Night on Bald Mountain.*

"53 Bytes in a Movement." Insight Media, 1998. Exploring the relationship between modern dance and high technology, this video shows how choreographer Wayne McGregor uses asynchronous transfer mode to present audiences and dances as part of a live, virtual performance that spans oceans.

"Fractions 1." Insight Media, 1978. In this Merce Cunningham production, four video monitors share space with the dancers. Dancers just outside of one camera's range are caught by other cameras and shown in smaller scale on one of the monitors within the screen. The frame is thus divided into "fractions" that demonstrate the relationship between subject and object.

"Invitation to the Dance." Directed and choreographed by Gene Kelly, MGM, 1956. A full-length feature, unfortunately unsuccessful for Kelly. In one sequence, he dances with animated cartoon characters again, as in his 1945 film with Tom and Jerry, "Anchors Aweigh."

"Shirley Clarke: Dances for the Camera." Insight Media, 1998. Clarke studied and performed with Martha Graham and Hanya Holm, and this video presents her *Dance in the Sun* with Daniel Nagrin, *In Paris Parks* and other dances with Anna Sokolow.

"Twyla Tharp: Making Television Dance." Insight Media, 1980. Explores the fusion of dance and television by demonstrating the freedoms of time, space and proximity available in the video medium.

"Video Dance." 2 vols. Insight Media, 1991–1992. Focus on choreographing dance for film and video by documenting a workshop conducted by the BBC director of dance. Include lectures that examine how the human eye sees dance and trace the path from a choreographer's notation to a shooting script, which then becomes a true mixture of dance and film—video dance!

"Video Dance: Three Dances for the Camera." Insight Media, 1998. *Wind,* by Eiko and Koma; *Bardo in Extremis,* with Molissa Fenley; and *My Grandfather Dances,* with Anna Halprin are directed by Douglas Rosenberg as he suspends each dance within a frame of elegant camera work.

"Whoopee!" Directed by Thornton Freeland, coproduced by Samuel Goldwyn and Florenz Ziegfeld, United Artists, 1930. Busby Berkeley's first onscreen choreography. Although the wonderful title song-and-dance number *Makin' Whoopee* is almost impossible to watch as Eddie Cantor struts in front of a dozen static chorus girls, with the camera equally inert, the dances *Stetson* and *Song of the Setting Sun* show Berkeley beginning to experiment with the fluid possibilities of the camera, using brief overhead kaleidoscope shots and bizarre choreography.

"The World of Alwin Nikolais." 5 vols. Princeton Book Company/Dance Horizons, 1996. Explores choreographer Alwin Nikolais's multimedia performance works in concert with computer music and other art forms.

Busby Berkeley

Most of Busby Berkeley's films are still available on videos that demonstrate many incredible kaleidoscopic camera angles and flights of fancy that still wow audiences today, especially if seen for the first time: "42nd Street" (1933, Warner Brothers), "Gold Diggers of 1933" (1933, Warner Brothers), "Footlight Parade" (1933, Warner Brothers), "Gold Diggers of 1935" (1935, Warner Brothers), "For Me and My Gal" (1942, MGM), "The Gang's All Here" (1943, 20th Century Fox), "Take Me Out to the Ball Game" (1948, MGM) and many others. A recent film that includes a song-and-dance number that harks back to Berkeley's style, is Joel Coen's "The Big Lebowski" (1988, Polygram/Working Title), specifically in the bizarre *Gutterball* number. Straight out of the "Gold Diggers" pictures, the number is set to Kenny Rogers's 1960s tune "Tried to See What Condition My Condition Was In."

Fred Astaire

Most of Fred Astaire's thirty-one film musicals are available on video, often through facets.com and Amazon.com, at your local video store or through the movie studies' Web sites. This list of all thirty-one films is presented in chronological order with their studio names. All of these films include at least three to five extraordinary dances by Astaire alone or in partnership with someone. The ten films marked by an asterisk are the ones costarring Ginger Rogers, his greatest partner.

"Dancing Lady" (1933, MGM); "Flying Down to Rio"* (1933, RKO); "The Gay Divorcee"* (1934, RKO); "Roberta"* (1935, RKO), "Top Hat"* (1935, RKO), "Follow the Fleet"* (1936, RKO), "Swing Time"* (1936, RKO), "Shall We Dance"* (1937, RKO), "A Damsel in Distress" (1937, RKO), "Carefree"* (1938, RKO), "The Story of Vernon and Irene Castle"* (1939, RKO), "Broadway Melody of 1940" (1940, MGM), "Second Chorus" (1940, Paramount), "You'll Never Get Rich" (1941, Columbia), "Holiday Inn" (1942, Paramount), "You Were Never

Lovelier" (1942, Columbia), "The Sky's the Limit" (1943, RKO), "Ziegfeld Follies" (1945–1946, MGM), "Yolanda and the Thief" (1945, MGM), "Blue Skies" (1946, Paramount), "Easter Parade" (1948, MGM), "The Barkleys of Broadway"* (1949, MGM), "Three Little Words" (1950, MGM), "Let's Dance" (1950, Paramount), "Royal Wedding" (1951, MGM), "The Belle of New York" (1952, MGM), "The Band Wagon" (1953, MGM), "Daddy Long Legs" (1955, 20th Century Fox), "Funny Face" (1957, Paramount), "Silk Stockings" (1957, MGM), "Finian's Rainbow" (1968, Warner Seven Arts).

CHAPTER TWELVE. Of Dainty Gorillas and Macho Sylphs: Dance and Gender   Janice LaPointe-Crump

Web Sites

For excellent examples of male chivalry and traditional gender roles in dance, see Princeton Book Company/Dance Horizon's extensive collection of classical 19th century ballets and pas de deux from *Swan Lake* (1895), *The Sleeping Beauty* (1890) and *The Nutcracker* (1892), at **www.dancehorizons.com**.

Videos

"Dancing for Mr. B: Six Balanchine Ballerinas." Princeton Book Company/ Dance Horizons, 1996. Excerpts of *Serenade*.

"Four by Ailey." Danmarks Radio/ZDF/RM Arts coproduction; Princeton Book Company/Dance Horizons, 1986. Features *Divining, Revelations, The Stack-up* and *Cry*.

"Grease." Directed by Randal Kleiser, Paramount Pictures, 1978. With Patricia Birch's original choreography from the 1972 Broadway show.

"Gotta Dance!" American Movie Classics (AMC), 1995. Fox-trot, waltz, swing, jitterbug, tango, cha-cha and more demonstrated by everyday folks out for a night of partner dancing to live big band music. Interviews with the dancers discussing gender roles on the dance floor are illuminating.

"The Hard Nut." Princeton Book Company/Dance Horizons, 1991. Mark Morris's sardonic, gender-bending version of *The Nutcracker.*

"Il Ballarino: The Art of Renaissance Dance." Princeton Book Company/Dance Horizons, 1991. Explores 16th century dance in couples and groups, with authentic costumes and music, based on the Italian dancing masters Caroso and Negri.

"Last Supper at Uncle Tom's Cabin/The Promised Land." Dance in America series, PBS; Princeton Book Company/Dance Horizons, 1991.

The Bill T. Jones/Arnie Zane Company tackles issues about gays, men, African Americans, ritual and community in this challenging and complicated dance work.

"The Men's Project." Insight Media, 1998. This video traces the progress of six male choreographers of international stature, commissioned by dancer Li Chiao-Ping, as they create solo dance works exploring how cultural, race, gender, age and sexuality issues affect their productions.

"Seven Brides for Seven Brothers." Directed by Stanley Donen, MGM, 1954. With choreography by Michael Kidd, macho males run rampant!

CHAPTER THIRTEEN. A FAILED MARRIAGE: DANCE AND PHYSICAL EDUCATION
MYRON HOWARD NADEL

"Dance and Grow." Princeton Book Company/Dance Horizons, 1994. Presents developmental activities for children ages three to eight, illustrating how children's awareness of rhythm, space and movement can be heightened in relation to their cognitive development.

"Early Dance: From the Greeks to the Renaissance." Princeton Book Company/Dance Horizons, 1995. Traces the history of dance from Greek theater to Elizabethan masques, with dancers in period costumes.

"Who's Dancin' Now?" Dance in America series, PBS, 1999. Jacques d'Amboise revisits the young dancers who participated in a 1983 National Dance Institute documentary to judge the effects of that educational experience sixteen years later.

CHAPTER FOURTEEN. TECHNIQUE: THE CRAFT OF DANCING   MYRON HOWARD NADEL

Many videos include demonstrations and instruction in a wide variety of dance style techniques, including ballet, modern, jazz, tap and world dances. Far from exhaustive, the selection here includes some of the most available and current videos.

"The Balanchine Essays: Arabesque, *Passé* and Attitude, Port de Bras and *Épaulement*." Nonesuch/Dance in America Series/NVC Arts; Princeton Book Company/Dance Horizons, 1996. Three separate videos detail George Balanchine's technique with demonstrations by many of his dancers.

"Ballet Floor Barre: A Warm-up and Conditioning Program." Princeton Book Company/Dance Horizons, 1995. This video features a sequential program of floor exercises that progressively warm up the body based on a ballet barre warm-up.

"Baryshnikov by Tharp." Dance in America series, PBS; Princeton Book Company/Dance Horizons, 1984. Interspersed between three different dances, Baryshnikov explains the value of classical ballet technique. He and members of American Ballet Theatre demonstrate the alphabet of technique A to Z. This video is a pleasant introduction to understanding ballet terminology as well as some modern steps and history, with large lettering and very clear dance examples.

"Cunningham Dance Technique: Elementary and Intermediate Levels." Insight Media, 1985, 1987. Presents the elements of the Cunningham technique, demonstrating sequential exercises and combinations, with Cunningham's commentary on each exercise.

"The Erick Hawkins Modern Dance Technique." Vols. 1 and 2. Princeton Book Company/Dance Horizons, 2000. Hawkins and members of his dance company demonstrate principles and movement ideas as developed from classroom exercises to full phrases with choreography.

"José Limón Technique." Insight Media, 1988. Daniel Lewis, principal member of the José Limón Company, teaches thirty-six invaluable exercises for actors and dancers.

"Lester Horton Technique: The Warm-up." Princeton Book Company/Dance Horizons, 1990. A modern dance pioneer, choreographer and teacher, Horton left a dance-training legacy cherished by such dancers and choreographers as Alvin Ailey, Bella Lewitzky and Joyce Trisler. This video features an actual Horton warm-up with Ailey commentaries.

"The Video Dictionary of Classical Ballet." Princeton Book Company/Dance Horizons, 1990. Provides a visual dictionary of every classical ballet movement, featuring dance greats Merrill Ashley, Denise Jackson, Kevin McKenzie and Georgina Parkinson.

CHAPTER FIFTEEN. SEEING CHOREOGRAPHY: SEPARATING THE DANCE FROM THE DANCER
MYRON HOWARD NADEL

"Behind the Scenes with David Parsons." Insight Media, 1999. Choreographer and dancer David Parsons demonstrates how dance transforms movement into patterns. He shows how the design of choreography can elevate the simplest of everyday movements into grace and excitement.

"Bill T. Jones: Dancing to the Promised Land." Princeton Book Company/ Dance Horizons, 1994. The video follows Jones's dancers through the development of *Last Supper at Uncle Tom's Cabin/The Promised Land*, interspersing rehearsal footage with performance clips and interviews with Jones and his dancers.

"Dance as an Art Form: Motion, Time, Space, Shape, the Body as an Instrument." 5 vols. Princeton Book Company/Dance Horizons, 1972. Modern dance choreographer Murray Louis's celebrated film series portrays artistic creation as the elevation of the commonplace into the aesthetic by means of careful selection, arrangement and performance. These videos illustrate five of the major elements necessary for choreographic composition and Louis's exploration of their interrelationships in the studio.

"Paul Taylor: Dancemaker." Princeton Book Company/Dance Horizons, 1999. Examines the creative collaboration between Taylor and his troupe, traveling from the first steps of a new dance through rehearsals to performance of *Piazzolla Caldera*.

"Principles of Choreography." Princeton Book Company/Dance Horizons, 1996. Hosted by choreographer and teacher Janet Roston, this video teaches the basic principles of choreography, including modern and jazz elements, space, time, energy, manipulation of a phrase and the power of a group.

"Sally Gross: Movement and Improvisation." Insight Media, 2001. A choreographer's choreographer, Gross was involved in the influential experiments at the Judson Church in the 1960s. This video profiles her work since the 1960s and describes her dance approach and weekly movement class, which often reaps choreographic material.

"Step by Step: An Amateur's Guide to Choreography." Insight Media, 1992. Teaches amateurs the basics of preparing for a theatrical production, explaining staging techniques and basic dance steps such as the grapevine, the chorus line kick and the three-step turn, as well as period dances such as the Charleston, the Lindy and disco.

CHAPTER SIXTEEN. WHAT IS DANCE NOTATION? ANN HUTCHINSON GUEST

"Intensive Course in Elementary Labanotation." 5 vols. Insight Media, 1988. Based on the book *Elementary Reading Studies*, this set teaches introductory Labanotation to dancers, students and company leaders. It also presents students in class learning the basic symbols, asking questions and performing dance exercises by reading notation scores.

"Laban for Actors: The Eight Effort Actions." Insight Media, 1997. Rudolf Laban's system of analyzing movement is explained according to three categories (direction, time and weight), yielding eight possible combinations that can define a movement. It shows acting students using Laban's eight effort actions to add variety and clarity to their physical work.

"The Search for Nijinsky's *Rite of Spring*." Dance in America series, PBS, 1989. In-depth account of the reconstruction of this important lost ballet based on the Labanotation score and interviews with people who danced and watched the ballet.

CHAPTER SEVENTEEN. COLLABORATION AMONG THE ARTS   MARC RAYMOND STRAUSS

"An American in Paris." Directed by Vincente Minnelli, MGM, 1951. This Oscar-winning film musical includes the brilliant seventeen-minute ballet finale, choreographed by Gene Kelly, with interpretations of impressionist French painters' works grandly displayed behind and around the dancers.

"Martha Graham: The Dancer Revealed." Princeton Book Company/Dance Horizons, 1994. Presents excerpts from a variety of Graham works, including *Night Journey*, with Noguchi's raised and tilted platform supporting a bonelike structure.

"Paris Dances Diaghilev." A&E Network; Princeton Book Company/Dance Horizons, 1990. Paris Opera Ballet dances ballets from Diaghilev's Ballets Russes, including reconstructions of *Petrouchka*, *Spectre de la rose*, *Les noces* and *L'après-midi d'un faune*. In the last dance, we see Léon Bakst's impressionist painting of a woodland scene on the back scrim as well as his costumes and décor, which match Debussy's evocative score perfectly.

"*Prodigal Son/Chaconne*." Dance in America series, PBS; Princeton Book Company/Dance Horizons, 1978. *Prodigal Son* includes stunning sets and costumes by the French artist Georges Rouault.

CHAPTER EIGHTEEN. SEEING FEELINGS—COSTUME DESIGN AND DANCE
CATHERINE F. NORGREN

Costuming, although integral to all Western theatrical traditions, is just as singular an art form in different periods and in all kinds of world, ethnic, social, African, Japanese or folk dances.

"Il Ballarino: The Art of Renaissance Dance." Princeton Book Company/Dance Horizons, 1991.

"Dancetime! 500 Years of Social Dance." Vols. 1 and 2. Princeton Book Company/Dance Horizons, 1997.

"Early Dance: The Baroque Era." Princeton Book Company/Dance Horizons, 1995.

"Early Dance: From the Greeks to the Renaissance." Princeton Book Company/Dance Horizons, 1995. Dancers in period costumes demonstrate the pavan, galliard, saltarello, *canarie* and *volta* in this video.

"How to Dance Through Time: The Majesty of Renaissance Dance, the Elegance of Baroque Social Dance." 2 vols. Princeton Book Company/Dance Horizons, 2000. Featuring period dress and music, these instructional programs demonstrate typical Renaissance dances as well as baroque dances such as the minuet, allemande and *contredanses*.

"Martha Graham: The Dancer Revealed." Princeton Book Company/ Dance Horizons, 1994. In *Lamentation*, Graham's signature 1930 solo piece, we see her own costume design in action—the "visual icon" of her struggling soul—the stretch fabric wrapped tightly around the sitting figure of Graham herself.

"Paris Dances Diaghilev." A&E Network; Princeton Book Company/Dance Horizons, 1990. Alexander Benois and Léon Bakst were two of Diaghilev's greatest set and costume designers. Here we see their elaborately re-created designs and costumes on display in *Petrouchka* and *Spectre de la rose*, respectively.

"Strictly Ballroom." Directed by Baz Luhrmann, Miramax, 1992.

"Tchaikovsky's *Swan Lake*." NVC Arts, 1998. Available through Amazon.com. Matthew Bourne's unique choreographic revival of this classic replaces the female corps of leggy, tutued swans with a flock of bare-chested blokes in feathery leggings. The costumes were created based on the idea of the production and complement that idea by sticking closely to the choreographer's intentions.

"The World of Alwin Nikolais." 5 vols. Princeton Book Company/Dance Horizons, 1996. These videos present numerous works of choreographer, lighting designer, music composer and costume designer Alwin Nikolais, who frequently transformed bodies into three-dimensional shapes and objects through his multimedia, multiarts compositions.

CHAPTER NINETEEN. "As a Fish Lives in Water, a Dancer Lives in Light"
RICK YEATMAN

"Lighting." Insight Media, 1991. Explains how lighting affects other aspects of stagecraft and provides detailed information about commonly used lighting instruments such as fresnels, ellipsoidals and the scoop. Shows how lighting affects the appearance of faces and costumes and provides tips for handling lighting instruments properly.

"Designing with Gobos." Insight Media, 1999. Lighting designer Neil Peter Jampolis demonstrates the use of gobos (specials) to create fire, rain, snow, reflected water, church windows, fireworks and pattern effects on a stage for both dance and theatrical productions.

"The World of Alwin Nikolais." 5 vols. Princeton Book Company/Dance Horizons, 1996.

CHAPTER TWENTY. Dance, Music and Theater in Theory and Practice Myron Howard Nadel

General

"Backstage at the Kirov." Pacific Arts Video Records, 1984. When this film was released, Jennifer Dunning of *The New York Times* wrote, "Rare and absorbing, 'Backstage at the Kirov' succeeds in recreating the magical atmosphere of the theatre, particularly in the wings, during a performance, in those moments when the performers are no longer quite themselves, nor yet the characters they portray."

"Baryshnikov by Tharp." Dance in America series, PBS; Princeton Book Company/Dance Horizons, 1984. Mikhail Baryshnikov performs in three distinct dances choreographed for him: *The Little Ballet*, *Sinatra Suite* and *Push Comes to Shove*. In all three, but particularly in the last two, Tharp effectively combines the purity of classical ballet technique as epitomized through Baryshnikov's consummate virtuosity with the appeal and entertainment value of contemporary popular theater, dance and music—an excellent example of several performing arts working well toward an artistically successful and popular goal.

"*Dido and Aeneas:* A Danced Opera." Insight Media, 1995. A fascinating version of an opera transformed into a modern dance is Mark Morris's fresh, controversial approach to Henry Purcell's 1689 baroque masterpiece *Dido and Aeneas*. Combining modern dance with the rich dramatic content of the original, Morris himself stars in the dual roles of lovestruck Queen Dido of Carthage and the evil Sorceress who plots her downfall.

"Martha Graham: The Dancer Revealed." Princeton Book Company/Dance Horizons, 1994. Film clips show Graham speaking about her art and in performance from *Heretic*, *Lamentation*, *Frontier*, *Appalachian Spring*, *Primitive Mysteries* and *Night Journey*. Aaron

Copland's commissioned score to *Appalachian Spring* in 1944 is an example of two arts that mutually complement each other.

"Romeo and Juliet." Directed by Paul Czinner, Princeton Book Company/ Dance Horizons, 1966. Excellent example of classical dance mixed with dramatic acting and danced mime, by two great 20th century interpreters of these forms, Margot Fonteyn and Rudolf Nureyev. The balcony scene is matched by the power of the dance drama in the crypt death scenes at the end of the film. Kenneth MacMillan was the choreographer.

"West Side Story." Directed by Robert Wise and Jerome Robbins, Mirisch Pictures, 1961. The definitive filmed dance musical adaptation of the classic Romeo and Juliet story, updated to the youth-gang 1950s streets of New York City.

Hollywood and Broadway Musicals

A short list of occasionally faithful Hollywood re-creations of Broadway musicals includes: "Kiss Me Kate" (MGM, 1953; Broadway, 1948), "Oklahoma!" (Magna/20th Century Fox, 1955; Broadway, 1943), "Carousel" (20th Century Fox, 1956; Broadway, 1945) and "A Chorus Line" (Embassy and PolyGram, 1985; Broadway, 1975).

"42nd Street" (Warner Brothers, 1933; Broadway, 1980) is one of just a few examples in which the Broadway production was created years after the film was released.

CHAPTER TWENTY-ONE. DANCE CRITICISM   MARC RAYMOND STRAUSS

"The Bolshoi Ballet." Dance in America Series, PBS, 1986. In this documentary about the Bolshoi, members of the company demonstrate their incredible athleticism and artistry.

"The Hard Nut." Princeton Book Company/Dance Horizons, 1992. Mark Morris's updated version of *The Nutcracker* makes for a fascinating discussion in relation to the original, from both historical and contextualized perspectives.

"Swing Time." Directed by George Stevens, RKO Pictures, 1936. This film stars Fred Astaire and Ginger Rogers. The song-and-dance number *Pick Yourself Up*, near the beginning of the film, is but one example of complex dancing that can be seen again and again.

APPENDIX

CONTRIBUTORS

FERNE YANGYEITIE CAULKER is a native of Sierra Leone, West Africa, and is a full professor in the Department of Theatre and Dance at the University of Wisconsin, Milwaukee, where she has taught since 1971. She is also the founder and artistic/executive director of the Ko-Thi Dance Company, a national and international African dance and music ensemble created in 1969. Caulker is the recipient of numerous awards for her creative influence as a mentor and cultural icon in the state of Wisconsin, including the Professional Dimensions 2001 Career Sacagewea Award and the Milwaukee Arts Board's Outstanding Artist of the Year award. As part of her ongoing mission to study the dance forms of Africa, she was named a 1994 Fulbright scholar, which allowed her to return to that continent for a three-month research sabbatical in Tanzania. She continues to serve on many regional and national panels and boards, speaking with a passion for the inclusion of the arts in education.

ROSA GUERRERO is recognized as one of the foremost leaders in education in El Paso and Texas. She received an M.A. in curriculum development and bilingual education from the University of Texas at El Paso. At Texas Woman's University, she was most influenced by the country's leading teacher of folk dance, Dr. Ashlai Duggan. Guerrero has taught dance and created innovative curricula for the El Paso schools as director of Inter-Cultural Programs. She takes her curricula ideas to communities all over the United States in lecture demonstrations. The El Paso School Board named an elementary school after her, and she has been honored with admission to the Texas Women's Hall of Fame. She created the International Ballet Folklorico in 1975, which, among its many performances, danced for President Reagan at the White House. Currently serving as artist-in-residence for the University of Texas at El Paso Chicano Studies Program, she continues to inspire children and adults to find success through dance and is a leader in developing solutions to community health problems. Her film "Tapestry II" (1998) tells her life story.

ANN HUTCHINSON GUEST, a specialist in systems of dance notation and a leading authority on Labanotation, has applied her professional knowledge and dance experience not only to recording important works of the present but also to reviving choreographic works of the past. As a notator, she has recorded works by Balanchine, Tudor, Robbins, Humphrey and other leading choreographers. She recorded both Margot Fonteyn's "Children's Syllabus" for the Royal Academy of Dancing in London and the Bournonville School method as taught by Kirsten Ralov, and has in preparation the complete Cecchetti method of ballet training. For her pioneering work in dance education and contributions to the art of dance, she has been awarded two honorary doctorates. She received an early National Endowment of the Humanities Rockefeller Foundation grant to decipher Vaslav Nijinsky's dance notation system and to revive his first ballet *L'après-midi d'un faune* from Nijinsky's own dance score. In 1997, she received a Lifetime Achievement Award from Motus Humanus and an Outstanding Contribution to Dance Research Award from the Congress on Research in Dance.

JANICE LAPOINTE-CRUMP is a professor of dance at Texas Woman's University in Denton, where she teaches courses in dance and women's studies. She also serves as a visiting professor at Texas Christian University in Fort Worth. A former professional dancer, she has choreographed and performed in modern dance, ballet and musical theater productions. Her published works include *Discovering Jazz Dance: America's Energy and Soul* (1992), *Encores II: Travels through the Spectrum of Dance, 1978–1987* (coedited with Ann Akins Severance, 1990) and *In Balance: Fundamentals of Ballet* (1985), as well as many articles in dance journals. She is a member of the editorial board of the Congress on Research in Dance, the vice president of the National Dance Association and a member of the Dance Council board of directors.

HELEN MYERS is an assistant professor at the State University of New York at Geneseo. She has taught at Ohio State University, Kent State University, Ohio Wesleyan, New Mexico State University and Eastern New Mexico University. She received her M.F.A. from Ohio State University and was awarded the national Graduate Research Award in 1992 for her research in dance expressionism. She was given the Award for Teaching Excellence in 1995 from the New Mexico secretary of state. Her choreography has been commissioned by the Mid-America Dance Company of St. Louis, the Fringe Festival of Independent Dance Artists of Toronto, the Universidad Autonoma of Ciudad Juárez, Mexico, the

Chashamafest of New York City, the American Southwest Theatre Company of New Mexico and the Crimson Coast Dance Society of British Columbia, among others.

MYRON HOWARD NADEL is a professor of dance and the associate dean for the arts in the College of Liberal Arts at the University of Texas at El Paso. He is a graduate of the Juilliard School and Columbia Teachers College; his teachers include José Limón, Betty Jones, Antony Tudor, Louis Horst, Lulu Sweigard and Martha Hill. His choreography has been performed by the Milwaukee and Maryland Ballets, CBS Repertory Workshop and companies in Australia and Norway. He has performed professionally as a dancer and actor since his youth. He was the founding chair of the dance department at the University of Wisconsin, Milwaukee, the coordinator for Music Theatre at Carnegie Mellon University and chair of performing arts at Buffalo State College. He wrote the first edition of *The Dance Experience* in 1969 with Constance Miller. He has written a musical, "The Ballet Man," and several minimusicals about the history of dance. He directs, acts, choreographs, teaches and lives with his wife, Jane Poss, D.N.S., in El Paso, Texas. He has been a member of the Actors Equity Association and the Society of Stage Directors and Choreographers, and currently serves as vice president of the Texas Council of the Arts in Education.

CATHERINE F. NORGREN is a member of the professional designers' union United Scenic Artists, Local 829. She earned her B.A. at Mount Holyoke College and her M.A. at Carnegie Mellon University. She is the national chair of the Kennedy Center American College Theater Festival and is an associate professor of theater and head of design and technology at the State University of New York at Buffalo, where she teaches and designs.

CAROL PARDO has been the New York correspondent for *DanceView* magazine since 1998. She received her B.A. in art history from Manhattanville College in 1977, an M.S. in library science in 1979 and an M.A. in art history from Columbia University in 1983. Pardo became hooked on dance by annual visits to George Balanchine's *Nutcracker* at the New York City Ballet and then had the opportunity to follow the Royal Danish Ballet, the Paris Opera Ballet, the Paul Taylor Dance Company and the Mark Morris Dance Group in some detail.

MARC RAYMOND STRAUSS has studied, performed, taught and choreographed in a variety of dance styles, including musical theater, jazz dance, ballet, folk dance, ballroom dance and women's gymnastics, since 1977. Formerly an associate dean in the College of Liberal Arts, he is currently a tenured associate professor of theater and dance at Southeast Missouri State University. His scholarly pursuits include dance criticism, dance history and aesthetics, with specialized interests in dance on film, Balanchine, Fred Astaire and Ginger Rogers, the Nicholas Brothers, Alfred Hitchcock, Gene Kelly, Bob Fosse and film musicals. He has published articles in *Dance Teacher* and in the new literary journal *Points of Entry: Cross-Currents in Storytelling*. He is also the only person he knows who is fortunate enough to have homes on two capes, one inland and one on a seacoast: Cape Girardeau, Missouri, and Cape Cod, Massachusetts.

EDWARD VILLELLA, America's most celebrated male dancer, did much to popularize the role of men in dance through the supreme artistry and virility he exhibited during his exceptional performing career. A graduate of the New York Maritime Academy, he obtained a B.S. degree in marine transportation, lettered in baseball and was a championship boxer. In 1957, he was invited to join the New York City Ballet, where he was quickly promoted to soloist in 1958 and then principal dancer in 1960. Mr. Villella originated many roles in the New York City Ballet repertory, created for him by George Balanchine, most significantly in *Tarantella* (1964), *Jewels* (1967) and *A Midsummer Night's Dream* (1962). Accepting the position of founding artistic director of Miami City Ballet in 1985, he achieved worldwide acclaim for the company in less than a decade. In recognition of his many accomplishments, he was named a Kennedy Center Honoree in 1997 and was presented the National Medal of Arts by President Clinton, the highest artistic award that a president of the United States can bestow.

CARL WOLZ was a professor of dance in the Graduate School of the Japan Women's College of Physical Education, located in Tokyo, and executive director of the World Dance Alliance International Secretariat until his death in early 2002. From 1983 to 1993, he was dean of dance at the Hong Kong Academy for Performing Arts. For twenty years prior to that, he taught at the University of Hawaii. Mr. Wolz was also a Labanotator and reconstructor. In the late 1990s, he was part of a team preparing a Japanese-English dictionary of dance terms and was coediting a volume of articles on dance in Japan.

RICK YEATMAN is in his seventh year at the University of Texas at El Paso Department of Theatre Arts and Film, where he teaches theatrical design and technical theater. He was previously at the University of

Kentucky as technical director of the Singletary Center for the Arts and lighting designer in the Theatre Arts Program. He earned a B.F.A. from the University of Southern Mississippi and an M.F.A. in scenic and lighting design from the University of Tennessee at Knoxville.

INDEX